ENCYCLOPEDIA
OF EMOTION

ENCYCLOPEDIA
OF EMOTION

VOLUME 2

Gretchen M. Reevy
with the assistance of
Yvette Malamud Ozer and Yuri Ito

 GREENWOOD

AN IMPRINT OF ABC-CLIO, LLC
Santa Barbara, California • Denver, Colorado • Oxford, England

Copyright 2010 by Gretchen M. Reevy

Library of Congress Cataloging-in-Publication Data

Reevy, Gretchen.
    Encyclopedia of emotion / Gretchen M. Reevy with the assistance of Yvette Malamud Ozer and Yuri Ito.
        v. cm.
    Includes bibliographical references and index.
    ISBN 978-0-313-34574-6 (hard copy set : alk. paper) — ISBN 978-0-313-34575-3 (ebook set) — ISBN 978-0-313-34576-0 (hard copy volume 1 : alk. paper) — ISBN 978-0-313-34577-7 (ebook volume 1) — ISBN 978-0-313-34578-4 (hard copy volume 2 : alk. paper) — ISBN 978-0-313-34579-1 (ebook volume 2)   1. Emotions.   I. Ozer, Yvette Malamud.   II. Ito, Yuri.   III. Title.
    BF531.R445   2010
    152.403—dc22   2010015899

ISBN: 978-0-313-34578-4
EISBN: 978-0-313-34579-1

14   13   12   11   10   1   2   3   4   5

This book is also available on the World Wide Web as an eBook.
Visit www.abc-clio.com for details.

Greenwood
An Imprint of ABC-CLIO, LLC

ABC-CLIO, LLC
130 Cremona Drive, P.O. Box 1911
Santa Barbara, California 93116-1911

This book is printed on acid-free paper ∞

Manufactured in the United States of America

This book discusses treatments (including types of medication and mental health therapies), diagnostic tests for various symptoms and mental health disorders, and organizations. The authors have made every effort to present accurate and up-to-date information. However, the entries in this book are not intended to recommend or endorse particular treatments or organizations, or substitute for the care of a qualified health professional. Specific situations may require specific therapeutic approaches not included in this book. For these reasons, we recommend that readers follow the advice of qualified health care professionals directly involved in their care.

To my parents, William R. Reevy and Carole M. Reevy, and to
my psychology professor at the University of North Carolina,
Chapel Hill, W. Grant Dahlstrom (1922–2006).
They taught me to love psychology.

CONTENTS

LIST OF ENTRIES

Contributors:
1 = Gretchen M. Reevy
2 = Yvette Malamud Ozer
3 = Yuri Ito

LIST OF ENTRIES BY TYPE

Individuals

Mary D. Salter Ainsworth (1913–1999)[1]
Aristotle (384–322 BC)[1]
Magda Arnold (1903–2002)[1]
Aaron T. Beck (1921–)[2]
John Bowlby (1907–1990)[2]
Walter Cannon (1871–1945)[1]
Charles Darwin (1809–1882)[1]
René Descartes (1596–1650)[1]
Dorothea Dix (1802–1887)[1]
Paul Ekman (1934–)[1]
Albert Ellis (1913–2007)[1]
Viktor Frankl (1905–1997)[1]
Anna Freud (1895–1982)[1]
Sigmund Freud (1856–1939)[1]
Phineas P. Gage (1823–1860)[2]
Harry Harlow (1905–1981)[1]
Karen Horney (1885–1952)[1]
William James (1842–1910)[1]
Arnold A. Lazarus (1932–)[2]
Abraham Maslow (1908–1970)[1]
Egas Moniz (1874–1955)[2]
Plato (427–347 BC)[1]
Carl Rogers (1902–1987)[1]
B. F. Skinner (1904–1990)[1]
John Watson (1878–1958)[1]
Edward O. Wilson (1929–)[1]

Disorders and Symptoms

Acute Stress Disorder[1]
Adjustment Disorder[3]
Alcohol Abuse and Alcoholism[1]
Alexithymia[2]
Anniversary Reaction[1]
Anomie[1]
Anxiety[1]
Aprosodia[2]
Autistic Spectrum Disorders[2]
Bipolar Disorder[2]
Birth Trauma[1]
Blunted Affect[1]
Borderline Personality Disorder[3]
Catathymia[2]
Cotard's Syndrome[2]
Culture-Related Specific Syndromes[2]
Depersonalization[1]
Depression[2]
Dissociation[1]
Dysphoria[2]
Dysthymia[3]
Egomania[1]
Endogenous Depression[3]
Generalized Anxiety Disorder (GAD)[3]
Grief[1]
Guilt[1]
Hedonism[3]
Histrionic[1]
Hopelessness[1]
Lability (Emotional)[1]
Learned Helplessness[1]
Major Depressive Disorder[2]
Mood Disorder[1]
Mood Swings[2]
Neuroticism[1]
Obsessive-Compulsive Disorder (OCD)[3]
Panic Disorder[3]
Parkinson's Disease[2]
Personality Disorder[1]
Phobia[3]
Postal[1]
Postpartum Depression[3]
Posttraumatic Stress Disorder (PTSD)[2]
Right Hemisphere Syndrome[2]
Road Rage[1]
Schizoaffective Disorder[2]
Schizophrenia[2]
Seasonal Affective Disorder (SAD)[2]

Contributors:

1 = Gretchen M. Reevy

2 = Yvette Malamud Ozer

3 = Yuri Ito

LIST OF ILLUSTRATIONS

I

Insula

The insular cortex (also known as the insula) is part of the cerebral cortex. It lies between the temporal and parietal lobes of the brain. It was first described by Johann-Christian Reil (1759–1813) in 1796 and later became known as the Island of Reil (Binder, Schaller, & Clusmann, 2007). The insula plays a role in functions linked to emotion and to regulation of the body's homeostasis (balance). The insula is thought to contain representations of external sensory and internal bodily states, incorporating information from visceral (guts), olfactory (smell), gustatory (taste), visual, auditory, and somatosensory (feeling) inputs (Beauregard, 2003). The insula is active in perception, motor control, and self-awareness.

Neuroimaging studies—such as functional magnetic resonance imaging and positron emission tomography scans—have yielded insight into the role of the insula. Research has implicated the insula specifically in the emotion of disgust. However, the insula is also activated with other basic emotions such as happiness, sadness, and fear. It can be activated by emotional recall as well as real-time experiencing of emotion (Phan, Wager, Taylor, & Liberzon, 2002). The insula is involved in the experiencing of social emotions, including admiration of virtue, feelings of compassion for social or psychological pain, and moral indignation (Immordino-Yang, McColl, Damasio, & Damasio, 2009). Anxiety-prone research participants had greater insula activation when shown pictures of emotional faces than did participants with lower anxiety (Stein, Simmons, Feinstein, & Paulus, 2007). The insula is activated during tic initiation in individuals with Tourette's syndrome (Lerner et al., 2009).

The insula has been implicated in conscious urges and addiction, showing activation during drug cravings and exposure to cues associated with drugs of abuse (e.g., cocaine, nicotine). In one study, damage to the insula was found to disrupt addiction to cigarette smoking. Research participants were smokers who had smoked at least five cigarettes a day for at least two years before the onset of an acquired brain injury (e.g., stroke). Those who had damage to the insula were more likely to quit smoking easily, immediately, without relapse, and without the urge to smoke (Naqvi, Rudrauf, Damasio, & Bechara, 2007).

See also anxiety, disgust, functional magnetic resonance imaging, positron emission tomography, substance abuse.

Further Reading:
Diamond, M. C., & Scheibel, A. B. (1985). *The human brain coloring book.* New York: HarperCollins.

References:
Beauregard, M. (2003). *Consciousness, emotional self-regulation and the brain.* Philadelphia: John Benjamins.
Binder, D. K., Schaller, K., & Clusmann, H. (2007). The seminal contributions of Johann-Christian Reil to anatomy, physiology, and psychiatry. *Neurosurgery, 61*, 1091–1096.
Immordino-Yang, M. H., McColl, A., Damasio, H., & Damasio, A. (2009). Neural correlates of admiration and compassion. *Proceedings of the National Academy of Sciences of the United States of America, 106*, 8021–8026.
Lerner, A., Bagic, A., Hanakawa, T., Boudreau, E. A., Pagan, F., Mari, Z., et al. (2009). Involvement of insula and cingulate cortices in control and suppression of natural urges. *Cerebral Cortex, 19*, 218–223.
Naqvi, N. H., Rudrauf, D., Damasio, H., & Bechara, A. (2007). Damage to the insula disrupts addiction to cigarette smoking. *Science, 315*, 531–534.
Phan, K. L., Wager, T., Taylor, S. F., & Liberzon, I. (2002). Functional neuroanatomy of emotion: A meta-analysis of emotion activation studies in PET and fMRI. *NeuroImage, 16*, 331–348.
Stein, M. B., Simmons, A. N., Feinstein, J. S., & Paulus, M. P. (2007). Increased amygdala and insula activation during emotion processing in anxiety-prone subjects. *American Journal of Psychiatry, 164*, 318–327.

International Affective Picture System

The International Affective Picture System (IAPS) is an in-progress database of color pictures that are intended to elicit emotions in research participants for the purposes of studying emotion and attention. The pictures are standardized, designed to evoke a wide range of emotions (from negative to positive and from low to high arousal) and for use internationally. The pictures vary in complexity, content (some human, some animal, some inanimate), amount of color, and size of image.

The IAPS is used widely in research on general emotion, emotional disorders, emotional experiences associated with different groups (such as younger vs. older participants), and special topics related to emotion such as music and emotion. Researchers from many different countries utilize the IAPS.

The earliest version of the IAPS was published by American psychologists Peter Lang and Mark Greenwald in 1988. The database is continually developed at the National Institute for Mental Health Center for Emotion and Attention at the University of Florida.

Further Readings:
Lang, P. J., Bradley, M. M., & Cuthbert, B. N. (2008). *International Affective Picture System (IAPS): Affective ratings of pictures and instruction manual* (Technical Report No. A-8). University of Florida, Gainesville.
NIMH Center for the Study of Emotion and Attention Web site: http://csea.phhp.ufl.edu/index. html

Reference:
Lang, P. J., & Greenwald, M. K. (1988). *The International Affective Picture System standardization procedure and initial group results for affective judgments: Technical report 1A.* Gainsville: Center for Research in Psychophysiology, University of Florida.

International Classification of Diseases

The *International Statistical Classification of Diseases and Related Health Problems*, commonly referred to as the *International Classification of Diseases* (*ICD*), is currently in its 10th edition (*ICD*-10; World Health Organization, 1990). The *ICD* has its origins in the 1850s. The statistical study of death (mortality) statistics began in London in the early 1600s in an attempt to estimate the percentage of children who died before the age of six years. Later disease (morbidity) classifications were written by French scientist François Bossier de Sauvages (1706–1777), Swedish biologist and physician Linnaeus (1707–1778), and Scottish doctor and chemist William Cullen, who wrote *Synopsis Nosologiae Methodicae* (1785). The first international classification was the *Bertillon Classification of Causes of Death*, which in 1898 was adopted by the registrars of Canada, Mexico, and the United States (World Health Organization [WHO], n.d.). The plan was to review and revise the classification every 10 years. Subsequent conferences to review the classification from 1900 through 1938 included the Health Organization of the League of Nations and delegates from more than 26 countries. The sixth revision included diseases (morbidity) as well as mortality figures. It was titled the *International Classification of Diseases, Injuries, and Causes of Death* (1948).

Having an internationally agreed-on classification system of diseases and disorders allows countries to assess the progress of health care and the control of disease. The *ICD* system has also become a widely used method to bill insurance, promote communication among health care providers, further health care and epidemiology research, and measure the effectiveness of health care interventions and treatments. The *ICD* is organized by parts of the body affected (e.g., respiratory, skin) and contains descriptions, diagnosis, and procedure codes. While some countries (e.g., Australia and Canada) have adopted *ICD*-10, the United States only uses it for reporting death (mortality) statistics. *ICD*-9-*CM* (9th version, Clinical Modification; WHO, 1988) is still used for morbidity (sickness and disease) in the United States. The *ICD* is available in the six official languages of WHO (Arabic, Chinese, English, French, Russian, and Spanish) as well as in 36 other languages.

In the area of mental health, systems comparable to the *ICD* include the *Diagnostic and Statistical Manual of Mental Disorders* (*DSM-IV-TR*; American Psychiatric Association, 2000) and—for young children—the *Diagnostic Classification System of Mental Health and Developmental Disorders of Infancy and Early Childhood* (DC:0–3R). There is considerable overlap between the *DSM* and the *ICD*, both of which contain criteria for mental health symptoms and disorders. *ICD* categories are very similar to *DSM* Axis I categories. The *DSM* is more widely used in the United States, and the *ICD* system is more widely used in Europe and the United Kingdom (Stirling, 1999).

Both *ICD* and *DSM* are categorical systems in which each mental illness is seen as a discrete diagnostic entity. Critics of categorical systems support an alternative dimensional approach in which symptoms are seen as exaggerations of normal emotions and feelings occurring along a continuum. The dimensional approach sees the distinction between normal and abnormal human experience (e.g., mental illness) as a matter of degree and somewhat arbitrary (Stirling, 1999). Supporters of both systems (dimensional and categorical) agree that it is important that individuals receive the appropriate treatment and that treatment be linked to the correct diagnosis.

See also Diagnostic and Statistical Manual of Mental Disorders, Diagnostic Classification System of Mental Health and Developmental Disorders of Infancy and Early Childhood.

Further Reading:
World Health Organization Web site: http://www.who.int/classifications/icd/en/

References:
American Psychiatric Association. (2000). *Diagnostic and statistical manual of mental disorders* (4th ed., text rev.). Washington, DC: Author.

Stirling, J. D. (1999). *Psychopathology*. London: Routledge.

World Health Organization. (1988). *International statistical classification of diseases and related health problems* (9th rev., Clinical Modification). Geneva, Switzerland: Author.

World Health Organization. (1990). *International statistical classification of diseases and related health problems* (10th rev.). Geneva, Switzerland: Author.

World Health Organization. (n.d.). *History of the development of the ICD*. Retrieved from http://www.who.int/classifications/icd/en/

Zero to Three. (2005). *Diagnostic classification of mental health and developmental disorders of infancy and early childhood* (rev. ed.). Washington, DC: Author.

Interpersonal Psychotherapy

The principles and general philosophy of interpersonal psychotherapy are based in the interpersonal theory of American psychiatrist and psychodynamic theorist Harry Stack Sullivan, who emphasized that personality difficulties arise primarily in relationships with others, and in attachment theory, which holds that interpersonal loss and attachment issues are at the core of psychological problems. The actual techniques and form of the therapy were developed by clinical researchers Gerald Klerman and Myrna Weissman in the 1970s and 1980s. They adapted techniques from both psychodynamic (Freudian and neo-Freudian) therapists and the more modern cognitive-behavioral therapists. The treatment was originally designed for adults diagnosed with moderate or severe clinical depression.

The basis of interpersonal psychotherapy is the idea that psychological problems are largely caused by interpersonal issues. According to the theory, one or more of four major areas of interpersonal problems may be associated with depression. The first is *interpersonal loss*. The client's grieving process following the death of a loved one may have become problematical (i.e., excessive or prolonged). The interpersonal therapist would encourage the client to explore the lost relationship and express feelings that may be unresolved. The client would create a new way of thinking about the lost person and, by the end of treatment, would be prepared to seek new connections and relationships with people. A second area is *interpersonal role disputes*, which may occur in romantic relationships, families, or work or other settings. In a romantic relationship, the client may find that she and her partner have different expectations of their relationship or different interaction styles that lead to conflict. For example, one partner may expect the partner to follow traditional sex roles while the other finds this expectation to be too restrictive. Treatment would involve questioning whether the beliefs of the client are realistic and constructive and teaching behavioral techniques such as new methods of communication and problem solving. A third area is *interpersonal role transition*. An individual may have experienced a major life change such as the birth of a child, moving across country, divorce, or marriage. It may be difficult to navigate the new roles that are required by these life changes. Therapy would encourage the person to seek out support from others (social support) and develop the skills that are required by the new role. A fourth area is *interpersonal deficits*, such as poor social skills or extreme shyness. Treatment would involve helping the client to see that he has a "problem" (e.g., engaging in role-play and showing the client how his behavior might be viewed or received by others). In addition, behavioral or cognitive-behavioral techniques would be used to teach the social skills that are required, for example, assertiveness or anger management.

Interpersonal psychotherapy is brief, typically designed for 12 to 16 one-hour, weekly sessions. According to the theory, three main issues that should be addressed in depression are symptom formation, social functioning, and personality. Interpersonal psychotherapy works on social functioning, which helps to reduce symptom formation. Personality is not directly a focus of treatment since this therapy is of short duration and personality restructuring is time-intensive. Sessions begin by collecting information from the client. The therapist interprets the client's presenting problems in an interpersonal context and explains the interpretations to the client. Treatment proceeds from this framework, using a variety of cognitive, behavioral, psychodynamic (Freudian), and other techniques. The goal of therapy is to create new ways of thinking, feeling, and behaving. The new person is (it is hoped) less vulnerable to future depressions.

Interpersonal psychotherapy is an effective treatment for depression. Several well-designed studies compared interpersonal psychotherapy to other treatments of demonstrated effectiveness (i.e., cognitive-behavioral therapy, antidepressant medication), and results revealed that interpersonal psychotherapy is at least as effective as the other treatments for depression (e.g., Elkin et al., 1989; Weissman et al., 1979). Interpersonal psychotherapy has been adapted to treat other conditions, including bipolar disorder, eating disorders, posttraumatic stress disorder, anxiety disorders, and substance use disorders. Studies of therapy effectiveness for several of these conditions are ongoing.

See also attachment, cognitive therapy and cognitive-behavioral therapy, depression, loss, psychoanalytic perspective, psychodynamic psychotherapy and psychoanalysis, relationships, shyness.

Further Reading:
International Society for Interpersonal Psychotherapy Web site: http://www.interpersonalpsychotherapy.org

References:
Elkin, I., Shea, M. T., Watkins, J. T., Imber, S. D., Sotsky, S. M., Collins, J. F., et al. (1989). National Institute of Mental Health Treatment of Depression Collaborative Research Program: General effectiveness of treatments. *Archives of General Psychiatry, 46,* 971–982.
Weissman, M. M., Prusoff, B. A., DiMascio, A., Neu, C., Goklaney, M., & Klerman, G. L. (1979). The efficacy of drugs and psychotherapy in the treatment of acute depressive episodes. *American Journal of Psychiatry, 136,* 555–558.

Intimacy

Intimacy is a generalized concept that encompasses feelings and behaviors and that occurs in the context of relationships between individuals. Being intimate means sharing one's innermost feelings and thoughts with another.

Intimacy involves a variety of positive and negative emotions. Being intimate usually means feeling love, joy, contentment, warmth, and possibly passion. According to American psychologist Robert Sternberg (1988), who proposed the triangular theory of love, love is composed of three main components: intimacy, passion, and commitment. Intimacy is emotional, involving warmth, connectedness, and feelings of closeness. Passion is a motivational component, including strong desire, often (but not always) sexual, and arousal. Commitment is cognitive; it is a decision to love another person and to secure and maintain a bond with that person. Sternberg argued that intimacy is the core, the fundamental component of love. Needless to say, intimacy can occur in relationships that do not involve passion, especially sexual passion, such as friendships and family relationships. Intimacy is clearly connected to the positive emotions joy and happiness. Shaver, Schwartz, Kirson, and O'Connor (1987) found that adults report the highest levels of happiness when they feel loved and accepted by others and when people praise them or show affection toward them.

As social psychologist Elaine Hatfield (1984) described, fear is an emotion that is often strongly linked to intimacy. Hatfield identified six types of fear commonly associated with intimacy: fear of exposure (revealing the true self and making oneself vulnerable), fear of abandonment, fear of angry attacks (that a partner will become angry and attack either physically or psychologically), fear of loss of control (that with closeness, another person will have too much control over one's own thoughts and feelings), fear of one's own destructive impulses, and fear of losing one's individuality. This latter fear, the fear that one's own self will be lost in a relationship, has been discussed by many interpersonal relationship scholars. For instance, Leslie Baxter (1988, 1990) introduced a theory she called *dialectics theory*. According to Baxter, people have strong needs for both intimacy and independence or autonomy. She called this the autonomy-connection dialectic. These intimacy and independence needs often conflict and lead to a push and pull in relationships. People also have needs to disclose to others and to keep some information private; these needs create another conflict. Baxter called this the *openness-closedness dialectic*. To achieve satisfaction in relationships, people must balance these opposing motives.

Scholars who have studied intimacy include psychologists, sociologists, communication researchers, and others. Miller, Perlman, and Brehm (2007) have written a comprehensive textbook, *Intimate Relationships*, describing theory and research on many topics related to intimacy, including nonverbal communication, attraction, sex and gender comparisons in intimacy, friendship, love, conflict, jealousy, and other topics.

See also family, friendship, loneliness, love, relationships, social support.

Further Readings:

Guerrero, L. K. (1999). Intimacy. In D. Levinson, J. J. Ponzetti, & P. F. Jorgensen (Eds.), *Encyclopedia of human emotions* (2nd ed., pp. 403–409). New York: Macmillan Reference USA.

Miller, R. S., Perlman, D., & Brehm, S. S. (2007). *Intimate relationships* (4th ed.). New York: McGraw-Hill.

References:

Baxter, L. A. (1988). A dialectical perspective on communication strategies in relationship development. In S. Duck, D. F. Hay, S. E. Hobfoll, W. Ickes, & B. M. Montgomery (Eds.), *Handbook of personal relationships: Theory, research, and interventions* (pp. 257–273). Oxford, England: John Wiley.

Baxter, L. A. (1990). Dialectical contradictions in relationship development. *Journal of Social and Personal Relationships, 7,* 69–88.

Hatfield, E. (1984). The dangers of intimacy. In V. J. Derlega (Ed.), *Communication, intimacy, and close relationships* (pp. 207–220). New York: Praeger.

Miller, R. S., Perlman, D., & Brehm, S. S. (2007). *Intimate relationships* (4th ed.). New York: McGraw-Hill.

Shaver, P., Schwartz, J., Kirson, D., & O'Connor, C. (1987). Emotion knowledge: Further exploration of a prototype approach. *Journal of Personality and Social Psychology, 52,* 1061–1086.

Sternberg, R. J. (1988). Triangulating love. In R. J. Sternberg & M. L. Barnes (Eds.), *The psychology of love* (pp. 119–138). New Haven, CT: Yale University Press.

Introversion

In the 1920s, eminent Swiss psychiatrist Carl Jung was the first of the modern personality theorists to clearly detail the difference between introversion and extraversion. He spoke of these attributes primarily in terms of sociability and of where one directs his energy (toward the self or toward an external object). Jung (Jung & Hull, 1992) described introversion and extraversion as follows:

> [Introversion] is normally characterized by a hesitant, reflective, retiring nature that keeps itself to itself, shrinks from objects, is always slightly on the defensive and prefers to hide behind mistrustful scrutiny. [Extraversion] is normally characterized by an outgoing, candid, and accommodating nature that adapts easily to a given situation, quickly forms attachments, and, setting aside any possible misgivings, will often venture forth with careless confidence into unknown situations. In the first case obviously the subject, and in the second the object, is all-important. (p. 44)

Jung stated that introversion-extraversion was the primary personality difference among people. According to him, we possess both characteristics but have a strong preference for one. If introversion is preferred, the individual becomes an adept introvert. He is capable of extraversion but utilizes this characteristic with awkwardness.

Jung was not alone in identifying introversion-extraversion as an important individual difference variable. The majority of the comprehensive theories of individual differences (i.e., those of Eysenck, Cattell, Tupes, and Christal) include introversion-extraversion as a primary trait. Additionally, most broad-based, general personality tests measure introversion-extraversion.

Many modern theorists view introversion-extraversion as being related to positive emotion, in addition to being related to sociability. Specifically, extraverts tend to experience high levels of positive emotion, whereas introverts generally feel low levels of positive emotion. This point has to be made clear, however: introverts are not necessarily high in negative emotion such as sadness, fear, or anger. Rather, introverts generally experience low levels of happiness, joy, excitement, and hedonistic feelings compared to extraverts. According to some psychologists (e.g., Watson & Clark, 1997), it is this high positive emotion that leads to the outgoing, assertive, active, and excitement-seeking behavior that is characteristic of extraverts. Introverts, without this outward-directed excitement and energy, are more solitary, withdrawn, and hesitant. The rewards they seek may be of a quieter variety such as the gratification that comes from doing solitary work, reading, hobbies, or individual sports such as swimming.

Results of some studies reveal that introverts are more sensitive to stimuli. According to a review by Eysenck (1990), introverts have lower pain thresholds than extraverts. Introverts salivate more than do extraverts when drops of lemon juice are placed on their tongues (Deary, Ramsay, Wilson, & Riad, 1988). Additionally, introverts are more difficult to sedate than are extraverts; they require higher dosages of sedative drugs (Wilson, 1978). The interest in introversion and extraversion has remained steady since the beginnings of modern psychology. In the last couple of decades, investigators have begun exploring the meanings of the emotional facets of these characteristics.

See also affective personality traits, extraversion, PEN model of personality, shyness.

References:
Deary, I.J., Ramsay, H., Wilson, J.A., & Riad, M. (1988). Stimulated salivation: Correlations with personality and time of day effects. *Personality and Individual Differences, 9*, 903–909.
Eysenck, H. J. (1990). Biological dimensions of personality. In L. A. Pervin (Ed.), *Handbook of personality: Theory and research* (pp. 244–276). New York: Guilford.
Jung, C.G., & Hull, R.F.C. (1992). *Two essays on analytical psychology* (Vol. 7). New York: Routledge.
Watson, D., & Clark, L.A. (1997). Extraversion and its positive emotional core. In R. Hogan, J. Johnson, & S. Briggs (Eds.), *Handbook of personality psychology* (pp. 767–793). San Diego, CA: Academic Press.
Wilson, G.D. (1978). Introversion-extraversion. In H. London & J.E. Exner Jr. (Eds.), *Dimensions of personality* (pp. 217–261). New York: John Wiley.

J

William James (1842–1910)

American psychologist and philosopher William James was one of the leading contributors to emotion theory during the 19th and 20th centuries. His James-Lange theory of emotion inspired thinking and research that continues to this day.

James was born in New York City in 1842, son of Henry James Sr. and Mary Walsh James. Since William James's grandfather had become rich buying and selling land, Henry Sr. did not need to work to earn a living. Henry Sr. valued education and all intellectual affairs and spent a great deal of his time with other intellectuals. He also used much of his wealth to provide the best possible education for his children. William, his brother Henry Jr. (who became a famous novelist), and the other three children were educated in Europe, at exclusive private universities in the United States, or both.

As a young man, William had a passion and talent for art and worked as a painter. After a short period, however, he decided to abandon art and to pursue medicine instead. It is not clear why he made this change, perhaps because his father suggested it. James entered Harvard in 1861 and graduated with a medical degree in 1869. He never practiced medicine; instead, he was hired in 1874 to teach a course about the relationship between physiology and psychology at Harvard University. In 1875, he also established a demonstrational lab in psychology there. Both of these were achievements for the psychology field. Most historians say that modern scientific psychology had its origins in the 1870s and 1880s in the United States and Europe. For several reasons—including this early course taught by James and his creation of a lab—some argue that James should be considered the father of modern psychology. In 1876, James was appointed to the rank of assistant professor at Harvard. In 1885 he was promoted to full professor of philosophy, and in 1889 to full professor of psychology.

James's theory of emotion is called the James-Lange theory because Danish psychologist Carl Lange introduced the same ideas at the same time. The James-Lange theory is based on the principle that emotional feeling is a result of physical reactions to a stimulus; the body reaction to a stimulus precedes the feeling aspect (subjective experience) of the emotion. Specifically, James and Lange suggested that the perception of a stimulus produces a specific body reaction and that the body reaction produces the emotional feeling. This sequence of emotional experience contradicts the common notion that emotion precedes the bodily reaction to a stimulus. In his article, James stated that "we feel sorry because we cry, angry because we strike, afraid because we tremble" (Lange & James, 1922, p. 13). A major point of this theory is that it does not assume any intervening cognition of emotion that comes after the physiological arousal. The arousal itself is considered the emotional feeling. An additional significant aspect of this theory is that different emotions might be associated with different physiological responses, although James and Lange did not specifically address this issue (Russell, 2003).

William James not only pioneered in the study of psychology in the United States but also achieved international fame as a philosopher with his doctrine of pragmatism, a method for determining truth by testing the consequences of ideas. (Library of Congress)

The James-Lange theory has had a tremendous impact on the development of emotion theory, for example, by inspiring research on whether differential physiological responses occur for the various emotions. This research is ongoing. However, the James-Lange theory has been heavily criticized. In particular, the theory was scientifically attacked by Walter Cannon, an American physiologist in the late 1920s. One criticism he made was that many of the necessary physiological responses to which James and Lange allude, particularly the hormonal action of the autonomic nervous system, are too slow to cause the emotional feeling.

Another highly significant contribution of James was his two-volume, 1,393-page book *The Principles of Psychology*, published in 1890. The books were a huge success; they were the standard psychology texts in the United States, England, Germany, France, and Italy for several years (Hothersall, 2004). The books were extremely well written and painstakingly researched. They had an appeal for academics, students, and general audiences. Psychologists today still praise these books highly. For instance, Peter Gray, who has written an introductory psychology text that has been successful for a couple of decades, called James's text the best introductory text ever written (Gray, 2002).

James was an outstanding writer and lecturer and an engaging teacher of psychology who enjoyed interaction with his students. He served two terms as president of the American Psychological Association (in 1894 and in 1904). He is widely recognized as a significant figure in psychology. For instance, in a 1970 poll of 1,000 members of the American Psychological Association, ranking psychologists for the influence they had on the development of psychology, James ranked sixth (Wright, 1970). However, in some ways, James was not fully devoted to the psychology field. For example, he did not devote much energy or time to research other than the research demonstrations that he did specifically for teaching. Additionally, during the last 10 years of his life, he moved away from psychology and devoted his scholarly pursuits to philosophy, publishing two influential books, *Pragmatism* in 1907 and *The Meaning of Truth* in 1909. For these reasons, in discussions of who should be denoted as father of modern psychology, support for James is lukewarm.

In 1878 (when he was 36), James married Alice Howe Gibbons, a Boston schoolteacher. Their marriage was largely a happy one; they shared many interests. They had five children. In the last 12 years of his life, James suffered from heart problems, and he died of a heart attack in 1910 at age 68.

See also autonomic nervous system, Walter Cannon; Cannon-Bard theory of emotion, James-Lange theory of emotion, stress, stress hormones, sympathetic nervous system.

Further Readings:

James, W. (1890). *The principles of psychology* (2 vols.). New York: Henry Holt.

Simon, L. (1998). *Genuine reality: A life of William James.* New York: Harcourt Brace.

William James Society Web site: http://wjsociety.org/

William James Web page at Emory University: http://www.des.emory.edu/mfp/james.html

References:

Gray, P. (2002). *Psychology* (4th ed.). New York: Worth.

Hothersall, D. (2004). *History of psychology.* San Francisco: McGraw-Hill.

James, W. (1890). *The principles of psychology* (2 vols.). New York: Henry Holt.

James, W. (1907). *Pragmatism: A new name for some old ways of thinking.* New York: Longman's, Green.

James, W. (1909). *The meaning of truth: A sequel to "pragmatism."* Oxford, England: Longmans, Green.

Lange, C. G., & James, W. (1962). *The emotions.* New York: Hafner. (Original work published 1922)

Russell, J. A. (2003). Core affect and the psychological construction of emotion. *Psychological Review, 110,* 145–172.

Wright, G. D. (1970). A further note on ranking the important psychologists. *American Psychologist, 25,* 650–651.

James-Lange Theory of Emotion

The James-Lange theory of emotion was independently developed in the late 19th century by American psychologist William James and Danish psychologist Carl Lange. James first discussed his view on the genesis of emotion in an article titled "What Is an Emotion?" published in the journal *Mind* in 1884. Later in his book *The Principles of Psychology*, published in 1890, he explicitly stated his theory of emotion. Around the same time, Lange published similar views and reaffirmed James's theory.

The James-Lange theory of emotion is based on the principle that emotion is a result of physical reactions to a stimulus; the body reaction to a stimulus precedes the feeling aspect (subjective experience) of the emotion. Specifically, James and Lange suggested that the perception of a stimulus produces a specific body reaction and that the body reaction produces the emotional feeling. This sequence of emotional experience contradicts the common notion that emotion precedes the bodily reaction to a stimulus. In his article, James stated that "we feel sorry because we cry, angry because we strike, afraid because we tremble" (Lange & James, 1922, p. 13). A major point of this theory is that it does not assume any intervening cognition of emotion that comes after the physiological arousal. The arousal itself is considered the emotional feeling. An additional significant aspect of this theory is that different emotions might be associated with different physiological responses, although James and Lange did not specifically address this issue (Russell, 2003).

James and Lange held the idea that physiological activity is necessary for the production of emotional experience. In their view, the emotion-provoking object itself is not strong enough to produce emotional experience. As some researchers have pointed out, some of James's statements were lacking in clarity, leading to some confusion about the theory. For instance, James said that when you see a bear, you first run away then feel fear, rather than feeling fear then running away (as common sense would suggest). But others have said that running away from a bear is not automatic: we would not run away from a bear in a zoo or a bear that we saw sleeping in the woods. As they say, some interpretation, or appraisal, of the situation is necessary for you to run. For example, Kalat and Shiota (2007) restate and clarify the James-Lange theory as shown in Table 6.

Table 6: James-Lange Theory of Emotion

Event	→	Appraisal of event	→	Action (both behavioral and physiological responses)	→	Emotional feeling
(threatening bear)	→	(this is threatening)	→	(running and stress reaction)	→	(fear)

The James-Lange theory has had a tremendous impact on the development of emotion theory, for example, by inspiring research on whether differential physiological responses occur for the various emotions. However, the James-Lange theory has been heavily criticized. In particular, the theory was scientifically attacked by Walter Cannon, an American physiologist in the late 1920s (e.g., see Cannon, 1915/1929). One criticism he made was that many of the necessary physiological responses that James and Lange refer or allude to, in particular, the hormonal action of the autonomic nervous system, are too slow to cause the emotional feeling. Another critique was that one would expect individuals with spinal cord injuries to experience relatively numbed emotions (since nervous system damage would mean a reduced physiological reaction to a stimulus), but research has produced mixed findings, with some results suggesting less intense emotional experience among spinal cord injury patients (e.g., Mack, Birbaumer, Kaps, Badke, & Kaiser, 2005) and other results indicating normal emotional experience (e.g., Cobos, Sanchez, Perez, & Vila, 2004).

See also autonomic nervous system, Walter Cannon, Cannon-Bard theory of emotion, feeling, William James, physiology of emotion, subjective experience of emotion, sympathetic nervous system.

References:

Cannon, W. B. (1929). *Bodily changes in pain, hunger, fear, and rage* (2nd ed.). New York: D. Appleton. (Original work published 1915)

Cobos, P., Sánchez, M., Pérez, N., & Vila, J. (2004). Effects of spinal cord injuries on the subjective component of emotions. *Cognition & Emotion, 18*, 281–287.

James, W. (1884). What is an emotion? *Mind, 9*, 188–205.

James, W. (1890). *The principles of psychology* (2 vols.). New York: Henry Holt.

Kalat, J. W., & Shiota, M. N. (2007). *Emotion.* Belmont, CA: Thomson Wadsworth.

Lange, C. G., & James, W. (1962). *The emotions.* New York: Hafner. (Original work published 1922)

Mack, H., Birbaumer, N., Kaps, H., Badke, A., & Kaiser, J. (2005). Motion and emotion: Emotion processing in quadriplegic patients and athletes. *Zeitschrift fur Medizinische Psychologie, 14*, 159–166.

Russell, J. A. (2003). Core affect and the psychological construction of emotion. *Psychological Review, 110*, 145–172.

Jealousy

Jealousy is the feelings, thoughts, and behaviors that occur when an individual perceives that a rival threatens his romantic relationship. The emotions involved in jealousy are anger, fear, and hurt (Guerrero & Andersen, 1998). Anger is present because the jealous individual thinks that he has been betrayed or could be betrayed. Fear arises from the perception that one could lose his partner, and sadness occurs due to the possible loss of trust in the relationship.

Scholars have viewed jealousy from diverse perspectives, including attachment theory and evolutionary theory. Scholars from both theoretical viewpoints have attempted to explain how jealousy is functional. According to attachment theory, adult romantic relationships involve *attachment* that is highly similar to the attachment of an infant and her caretaker (Sharpsteen, 1999). Young infants become attached to a single person, often the mother. The attachment is expressed in behavior, meaning that the infant desires and makes efforts to maintain close proximity to the attachment figure. Additionally, attachment is an emotional bond. During particular developmental periods, the infant will scream and cry when separated from the mother; the crying is not only an emotional expression but also an attempt to encourage the mother to return. Scholars studying jealousy make note that infant behavior surrounding the experiences of separating from and reuniting with mother meets the description of jealousy. Specifically, they show fear when the mother leaves, may show anger when she returns (perhaps hitting Mom or having a mini temper tantrum), and demonstrate sadness/hurt if the separation is prolonged.

According to the attachment perspective on jealousy, adults become attached to other adults, and jealousy feelings and behaviors may be the adult counterpart of the feelings and behaviors that an infant has when threatened by separation from her mother. The adult expressions of fear, anger, and sadness may be designed to maintain the physical and psychological attachment between two individuals, just as these behaviors function the same way in the infant-mother attachment bond.

Evolutionary psychologists have a somewhat different perspective on the function of jealousy. According to Buss (2000), jealousy evolved to motivate people to act in ways that are likely to protect their close relationships. Close relationships are advantageous from an evolutionary perspective because they enhance the survival of people's offspring, thus ensuring survival of their genetic material. Buss argues that early humans who reacted strongly to potential romantic rivals by vigilantly scanning for potential threats, discouraging rivals, and keeping their mates happy and satisfied were more likely to keep their relationships and reproduce more than people who were apathetic when a potential rival came along. Therefore jealousy is currently a part of our genetic makeup because it led to a reproductive advantage in the past. Jealousy scholars have reviewed research on a wide variety of topics related to jealousy such as individual characteristics that make one prone to jealousy, sex differences in jealousy, various events and circumstances that tend to evoke jealousy, and how to cope with jealousy (e.g., Miller, Perlman, & Brehm, 2007; Pines, 1998).

See also anger, attachment, evolutionary psychology (human sociobiology), fear.

Further Readings:

Buss, D. M. (2000). *The dangerous passion: Why jealousy is as necessary as love and sex.* New York: Free Press.

Pines, A. M. (1998). *Romantic jealousy: Causes, symptoms, cures.* New York: Routledge.

References:

Buss, D. M. (2000). *The dangerous passion: Why jealousy is as necessary as love and sex.* New York: Free Press.

Guerrero, L. K., & Andersen, P. A. (1998). Jealousy experience and expression in romantic relationships. In P. A. Andersen & L. K. Guerrero (Eds.), *Handbook of communication and emotion* (pp. 155–188). San Diego, CA: Lawrence Erlbaum Associates.

Miller, R. S., Perlman, D., & Brehm, S. S. (2007). *Intimate relationships* (4th ed.). New York: McGraw-Hill.

Pines, A. M. (1998). *Romantic jealousy: Causes, symptoms, cures.* New York: Routledge.

Sharpsteen, D. J. (1999). Jealousy. In D. Levinson, J. J. Ponzetti, & P. F. Jorgensen (Eds.), *Encyclopedia of human emotions* (2nd ed., pp. 413–418). New York: Macmillan Reference USA.

Joy

Joy is one of the variety of positive emotions or affective states that also include happiness, contentment, pleasure, excitement, satisfaction, gladness, ecstasy, and others. According to Bagozzi (1999), the English language has about 40 words that describe states that are variants of happiness.

The word *joy* is sometimes used generically to describe a pleasant emotional or affective state. However, psychologists have attempted to distinguish the variety of positive states in an effort to provide clear descriptions of each individual state. The states can be categorized as other-directed (interpersonal) or self-directed (intrapersonal; DeRivera & Grinkis, 1986). Love is an example of an other-directed state, whereas most of the positive emotion terms, including joy, refer to self-directed states. Emotions and affective states may also be distinguished by degree of arousal (e.g., Russell, 1980). Some positive states involve high arousal, such as ecstasy, and others involve low arousal, such as tranquility or contentment. Joy falls in between these extremes, with moderate arousal. Another way to understand affective experience is to consider whether a particular type of experience is a reaction to an immediate event or whether it describes an individual's typical or customary way of feeling (the latter may indicate a personality trait). Applying this distinction, joy is usually used to mean a positive emotional experience that occurs as a reaction to a particular event, whereas according to some emotion researchers (e.g., Kalat & Shiota, 2007), the term *happiness* is more appropriate for an affective state that one has more consistently; thus some people can be said to have happy personalities.

Schumm (1999) distinguishes between four positive emotional states: pleasure, satisfaction, happiness, and joy. The main difference between the four states has to do with what causes the state. Pleasure is usually associated with the occurrence of something tangible such as eating good food, using a drug, or finding a $100 bill on the street. The cause of pleasure is not necessarily related to anything that the individual experiencing the pleasure has achieved or earned (although it can be). The feeling of pleasure is short-lived; it tends to go away soon after the event that caused it. Satisfaction is more complex than pleasure because it involves thinking. Someone experiences satisfaction when he achieves what he has set out to achieve or what he feels he deserves. For instance, a person may feel satisfaction when he has won an award that he thought he deserved for the poem that he wrote. Since satisfaction involves thinking (cognition), it may be either fairly easy or fairly difficult for a particular individual to experience it; some people may hold very high standards for feeling satisfaction, for instance, by requiring high absolute performance or requiring oneself to continually achieve more and more over time or requiring oneself to be better than all competitors. Happiness is less cognitive and more emotional than satisfaction; Schumm (1999) and others have described happiness as the emotional aspect of a general sense of well-being, whereas satisfaction is the cognitive aspect. Additionally, happiness is often described as being largely derived from the quality of one's interpersonal relationships with friends and family. Joy is usually associated with transcendent experiences. Most often, these experiences are religious or spiritual or the result of involvement in meaningful work. Csikszentmihalyi (1997) has described the feeling of "flow," intense concentration and full involvement, that occurs when an individual is engaged in much-loved work and is making nearly full use of his capabilities. A significant component of flow is joy.

See also flow, happiness, pleasure, positive emotions, satisfaction.

References:

Bagozzi, R. P. (1999). Happiness. In D. Levinson, J. J. Ponzetti, & P. F. Jorgensen (Eds.), *Encyclopedia of human emotions* (2nd ed., pp. 317–324). New York: Macmillan Reference USA.

Csikszentmihalyi, M. (1997). *Finding flow: The psychology of engagement with everyday life.* New York: Basic Books.

de Rivera, J., & Grinkis, C. (1986). Emotions as social relationships. *Motivation and Emotion, 10*, 351–369.

Kalat, J. W., & Shiota, M. N. (2007). *Emotion.* Belmont, CA: Thomson Wadsworth.

Russell, J. A. (1980). A circumplex model of affect. *Journal of Personality and Social Psychology, 39*, 1161–1178.

Schumm, W. R. (1999). Satisfaction. In D. Levinson, J. J. Ponzetti, & P. F. Jorgensen (Eds.), *Encyclopedia of human emotions* (2nd ed., pp. 583–590). New York: Macmillan Reference USA.

L

Lability (Emotional)

Lability, which is instability or changeability, applies to a number of emotion concepts. Lability is an aspect of the emotion concept itself. From a psychological point of view, an emotion is an immediate, temporary reaction to an event or experience. Thus an emotion tends to last a few minutes or hours, then subsides, and other emotions surface.

Emotional lability is a central feature in a number of psychological disorders. Bipolar disorder (formerly called manic depression) involves a cycling between periods of depression, periods of mania (which involve grandiosity and high energy, and often elevated mood), and periods of "normalcy." Borderline personality disorder is also characterized by emotional lability; in this condition, an individual has major mood shifts, unstable self-perceptions and perceptions of others (e.g., idealizing someone one day and vilifying him the next), and unstable relationships.

Emotional lability may be associated with traumatic brain injury, Alzheimer's disease, stroke, autistic spectrum disorders, and attention-deficit hyperactivity disorder. Emotional lability characterizes some common psychological states or experiences outside of the realm of psychological disorders. Emotional lability may be associated with hormonal changes (e.g., during puberty, pregnancy, and after childbirth). Experiencing menopause often means experiencing increased mood swings (Xu et al., 2005). Additionally, a component of the general personality trait "neuroticism" is moodiness and emotional instability.

See also bipolar disorder, borderline personality disorder, menopause, mood, mood swings, neuroticism, personality disorder.

Reference:
Xu, J., Bartoces, M., Neale, A. V., Dailey, R. K., Northrup, J., & Schwartz, K. L. (2005). Natural history of menopause symptoms in primary care patients: A MetroNet study. *Journal of the American Board of Family Practice, 18*, 374–382.

Arnold A. Lazarus (1932–)

Arnold Lazarus is a pioneer in the field of psychotherapy. He is probably best known for developing multimodal therapy (MMT), a multifaceted approach to psychotherapy based on cognitive-behavioral therapy (CBT).

Dr. Lazarus was born in Johannesburg, South Africa, in 1932. He attended the University of Witwatersrand in Johannesburg, where he earned his bachelor's and master's degrees, receiving a PhD in clinical psychology in 1960. In 1958 (while still a graduate student), Lazarus originated the term *behavior therapy* in a paper published in the *South African Medical Journal*. He started a private psychotherapy practice in Johannesburg in 1959. In 1966, while director of the Behavior Therapy Institute in Sausalito, California, he published *Behavior Therapy Techniques* with Joseph Wolpe.

Dr. Lazarus has been an innovator, utilizing novel approaches to psychotherapy: Lazarus and Abramowitz were the first psychologists to use emotive imagery (a desensitization method utilizing imagery and relaxation to overcome fears and phobias) with children, and Lazarus was the first to use desensitization techniques to treat phobias in group settings (Alic, 2001). Lazarus has long been a proponent of a multifaceted (broad spectrum) approach to psychotherapy. In 1958, Lazarus stated that "the emphasis in psychological rehabilitation must be on a *synthesis* which would embrace a diverse range of effective therapeutic techniques, as well as innumerable adjunctive measures, to form part of a wide and all-embracing re-educative programme" (Lazarus, 1958, p. 710). In *Behavior Therapy and Beyond* (Lazarus, 1971), the book that laid the foundations for CBT, Lazarus again advocated a broad-spectrum approach to psychotherapy.

In his research on the long-term results of CBT, Lazarus found high relapse rates for patients who underwent CBT for panic and anxiety disorders, obsessive-compulsive problems, depression, and marriage and family problems. So Lazarus developed a distinctive therapeutic orientation, MMT, between 1970 and 1973. MMT is a comprehensive appraisal that looks at seven arenas of human functioning, including behavior (B), affect (A), sensation (S), imagery (I), cognition (C), interpersonal relationships (I.), and drugs/biology (D.). From these seven areas comes the MMT acronym BASIC I.D. MMT has been utilized in diverse environments, including schools, psychiatric hospitals, and residential facilities.

MMT has been refined since its development, and training in MMT has been part of the clinical doctoral program at Rutgers since 1972. In 1976, Lazarus established the Multimodal Therapy Institute in Kingston, New Jersey; he is currently executive director of the Lazarus Institute in Skillman, New Jersey. Nine books, many chapters, and numerous articles have been published on MMT.

Dr. Lazarus has authored 18 books and hundreds of scientific publications. He has received the American Psychological Association's Distinguished Psychologist and Distinguished Professional Contributions awards, the American Board of Professional Psychology's Distinguished Service Award, and the first Annual Cummings PSYCHE Award, among others. Dr. Lazarus has been a faculty member of Stanford University, Temple University Medical School, and Yale University and has maintained an active psychotherapy practice since 1959.

See also behavior therapy, cognitive therapy and cognitive-behavioral therapy, multimodal therapy: BASIC I.D., systematic desensitization.

Further Readings:

Lazarus, A. A. (2007). Multimodal therapy. In R. J. Corsini & D. Wedding, *Current psychotherapies* (8th ed., pp. 368–401). Belmont, CA: Wadsworth.

Lazarus Institute Web site: http://www.thelazarusinstitute.com/

References:

Alic, M. (2001). Lazarus, Arnold Allan (1932–). In B. B. Strickland (Ed.), *Gale encyclopedia of psychology* (2nd ed.). Farmington Hills, MI: Gale Group.

Lazarus, A. A. (1958). A psychological approach to alcoholism. *South African Medical Journal, 30,* 707–710.

Lazarus, A. A. (1971). *Behavior therapy and beyond.* New York: McGraw-Hill.

Lazarus, A. A., & Wolpe, J. (1966). *Behavior therapy techniques: A guide to the treatment of neuroses.* New York: Pergamon Press.

Learned Helplessness

In the 1960s, Martin Seligman, a young graduate student at the University of Pennsylvania, became interested in people who possess an attitude and behavior tendency that often causes suffering for themselves and those around them. His interest was in passivity, the tendency that some people have to resign themselves to their fates, to do nothing to solve their problems, even when they likely have the physical and cognitive capacities to improve their circumstances. Seligman set out to learn why some individuals possess this level of apathy.

His interest did not develop out of thin air; research that his graduate lab was conducting at the University of Pennsylvania inspired Seligman's musings. In the laboratory research supervised by Seligman's graduate school advisor, dogs were being trained to associate a tone with a shock. The purpose of these studies was to see if the dogs could learn to anticipate the shock once they heard the tone and then take action to escape the shock. In the experiment, which left the researchers baffled, the dogs that had been previously conditioned to associate the tone and shock reacted in an opposite way than predicted; when shocked, instead of moving around so that they could jump over a barrier and escape the shock, the dogs lay down and whimpered, accepting the painful shock. In a moment of insight, Seligman realized that the conditioning had actually occurred differently than expected. During the experiment, the dogs, in addition to learning that the tone and the shock occur together, may have also learned (Seligman speculated) that they have no ability to prevent the unpleasant event (the shock) from occurring. This learning would have occurred because as the tone and shock were presented together during conditioning, the dogs were restrained and thus unable to escape the shock. As a result, when the same dogs were put in a new situation in which they actually could escape, they did not try to escape.

In the 1960s and 1970s, in a series of classic studies, Seligman, fellow student Steven Maier, another colleague, Bruce Overmier, and others set out to test Seligman's new hypotheses directly. In a key study, dogs, one at a time, were placed in a cage and restrained. They received a series of shocks on their feet through the floor. Then each dog, and other dogs that had not had the initial experience, were placed in a new large cage where a light would turn on periodically. Each time the light was presented, it was followed ten seconds later by a shock to the feet. All animals learned to associate the light with the shock. The dogs that had not experienced the earlier experimental situation (being shocked while restrained) would run around nearly in a panic. They would soon learn that if they jumped over a fence to another part of the cage, they would escape the shock. Conversely, the dogs that had experienced the initial experimental treatment of restraint while being shocked would not even try to escape; they would passively accept the shock that followed. Seligman and his colleagues concluded that the dogs who did not try to escape had formed an expectation that their behavior did not matter, their behavior had no effect—these dogs had learned to be helpless (e.g., Overmier & Seligman, 1967; Seligman & Maier, 1967).

Seligman and colleagues generalized this finding with dogs to humans. They suggested that depression, rather than being an inability to cope or being caused by other factors, may be due to an attitude that the individual learned from his life experiences—learned helplessness. Other psychologists and psychiatrists quickly refuted this claim, some stating that many people experience frustrating situations in which their immediate behavior has no effect, but not everyone becomes depressed, and others criticized Seligman and his colleagues' research methodology (e.g., Costello, 1978).

Seligman sought to find a response to the criticisms, still believing that his learned helplessness explanation had merit. He worked together with a psychologist who had criticized him, John Teasdale, and another psychologist, Lyn Abramson. They reasoned that individual difference variables work in conjunction with experiences of uncontrollable events to induce depression. As Abramson, Seligman, and Teasdale (1978) described, we all sometimes experience failures or distressing experiences about which we can do nothing, but we have different ways of making sense of these experiences and of predicting future events based on the experiences. In their new model of depression, they suggested that one of the important factors affecting the probability of developing depression in the face of uncontrollable events is whether the individual believes that the uncontrollable events that are likely to occur say something about her self-worth. For example, if a person fails an exam and perceives that that exam and future exams with that teacher are uncontrollable, she will be more likely to become depressed if the past failure and perceived future failures are believed to be caused by her lack of intellectual ability rather than by the extreme difficulty of the tests.

Seligman and colleagues continued to develop the learned helplessness theory. Peterson, Maier, and Seligman's book *Learned Helplessness: A Theory for the Age of Personal Control* (1993), describes the decades of research on learned helplessness that fleshes out the complexity of learned helplessness theory and situations in which learned helplessness applies. For instance, in addition to explaining depression, learned helplessness has been used to explain poor achievement and poor health.

Beginning in about the 1990s, Seligman and his colleagues began to frame their learned helplessness research and theory in more positive terms, speaking of the converse of learned helplessness, which is optimism. This reframing is consistent with a relatively modern movement in psychology that focuses on what is best in human nature: *positive psychology*.

See also depression, locus of control, motivation, optimism, positive psychology.

Further Readings:
Peterson, C. (1999). Helplessness. In D. Levinson, J. J. Ponzetti Jr., & P. F. Jorgensen (Eds.), *Encyclopedia of human emotions* (2nd ed., pp. 343–347). New York: Macmillan Reference USA.
Peterson, C., Maier, S. F., & Seligman, M.E.P. (1993). *Learned helplessness: A theory for the age of personal control.* New York: Oxford University Press.

University of Plymouth, Department of Psychology. (n.d.). *Depression and learned helplessness*. Retrieved from http://www.flyfishingdevon.co.uk/salmon/year2/psy221depression/psy221depression.htm#learnedhelplessnesstheory

References:

Abramson, L., Seligman, M., & Teasdale, J. (1978). Learned helplessness in humans: Critique and reformulation. *Journal of Abnormal Psychology, 87*, 49–74.

Costello, C. (1978). A critical review of Seligman's laboratory experiments on learned helplessness and depression in humans. *Journal of Abnormal Psychology, 87*, 21–31.

Overmier, J. B., & Seligman, M.E.P. (1967). Effects of inescapable shock upon subsequent escape and avoidance responding. *Journal of Comparative and Physiological Psychology, 63*, 28–33.

Peterson, C., Maier, S. F., & Seligman, M.E.P. (1993). *Learned helplessness: A theory for the age of personal control*. New York: Oxford University Press.

Seligman, M.E.P., & Maier, S. F. (1967). Failure to escape traumatic shock. *Journal of Experimental Psychology, 74*, 1–9.

Libido

Sigmund Freud coined the term *libido* in the early 1900s. Libido means sensual desire or the drive for physical pleasure seeking. According to Freud, it is one of three primary motivational forces in people, along with the drive for self-preservation and a destructive drive.

Freud (1905/1953, 1916/1961, 1963/1997) famously and elaborately described the way that libido is linked to human psychological development. According to his theory of psychosexual development, children derive sensual pleasure from particular objects and activities during each of the stages of their psychological development. The stages are named *oral, anal, phallic, latency*, and *genital*; each of these labels identifies the main area of the body around which pleasure is centered during that particular stage. (*Latency* refers to the idea that libido is repressed during this stage, and therefore pleasure is not centered around any part of the body at all.) For instance, in the first stage of development, the oral stage, the infant/young child's pleasure is centered around oral activities: sucking, placing objects in the mouth, and so on. A primary source of enjoyment is the mother's breast. The child not only obtains pleasure from the object (in this case, the breast) but also develops a psychological attachment to the object from which it receives pleasure. These same principles of pleasure and attachment apply to the remaining stages (except latency). The final stage, genital, is psychological maturity. According to Freud, if development has progressed adequately, the individual's libido will be directed toward an opposite-sexed partner during this final stage. Like the other stages, pleasure and attraction are linked with attachment to the object (opposite-sexed partner); pleasure and love are linked. Put another way, according to Freud, sex and love are intimately associated with one another (see Freud, 1963/1997, for further discussion of the connection between sex and love).

Freud (1963/1997) emphasized the role that sensual desire plays in mental illness, particularly *neurosis*, a large class of mental illnesses that are generally less severe than psychosis but that can involve significant suffering, for instance, depression and the wide variety of anxiety disorders. In Freud's theory, development has a goal, which is that the individual reach the genital stage, where the individual becomes capable of experiencing love toward, intimacy with, and desire for sexual activity with a heterosexual partner. Freud went so far as to say that the most normal development in the genital stage is behavioral heterosexual monogamy (which does not mean that people do not have sexual desire outside of the monogamous bond but means that people, if they are psychologically strong, will tend to choose to behave within the bond). According to Freud, this is the normal and ideal development because it ensures survival of the species. People will mate with someone with whom they can reproduce, an opposite-sexed partner. Furthermore, pair bonding is beneficial for one's offspring and helps to keep societies stable. Although the genital stage is the goal, most people do not arrive at the goal unscathed. Since libido involves both pleasure seeking and love/attachment, the potential exists for both frustration of pleasure and psychological hurt, for example, through feeling rejected by a loved object. In the oral stage, for instance, the child may experience some extreme in breast feeding—overindulgence or deprivation—or the child may have had experiences with the mother that led to mistrust. Under these circumstances, the child will, to some extent, become "stuck" at that stage, leaving less energy (libido) for the child to direct toward the upcoming stages. Freud said that libido is a fixed or limited amount of energy. If libido is directed in one direction (e.g., toward oral interests), there is less libido remaining for another direction (e.g., toward a heterosexual partner).

Being stuck at a stage is called a *fixation*. Fixations are sources of mental illness symptoms. For example, during the oral stage, an individual is passive and dependent. If the caretaker overindulges the child in regard to breast-feeding and other situations, the child may become fixated here, resulting in a number of possible outcomes such as passivity and dependency in adulthood, an eating disorder, oral behaviors such as smoking, and so forth.

Like so many of Freud's theories, aspects of the libido theory have received support and other aspects have not. For instance, many psychologists agree that pleasure seeking is a powerful motive for people (e.g., Skinner, 1938). However, whether pleasure seeking exists in exactly the way Freud most often presented it (almost exclusively sensual) is questionable. Additionally, the idea of whether pleasure-seeking energy is fixed is debatable. Scholars who were initially followers of Freud and who later broke off and developed independent theories, such as Carl Jung and Alfred Adler, revised the libido concept, viewing it as a general creative life force.

See also desire, developmental crisis, Sigmund Freud, Karen Horney, human development, human life span, love, lust, motivation, pleasure, psychoanalytic perspective, the unconscious mind.

Further Readings:
Freud, S. (1953). The ego and the id. In J. Strachey (Ed. & Trans.), *The standard edition of the complete psychological works of Sigmund Freud* (Vol. 19). London: Hogarth Press. (Original work published 1923)
Freud, S. (1997). *Sexuality and the psychology of love.* New York: Touchstone. (Original work published 1963)

References:
Freud, S. (1953). Three essays on the theory of sexuality. In J. Strachey (Ed. & Trans.), *The standard edition of the complete psychological works of Sigmund Freud* (Vol. 7, pp. 123–213). London: Hogarth Press. (Original work published 1905)
Freud, S. (1961, 1963). Introductory lectures on psychoanalysis. In J. Strachey (Ed. & Trans.), *The standard edition of the complete psychological works of Sigmund Freud* (Vols. 15 & 16). London: Hogarth Press. (Original work published 1916)

Freud, S. (1997). *Sexuality and the psychology of love.* New York: Touchstone. (Original work published 1963)

Skinner, B. F. (1938). *The behavior of organisms: An experimental analysis.* New York: Macmillan.

Light Therapy

Sunlight has been used for healing purposes since ancient Greece, when Hippocrates prescribed exposure to sunlight to treat various illnesses. In the late 19th and early 20th centuries, bright light was prescribed to treat several mood and stress disorders, and hospitals were built with solariums (sun rooms) so patients could recuperate in the sunshine (Gale Group, 2006). Light therapy is most often used to treat seasonal affective depressive disorder (SAD) and subsyndromal SAD (winter doldrums). It has also been used to treat other major depressive disorders, including nonseasonal (chronic) depression, premenstrual dysphoric disorder, postpartum depression, depression associated with bulimia, and seasonal manifestations of adult attention-deficit disorder. Light therapy has also been explored to assist with jet-lag adjustments, to help shift workers adapt to rotations, to prevent postoperative delirium (Taguchi, Yano, & Kido, 2007), and to treat premenstrual syndrome. Light therapy is used either by itself or in conjunction with other treatments such as pharmacotherapy (e.g., antidepressant medications), cognitive-behavioral therapy, psychodynamic (talk) therapy, wake therapy (sleep deprivation), or physical exercise.

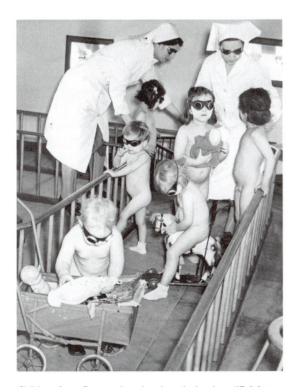

Children from Bermondsey London playing in artificial sunlight in a solarium with a sunlamp providing the "sunshine," March 2, 1942. Light therapy is most often used to treat seasonal affective depressive disorder (SAD) and subsyndromal SAD as well as other major depressive disorders. (Fox Photos/Getty Images)

Light therapy involves exposure to light of a specified intensity and type for a prescribed duration (dosage), often at a specific time of day. Most research has involved bright-light therapy, although research has been conducted with dim lights. Early light therapy utilized full-spectrum fluorescent lamps, which closely approximate the color composition of outdoor daylight, but ordinary fluorescent bulbs have been found to yield similar results. Morning treatment has generally demonstrated more benefits than evening treatment for people with seasonal depression (Terman & Terman, 2005). Some studies claim that people experience antidepressant benefits from light therapy in only a few days (Terman & Terman, 2005), while other studies claim it takes several weeks before light therapy shows statistically significant benefits over placebo treatments (Eastman, Young, Fogg, Liu, & Meaden, 1998). While many claims have been made about the effectiveness of light therapy, randomized, controlled studies have demonstrated the effectiveness of bright-light treatment and dawn simulation for SAD and bright-light therapy for nonseasonal depression (Golden et al., 2005). More research is needed to further explore the effectiveness of light therapy (Even, Schröder, Friedman, & Rouillon, 2008).

Side effects of light therapy may include eye strain or visual disturbances, nausea, headache, sweating, sedation, sleep disturbances, and unusual uterine bleeding. Light therapy, especially when used with a selective serotonin reuptake inhibitor (SSRI), may cause mania or hypomania as well as serotonin syndrome (which can cause diarrhea, nausea, hyperthermia, agitation, and disorientation). Light therapy can adversely interact with medications that cause photosensitivity, including some psychiatric medications (e.g., imipramine, phenothiazine, and lithium), supplements (e.g., St. John's wort, melatonin), and other medications (e.g., chloroquine, tetracycline). Anyone considering trying light therapy should have an eye exam; light therapy is not recommended for people with cataracts, glaucoma, or retinopathies. If sleep disturbances (including insomnia) or hyperactivity emerge after the initiation of treatment, the timing, dosage, and intensity of light therapy treatment may need to be adjusted.

See also complementary and alternative medicine, major depressive disorder, seasonal affective disorder.

Further Readings:

Even, C., Schröder, C. M., Friedman, S., & Rouillon, F. (2008). Efficacy of light therapy in nonseasonal depression: A systematic review. *Journal of Affective Disorders, 108*, 11–23.

Golden, R. N., Gaynes, B. N., Ekstrom, R. D., Hamer, R. M., Jacobsen, F. M., Suppes, T., et al. (2005). The efficacy of light therapy in the treatment of mood disorders: A review and meta-analysis of the evidence. *American Journal of Psychiatry, 162*, 656–662.

Terman, M., & Terman, J. S. (2005). Light therapy for seasonal and nonseasonal depression: Efficacy, protocol, safety, and side effects. *CNS Spectrums, 10*, 647–663.

References:

Eastman, C. I., Young, M. A., Fogg, L. F., Liu, L., & Meaden, P. M. (1998). Bright light treatment of winter depression: A placebo-controlled trial. *Archives of General Psychiatry, 55*, 883–889.

Even, C., Schröder, C. M., Friedman, S., & Rouillon, F. (2008). Efficacy of light therapy in nonseasonal depression: A systematic review. *Journal of Affective Disorders, 108*, 11–23.

Gale Group Inc. (2006). Light therapy. *Encyclopedia of Alternative Medicine.* Retrieved from http://www.enotes.com/alternative-medicine-encyclopedia/light-therapy

Golden, R. N., Gaynes, B. N., Ekstrom, R. D., Hamer, R. M., Jacobsen, F. M., Suppes, T., et al. (2005). The efficacy of light therapy in the treatment of mood disorders: A review and meta-analysis of the evidence. *American Journal of Psychiatry, 162*, 656–662.

Taguchi, T., Yano, M., & Kido, Y. (2007). Influence of bright light therapy on postoperative patients: A pilot study. *Intensive and Critical Care Nursing, 23*, 289–297.

Terman, M., & Terman, J. S. (2005). Light therapy for seasonal and nonseasonal depression: Efficacy, protocol, safety, and side effects. *CNS Spectrums, 10*, 647–663.

Limbic System

The limbic system is a group of brain areas including the hypothalamus, anterior thalamus, cingulate gyrus, hippocampus, amygdala, septal nuclei, orbitofrontal cortex, and portions of the basal ganglia. In the late 1940s and early 1950s, American physician and neuroscientist Paul MacLean (1949, 1952) proposed that these structures constitute the *emotional brain*.

The relationship between emotion and several of the limbic system structures (specifically, the hypothalamus, anterior thalamus, cingulate gyrus, and hippocampus) was first proposed by American neuroanatomist Dr. James Papez in his theoretical paper in 1937. These four brain structures were called the *Papez circuit* because they form a circuitous chain. In developing his theory, Papez built on information from at least three sources. First, research by Cannon (1915/1929) and Bard (1929), in which they systematically damaged or removed parts of the brain in animals, demonstrated that the hypothalamus is necessary for an animal to produce an integrated emotional expression (e.g., a cat's behavior when threatened of crouching down, hissing, with ears back, claws ready). Without the hypothalamus, the animal may produce some but not all behaviors characteristic of a particular emotional expression. Second, anatomist C. Judson Herrick (1933) had proposed a theory that distinguished between two parts of the cortex: the lateral (newer, from an evolutionary point of view) and medial (older). According to Herrick, the lateral cortex was responsible for sensation, motor function, and higher-order thinking in humans, while the medial cortex was involved with more primitive functions. Third, Papez had learned about research on damage to the medial cortex resulting in emotional dysfunction.

The Limbic System

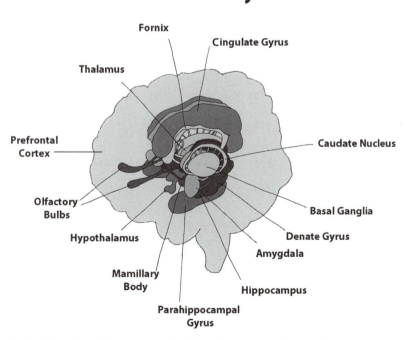

The limbic system of the human brain. The limbic system is the set of brain structures that forms the inner border of the cortex and is believed to support a variety of functions including emotion, behavior, long-term memory, and olfaction. (ABC-CLIO)

Papez theorized that the neural circuit for behavioral expression of emotion was primarily governed by the hypothalamus, while the actual experience (subjective feeling) of emotion was produced through the interactions among different structures in the Papez circuit. These other structures were part of the medial cortex, which presumably was a part of the cortex common across mammal species and which was relatively "primitive," as Herrick had said. These structures would not have language processing as a focus and were candidates for emotional experience, which can occur viscerally, without verbal labels or higher-order thinking.

Over 10 years later, MacLean integrated Papez's theory and other work, proposing the limbic system, the "emotional brain." As previously described, the limbic system includes the brain structures of the Papez circuit plus additional structures. MacLean discussed the importance of the hypothalamus in behavioral expression of emotion and the cerebral cortex in the experience of emotion. Starting with the hypothalamus as the center, and as a part of the brain with demonstrated involvement in emotion, he reasoned that other parts of the brain that are involved with emotion must be connected (by nerve fibers) to the hypothalamus. Most of the newer (more recently evolved) cortex did not have strong connections to the hypothalamus, but many parts of the medial cortex did. Based on both the observation of neural connections to the hypothalamus and clinical evidence, MacLean thus added brain structures to Papez's circuit. Other than the hypothalamus, MacLean suggested the hippocampus was the primary brain structure involved in emotional experience, because of both its location and its anatomy (LeDoux, 1996). The nerve cells (neurons) of the hippocampus are large and located next to one another in an orderly fashion. MacLean referred to the hippocampal neurons as an "emotional keyboard," the firing of particular neurons being associated with particular emotions. As hippocampal neurons lack the analyzing capacity of other neurons associated with more advanced anatomy, experience associated with stimulation of hippocampal neurons is relatively crude.

MacLean's theory was extremely influential and has played a large role in the development of knowledge about human emotion. However, the limbic system theory—at least as MacLean presented it—is largely unsupported. LeDoux (1996) describes a number of shortcomings with this theory. First, research indicates that the hippocampus plays a more significant role in memory than it does in emotion. Second, if one uses the criterion of nerve connections with the hypothalamus to identify whether a structure is involved with emotion, then most of the brain would qualify as the emotional brain. Third, at present, only particular brain structures have been clearly indicated in emotion, in particular, the amygdala, which is involved in fear. Thus LeDoux says that there really is no limbic system; there are clearly brain structures that are involved in emotion, and we have not yet identified all of them and their roles, but the limbic system concept is outdated.

While the limbic system concept as MacLean originally conceptualized it lacks support, it has led to some illuminating research regarding the brain and emotion. Results from neuroimaging studies (e.g., functional magnetic resonance imaging) continue to shed light on various theories of emotion processing. In addition to the limbic system concept, other theories have focused on the role of the brain's right hemisphere in emotion processing and the association between specific brain regions and emotions. For example, the amygdala is strongly associated with fear, the insula with disgust, and anger with the lateral orbitofrontal cortex (Murphy, Nimmo-Smith, & Lawrence, 2003).

See also amygdala, functional magnetic resonance imaging, hippocampus, hypothalamus, physiology of emotion, triune brain.

Further Reading:
LeDoux, J. (1996). *The emotional brain: The mysterious underpinnings of emotional life.* New York: Touchstone.

References:
Bard, P. (1929). The central representation of the sympathetic system, as indicated by certain physiologic observations. *Archives of Neurology and Psychiatry, 22*, 230–246.
Cannon, W. B. (1929). *Bodily changes in pain, hunger, fear, and rage* (2nd ed.). New York: D. Appleton. (Original work published 1915)
Herrick, C. J. (1933). The functions of the olfactory parts of the cerebral cortex. *Proceedings of the National Academy of Sciences of the United States of America, 19*, 7–14.
LeDoux, J. (1996). *The emotional brain: The mysterious underpinnings of emotional life.* New York: Touchstone.
MacLean, P. D. (1949). Psychosomatic disease and the "visceral brain": Recent developments bearing on the Papez theory of emotion. *Psychosomatic Medicine, 11*, 338–353.
MacLean, P. D. (1952). Some psychiatric implications of physiological studies on frontotemporal portion of limbic system (visceral brain). *Electroencephalography and Clinical Neurophysiology, 4*, 407–418.
Murphy, F. C., Nimmo-Smith, I., & Lawrence, A. D. (2003). Functional neuroanatomy of emotions: A meta-analysis. *Cognitive, Affective, & Behavioral Neuroscience, 3*, 207–233.
Papez, J. W. (1937). A proposed mechanism of emotion. *Archives of Neurology and Psychiatry, 38*, 725–743.

Lithium Therapy

Compounds of the chemical element lithium (i.e., lithium carbonate, lithium citrate) are common pharmaceutical treatments for the psychiatric condition bipolar disorder (formerly known as manic depression). People suffering from bipolar disorder alternate between episodes of depression, episodes of mania (typically characterized by elevated mood, high self-esteem, and high energy), and periods of normal mood and energy levels. Lithium treatments stabilize mood and help prevent future episodes of mania or depression in many people with bipolar disorder.

Lithium compounds were used in the 19th century to treat anxiety, seizures, and gout (Preston, O'Neal, & Talaga, 2008). In the 1940s, lithium was discovered as an effective treatment for bipolar disorder by Australian psychiatrist John Cade. Cade thought that mania was caused by an overabundance of a toxin circulating in the bloodstream and that the depression in bipolar disorder was caused by having too little of an unknown substance. Cade engaged in a tireless search for this hypothetical substance. In what he admitted was a fairly crude investigative approach, he injected the urine from manic patients into guinea pigs. He found that urine from manic patients was much more toxic than urine from other sources, killing the guinea pig more quickly. Cade next separated urine into its chemical components to identify the specific toxin. The discovery of lithium as a treatment was then fortuitous. Cade found that studying one of the components, uric acid, was difficult because crystals of uric acid are insoluble in water. To be able to dissolve uric acid, Cade added lithium to it, forming lithium urate. When he injected lithium urate, along with urea (another component of urine, which he had already found was highly toxic) into guinea pigs, he expected that the lithium urate would make urea even more toxic. Instead, urea was less toxic. Cade had identified lithium as a substance that reduced toxicity of another substance (Cade, 1949).

To investigate the helpful role of lithium, Cade injected it into guinea pigs without also injecting urea. He used lithium carbonate rather than lithium urate to reduce the possibility of side effects. When he injected lithium carbonate into the guinea pigs, they became sedate, a marked contrast to their typical frenetic behavior. Cade hypothesized that lithium could also have a calming effect on manic patients. His next step was to try the substance on himself to make sure it was safe. He suffered no ill effects and then tried lithium on 10 manic patients. His experiment was a success: the patients improved on the medication. In 1949, Cade published his findings in an article in the *Medical Journal of Australia* titled "Lithium Salts in the Treatment of Psychotic Excitement."

Lithium was a true success story in terms of treatment of psychiatric disorders; most medications in the 1940s and early 1950s were not very effective, and lithium not only alleviated current symptoms but could also prevent future episodes of mania or depression. It was used in many countries following the publication of Cade's paper but was not widely utilized in the United States until its approval by the U.S. Food and Drug Administration in 1970. Lithium is still used as a medication for bipolar disorder; 60 percent of patients who suffer manic episodes experience improvements (Carney & Goodwin, 2005). Depressive episodes also respond to lithium, although less markedly. Lithium is not effective for all individuals with bipolar disorder, and side effects are potentially very serious. Lithium should not be taken during pregnancy as it can cause birth defects (Preston et al., 2008). Some newer medications have comparable effectiveness as lithium with fewer side effects. Other mood stabilizers used in the treatment of bipolar disorder include valproic acid, carbamazepine, and lamotrigine. Medications used in addition to mood stabilizers to treat bipolar disorder include antidepressants, benzodiazepines (e.g., Valium), and antipsychotics (e.g., olanzapine; Preston et al., 2008). In 1998, valproic acid (divalproex, Depakote) replaced lithium as the most frequently prescribed drug for bipolar disorder (University of Texas Medical Branch, 1999).

It is not entirely clear how lithium achieves its therapeutic effect. One theory is that lithium may bring about changes within neurons, operating on substances called *second messengers* that prepare neurons for firing (Julien, 2007). Other evidence suggests that lithium increases the activity of particular proteins and other chemicals within neurons, thereby improving the health of these neurons (Gray, Zhou, Du, Moore, & Manji, 2003). Lithium's mechanism of action may operate through multiple routes. Ongoing research may determine how lithium and other mood-stabilizing medications help to stabilize the moods of bipolar patients.

See also antimanic, bipolar disorder, mood stabilizer.

Further Readings:
Healy, D. (2008). *Mania: A short history of bipolar disorder.* Baltimore: Johns Hopkins University Press.

Lewis, J. (Producer), & Smith, D. K. (Director). (2004). *Troubled minds: The lithium revolution* [Motion picture]. (Available from Screen Australia, GPO Box 3984, Sydney, NSW 2001, Australia).

References:
Cade, J. F. (1949). Lithium salts in the treatment of psychotic excitement. *Medical Journal of Australia, 2*, 349–352.
Cade, J. F. (1999). John Frederick Joseph Cade: Family memories on the occasion of the 50th anniversary of his discovery of the use of lithium in mania. *Australian and New Zealand Journal of Psychiatry, 33*, 615–618.
Carney, S. M., & Goodwin, G. M. (2005). Lithium—a continuing story in the treatment of bipolar disorder. *Acta Psychiatrica Scandinavica, 111*(Suppl. 426), 7–12.
Gray, N. A., Zhou, R., Du, J., Moore, G. J., & Manji, H. K. (2003). The use of mood stabilizers as plasticity enhancers in the treatment of neuropsychiatric disorders. *Journal of Clinical Psychiatry, 64*(Suppl. 5), 3–17.
Julien, R. M. (2007). *A primer of drug action* (11th ed.). New York: Worth.
Mitchell, P. B., & Hadzi-Pavlovic, D. (2000). Lithium treatment for bipolar disorder. *Bulletin of the World Health Organization, 78*, 515–518.
Preston, J. D., O'Neal, J. H., & Talaga, M. C. (2008). *Handbook of clinical psychopharmacology for therapists* (5th ed.). Oakland, CA: New Harbinger.
University of Texas Medical Branch at Galveston. (1999, May 14). *Mania drugs cut hospitalization costs.* Study presented at the meeting of the American Psychiatric Association, Washington, D.C.

Australian psychiatrist John Frederick Joseph Cade (1912–1980) discovered lithium carbonate, used as a mood stabilizer in the treatment of bipolar disorder. Cade's father, physician David Cade, suffered from depression and "war weariness" after serving in Gallipoli in World War I. Unable to maintain his medical practice, David Cade accepted a position with the Mental Hygiene Department, working at several Victorian mental hospitals. Thus John F. Cade and his brothers grew up living on the grounds of several mental institutions. This had a great bearing on John's future interest in treatments for the mentally ill. Cade was also influenced by his own experiences in Changi prison camp in Singapore during World War II (Cade, 1999).

As lithium salt is a naturally occurring chemical, it cannot be patented. Because of its limited commercial viability and toxicity, it was not widely accepted in psychiatry until its approval by the U.S. Food and Drug Administration in 1970 (Mitchell & Hadzi-Pavlovic, 2000).

Locus of Control

Locus of control is a personality trait identified by psychologist Julian Rotter (1966) that has been associated with health and other outcomes. People with an internal locus of control believe that they have control over their own lives. People with an external locus of control believe that something other than themselves (i.e., other people, the environment, fate, luck, the government) determines what happens to them. Locus of control exists on a continuum and thus an individual may be strongly internal or strongly external, or anywhere in between.

Overall, an internal locus of control has been associated with positive outcomes. For instance, compared to external control, those with internal control have less severe physical illness, are less likely to abuse substances such as drugs or alcohol, are more successful in quitting negative habits such as smoking, are higher achievers, have better overall psychological adjustment, cope better with stress, and many other examples. In her book *Control and the Psychology of Health*, Walker (2001) does a good job of explaining the role of control, including locus of control, in physical and psychological health. She discusses some of the research findings mentioned earlier. Additionally, and not surprisingly, internal locus of control is associated with positive emotions, and external locus of control tends to be correlated with negative emotions (e.g., Masters & Wallston, 2005).

Locus of control develops in the context of our life experiences. One factor that affects locus of control is the manner in which parents have reinforced or punished us as children. Parents who attend to and approve their children's positive behaviors tend to produce children with internal locus of control. When parents devalue children without any relation to the children's behavior, external locus of control is likely to develop (Krampen, 1989). Another variable that affects locus of control is social class; higher socioeconomic class is associated with internal locus of control.

Since Rotter identified locus of control in the 1960s, research on the topic has advanced at a steady pace. Now researchers recognize that locus of control is multidimensional; that is, an individual may possess internal control in one area (i.e., academics—believing that she can control her academic outcomes) and external control in another arena (e.g., social relationships).

See also attitude, learned helplessness, positive emotions.

References:
Krampen, G. (1989). Perceived childrearing practices and the development of locus of control in early adolescence. *International Journal of Behavioral Development, 12*, 177–193.
Masters, K. A., & Wallston, K. S. (2005). Canonical correlation reveals important relations between health locus of control, coping, affect, and values. *Journal of Health Psychology, 10*, 719–731.
Rotter, J. B. (1966). Generalized expectancies for internal versus external control of reinforcement. *Psychological Monographs: General and Applied, 80*, 1–28.
Walker, J. (2001). *Control and the psychology of health: Theory, measurement, and applications.* Buckingham, England: Open University Press.

Logotherapy

Logotherapy is an approach to psychotherapy introduced by humanistic/existentialist psychologist and psychiatrist Viktor Frankl. Frankl, who had begun his psychiatric career in the 1930s, was captured by Nazis in 1942 and spent several years in four death camps, including Auschwitz and Dachau. After surviving the camps, he wrote a now world-famous book, *Man's Search for Meaning* (1962), originally published under the title *From Death-Camp to Existentialism* (1946), in which he introduced and popularized his approach to psychotherapy and his approach to life, *logotherapy*.

Logotherapy is derived from the Greek word *logos* (meaning) and the word *therapy* (signifying treatment). According to Frankl, humans are motivated to seek meaning in their lives. In his book, Frankl cites research supporting his contention that meaning finding is a primary motivation for people. According to logotherapy, people can find meaning in three main ways: "1) by creating a work or doing a deed;

2) by experiencing something or encountering someone; and 3) by the attitude we take toward unavoidable suffering" (Frankl, 1962, p. 133). To elaborate on each of these, first, we may find meaning through accomplishment or achievement. Second, meaning may be felt when experiencing much in life such as nature, beauty, goodness, or the loving of another human being. The last source of meaning requires further explanation. As Frankl describes, suffering is unavoidable in life. But we have a "uniquely human potential . . . to transform a personal tragedy into a triumph, to turn one's predicament into a human achievement" (Frankl, 1962, p. 135). He gives an example of a man who was suffering because his wife, whom he dearly loved, died. The man looked to Frankl for comfort and solace and, as is revealed through the session, for meaning. Frankl, after listening to the man's story of pain, rather than telling him something, asked a question: what would have happened if he had died and his wife had lived? The man replied that his wife would have suffered and mourned greatly. Frankl responded that since she died first, this suffering has been spared her. Viewing the situation this way, according to Frankl, the man was able to see the meaning in his experience: he had made a sacrifice, the sacrifice of suffering, so that his wife may not suffer.

As Frankl explains, the therapy worked not through changing an actual situation but rather through changing the attitude or point of view of the patient. Other psychotherapy approaches and general psychological theories also advocate healing and well-being through changing attitudes or beliefs. Examples include cognitive therapy and appraisal theory. Logotherapy is an effective form of psychotherapy. The Viktor Frankl Institute Web site is devoted to describing and promoting logotherapy and is a repository for logotherapy research studies and discussion of these studies.

See also appraisal, cognitive therapy and cognitive-behavioral therapy, humanistic psychotherapy, existential psychotherapy, Viktor Frankl.

Further Readings:
Frankl, V. E. (1962). *Man's search for meaning.* New York: Washington Square.
Frankl, V. E. (1988). *The will to meaning: Foundations and applications of logotherapy.* New York: Penguin Books.
Viktor Frankl Institute Web site: http://logotherapy.univie.ac.at/

Reference:
Frankl, V. E. (1962). *Man's search for meaning.* New York: Washington Square.

Loneliness

Loneliness is an unpleasant emotional state that occurs because of dissatisfaction with the quality of one's relationships. Lonely people may feel emotional pain, sadness, and emptiness and feel distanced from and misunderstood by other people. More technically, loneliness can be defined as a discrepancy between an individual's *desired* level and *actual* level of social contact. Loneliness is a subjective experience; therefore one can be alone but not lonely. Conversely, one may have many friends and other social contacts but still feel lonely.

Weiss (1973) identified two types of loneliness. *Emotional* loneliness occurs when an individual fails to have a close relationship or confidant such as a romantic partner or very close friend. *Social* loneliness arises when a person has no ties to a social group such as a group of friends or a social organization. Anyone may suffer from either type of loneliness or both. Improving the quality of one type of relationship (social or emotional) does not typically ameliorate the other type of loneliness.

Miller, Perlman, and Brehm (2007) review the research on personal demographic and social characteristics associated with loneliness. Loneliness occurs with greater frequency in some countries than in others. In one study that compared 18 countries, Italians and Japanese reported the highest levels of loneliness while people from Denmark reported the lowest levels. Citizens of the United States also reported high levels (ranking fourth; Stack, 1995, 1998). Unmarried people are more lonely than married people, but divorced and widowed people are more lonely than those who never married. When unmarried people are asked indirectly about loneliness (i.e., asking about relationships and feelings without actually using the word *lonely*), men report more loneliness than women. When asked directly, women report more loneliness than men (Pinquart, 2003). Most researchers consider indirect measures of loneliness more valid. The explanation for men's underreporting of loneliness when asked directly is that the stigma associated with loneliness is greater for men than for women. For men, emotional loneliness is most often remedied through a relationship with a woman; men's relationships with one another tend to involve relatively little self-disclosure and emotional closeness. Women's friendship relationships with other women can be quite close, involving a great deal of disclosure, and emotional loneliness for women may typically be remedied through either a romantic relationship with a man (or woman) or a friendship relationship with a woman.

Age is related to loneliness. Perlman's (1990) review of six surveys involving 18,000 people in North America revealed that in general, people are lonelier when they are adolescents or young adults than when they are middle-aged. Beyond the age of 40, loneliness tends to be associated with divorce, death of a spouse, or poor health.

Loneliness may be caused by both situational factors and an individual's personal characteristics. In a national survey of loneliness in the United States, people provided five major reasons why they were lonely (Rubenstein & Shaver, 1982): (1) having no spouse or sexual partner, (2) feeling different or misunderstood or having no close friendships, (3) being alone, particularly coming home to a house with no one there, (4) being forced into isolation (due to being homebound, hospitalized, or having no transportation), and (5) being dislocated (from moving, starting a new job or school, or traveling frequently). Notice that the research participants mentioned both situational causes (e.g., forced isolation, dislocation) and causes that are more likely related to personal characteristics (e.g., feeling different or misunderstood, no close friends, or no spouse or partner). Additionally, the participants described both emotional loneliness and social loneliness situations.

Personal characteristics associated with loneliness are both cognitive (thoughts, attitudes) and behavioral. Lonely people may have low self-esteem, viewing themselves as unworthy or unlovable; as a result, they may be resigned to their loneliness (McWhirter, 1997). People who are lonely may have negative views and attitudes toward other people (e.g., Check, Perlman, & Malamuth, 1985). They may have an attitude of mistrust toward others and a general negative attitude toward others (including disliking others). Negative or mistrustful attitudes may manifest in behaviors such as being unresponsive in interactions with others (e.g., Solano & Koester, 1989), failing to ask questions, responding slowly to what other people say, changing topics at inappropriate times, or a lack of personal disclosure. Even individuals who generally dislike other people crave social interaction and contact and experience emotional distress when lonely.

Lonely people can take action to attempt to improve their situations. Miller, Perlman, and Brehm (2007) make several helpful suggestions. First, lonely people can question their attitudes. A fear of rejection or disappointment may result in social withdrawal. However, little is lost if one forces oneself to interact, show interest in others, or engage in some self-disclosure. Adopting a positive attitude may result in positive social interactions. People tend to blame loneliness on their own personal inadequacies; however, situational factors likely play a part as well. It may be beneficial to consider situational factors that may be contributing to loneliness; it is generally not constructive to put all the blame on oneself. Third, once lonely people have considered and identified situational factors, they may think about how their attitudes are contributing to the problem and reconsider those attitudes. Individuals who think that people are selfish, uncaring, and untrustworthy may be creating a self-fulfilling prophecy. Instead, it is more helpful to try to find the positive qualities in others. Fourth, if the preceding advice does not lead to positive results, social skills training may be helpful. Another useful exercise involves reexamining one's attitudes and behaviors. For example, an individual who is attempting to heal loneliness by searching for a romantic partner might find a close friendship to be emotionally satisfying and personally enriching.

See also friendship, intimacy, relationships, shyness, social support.

Further Reading:
Miller, R. S., Perlman, D., & Brehm, S. S. (2007). *Intimate relationships.* New York: McGraw-Hill.

References:
Check, J. V.P., Perlman, D., & Malamuth, N. M. (1985). Loneliness and aggressive behavior. *Journal of Social and Personal Relationships, 2,* 243–252.
McWhirter, B. T. (1997). Loneliness, learned resourcefulness, and self-esteem in college students. *Journal of Counseling and Development, 75,* 460–469.
Miller, R. S., Perlman, D., & Brehm, S. S. (2007). *Intimate relationships* (4th ed.). New York: McGraw-Hill.
Perlman, D. (1990, August 10–14). *Age differences in loneliness: A meta-analysis.* Paper presented at the 98th annual convention of the American Psychological Association, Boston, MA. (ERIC Document Reproduction Service No. ED326767).
Pinquart, M. (2003). Loneliness in married, widowed, divorced, and never-married older adults. *Journal of Social and Personal Relationships, 20,* 31–53.
Rubenstein, C. M., & Shaver, P. (1982). *In search of intimacy.* New York: Delacorte Press.
Solano, C. H., & Koester, N. H. (1989). Loneliness and communication problems: Subjective anxiety or objective skills? *Personality and Social Psychology Bulletin, 15,* 126–133.
Stack, S. (1995). *Gender, marriage and loneliness: A cross-national study.* Unpublished manuscript, Wayne State University.
Stack, S. (1998). Marriage, family and loneliness: A cross-national study. *Sociological Perspectives, 41,* 415–432.
Weiss, R. L. (1973). *Loneliness.* Cambridge, MA: MIT Press.

Loss

Bereavement is a state of sorrow over a loss or death of a loved one; to be *bereft* is to be left alone or to experience a loss. According to Merriam-Webster, *grief* is distress caused by bereavement (by experiencing loss). Loss is associated with many life events and transitions, including illness, disability, infertility, miscarriage, loss of housing or employment, educational failure, war or natural disasters, abuse, relationship breakdown, divorce, addiction, migration, aging, and death of a loved one.

There are many ideas about the grieving process, among them theories about grief occurring in phases or stages. In 1961, British psychiatrist John Bowlby described three stages of grief based on young children's reactions to separation from parents: protest, despair, and detachment. Later he refined his stages and added a fourth to his theory of grieving in adults: numbness and disbelief, yearning and searching, disorganization and despair, and finally reorganization or recovery from bereavement (see Bowlby, 1980). In 1969, Swiss-born psychiatrist Elisabeth Kübler-Ross published *On Death and Dying*, which suggested that there are five stages when facing one's own terminal illness: denial, anger, bargaining, depression, and acceptance. Kübler-Ross's five-stage model has gained popularity, has been extended to dealing with any sort of loss (including death of a loved one), and has been incorporated into many mental health practitioners' treatment practices. However, most researchers now recognize that the five-stage model lacks empirical support. Responses to loss may include many different reactions, including those in the five-stage model. Reactions may occur in many orders or combinations and may vary depending on the bereaved person's mental state and circumstances (Archer, 1998).

Grieving is a normal process; it is an individual, unique, and highly personal experience. Depending on social context and personal experience, grief has potential for both personal deterioration and personal growth. Unless symptoms of grief become debilitating, causing significant distress over a prolonged period of time, grief will resolve on its own, without the need for intervention from a mental health practitioner. Complicated grief, on the other hand, does benefit from therapy. According to Australian psychologist Judith A. Murray (2001), complicated grief is more likely when the bereaved individual loses a child (including an unborn child), has an intellectual disability or other mental health disorder, sustains multiple losses simultaneously, sustains losses that occur through trauma or violence, or experiences a sudden loss (without time to prepare). Circumstances surrounding a loss—including cultural, social, and family contexts—influence the stress accompanying the grief reaction. For example, the response to a suicide may be different among members of cultures or religions that consider suicide a sin versus those that consider suicide an honorable action. Loss may threaten a person's sense of safety, security, and control (Murray, 2001).

Grief may by accompanied by many symptoms, including depressions, somatic symptoms (physical illness), and a higher risk for suicide. John Bowlby's work on attachment theory showed that even people who cannot fully understand the finality of death (e.g., young children and individuals with intellectual disabilities) are capable of experiencing grief. Individuals with intellectual disabilities may have a more complex grieving process, with a higher risk for emotional disturbance (e.g., sadness, anger, anxiety) and behavioral disturbance (e.g., irritability, lethargy, hyperactivity; Brickell & Munir, 2008). Multiple losses, which can complicate the grieving process, may affect individuals' health, marriages, employment, finances, and emotions (Mercer & Evans, 2006).

Ambiguous loss—such as when a loved one is missing or is presumed to be dead but no body has been found—freezes the grieving process. This can occur in the context of an abduction or a soldier who is missing in action. It can be especially difficult if some family members are still holding out hope that their missing loved one will be found, while other family members want to accept the loss to move forward with their lives. This type of ambiguity can be emotionally devastating for individuals as well as putting a great strain on families and relationships. Closure is impossible; family members have no choice but to live with uncertainty (Boss, 2007). An extended period of preparation for an expected loss is known as *anticipatory loss.* For example, caregivers of family members with dementia or terminal illness know that their loved one is expected to die but may not know how soon. Anticipatory loss may be accompanied by a complex mix of emotions, including sadness, anger, and feeling overwhelmed, tired, trapped, guilty, frustrated, and relieved. Individuals anticipating loss may feel powerless in the face of the inevitability of the loss (Green, 2006).

See also John Bowlby, depression, grief.

Further Readings:

Archer, J. (1998). *Nature of grief: The evolution and psychology of reactions to loss.* Florence, KY: Brunner-Routledge.

Bowlby, J. (1980). *Attachment and loss: Vol. 3. Loss: Sadness and depression.* New York: Basic Books.

Kübler-Ross, E. (1969). *On death and dying.* New York: MacMillan.

References:

Archer, J. (1998). *The nature of grief: The evolution and psychology of reactions to loss.* Florence, KY: Brunner-Routledge.

Boss, P. (2007). Ambiguous loss theory: Challenges for scholars and practitioners. *Family Relations, 56,* 105–111.

Bowlby, J. (1980). *Attachment and loss: Vol. 3. Loss: Sadness and depression.* New York: Basic Books.

Brickell, C., & Munir, K. (2008). Grief and its complications in individuals with intellectual disability. *Harvard Review of Psychiatry, 16,* 1–12.

Green, S. (2006). "Enough already!": Caregiving and disaster preparedness—Two faces of anticipatory loss. *Journal of Loss and Trauma, 11,* 201–214.

Kübler-Ross, E. (1969). *On death and dying.* New York: MacMillan.

Mercer, D. L., & Evans, J. M. (2006). The impact of multiple losses on the grieving process: An exploratory study. *Journal of Loss and Trauma, 11,* 219–227.

Murray, J. A. (2001). Loss as a universal concept: A review of the literature to identify common aspects of loss in diverse situations. *Journal of Loss and Trauma, 6,* 219–241.

Love

Love has interested thinkers from diverse disciplines since the beginning of writing (or before). The word *love* can mean many things, including feelings one has about people, animals, one's country, activities, foods, books, and much more. Scholars and researchers have tended to focus on love in the context of relationship. Love experts Reis and Aron (2008) have defined *love* as "a desire to enter, maintain, or expand a close, connected, and ongoing relationship with another person or other entity" (p. 80).

Early love researchers created love taxonomies. A widely known distinction between types of love, first proposed by Berscheid and Walster (1978), is between passionate love ("a state of intense longing for union with another," p. 9) and companionate love ("the affection we feel for those with whom our lives are deeply entwined," p. 9). The usefulness of this categorization has been supported by research at various levels, including laypeople's conceptions of love, behavioral studies, and biological research. Another expedient theory has been Sternberg's (1986), which identified components of love: passion (an arousal state and longing for another person), intimacy (closeness to and emotional investment in another person), and commitment (attachment to a person and decision to be with her). In general, passion tends to be associated with passionate love, and intimacy and commitment tend to be associated with companionate love, although any of the three love features can be associated with either type of love (e.g., an individual can feel a sort of passion for a platonic friend—the passion is nonsexual and occurs primarily in a companionate relationship).

Leading figures in the history of science have explored concepts related to or processes involving love. John Bowlby and Harry Harlow, studying infant attachment, argued and provided evidence that the bond between infant and mother may set the stage for future love relationships for the child. Sigmund Freud ("the love doctor") proposed that our childhood experiences create our love templates. For him, an individual's first romantic relationship occurs around ages four to six, when the child develops an attachment to the opposite-sexed parent. The attachment is sensual and includes a passionate desire to possess the parent exclusively. The particular dynamic between child and opposite-sexed parent and child and same-sexed parent (who is the child's rival) will to some extent play out again in future romances. Charles Darwin asserted that sexual attraction is necessary for the survival of our species and thus sexual love is functional. This theorizing about the evolutionary basis of love opened up a large research area, leading to comparisons across species and studies on topics such as mate preferences and sexual mating strategies in both humans and other animals.

An evolutionary perspective on love has gained popularity. Theorists (e.g., Reis & Aron, 2008) have applied Berscheid and Walster's (1978) dichotomy within an evolutionary approach and have argued that both passionate and companionate love are helpful for survival of the species. Passionate love leads to attraction, which can be associated with individuals entering into mating relationships that are relatively long term—at least, long enough to lead to successful reproduction. Companionate love, which includes love between parents and love of parents for their children, increases the probability of survival of the child.

Recently, research on love has met with a resurgence. Reis and Aron (2008) predict that research will continue to be popular, addressing issues such as specific biological mechanisms associated with love, how love is related to culture, and love outside of romantic relationships. Reis and Aron also point out that love is associated with some negatives, which they call the "dark side" of love, including bereavement, unrequited love, jealousy, abandonment, and violence, and that these topics also need further study.

See also attachment, John Bowlby, Charles Darwin, evolutionary psychology (human sociobiology), Sigmund Freud, friendship, Harry Harlow, intimacy, jealousy, relationships.

Further Reading:

Hendrick, S., & Hendrick, C. (1992). *Liking, loving, and relating* (2nd ed.). Pacific Grove, CA: Brooks/ Cole.

References:
Berscheid, E., & Walster, E. H. (1978). *Interpersonal attraction* (2nd ed.). Reading, MA: Addison Wesley.
Reis, H. T., & Aron, A. (2008). Love: What is it, why does it matter, and how does it operate? *Perspectives on Psychological Science, 3,* 80–86.
Sternberg, R. J. (1986). A triangular theory of love. *Psychological Review, 93,* 119–135.

Lust

Lust is sexual desire: an interest in sexual contact with another person or even with other objects (e.g., animals, inanimate objects). Scholars have taken different positions regarding the origins of lust. Sigmund Freud (e.g., Freud, 1905/1910) and more modern theorists such as Kaplan (1979) viewed lust as a drive that originates within the individual who experiences it, possibly from biochemical sources. Other modern theorists (e.g., Verhulst & Heiman, 1979) have argued that lust is caused by the external object, for instance, an attractive person. A third view is that lust has both internal and external origins.

Lust differs from individual to individual. As Regan and Berscheid (1999) discuss, lust varies in both frequency and intensity across people. Additionally, people differ in regard to the specific types of sexual activities that they prefer and in the number of preferred sexual activities (i.e., some prefer more variety than others). Also, different people have different objects of desire. The list of possible objects is long: other people (same or opposite sex or both), numbers of other people (i.e., some are attracted to more people than others), specific body parts (e.g., one may have a fetish for feet), children, animals, inanimate objects, and so forth.

Scholars disagree about whether lust is technically an emotion. However, most agree that lust is often closely associated with an emotion: romantic love. Both Sigmund Freud and the early sexologist Havelock Ellis (1933/1963) believed that lust was a significant part of romantic love. Some researchers have studied the relationship between lust and romantic love. For example, Meyers and Berscheid (1997) asked research participants to identify people with whom they were in love and those to whom they felt a sexual attraction. They found that most people's list of attractive people was longer than their list of people toward whom they felt romantic love; they nearly always said that they were sexually attracted to people with whom they were in love but did not necessarily say that they were in love with people to whom they were attracted.

See also desire, Sigmund Freud, libido, love.

Further Readings:
Berscheid, E., & Heller, M. (1999). Desire. In D. Levinson, J. J. Ponzetti, & P. F. Jorgensen (Eds.), *Encyclopedia of human emotions* (2nd ed., pp. 184–188). New York: Macmillan Reference USA.
Regan, P. C., & Berscheid, E. (1999). *Lust: What we know about human sexual desire.* Newbury Park, CA: Sage.

References:
Ellis, H. (1963). *Psychology of sex.* New York: New American Library of World Literature. (Original work published 1933)
Freud, S. (1910). *Three contributions to the sexual theory* (A. A. Brill, Trans.). New York: Journal of Nervous and Mental Disease. (Original work published 1905)

Kaplan, H.S. (1979). *Disorders of sexual desire and other new concepts and techniques in sex therapy.* New York: Simon and Schuster.

Meyers, S. A., & Berscheid, E. (1997). The language of love: The difference a preposition makes. *Personality and Social Psychology Bulletin, 23*, 347–362.

Regan, P.C., & Berscheid, E. (1999). *Lust: What we know about human sexual desire.* Newbury Park, CA: Sage.

Verhulst, J., & Heiman, J.R. (1979). An interactional approach to sexual dysfunctions. *American Journal of Family Therapy, 7*, 19–36.

M

Machover Draw-A-Person Test

The Machover Draw-A-Person (DAP) test is a projective personality test developed by American psychologist Karen Machover in 1949. In a projective test, an assessee (person taking a test) is presented with unstructured stimuli (inkblots, pictures of people) or tasks and asked to respond in some way (e.g., draw a picture, tell a story, complete a sentence). The assumption is that the assessee's responses will reveal something about her personality.

In the DAP, the assessee (either an adult or a child) is given a blank piece of paper and a pencil and is asked to draw a person. On a second sheet of paper, the assessee is asked to draw a person of the opposite sex. Next, the assessee may be asked any of a number of questions about the drawing, which Machover called *associations*, for example, asking about the age, marital status, schooling, self-concept, wishes, and habits of the person drawn. Machover made specific recommendations for interpretation of the test responses, utilizing the *sign approach*, wherein specific aspects of the drawing have very specific meanings. Machover instructed that general "feature placements" be evaluated, that is, size of the drawing, positioning, clothing, and so on. Particular characteristics of the figures are significant, for instance, large ears or eyes indicate paranoia, poorly drawn facial features indicate depression, dark shading indicates aggression, general lack of details may indicate psychosis or brain damage, and so forth.

The sign approach to interpretation has been strongly criticized (e.g., Lilienfeld, Wood, & Garb, 2000, 2001). Using a global approach may be more valid (Swenson, 1957; Lilienfeld et al., 2001). Rather than assuming that specific drawing features correspond directly to particular psychological problems, psychologists employing a global approach form a general idea of the assessee's overall adjustment through combining many features of the drawing. Thus the DAP likely has some validity for determining overall adjustment or mental health but has not demonstrated validity in terms of identifying particular psychological issues or providing specific diagnoses.

In 1991, Naglieri, McNeish, and Bardos published *Draw-A-Person: Screening Procedures for Emotional Disturbance*, a new scoring procedure to be used with children with suspected emotional or behavior problems. This use of the DAP is helpful in identifying children with such issues (Naglieri & Pfeiffer, 1992). The DAP is not among the 20 most commonly used tests by clinical psychologists; however, a similar drawing test that was developed later, the House-Tree-Person Technique, ranks in the top 10, as do two other projective techniques, the Rorschach Psychodiagnostic Technique and the Thematic Apperception Test (Camara, Nathan, & Puente, 2000).

See also projective tests, Rorschach Psychodiagnostic Technique, Thematic Apperception Test.

Further Reading:
Lilienfeld, S. O., Wood, J. M., & Garb, H. N. (2001). What's wrong with this picture? *Scientific American, 284*, 80–87.

References:
Camara, W. J., Nathan, J. S., & Puente, A. E. (2000). Psychological test usage: Implications in professional psychology. *Professional Psychology: Research and Practice, 31*, 141–154.
Lilienfeld, S. O., Wood, J. M., & Garb, H. N. (2000). The scientific status of projective techniques. *Psychological Science in the Public Interest, 1*, 27–66.
Lilienfeld, S. O., Wood, J. M., & Garb, H. N. (2001). What's wrong with this picture? *Scientific American, 284*, 80–87.
Machover, K. (1949). *Personality projection in the drawing of the human figure.* Springfield, IL: C. C. Thomas.
Naglieri, J. A., McNeish, T., & Bardos, A. (1991). *Draw-A-Person: Screening Procedure for Emotional Disturbance.* Austin, TX: Pro-ed.
Naglieri, J. A., & Pfeiffer, S. I. (1992). Performance of disruptive behavior disordered and normal samples on the Draw A Person: Screening Procedure for Emotional Disturbance. *Psychological Assessment, 4*, 156–159.
Swenson, C. H., Jr. (1957). Empirical evaluations of human figure drawings. *Psychological Bulletin, 54*, 431–466.

Major Depressive Disorder

Major depressive disorder (MDD) is a type of clinical depression. Like other types of clinical depression (e.g., bipolar disorder, seasonal affective disorder), MDD is characterized by sadness, feelings of emptiness, despair, anhedonia (loss of ability to experience pleasure), low self-esteem, apathy, low motivation, social withdrawal, negative or pessimistic thinking, irritability, and/or suicidal thoughts or attempts (Preston, 2006). Other symptoms may include sleep or appetite disturbances, weight gain or loss, early morning awakening, or agitation. Clinicians use the *Diagnostic and Statistical Manual of Mental Disorders* (*DSM-IV-TR*; American Psychiatric Association, 2000) criteria, clinical interviews, and other tools (e.g., Beck Depression Inventory, Children's Depression Inventory, Hamilton Depression Scale) to diagnose MDD. According to *DSM-IV-TR* criteria, symptoms must have persisted for at least two weeks and be accompanied by significant distress or impairment in functioning (e.g., social, vocational; American Psychiatric Association, 2000). In children, the predominant mood may present as irritability rather than sadness. Individuals with MDD may exhibit tearfulness, crying, brooding, anxiety, phobias, and physical complaints (e.g., headaches, stomach aches, joint pain). When depression is caused by outside situations or circumstances (e.g., death of a loved one, loss of a job), it is known as *exogenous* depression; when there are no identifiable upsetting circumstances, it is known as *endogenous* depression. Depression that is primarily caused by a drug (e.g., alcohol, cocaine withdrawal), as a side effect of medication (e.g., steroids), through exposure to toxins, or as a direct result of a physiological disorder (e.g., thyroid disease) is not considered MDD. MDD that is precipitated by childbirth is known as MDD with postpartum onset (or postpartum depression).

Current estimates of lifetime prevalence of MDD range from 16 to 18 percent among adults in the United States (Kessler et al., 2003; Williams et al., 2007). MDD occurs twice as much in women as in men. Rates of MDD appear to be similar among ethnic groups; however, treatment rates are much higher among whites than some ethnic minorities (Williams et al., 2007). While only one-third of people in the United States seek treatment for symptoms of depression, treatment can be effective in up to 80 percent of those who seek treatment (Preston, O'Neal, & Talaga, 2008).

Depression is thought to be related to a number of factors, including environmental, biological, genetic, hormonal, and neurochemical factors. Depression may involve imbalance of certain neurotransmitters (chemical messengers in the brain), including serotonin, norepinephrine, dopamine, acetylcholine, and gamma-aminobutyric acid (GABA). Some depressed people have been found to have elevated levels of cortisol (a stress hormone), deficiencies in brain-derived neurotrophic factor (a substance involved in keeping neurons healthy), cell death in the hippocampus (a brain structure), or atrophy in the anterior cingulate (in the frontal lobe of the brain; Preston et al., 2008). Extreme stress (including severe early abuse or neglect), poor nutrition, decreases in physical exercise, and reduced exposure to sunlight can result in or exacerbate depression (Preston et al., 2008).

The biopsychosocial model of depression considers (and treats) biological (e.g., genetic, hormonal), psychological, and social (e.g., family, interpersonal) factors. Effective treatments for depression involve a combination of psychotherapy (e.g., psychodynamic, cognitive-behavioral), physical exercise, and medications. Antidepressant medications include selective serotonin reuptake inhibitors, tricyclics, monoamine oxidase inhibitors, and atypical antidepressants. Troublesome medication side effects may occur well before the onset of therapeutic benefits. Working closely with a qualified health care professional can help minimize side effects and increase benefits from medications and adjunctive therapies. Natural or complementary alternatives that have been explored for the treatment of depression include St. John's wort (*Hypericum perforatum*) and SAMe (S-adenosyl-L-methionine). Evidence supports the use of St. John's wort as an effective treatment for mild to moderate depression; it has not been found to be effective in treating severe depression (National Center for Complementary and Alternative Medicine, 2004). Studies found that SAMe was more effective than placebo but no more effective than standard antidepressant medication (Agency for Healthcare Research and Quality, 2002). There is a great deal of controversy regarding the efficacy, side effects, and potential drug interactions of other complementary treatments such as L-tryptophan (a natural antidepressant found in foods such as turkey, potatoes, and milk), 5-hydroxytryptophan, melatonin, tyrosine, amino acids, vitamins, and minerals. Electroconvulsive therapy has been found to be effective in severe treatment-resistant cases of depression (Preston et al., 2008). Experimental treatments include vagus nerve stimulation and repetitive transcranial magnetic stimulation. Some individuals and their families find information and help through support groups (e.g., National Alliance on Mental Illness).

See also anhedonia, antidepressant, cognitive therapy and cognitive-behavioral therapy, complementary and alternative medicine, dysphoria, dysthymia, electroconvulsive therapy, endogenous depression, grief, light therapy, mood disorder, nutritional therapies, physical activity (exercise) for depression, postpartum depression, Prozac (fluoxetine), psychodynamic psychotherapy and psychoanalysis, sadness, seasonal affective disorder, selective serotonin reuptake inhibitor, serotonin, St. John's wort.

Further Readings:
Casey, N. (2002). *Unholy ghost: Writers on depression.* New York: Harper Perennial.
National Alliance on Mental Illness Web site: http://www.nami.org/
Solomon, A. (2001). *The noonday demon.* New York: Touchstone.

References:
Agency for Healthcare Research and Quality. (2002). *S-adenosyl-L-methionine for treatment of depression, osteoarthritis, and liver disease* (Evidence Report/Technology Assessment No. 64). Retrieved from http://www.ahrq.gov/clinic/epcsums/samesum.pdf
American Psychiatric Association. (2000). *Diagnostic and statistical manual of mental disorders* (4th ed., text rev.). Washington, DC: Author.
Kessler, R. C., Berglund, P., Demler, O., Jin, R., Koretz, D., Merikangas, K. R., et al. (2003). The epidemiology of major depressive disorder: Results from the National Comorbidity Survey Replication (NCS-R). *Journal of the American Medical Association, 289,* 3095–3105.
National Center for Complementary and Alternative Medicine. (2004). *St. John's wort (Hypericum perforatum) and the treatment of depression* (NCCAM Publication No. D005). Retrieved from http://nccam.nih.gov/health/stjohnswort/sjwataglance.htm
Preston, J. D., O'Neal, J. H., & Talaga, M. C. (2008). *Handbook of clinical psychopharmacology for therapists* (5th ed.). Oakland, CA: New Harbinger.
Williams, D. R., González, H. M., Neighbors, H., Nesse, R., Abelson, J. M., Sweetman, J., et al. (2007). Prevalence and distribution of major depressive disorder in African Americans, Caribbean Blacks, and non-Hispanic whites. *Archives of General Psychiatry, 64,* 305–315.

- Major depressive disorder (MDD) is the leading cause of disability in the United States for ages 15–44.
- MDD affects approximately 14.8 million American adults, or about 6.7 percent of the U.S. population aged 18 and older, in any given year.
- While MDD can develop at any age, the median age at onset is 32.
- MDD is more prevalent in women than in men.

Source: http://www.nimh.nih.gov/health/publications/the-numbers-count-mental-disorders-in-america.shtml

Abraham Maslow (1908–1970)

Abraham Maslow was born in Brooklyn, New York, the first of seven children. His parents were Russian Jewish immigrants, and his father owned a barrel manufacturing company. He was lonely and bookish as a child. He reported that neither parent showed him much attention or warmth; his anger about the perceived neglect was directed most at his mother, whom he described as "a pretty woman—but not a nice one" (Wilson, 1972, p. 31).

Although his parents were uneducated, they encouraged education in their children. Maslow and his new bride, Bertha (a first cousin), moved to Wisconsin so that he could attend the University of Wisconsin, where he earned a BA, an MA, and a PhD, all in psychology. Maslow was Harry Harlow's first PhD student, and his dissertation focused on dominance hierarchies in monkeys. After completing his education in 1934, he returned to the East Coast, taking a teaching position at Brooklyn College after a few years of research work at Columbia University. Years later, he moved to Brandeis University, where he served as chair of the psychology department from 1951 to 1969.

Maslow's marriage to Bertha was a happy one, and they had two daughters. After the birth of their first child, Maslow began to change his approach to psychology, moving away from his behavioral training and toward a new approach in psychology, humanism, which emphasizes that people are basically good and possess free will. He developed an interest in the healthy person, the "best specimens." He idealized some of his professors, in particular, anthropologist Ruth Benedict and Gestalt psychologist Max Wertheimer. He saw them as truly wonderful people, a contrast to his parents, who so disappointed him. He tried to understand Benedict and Wertheimer through thinking and writing about them. He began to see that the two had much in common. This realization led him to believe that there might be a prototype of a healthy person, and he began to look for commonalities among people whom he viewed as healthy.

Maslow himself suffered from anxiety and insecurities. Although he had earned the respect of many of his peers—he was elected president of the American Psychological Association (APA), for example—he nonetheless experienced intense stage fright. After a public presentation of his work, he sometimes had to take bed rest for several days (A. H. Maslow, 1979, p. 99). He resigned from the APA presidency after only one year (the usual term is two years), an unprecedented action, because of his fear of public speaking. In 1970, within two years of his resignation from the APA presidency, Maslow died of a heart attack at age 62.

Maslow is well known across academic disciplines for two main contributions. The first is his theory of motivation, the hierarchy of needs. Maslow identified needs that motivate all humans: physiological needs (e.g., hunger, safety, and security), belongingness and love needs, esteem needs (including self-esteem and esteem from others), and the need for self-actualization (the desire to achieve one's full potential). These motives are arranged in a pyramid or hierarchy such that the lower needs (beginning with the physiological) must be sufficiently addressed before higher ones arise and become the focus of an individual's being and experience. Maslow was most interested in the highest level of needs, the self-actualization needs, which he believed are natural to humans but whose realization depend on the lower needs being met. Thus one can become somewhat stuck at a lower level, making it difficult to self-actualize. For instance, some individuals become obsessed with safety and security and devote much energy to saving money, worrying about physical safety, and so on. In fact, since safety and security largely consume their conscious thoughts, these individuals do not even think about self-actualizing. As another example, some people become stuck at the love and belongingness stage, feeling that they have never really been unconditionally loved or accepted. The consciousness of these individuals is filled with regret regarding a perceived lack of love, and self-actualization does not enter much into their experience. Maslow was interested in helping people to become unchained from obsessions such as these and to free themselves to their natural self-actualization.

Maslow's other major contribution is his description of the healthy personality, also called the *fully functioning person* or the *self-actualizing person*. This approach in psychology was a fairly novel one—Maslow was focusing on the best qualities of humans rather than on psychopathology. After considering the commonalities of his admired professors, Benedict, Wertheimer, and several others whom Maslow viewed as healthy, he identified 20 characteristics of the fully functioning person. Examples include a more accurate perception of reality (neither too optimistic nor too pessimistic), an acceptance of self and others (does not expect perfection, accepts human foibles), an unhostile sense of humor, and social interest (a desire to help others).

Maslow, like Carl Rogers, was one of the founders of the humanistic psychology movement that began in full in the 1940s and 1950s, a true alternative approach to Freudian psychology or behaviorism. Additionally, the modern interests in the healthy personality and in positive psychology can be at least partially traced to Maslow. Maslow authored numerous books and articles. Some of the most informative and provocative books by or about him include *The Healthy Personality* (A. H. Maslow, 1977), *The Farther Reaches of Human Nature* (A. H. Maslow, 1993), and *Abraham H. Maslow: A Memorial Volume* (B. G. Maslow, 1972).

See also behaviorism, Harry Harlow, humanistic psychotherapy, motivation, positive psychology, Carl Rogers.

Further Readings:
Maslow, A. H. (1977). *The healthy personality.* New York: Van Nostrand.
Maslow, A. H. (1979). *The journals of Abraham Maslow* (R. J. Lowry, Ed.). Lexington, MA: Lewis.
Maslow, A. H. (1993). *The farther reaches of human nature.* New York: Arkana.
Maslow, B. G. (1972). *Abraham H. Maslow: A memorial volume.* Monterey, CA: Brooks/Cole.

References:
Maslow, A. H. (1977). *The healthy personality.* New York: Van Nostrand.
Maslow, A. H. (1979). *The journals of Abraham Maslow* (R. J. Lowry, Ed.). Lexington, MA: Lewis.
Maslow, A. H. (1993). *The farther reaches of human nature.* New York: Arkana.
Maslow, B. G. (1972). *Abraham H. Maslow: A memorial volume.* Monterey, CA: Brooks/Cole.
Monte, C. F. (1980). *Beneath the mask: An introduction to theories of personality.* New York: Holt, Rinehart, and Winston.
Wilson, C. (1972). *New pathways in psychology.* New York: Taplinger Publishing.

Abraham Maslow worked hard to establish recognition for humanistic psychology as an independent discipline—equal in worth to the Freudian and behaviorist disciplines in psychology—within the American Psychological Association. His fight was, by his account, a tough one. In a seminar that he gave at Brandeis University in 1963, he displayed a Saul Steinberg drawing and presented his feelings and associations to the drawing. On the right side of the drawing is a figure on horseback, holding a spear. The horse, person, and spear are all simply drawn in stick-figure style. On the left side is a collection of eight large, three-dimensional geometric figures (cube, sphere, triangle, etc.). The figure on horseback is riding toward the geometric figures, ready to attack them with his (or her) flimsy spear. Maslow revealed that when he first saw the drawing, he laughed his head off. He said that it reminded him of himself, in particular, his fight with the American Psychological Association. Maslow said that the geometric figures were cold and mechanistic, like the incarnation of the American Psychological Association against which he was fighting. The figure on horseback was a hero (himself), tragic in some ways because, at least on the surface, he would lose the battle against the much stronger foe. Maslow believed that fighting for what one believed, even in instances where the odds seem overwhelming, is nonetheless admirable and worthwhile (Monte, 1980).

Meditation

Meditation is a practice that involves calming the mind and the body and has a history of at least 2,000 years, having descended from Zen Buddhism and yoga. Examples of practices include Zen meditation, Chakra yoga, mantra meditation, transcendental meditation, breath-counting meditation, walking meditation, and others. Meditation involves a control of one's attention such that the attention is either focused or expanded. In focused attention, the meditator may concentrate on a sound or a single visual stimulus. Mantra meditation, silently repeating a sound (i.e., "peace," "om," or another word or phrase) to oneself, is the most common form of meditation throughout the world (Davis, Eshelman, & McKay, 2008). Visually concentrating on a mandala, a colorful geometric figure, is another type of focused meditation. Walking meditation is usually practiced as a form of expanding one's attention; as the meditator walks, she attends to all stimuli external to her own thoughts or feelings— the surrounding environment, the act of walking, physical sensations of walking, and so on. Goldstein (2003) stated that three central concepts unify the diverse meditation approaches: mindfulness (awareness), compassion, and nonclinging.

A goal of meditation is to allow an individual to simply "be" in the present moment, focusing on something outside of the self without worrying about the past or future. While meditating, one reduces the typical mental chatter that includes worrying, planning, fantasizing, and remembering. The idea is that practicing meditation regularly leads to a calmer state of mind that extends to all of one's life experience. A number of books provide how-to instructions for various types of meditation, including Girdano, Dusek, and Everly's (2009) *Controlling Stress and Tension*, Davis et al.'s (2008) *The Relaxation and Stress Reduction Workbook*, and Yogi's (1963/1995) *Science of Being and Art of Living: Transcendental Meditation.* Practicing most types of meditation involves sitting quietly in a comfortable position (ideally, in a quiet environment). Stretching muscles or performing progressive muscle relaxation (tensing and relaxing of muscles) can help ensure that the muscles are relaxed. It is probably best

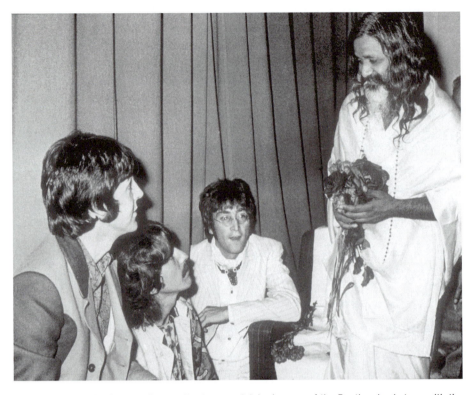

Left to right: Paul McCartney, George Harrison, and John Lennon of the Beatles, backstage with the Maharishi Mahesh Yogi after he gave a lecture on transcendental meditation at the Hilton hotel in London, August 25, 1967. Attention from celebrities such as the Beatles increased the popularity of meditation in North America in the 1960s and 1970s. (Hulton Archive/Getty Images)

for inexperienced meditators to close their eyes. Next, one should focus on quieting the mind. This is an area where practices may differ. One approach is to focus on a mantra, a relaxing word one states to oneself. The individual should try not to get carried away with thoughts, simply focusing on the mantra. If she notices that she is having a thought, she may push it away gently or allow it to pass through her. This is the attitude that one should have for the duration of the meditation. An individual may meditate for only 5 minutes if that is what works, but ideally, meditation should last at least 20 to 30 minutes. The preceding description is consistent with transcendental meditation, which was developed in the 1950s by Maharishi Mahesh Yogi to make meditation more accessible to Western cultures.

Regular meditation is beneficial in a wide variety of ways. Roth (1994) reviewed 500 studies from 35 different countries spanning 25 years and concluded that meditation can reduce stress, reduce insomnia, increase happiness and self-esteem, reduce anxiety and depression, and produce a number of other positive effects. The benefits of meditation were discussed at the 2004 annual meeting of the Mind and Life Institute on Destructive Emotions, a meeting of scientists and spiritual leaders including the Dalai Lama. As science writer Begley (2007), who attended the conference, states, some types of meditation can effectively treat depression and obsessive-compulsive disorder. Additionally, she describes how meditation appears to change the structure of the brain. The right prefrontal cortex, which tends to be associated with a state of happiness, is larger in meditators than in nonmeditators. Additionally, the left prefrontal cortex, which is associated with negative emotions, is smaller in meditators. Continued study in this general field, neuroplasticity (the changing of brain structure, including growth of new brains cells), may reveal additional findings that support the positive attributes of meditation and other stress-management techniques.

See also Buddhism, mindfulness, stress, yoga.

Further Readings:

Begley, S. (2007). *Train your mind, change your brain.* New York: Ballantine.

Davis, M., Eshelman, E. R., & McKay, M. (2008). *The relaxation and stress reduction workbook* (6th ed.). Oakland, CA: New Harbinger.

Girdano, D. A., Dusek, D. E., & Everly, G. S., Jr. (2009). *Controlling stress and tension* (8th ed.). San Francisco: Benjamin Cummings.

Mind and Life Institute Web site: http://www.mindandlife.org/

Roth, R. (1994). *Maharishi Mahesh Yogi's transcendental meditation.* New York: Primus.

Transcendental Meditation Program Web site: http://www.tm.org/

References:

Begley, S. (2007). *Train your mind, change your brain.* New York: Ballantine.

Davis, M., Eshelman, E. R., & McKay, M. (2008). *The relaxation and stress reduction workbook* (6th ed.). Oakland, CA: New Harbinger.

Girdano, D. A., Dusek, D. E., & Everly, G. S., Jr. (2009). *Controlling stress and tension* (8th ed.). San Francisco: Benjamin Cummings.

Goldstein, J. (2003). *One Dharma: The emerging Western Buddhism.* San Francisco: Harper.

Roth, R. (1994). *Maharishi Mahesh Yogi's transcendental meditation.* New York: Primus.

Yogi, M. M. (1995). *Science of being and art of living: Transcendental meditation.* New York: Meridian Books. (Original work published 1963)

Memory and Emotion

Conscious recollections of experiences are known as *declarative* or *explicit* memories. Explicit memories can be recalled and described verbally. *Implicit* (nondeclarative) memories are created subconsciously, for example, through fear conditioning. Implicit memories may form in response to dangerous or threatening situations. Stress and severe trauma are imprinted on the brain, sometimes bypassing explicit memory circuits and imprinting on implicit memory systems. Emotional memories (implicit memories that evoke emotional feelings) and memories of emotional experiences (explicit memories) sometimes occur together, but they activate different systems in the brain. Explicit memory formation involves the hippocampus and temporal lobe of the brain, while implicit memories involve the amygdala. So when recalling the circumstances of a trauma (e.g., an auto accident), the explicit memory system (temporal lobe and hippocampus) is engaged. When remembering how frightening the auto accident was, with accompanying physiological changes (heart pounding, sweating), the implicit memory system (amygdala) is activated (LeDoux, 1996).

Posttraumatic stress disorder symptoms in individuals suffering from this condition may be triggered by situations that are perceived as associated with a previously experienced traumatic event. There is controversy about the accuracy of traumatic memories. Some researchers question the accuracy of explicit traumatic memories. Other research finds that the explicit details of a traumatic event tend to be accurate, but implicit memory for the associated emotions and context is less accurate. Some research shows that intense, negative implicit memories (e.g., fear, horror) are accurate and stable over time, while implicit memories of other emotions are less accurate (Zoellner, Sacks, & Foa, 2001).

Individuals with phobias (and other anxiety disorders) repeatedly experience situations or objects as threatening. Certain types of psychotherapy (e.g., systematic desensitization) may help desensitize individuals who have phobias from responding to triggering situations as threats. While the fear is under control, the memory that originally provoked the fear response remains. A new stress or traumatic experience can rekindle the learned fear, causing the phobia to return (LeDoux, 1996).

Emotional life events are often remembered more vividly than everyday events. *Item memory* describes memory for content (e.g., names, faces, pictures, words), while *source memory* is memory for context (the time, place, situation, perceptions, tone of voice, emotional context). Overall, older adults perform more poorly on memory tasks than younger adults. Generally, source (context) memory tasks are more difficult than item memory tasks—it is easier to remember what someone said in a situation than to remember the context (sounds, smells, and feelings) of the situation. A study with young adults (average age 21 years) and older adults (average age 75 years) found that emotionally charged items (words and sentences) were better remembered than neutral (nonemotional) ones. In one experiment, sentences were spoken in an emotional or neutral tone of voice. Emotional tone of voice enhanced source (context) memory, more so for young adults than older adults. However, the content of the sentences (whether they were neutral or emotional) had no effect on source memory for either age group (Davidson, McFarland, & Glisky, 2006).

In developmental studies of memory and emotion with children aged 6 through 11 years, children were told stories and shown accompanying illustrations; then they were asked what happened in the stories. It was found that children remembered negative emotions (e.g., madness, guilt) more easily than positive emotions (e.g., happiness, pride) and that girls were more likely to remember emotions than boys (Davidson, 2006).

Individuals with major depressive disorder (MDD) have more difficulties with memory and emotion-processing tasks than individuals without depression. It has been found that individuals with MDD have poorer memory overall and selectively recall more negative than positive information (known as *emotional memory bias*). While overall memory deficits in individuals with MDD are more pronounced in elderly people than in younger individuals, both young and older individuals with MDD exhibit emotional memory bias (Pine et al., 2004).

Neurological disorders that affect memory (e.g., dementia, Alzheimer's disease, traumatic brain injury) may be accompanied by difficulty regulating or controlling emotions. Similarly, disorders or conditions that affect emotions (e.g., depression, anxiety) may affect memory abilities. Studies of these disorders have highlighted the interconnections between the emotion (e.g., limbic system, amygdala, hippocampus) and memory systems in the brain (LeDoux, 1996).

See also amygdala, fear, hippocampus, major depressive disorder, phobia, posttraumatic stress disorder, stress, systematic desensitization.

Further Readings:

Kensinger, E. A. (2008). *Emotional memory across the adult lifespan.* New York: Psychology Press.

Reisberg, D., & Hertel, P. (2003). *Memory and emotion.* New York: Oxford University Press.

References:

Davidson, D. (2006). The role of basic, self-conscious and self-conscious evaluative emotions in children's memory and understanding of emotion. *Motivation and Emotion, 30,* 232–242.

Davidson, P.S.R., McFarland, C. R., & Glisky, E. L. (2006). Effects of emotion on item and source memory in young and older adults. *Cognitive Affective & Behavioral Neuroscience, 6,* 306–322.

LeDoux, J. (1996). *The emotional brain: The mysterious underpinnings of emotional life.* New York: Touchstone.

Pine, D. S., Lissek, S., Klein, R. G., Mannuzza, S., Moulton, J. L., Guardino, M., et al. (2004). Face-memory and emotion: Associations with major depression in children and adolescents. *Journal of Child Psychology and Psychiatry, 45,* 1199–1208.

Zoellner, L. A., Sacks, M. B., & Foa, E. B. (2001). Stability of emotions for traumatic memories in acute and chronic PTSD. *Behaviour Research and Therapy, 39,* 697–711.

Menopause

When a woman's ovaries stop producing eggs and female hormone levels drop, her menstrual periods cease, and she experiences menopause. Menopause—signaling the cessation of reproductive fertility—usually occurs during midlife (usually between the ages of 45 and 55; Xu et al., 2005). Menopause can occur as a normal part of aging or can be a result of surgery (e.g., hysterectomy), chemotherapy, or radiation. Menopause, from the Greek roots *men* (month) and *pauein* (to bring to an end), literally means "end of monthly cycles." The period of time leading up to menopause, known as *perimenopause*, is marked by irregular menstrual cycles. Other menopause symptoms may occur during perimenopause. The perimenopause period may last between 1 and 10 years (average is 4 to 5 years). Menopause (or *postmenopause*) is said to have occurred after there have been no menstrual periods for 12 consecutive months (Twiss et al., 2007).

Estrogen (estradiol) and progesterone are female hormones (although estrogen is also found in males, as testosterone is found in females). Female hormones serve many functions. These include promoting the formation of female secondary sexual characteristics (e.g., breast development), onset of menstruation, supporting pregnancy, metabolism, and maintenance of bone density. Estrogen levels in females may affect energy level and mood. Fluctuating levels of estrogen and other (e.g., serotonin and beta-endorphins) hormones may manifest as mood swings, depression, anxiety, or irritability at different points in the menstrual cycle (Dickerson, Mazyck, & Hunter, 2003). Female hormones decrease naturally with age.

While some women experience menopause symptoms, including depression, irritability, mood swings, decreased libido, sleep problems, night sweats, and hot flashes, many women have no symptoms (Liu et al., 2009). Women may also experience loss of bone density during and after menopause. Symptoms may vary according to overall health or the existence or severity of preexisting symptoms (e.g., premenstrual syndrome). Menopause symptoms may also vary by culture, social group, and ethnicity (Xu et al., 2005).

Some women use hormone replacement therapy (HRT) to treat menopause symptoms. HRT consists of female hormones, usually in pill or skin patch form. HRT has been promoted as a means to treat menopause symptoms and prevent loss of bone density. However, a large study in 2002—the Woman's Health Initiative—raised concerns about the long-term safety of HRT and breast cancer (Rossouw et al., 2002). Some women use natural treatments for menopause symptoms, including botanicals (black cohosh, dong quai root, ginseng, kava, red clover, and soy) and dehydroepiandrosterone (DHEA), a dietary supplement. However, there is little good-quality research to support the safety and effectiveness of these alternative treatments (National Center for Complementary and Alternative Medicine, 2009). Women may also use physical exercise, calcium supplements, and social support to help them deal with the symptoms and risks associated with menopause.

The male equivalent of menopause, known as *andropause*, is a midlife condition experienced by some men. Although men do not have monthly menstrual cycles, their testosterone (male hormone) levels drop. Male testosterone levels affect sexual functioning, energy level, physical agility, bone health, and mood.

See also hormones, mood swings.

Further Reading:

National Center for Complementary and Alternative Medicine. (2009, February). *Menopausal symptoms and CAM* (National Institutes of Health Publication No. D406). Retrieved from http://nccam.nih.gov/health/menopause/D406.pdf

References:

Dickerson, L. M., Mazyck, P. J., & Hunter, M. H. (2003). Premenstrual syndrome. *American Family Physician, 67,* 1743–1752.

Liu, D., Lu, Y., Ma, H., Wei, R.-C., Li, J., Fang, J., et al. (2009). A pilot observational study to assess the safety and efficacy of Menoprogen for the management of menopausal symptoms in Chinese women. *Journal of Alternative and Complementary Medicine, 15,* 79–85.

National Center for Complementary and Alternative Medicine. (2009, February). *Menopausal symptoms and CAM* (National Institutes of Health Publication No. D406). Retrieved from http://nccam.nih.gov/health/menopause/D406.pdf

Rossouw, J. E., Anderson, G. L., Prentice, R. L., LaCroix, A. Z., Kooperberg, C., Stefanick, M. L., et al. (2002). Risks and benefits of estrogen plus progestin in healthy postmenopausal women: Principal results from the Women's Health Initiative randomized controlled trial. *Journal of the American Medical Association, 288,* 321–333.

Twiss, J. J., Wegner, J., Hunter, M., Kelsay, M., Rathe-Hart, M., & Salado, W. (2007). Perimenopausal symptoms, quality of life, and health behaviors in users and nonusers of hormone therapy. *Journal of the American Academy of Nurse Practitioners, 19,* 602–613.

Xu, J., Bartoces, M., Neale, A. V., Dailey, R. K., Northrup, J., & Schwartz, K. L. (2005). Natural history of menopause symptoms in primary care patients: A MetroNet study. *Journal of the American Board of Family Practice, 18,* 374–382.

Millon Clinical Multiaxial Inventory

The Millon Clinical Multiaxial Inventory (MCMI), developed by American psychologist Theodore Millon and first published in 1969, is one of the most widely used of all personality tests. Its primary utility is to aid in diagnosis of mental disorders. The MCMI is now the main competitor to the Minnesota Multiphasic Personality Inventory (MMPI), which has been the most commonly used diagnostic personality test for several decades.

The MCMI consists of 175 test items that assessees (people taking a test) complete, typically taking about 25 minutes. The items are scored on 27 primary scales.

Most of the scales measure mental disorders that are listed and described in the official diagnostic manual for mental disorders in the United States and some other countries, the *Diagnostic and Statistical Manual of Mental Disorders* (*DSM-IV*; American Psychiatric Association, 1994). The scales are classified into five categories: clinical personality patterns and severe personality pathology (each represents *DSM-IV* personality disorders), clinical syndromes and severe clinical syndromes (each represents *DSM-IV* clinical disorders), and modifying indices. Modifying indices provide general characteristics of the assessee that may interact with disorders, rather than listing disorders per se. These general characteristics may provide useful information so the clinician may more thoroughly understand the client to provide appropriate treatment. Examples of scales include the personality disorders Avoidant, Antisocial, Compulsive, Borderline, and Paranoid, the clinical disorders Anxiety, Bipolar: Manic, Alcohol Dependence, Major Depression, and Delusional Disorder, and the modifying indices Disclosure and Debasement.

Compared to utilizing the MMPI for diagnosis, use of the MCMI is associated with a few advantages, as described by Hogan (2008). First, MCMI scale scores that are generated are highly compatible with *DSM-IV* classifications. Second, the MCMI is much shorter than the MMPI (176 items compared to 567 items). This is important. A typical person may be loathe to complete a questionnaire with 567 items (which usually takes about 60 to 90 minutes), and this task may be even more challenging for some individuals who are diagnosable with a mental disorder. Third, the MCMI utilizes base-rate scores for its scales, which the MMPI generally fails to do. MMPI scale scores are flagged as potentially clinically significant on any scale (Depression scale, Schizophrenia scale, Paranoia scale, etc.) equally, regardless of the frequency with which the disorder exists in the population. Typically, a score is flagged for an individual if it is within the top 2 to 7 percent or so of scores on that scale. Disorder rates vary greatly in the population; about 0.5 to 1 percent of the population is diagnosable for schizophrenia, whereas major depression is exceedingly more common, affecting up to one-third of the population in terms of lifetime risk. When MCMI scores are identified as potentially clinically significant, the base-rate information has already been considered prior to the identification.

A disadvantage of the MCMI is its close connection to the *DSM*. The *DSM* itself has been criticized, and many flaws of the *DSM* are reflected in the MCMI. For instance, Cooper (2005) has criticized the categorical system of mental disorder classification utilized in the *DSM*. Additionally, the *DSM* changes regularly, and with these changes, the MCMI must change. Thus the MCMI-I was published after *DSM-II* was published. When the *DSM-III* came out, the MCMI-II was published. In 1994, The MCMI-III was created to coincide with the *DSM-IV.* As Hogan (2008) states, the new MCMI versions are produced as counterparts to the *DSM*, without attention to a critical evaluation of the changes that occurred to the *DSM*; Millon and his colleagues place a great deal of faith in the validity of the *DSM*. A second disadvantage is the large number of scales (27) that are derived from relatively few items (176). This creates some conceptual and statistical issues that are beyond the scope of this book.

The MCMI ranks as the 10th most frequently used test by clinical psychologists (the MMPI is second and the Wechsler Adult Intelligence Scale is first; Camara, Nathan, & Puente, 2000). Time will tell whether the strengths of the MCMI are sufficient to convince clinicians to utilize it more frequently than they employ the longtime standby in clinical personality assessment, the MMPI.

See also Diagnostic and Statistical Manual of Mental Disorders, Minnesota Multiphasic Personality Inventory.

Further Readings:

Cooper, R. (2005). *Classifying madness: A philosophical examination of the Diagnostic and Statistical Manual of Mental Disorders.* Dordrecht, Netherlands: Springer.
Millon, T. (Ed.). (1997). *The Millon Inventories: Clinical and personality assessment.* New York: Guilford.
Millon, T., & Davis, R. D. (1996). The Millon Clinical Multiaxial Inventory–III (MCMI-III). In C. S. Newmark (Ed.), *Major psychological assessment instruments* (2nd ed., pp. 108–147). Needham Heights, MA: Allyn and Bacon.
Pearson Assessments sample MCMI-III profile: http://www.pearsonassessments.com/hai/images/pa/pdfs/mcmi3profile.pdf

References:

American Psychiatric Association. (1994). *Diagnostic and statistical manual of mental disorders* (4th ed.). Washington, DC: Author.
Camara, W. J., Nathan, J. S., & Puente, A. E. (2000). Psychological test usage: Implications in professional psychology. *Professional Psychology: Research and Practice, 31,* 141–154.
Cooper, R. (2005). *Classifying madness: A philosophical examination of the Diagnostic and Statistical Manual of Mental Disorders.* Dordrecht, Netherlands: Springer.
Hogan, T. P. (2008). *Psychological testing: A practical introduction.* Hoboken, NJ: John Wiley.

Mindfulness

Being mindful means being aware in the present moment. The awareness may be of one or more aspects of the inner world (body sensations, emotions, or thoughts) or of what is going on in the outer world. One experiences this awareness as if one is a detached observer, with acceptance, with compassion, and without judgment. A purpose of practicing mindfulness is to realize that all the experiences and stimuli of which one is aware are transitory, and they do not define the person (i.e., "thoughts are just thoughts"). If one is able to practice being an objective, impartial observer, one is less likely to get caught up in negative thoughts and emotions, which may play over and over in the mind like a tape recorder. Ultimately, the purpose of mindfulness is a positive state of being, which includes feelings of peace and acceptance.

The concept of mindfulness dates back 2,500 years ago to ancient Buddhism. Various forms of meditation involve achieving a state of mindfulness. In the past few decades, Western scientists and mental health practitioners have adapted mindfulness philosophy and practices to improve the quality of life of people in the modern world.

In *Thoughts & Feelings: Taking Control of Your Moods and Your Life*, McKay, Davis, and Fanning (2007) describe many examples of mindfulness techniques that are accessible for most people. One simple example is "mindful breathing." To begin, one lies down and closes one's eyes. Breathing should be deep but natural. When breathing has become rhythmic, one should observe as much about one's breathing as possible. Notice how cool the air is as it passes through the nose, then throat, then lungs. Pay attention to the sensations of the diaphragm and belly. Listen to any quiet noises that the air may make when passing through the nose, throat, or lungs. If it is helpful, one may add a mantra such as saying "accept this moment" or "peace" during inhalations and exhalations. McKay, Davis, and Fanning recommend doing this technique twice a day. It is hoped that after a few days, one's spontaneous thoughts and emotions may change in positive ways.

Positive psychologists, who study the best in human nature and who promote positive psychological functioning, have developed an interest in mindfulness. They view mindfulness as a means to increase novelty in people's lives. Being mindful can help people to view the world and themselves in new ways, which may mean breaking away from automatic, negative habits and becoming creative; people may begin to see things from outside the box. For example, a mindless person would approach a problem the same way each time, in an unthinking, automatic fashion, even if the approach results in negative consequences. People's interpersonal relations sometimes operate in this way. A mindless person who is frustrated by the spending habits of her spouse may try to solve the problem with threats and continue to use threats for years, even though this never works. A mindful person would step back from the problem and try something different such as rewarding her spouse for good (thrifty) behavior.

In addition to positive psychologists, other psychologists have seen the value and potential applications of mindfulness. Timothy Miller, in *How to Want What You Have* (1996), argues the merits of an attitude that includes attention (his word for mindfulness), compassion, and gratitude. He says that it is difficult for humans to end the cycle of constantly wanting more but that learning how to appreciate what one has is worth the effort. Cognitive and cognitive-behavioral psychotherapies apply principles of mindfulness; the mechanism for personal change in these therapies is modifying one's ways of thinking through first becoming mindful of the ways of thinking.

More recently, applications of mindfulness have been put to empirical test. A frequently studied form of treatment based on mindfulness, *mindfulness-based stress reduction*, developed by Stanford psychologist Jon Kabat-Zinn, has been studied as an effective treatment for a variety of conditions, including anxiety, depression, and chronic pain (i.e., Grossman, Tiefenthaler-Gilmer, Raysz, & Kesper, 2007). In a review of studies on mindfulness, Bishop (2002) concluded that mindfulness techniques and treatments are promising, but very few studies have been rigorous, utilizing randomized, controlled designs. Interest in mindfulness has now spanned centuries, cultures, and disciplines.

See also acceptance, Buddhism, cognitive therapy and cognitive-behavioral therapy, meditation, positive psychology, rational emotive behavior therapy.

Further Readings:

Kabat-Zinn, J. (2005). *Wherever you go, there you are: Mindfulness meditation in everyday life.* Concord, NH: Hyperion.

McKay, M., Davis, M., & Fanning, P. (2007). *Thoughts & feelings: Taking control of your moods and your life* (3rd ed.). Oakland, CA: New Harbinger.

Miller, T. R. (1996). *How to want what you have.* New York: Harper Perennial.

References:

Bishop, S. R. (2002). What do we really know about mindfulness-based stress reduction? *Psychosomatic Medicine, 64*(1), 71–83.

Grossman, P., Tiefenthaler-Gilmer, U., Raysz, A., & Kesper, U. (2007). Mindfulness training as an intervention for fibromyalgia: Evidence of postintervention and 3-year follow-up benefits in well-being. *Psychotherapy and Psychosomatics, 76*, 226–233.

McKay, M., Davis, M., & Fanning, P. (2007). *Thoughts & feelings: Taking control of your moods and your life* (3rd ed.). Oakland, CA: New Harbinger.

Miller, T. R. (1996). *How to want what you have.* New York: Harper Perennial.

Minnesota Multiphasic Personality Inventory

The Minnesota Multiphasic Personality Inventory (MMPI), a success when it was initially published in 1942, remains the most widely used of all measures of abnormal personality in the world. The authors, psychologist Starke Hathaway and neuropsychiatrist J. Charley McKinley, developed the test to aid in the diagnosis and understanding of individual psychiatric patients. Currently the MMPI has many uses. Consistent with Hathaway and McKinley's purposes, it is a common tool in clinical assessment of psychiatric inpatients, outpatients receiving psychiatric or psychotherapy services, and students who utilize college counseling centers. The MMPI is also commonly used in employment contexts, for instance, for screening applicants for jobs that have a public safety element such as law enforcement, nuclear power plant operation, and piloting of airplanes. The MMPI has a number of forensic applications, including assessments of competency to stand trial, insanity, and parental fitness (i.e., child custody cases) and evaluations for personal injury and disability claims. It may also be utilized as part of a test battery (a collection of tests as part of a comprehensive assessment) assessing neuropsychological functioning.

One of the two current versions of the MMPI, the MMPI-2, published in 1989, is an inventory consisting of 567 statements to which the assessee (person taking the test) responds with "true" or "false" (Butcher, Dahlstrom, Graham, Tellegen, & Kaemmer, 1989). Examples of items on the original MMPI include "At times I feel like picking a fist fight with someone," "I prefer to pass by school friends, or people I know but have not seen for a long time, unless they speak to me first," "I sometimes tease animals," "Often I feel as if there were a tight band around my head," and "Everything is turning out just like the prophets of the Bible said it would." The items are typically scored by a computer, and a profile on the assessee is created. The standard profile consists of scores on 10 clinical scales and 4 validity scales. Eight of the clinical scales measure psychiatric categories that existed in 1942 and that currently exist, although not necessarily with the same label: hypochondriasis, depression, hysteria, psychopathic deviate, paranoia, psychasthenia, schizophrenia, and hypomania. The two remaining clinical scales, Masculinity-Femininity and Social Introversion, although not intended as measures of psychopathology per se, are helpful in gaining an understanding of the assessee. For instance, each of these scales interacts with other scales in ways that help clarify the individual's pathology or presenting problems.

The presence of validity scales is one of the aspects of the MMPI that contributed to its extreme popularity. These scales are used to identify ways in which the profiles may have questionable validity. One of the validity scales, Infrequency, assesses an individual's tendency to appear psychopathological or unfavorable, or problems with taking the test (e.g., reading problems, careless responding). Other validity scales are Lie, which measures the assessees' attempts to appear highly moral, and Correction, which assesses an individual's tendency to limit disclosure to others.

The method used to develop the MMPI and MMPI-2, called empirical criterion keying, became a standard method of test construction. This approach was motivated by the awareness that an individual who is taking a test of abnormal personality may respond in a dishonest fashion. In the empirical criterion keying method, no assumptions are made that the assessee is being honest or that responses are consistent with the assessee's true behavior, feelings, or thoughts.

The development of the MMPI (and later the MMPI-2) began with the creation of hundreds of items. Hathaway and McKinley wrote some items because they believed the items would differentiate between people with mental disorders and those without mental disorders. Other items were simply made up. Next, in creating each scale of the MMPI and MMPI-2, two groups of people were utilized. The *clinical* group consisted of individuals who had been diagnosed with the mental disorder represented by the scale (e.g., depression); the second (*normative*) group was presumed to represent the general population. Both groups were given the hundreds of statements that Hathaway and McKinley had written. If a particular statement differentiated clinical (e.g., depressed) people from the general population, the statement was retained for that particular clinical scale. Take, for example, the statement "I like to go shopping on the weekend." If depressed people tended to respond in a particular direction (e.g., false) and the general population tended to respond in the opposite direction (e.g., true), then that statement became a part of the Depression scale. Hathaway and McKinley were not concerned with why a clinical sample reliably responded to a particular item in a particular way, only that their responses distinguished them from the general (normative) population sample. Thus validity was automatically built in to the MMPI. At the same time, this method of test construction has been criticized by people who are interested in understanding why.

By the 1970s, it became clear that there were problems with the original MMPI, prompting creation of the MMPI-2. One issue was the original comparison or normative group. This group was unrepresentative of the general population, coming largely from the Minneapolis, Minnesota, area. All were white, and most were married, averaging age 35, with eight years of education. A second issue was the content of some of the test items. Some were outdated and people did not understand them (e.g., "I like to play drop-the-handkerchief"); some included sexist language; and a disproportionate number referred to Christian beliefs, sexual behaviors, or bladder or bowel functions. Thus the MMPI restandardization project was created in the early 1980s by the publisher of the MMPI. This project focused on producing a representative sample of the population as a comparison group for developing the scales and on updating and reinvestigating the test items. The final sample was ethnically diverse, ranging in age from 18 to 85, with a range in amount of formal education, and coming from several U.S. states: California, Minnesota, North Carolina, Ohio, Pennsylvania, Virginia, and Washington. The general demographic composition of the sample was based on U.S. Census data from 1980. A number of test items were slightly rewritten, 550 original items were retained, and 154 new items were added to the pool. Next, creation of each scale paralleled the original method: items were administered to both clinical and normative (comparison) samples. Those items that differentiated the particular clinical group (e.g., depressed people) from the general population sample were retained for the relevant (e.g., Depression) scale.

The MMPI-2 is appropriate for people 18 years and older who read at the eighth-grade level or better. In addition to the 10 clinical scales and 4 validity scales described earlier, other scale scores can be derived from the MMPI items. These additional scales include the MacAndrews Alcoholism Scale, the Anxiety Scale, the Repression Scale, and the Marital Distress Scale.

Compared to other measures of abnormal personality, use of the MMPI-2 has both benefits and drawbacks, as discussed by Nichols (2001). Some benefits include that (1) the test was developed in a sophisticated fashion, creating built-in validity of the scales; (2) the standardization sample (comparison group of people used to test the items) was ethnically, socioeconomically, and geographically diverse; (3) a large number of studies (over 10,000) has assessed the reliability and validity of the test, and most experts conclude that it is a sound test; and (4) test results produce a great deal of clinical information about the assessee. Some drawbacks include the following: (1) accurate results require at least an eighth- or ninth-grade education and some degree of cooperativeness on the part of the assessee; (2) meaning of high scores on scales is not entirely clear—high scores may indicate either high probability of the disorder or greater severity of the disorder; and (3) most test items appear on more than one scale, leading to high intercorrelation between scales.

The second current version of the MMPI is the MMPI-2-RF (*RF* stands for "Restructured Form"), released by Pearson Assessments in 2008. This version was developed with statistical methods that were not utilized during the standardization in the 1980s. It consists of 338 items scored on a set of scales different from but related to the MMPI and MMPI-2 scales. The nine restructured clinical scales that replaced the MMPI and MMPI-2 clinical scales are Demoralization, Somatic Complaints, Low Positive Emotions, Cynicism, Antisocial Behavior, Ideas of Persecution, Dysfunctional Negative Emotions, Aberrant Experiences, and Hypomanic Activation. Both the MMPI-2 and the MMPI-2-RF are currently in use. Some experts prefer the MMPI-2 to the MMPI-2-RF for a variety of reasons, including that decades of research are available on MMPI-2 scales. Other experts prefer the newer MMPI-2-RF, arguing that the scales are superior, more pure (statistically more sound) versions of the original scales, leading to more comprehensible interpretation of abnormal personality. A special issue of the peer-reviewed *Journal of Personality Assessment* (Meyer, 2006) was devoted to a debate between proponents of the two versions.

The fate of the MMPI-2 versus the MMPI-2-RF remains unclear. However, the MMPI and its progeny remain the most widely researched and widely used of all measures of abnormal personality in the world.

See also Millon Clinical Multiaxial Inventory.

Further Readings:

Paul, A. M. (2004). *The cult of personality: How personality tests are leading us to miseducate our children, mismanage our companies, and misunderstand ourselves.* New York: Free Press.

Pearson Assessments, MMPI-2: http://www.pearsonassessments.com/tests/mmpi_2.htm

Tellegen, A., Ben-Porath, Y. S., McNulty, J. L., Arbisi, P. A., Graham, J. R., & Kaemmer, B. (2003). *The MMPI-2 Restructured Clinical Scales: Development, validation, and interpretation.* Minneapolis, MN: University of Minnesota Press.

References:

Butcher, J. N., Dahlstrom, W. G., Graham, J. R., Tellegen, A., & Kaemmer, B. (1989). *Minnesota Multiphasic Personality Inventory MMPI-2: Manual for administration and scoring.* Minneapolis: University of Minnesota Press.

Hathaway, S. R., & McKinley, J. C. (1943). *Manual for the Minnesota Multiphasic Personality Inventory.* New York: Psychological Corporation.

Meyer, G. J. (2006). The MMPI-2 Restructured Clinical Scales [Special issue]. *Journal of Personality Assessment, 87*(2).

Nichols, D. S. (2001). *Essentials of MMPI-2 Assessment.* New York: John Wiley.

Sullivan, L., & Arnold, D. W. (2000, October). *Invasive questions lead to legal challenge, settlement and use of different test.* Retrieved from Society for Industrial & Organizational Psychology (American Psychological Association Division 14) Web site: http://www.siop.org/tip/backissues/TipOct00/24Sullivan.aspx

- Three major test publishers initially rejected the MMPI; University of Minnesota Press agreed to publish it if the authors would pay for half the publication cost.
- Hathaway suffered a cerebral hemorrhage in 1945 at age 53, losing the ability to express emotion. Hathaway attempted suicide by cutting his throat; he was unsuccessful and died five years later.
- In 1991, Target retail stores were sued for using the MMPI as part of a screening test for hiring unarmed security guards (*Soroka v. Dayton Hudson*, California Court of Appeals, 1991). Plaintiffs alleged that the personality test was a violation of their privacy. The parties settled out of court. In another case, two former Rent-a-Center (RAC) employees sued RAC for use of a management test that included the MMPI (*Staples, Hadley, Ferrando, Allen and Fralin v. Rent-A-Center, Inc.*, No. C 99-2987 MMC, 1999). Plaintiffs expressed concern about the MMPI's inquiries about sexual practices, religious beliefs, and sexual orientation. They also objected that profiles based on test results contained gross and unfounded generalizations about test takers' personalities and abilities. RAC discontinued use of the management test containing the MMPI in California and agreed to pay a settlement of $2 million, to be divided among 1,200 test takers in California (Sullivan & Arnold, 2000).

Egas Moniz (1874–1955)

António Caetano de Abreu Freire Egas Moniz was a Portuguese neurologist and dean of Medicine at the University of Lisbon. Moniz was awarded the 1949 Nobel Prize in Physiology or Medicine for his development of the prefrontal leucotomy, a type of psychosurgery. He was nominated for Nobel prizes—in 1928 and 1933—for his development of cerebral angiography, a method of making blood vessels in the brain visible on X-rays. He was also a distinguished politician. He was elected to the Portuguese parliament in 1900 and was ambassador to Spain during World War I. As minister for external affairs, he represented Portugal at the Versailles Peace Conference in 1918 (Tierney, 2000). He was a prolific and diverse author, writing on such subjects as sexology (which shocked his religious countrymen), the history of playing cards (1942), clinical neurology, and neurological war injuries. He wrote several biographies. By 1934, he had written 112 articles and two books about angiography (Tierney, 2000).

Moniz was born to parents Fernando de Pina Rezende Abreu and Maria do Rosario de Almeida e Sousa in the northern Portuguese town of Avança, at Casa do Marinheiro, an estate that had belonged to his aristocratic family for 500 years. He was baptized António Caetano de Abreu Freire. His godfather, an admirer of the 12th-century Portuguese hero Egas Moniz, added "Egas Moniz" to his name. Moniz attended Coimbra University, where he studied medicine and developed an interest in politics. He supported a republican form of government, which differed from his family's long-standing support of the monarchy; he was arrested several times for his political activities. After graduating from medical school in 1899, he lectured at Coimbra for 12 years before being appointed professor of neurology at the University of Lisbon in 1911. In 1902, he married Elvira de Macedo Dias. He retired from his professorship at the University of Lisbon in 1944. He died in 1955, at the age of 81.

Moniz's interest in psychosurgery was sparked by a presentation by American physiologists John F. Fulton and Carlyle Jacobsen at the 1935 Second World Congress of Neurology. In the 1930s, Fulton and Jacobsen found that creating lesions (wounds) in part of the frontal lobes of chimpanzees produced behavioral changes. After the surgery, a chimp who was previously agitated became docile. Moniz, an attendee at the 1935 congress, proposed using frontal cortex surgery in human psychiatric patients: "if frontal lobe removal prevents the development of experimental neuroses in animals and eliminates frustrational behavior, why would it not be feasible to relieve anxiety states in man by surgical means?" (Tierney, 2000, p. 27). Moniz and Portuguese neurosurgeon Almeida Lima began testing the prefrontal leucotomy on patients with psychoses. Because Moniz suffered from severe gout, he never performed leucotomies himself. The procedure involved severing nerve fibers in the frontal lobes as a treatment for depression, anxiety, and agitation associated with obsessive-compulsive disorder and schizophrenia. Moniz coined the term *psychosurgery*. Initial response to the leucotomy was positive; patients seemed to have reduced anxiety and agitation, and language and memory remained intact. However, patients also exhibited personality changes, lack of motivation, and flattened affect (expressing little or no emotion). Some patients were returned to asylums and never seen again (Mashour, Walker, & Martuza, 2005).

In 1936 (after Moniz's initial reports), American neurologist Walter Freeman and American neurosurgeon James Watts started performing the treatment in the United States, which they modified and renamed *prefrontal lobotomy*. The lobotomy, which was much more destructive than the leucotomy, was practiced in the United States until the 1970s.

See also prefrontal cortex, prefrontal lobotomy, psychosurgery.

Further Reading:
Museu Egas Moniz Web site (in Portuguese): http://museuegasmoniz.cm-estarreja.pt/

References:
Mashour, G. A., Walker, E. E., & Martuza, R. L. (2005). Psychosurgery: Past, present, and future. *Brain Research Reviews, 48*, 409–419.
Tierney, A. J. (2000). Egas Moniz and the origins of psychosurgery: A review commemorating the 50th anniversary of Moniz's Nobel Prize. *Journal of the History of the Neurosciences, 9*, 22–36.

Monoamine Oxidase Inhibitor

The first antidepressants were discovered inadvertently in the 1950s when a tuberculosis medication, iproniazid, was found to improve patients' moods (Preston, O'Neal, & Talaga, 2008). Iproniazid (Marsilid, Iprozid, Rivivol) and other monoamine oxidase inhibitors (MAOIs) block MAO, a substance that breaks down the norepinephrine, serotonin, and dopamine stored at the ends of neurons. This makes more of these neurotransmitters (chemical messengers) available for neurotransmission (communication between neurons; Preston et al., 2008). This discovery led to the development of the first class of antidepressant medication, the MAOIs. MAOIs include iproniazid, isocarboxazid (Marplan), pargyline (Eutonyl), phenelzine (Nardil), selegiline (Deprenyl, Emsam), and tranylcypromine (Parnate). In addition to the MAOIs, other types of antidepressants include tricyclics, selective serotonin reuptake inhibitors (SSRIs), serotonin and norepinephrine reuptake inhibitors (SNRIs), norepinephrine reuptake inhibitors, and atypical antidepressants. One type of atypical antidepressant is the reversible inhibitor of monoamine oxidase A (RIMA), which is a variant of the MAOI.

MAOI antidepressants are used to treat clinical depression and anxiety (e.g., social anxiety, generalized anxiety, panic disorder, posttraumatic stress disorder, and bulimia). Some MAOIs (e.g., Selegiline, an MAO-B inhibitor) are used in the treatment of Parkinson's disease. MAOIs are particularly useful to treat refractory (treatment-resistant) depression. Owing to potentially fatal severe hypertensive (high blood pressure) reactions, MAOIs are generally used only after other antidepressants have failed. Severe hypertensive reactions can be caused by taking MAOIs with decongestants or other antidepressants or by eating foods high in tyramine (e.g., salami, chicken liver, some sausages, some types of fish, bologna, beef bouillon, sauerkraut, some types of beer or wine). Other side effects of MAOIs may include sedation, agitation, confusion, insomnia, sudden drop in blood pressure, and edema (Preston et al., 2008).

Combining MAOIs with other antidepressants or drugs, such as opioids, stimulants (e.g., amphetamines, cocaine), psychedelics (e.g., MDMA or Ecstasy), or herbs (e.g., St. John's wort), can cause serotonin syndrome—a potentially lethal condition resulting from toxic levels of serotonin in the central nervous system. Symptoms of serotonin syndrome may include rapid heart rate, sweating, shivering, dilated pupils, tremor or twitching, muscular rigidity, elevated temperature, confusion, agitation, delirium, hallucinations, coma, or death.

Sudden discontinuation of MAOIs can result in withdrawal symptoms, which may include dizziness, nausea, sweating, insomnia, tremor, or confusion. A schedule for tapering off antidepressants should be discussed with a doctor. Risk of taking MAOIs while pregnant (including harm to the mother or to the fetus) cannot be ruled out (Preston et al., 2008). To avoid potentially harmful side effects and drug interactions, health care consumers should be sure that their doctors and pharmacist are aware of *all* medications they are taking, including over-the-counter medications, herbs and natural remedies, and dietary supplements.

See also antidepressant, atypical antidepressants, depression, neurotransmitter, Prozac (fluoxetine), selective serotonin reuptake inhibitor, St. John's wort, tricyclic antidepressant.

Further Readings:

American Psychiatric Association—Healthy Minds Web site: http://www.healthyminds.org/

Depression and Bipolar Support Alliance Web site: http://www.dbsalliance.org/

National Alliance on Mental Illness Web site: http://www.nami.org/

Reference:

Preston, J. D., O'Neal, J. H., & Talaga, M. C. (2008). *Handbook of clinical psychopharmacology for therapists* (5th ed.). Oakland, CA: New Harbinger.

Mood

A mood is a type of emotional experience. It is relatively long-lasting, persisting for up to several weeks or months, and there is no particular object toward which the feeling is directed; a mood is free floating. A good way to understand mood is to contrast it with the related concept of *emotion* (also called an *emotion episode*). An emotion episode is an immediate, temporary reaction to an event or experience (or an imagined event or experience). When a person experiences an emotion, she feels something toward a particular object, for example, she may be mad at a particular person or circumstance. When a person is experiencing a mood, she probably does not know why she feels that way, and the feeling is not directed toward anyone or anything in particular—she is just mad.

Emotions are temporary experiences. What exactly is meant by temporary is not rigidly determined. However, when research participants are asked to report on their emotional reactions to events, they typically state that the emotional episode lasts between several minutes and several hours. Moods tend to last for minutes, hours, days, or weeks, as a background to emotional experience. It is often unclear when exactly the mood started or ended.

For several decades, researchers have been studying the effects of moods on other experiences. For instance, mood can affect perception. In studies conducted by Niedenthal and Setterlund (1994), it was found that people pay more attention to stimuli or events that are consistent with their already-existing mood. In their studies, they induced mood by playing different types of classical music to participants. One group heard *happy* classical music such as Vivaldi's Concerto in C Major. The second group listened to *sad* music such as *Adagietto* by Mozart. All participants were asked to do a task on the computer, which was to respond to strings of letters. Some strings of letters were words and some were not words (simply strings of letters that were pronounceable in English). There were five different types of words: happy, positive (but not happy), sad, negative (but not sad), and neutral. Participants were presented with these different words or nonwords one at a time. The task was to indicate whether the stimulus was a word or nonword. Reaction time was measured for each response. Consistent with their hypothesis, people responded more quickly to words that were congruent with the quality of classical music to which they were listening (which presumably affected mood). Specifically, people who listened to happy music responded more quickly to happy words than to all other words, and people who listened to sad music responded more quickly to sad words than to all other words. Niedenthal and Setterlund concluded that one's current mood can affect perception or what one attends to. They suggested that this may be one mechanism through which moods tend to persist: what we see in the world reinforces the way we already feel, and we are relatively unperceiving of stimuli that are inconsistent with our moods.

Mood has been studied in relation to other experiences or behavior, including memory, general cognition, and social behavior. Eich, Kihlstrom, Bower, Forgas, and Niedenthal (2000) review some of the research in the broad area of cognition in their book *Cognition and Emotion*.

See also affect, euthymic mood, music.

References:

Eich, E., Kihlstrom, J. F., Bower, G. H., Forgas, J. P., & Niedenthal, P. M. (2000). *Cognition and emotion*. New York: Oxford University Press.

Niedenthal, P. M., & Setterlund, M. B. (1994). Emotion congruence in perception. *Personality and Social Psychology Bulletin, 20,* 401–411.

Mood Disorder

Mood disorders are a category of mental disorders described in the *Diagnostic and Statistical Manual of Mental Disorders* (*DSM-IV-TR*; American Psychiatric Association, 2000), a guide to classification of mental health disorders used primarily in the United States. The predominant feature of mood disorders is a disturbance in mood. Mood disorders are divided into depressive disorders (unipolar depression), bipolar disorders, disorders due to a general medical condition, and substance-induced mood disorders.

The building blocks for diagnosis of mood disorders are *mood episodes*, including major depressive, manic, hypomanic, or mixed episodes. Mood disorders are diagnosed based on the presence (or absence) of mood episodes. *Manic episodes* are characterized by abnormally elevated, expansive, or irritable mood, accompanied by inflated self-esteem or grandiosity, decreased need for sleep, pressured speech, flight of ideas, distractibility, increased involvement in goal-directed activities, or excessive involvement in risky behaviors. Manic episodes may also be accompanied by psychotic symptoms (e.g., hallucinations or delusions). Symptoms of *hypomanic episodes* are similar to those of manic episodes but are not accompanied by psychotic symptoms. Hypomanic episodes are less severe than manic episodes, which may cause marked impairment in social or occupational functioning and may require hospitalization. *Mixed episodes* include symptoms of both manic and depressive episodes occurring nearly every day for at least a week (American Psychiatric Association, 2000).

Depressive disorders include major depressive disorder, dysthymic disorder, and depressive disorder not otherwise specified (NOS). Depressive episodes are characterized by depressed mood or lack of interest or pleasure in most activities (anhedonia). Depressive episodes may also include changes in sleep, weight or appetite, decreased energy, feelings of worthlessness or guilt, difficulty concentrating or making decisions, or recurrent thoughts of death or suicide. Depression may be seasonal (e.g., seasonal affective disorder) or associated with hormonal changes (e.g., postpartum depression). In depressive disorders, there is no history of having had manic, hypomanic, or mixed episodes (a distinguishing feature of bipolar disorders). Depression may be accompanied by psychotic features such as hallucinations or delusions.

Bipolar disorders include bipolar I, bipolar II, cyclothymic disorder, and bipolar disorder NOS. Bipolar disorders involve the presence of manic, hypomanic, or mixed episodes, usually alternating with depressive episodes.

In mood disorder due to a general medical condition, mood episodes are determined to be a direct physiological consequence of a medical condition (e.g., diabetes, thyroid disease). In substance-induced mood disorder, the mood disturbance is a direct physiological consequence of a medication, drug of abuse, or exposure to a toxin.

See also anhedonia, bipolar disorder, depression, dysthymia, endogenous depression, major depressive disorder, postpartum depression, seasonal affective disorder.

Reference:
American Psychiatric Association. (2000). *Diagnostic and statistical manual of mental disorders* (4th ed., text rev.). Washington, DC: Author.

- Approximately 20.9 million American adults, or about 9.5 percent of the U.S. population aged 18 and older in a given year, have a mood disorder.
- The median age of onset for mood disorders is 30 years.
- Depressive disorders often co-occur with anxiety disorders and substance abuse.

Source: http://www.nimh.nih.gov/health/publications/the-numbers-count-mental-disorders-in-america.shtml

Mood Ring

Mood rings, introduced in the early 1970s, are rings containing liquid crystals that change color. The color of the ring was supposed to indicate the emotional state, or mood, of the ring's wearer. Mood rings cannot actually reflect emotions; they change color depending on the wearer's peripheral skin temperature. Warm skin temperatures produce brighter colors, presumably indicating a happy mood, while cold temperatures produce darker colors, presumably indicating a darker mood.

Mood rings are calibrated to have a blue or green color at the average person's resting peripheral skin temperature (about 82 degrees Fahrenheit or 28 degrees Celsius). Peripheral skin temperature tends to increase with passion or happiness, causing the ring color to move toward blue or violet. Stress may result in decreased skin temperature, twisting the liquid crystals in the other direction, resulting in a yellower color. According to information provided with the mood ring, colors were said to indicate the following moods: violet blue (happy, romantic), blue (calm, relaxed), green (average, not much going on), yellow/amber (tense, excited), brown/gray (anxious, nervous), black (depressed, down). In cold weather, or if the mood ring is damaged, the color will turn black (Berg, 2002).

While the mood ring's popularity died out in the middle to late 1970s, offshoots of it appear from time to time. Currently available are the Shoji mood lamp, said to assess the mood of an entire room by gathering data about temperature, humidity, and people's movement in the room. The mood phone changes color and brightness based on analysis of voice patterns and tones. The mood phone was designed to improve social interactions, especially for people with autistic spectrum disorders such as Asperger's syndrome. Mood artwork, created by researchers at the Boston University and the University of Bath, is displayed on a video screen that alters the artwork's color and brush strokes based on changes in a viewer's facial expressions (Stanton, 2007).

Further Reading:
University of Bath (2006, Aug 3). Scientists develop artwork that changes to suit your mood. *Press Release.* http://www.bath.ac.uk/news/articles/archive/artmodd030806.html

References:
Berg, T. (2002). Mood rings. In *Bowling, Beatniks, and bell bottoms: Pop culture of 20th century America* (pp. 958–959). n.p.: Gale/Cengage Learning.
Duke University. (2006, January 1). *Mood phone concept wins Motorola competition.* [News release] Retrieved from http://www.pratt.duke.edu/news/?id=520
Stanton, D. (2007). Mood ring reincarnated. *Psychology Today, 40,* 19.

Mood Stabilizer

Mood stabilizers are medications used in the treatment of bipolar disorder (formerly called *manic depressive disorder*). The term *mood stabilizer* (which is not officially recognized by the U.S. Food and Drug Administration, or FDA) is used interchangeably with the terms *bipolar medications* and *antimanic.* Bipolar disorder is a condition characterized by alternating episodes of mania (e.g., elevated mood, high energy, inflated self-esteem, grandiosity, risk-taking behavior), depression, and periods of normal mood and energy (also known as *euthymia*). Depending on the type of bipolar disorder, an individual may experience a combination of episode types: manic, depressive, or mixed (features of both mania and depression in the same episode). Some medications are more effective for treating manic symptoms, others are used primarily to treat depressive symptoms, and some medications are effective on multiple symptoms. Since individuals respond differently to medications, treatment regimens must be individually tailored and closely monitored for effectiveness, treatment of target symptoms, and any side effects.

Lithium, reported by Australian psychiatrist John Cade in 1949 and approved by the FDA in 1970, was the first effective treatment for bipolar disorder (Patterson, 2006). The anticonvulsants carbamazepine and valproic acid have also been used effectively as mood stabilizers for many years. Current treatment of bipolar disorder may include multiple mood stabilizers, antidepressants, antipsychotics, and benzodiazepines (Patterson, O'Neal, & Talaga, 2008). While all these medications are used to treat the symptoms of bipolar disorder, *mood stabilizers* typically refer to lithium, anticonvulsants, and any medications that help prevent switching into a manic or depressive episode. *Antimanic* more often refers to those medications that treat symptoms or prevent occurrences of mania.

Lithium is a relatively safe treatment and is effective in the treatment of acute mania and prevention of manic and depressive episodes in 60 to 80 percent of cases (Preston et al., 2008). Lithium has a narrow therapeutic window—the difference between a therapeutically effective dose and a toxic one is very small—and therefore frequent monitoring of blood level lithium concentrations is necessary (Preston et al., 2008). After initiating lithium treatment, it may take from five days to two weeks before experiencing therapeutic benefits. Side effects of lithium may include gastrointestinal effects (nausea, vomiting, diarrhea), headache, lethargy, muscle weakness, hand tremors, rash, acne, and weight gain. Some side effects, such as confusion, stupor, slurred speech, or worsening tremor or gastrointestinal symptoms, may be signs of lithium toxicity, which can cause seizures, coma, or death. Lithium can cause some hormonal changes, so periodic monitoring of thyroid function is recommended. Since lithium depends on the kidneys for excretion, it is important for individuals taking lithium to stay well hydrated (Preston et al., 2008). Lithium should not be taken during pregnancy. The mechanism of action for lithium is not clearly understood. It may work through its ability to stabilize cell membranes; its effects on the neurotransmitters (chemical messengers) dopamine, norepinephrine, and serotonin; or its neuroprotective properties (protecting against destructive consequences of certain biochemical processes in the brain; Preston et al., 2008).

The anticonvulsants carbamazepine (Tegretol Equetro), valproic acid (divalproex, Depakote), and lamotrigine (Lamictal) are all effective mood stabilizers. Other anticonvulsants used as mood stabilizers include gabapentin (Neurontin), topiramate (Topamax), tiagabine (Gabatril), oxcarbazepine (Trileptal), and pregabilin (Lyrica). The mechanisms of action for the anticonvulsants have not been conclusively identified. Some anticonvulsants have demonstrated neuroprotective properties. Anticonvulsants are believed to affect the activity of certain neurotransmitters (chemical messengers), increasing the activity of gamma-aminobutyric acid (GABA) or inhibiting the activity of glutamate (Preston et al., 2008). Side effects vary by anticonvulsant but may include sedation, dizziness, drowsiness, blurred vision, incoordination, gastrointestinal symptoms (nausea, vomiting, diarrhea, abdominal pain), rash, or hives. Blood levels should be monitored frequently to identify potential toxicity (Preston et al., 2008). Some anticonvulsants (e.g., Topamax) can cause confusion or memory loss (Dulcan, 2007). Use of some anticonvulsants (e.g., Depakote) during pregnancy has been associated with neural tube defects; risk cannot be ruled out for other effects (e.g., Tegretol; Preston et al., 2008)

Atypical antipsychotics used (alone or in conjunction with other medications) to treat mania, depression, and for relapse prevention include olanzapine (Zyprexa), risperidone (Risperdal), ziprasidone (Geodon), aripiprazole (Abilify), quetiapine (Seroquel), and clozapine (Clozaril). Treatment may also include benzodiazepines (e.g., Ativan, Klonopin) or antidepressants (Patterson, 2006; Preston et al., 2008). There are concerns that antidepressants (both selective serotonin reuptake inhibitors and other antidepressants) may trigger a switch to a manic episode, so antidepressants are generally used together with a mood stabilizer (Patterson, 2006).

Omega-3 fatty acids, found in seafood, flax seeds, and eggs, have been studied for the treatment of bipolar disorder. Some studies support the effectiveness of omega-3 fatty acids in treating the depressive symptoms of bipolar disorder. Studies demonstrated no effect of omega-3 fatty acids on manic symptoms. Research conclusions should be interpreted with caution due to small sample sizes, concerns about study design, and conflicting results (Peet & Stokes, 2005; Ross, Seguin, & Sieswerda, 2007). St. John's wort (*Hypericum perforatum*) has been primarily studied for its effects on depression. Research does not support the effectiveness of St. John's wort as a treatment for bipolar disorder, and researchers have issued warnings about harmful interactions between St. John's wort and bipolar medications (U.S. Food and Drug

Administration, 2000) as well as concerns about St. John's wort triggering manic episodes (Nierenberg, Burt, Matthews, & Weiss, 1999).

See also antidepressant, antimanic, antipsychotic, benzodiazepine, bipolar disorder, complementary and alternative medicine, lithium therapy.

Further Readings:
Depression and Bipolar Support Alliance Web site: http://www.dbsalliance.org/
Jamison, K. R. (1995). *An unquiet mind: A memoir of moods and madness.* New York: Random House.

References:
Dulcan, M. K. (2007). *Helping parents, youth, and teachers understand medications for behavioral and emotional problems.* Arlington, VA: American Psychiatric.
Nierenberg, A. A., Burt, T., Matthews, J., & Weiss, A. P. (1999). Mania associated with St. John's wort. *Biological Psychiatry, 46,* 1707–1708.
Patterson, J. (2006). *Therapist's guide to psychopharmacology: Working with patients, families, and physicians to optimize care.* New York: Guilford.
Peet, M., & Stokes, C. (2005). Omega-3 fatty acids in the treatment of psychiatric disorders. *Drugs, 65,* 1051–1059.
Preston, J. D., O'Neal, J. H., & Talaga, M. C. (2008). *Handbook of clinical psychopharmacology for therapists* (5th ed.). Oakland, CA: New Harbinger.
Ross, B. M., Seguin, J., & Sieswerda, L. E. (2007). Omega-3 fatty acids as treatments for mental illness: Which disorder and which fatty acid? *Lipids in Health and Disease, 6,* 21–39.
U.S. Food and Drug Administration. (2000, February 10). *Risk of drug interactions with St John's wort and indinavir and other drugs* (FDA Public Health Advisory). Retrieved from http://www.fda.gov/cder/drug/advisory/stjwort.htm

Mood Swings

A mood swing is a rapid (or extreme) change of mood. Mood swings may be a feature of emotional lability, which involves marked, intense emotional fluctuations. Mood swings are associated with bipolar disorder, where individuals alternate between manic (or hypomanic) and depressive states. Mood swings may also be associated with traumatic brain injury (Brain Injury Resource Foundation, n.d.), Alzheimer's disease, stroke, autistic spectrum disorders, and attention-deficit hyperactivity disorder. Mood swings can accompany hormonal changes such as those occurring during puberty, pregnancy, postpartum (after childbirth), and menopause. Mood swings can be a feature of premenstrual syndrome (PMS). Some drugs and medications (e.g., steroid use, withdrawal from stimulants) can cause mood swings. Generally, after the effects of the drugs wear off (or after withdrawal), moods—and the ability to regulate them—will return to normal. In conditions that have accompanying mood swings (such as bipolar disorder), mood-stabilizing medications may help even out moods. These include antimanic or anticonvulsant medications (e.g., lithium or valproic acid) and some antidepressants.

See also antimanic, autistic spectrum disorders, bipolar disorder, hormones, lability (emotional), lithium therapy, menopause, mood stabilizer, postpartum depression, traumatic brain injury.

Reference:
Brain Injury Resource Foundation. (n.d.). *Frequently asked questions: What can be done to help with mood and behavior disorders caused by brain injury?* Retrieved from http://www.birf.info/home/about/faq-behav.html

Motivation

Motivation is the drive, energy, or activation to engage in goal-oriented behaviors. Motivation may be external (extrinsic) or internal (intrinsic). *Intrinsic* motivation comes from the rewards inherent to a task or activity, for example, the pleasure, interest, or enjoyment of playing a musical instrument, painting a picture, or learning for its own sake. *Extrinsic* motivation comes from an external source. External motivation may be positive, such as reaping a reward (earning money, getting a good grade, making the football team), or negative (e.g., avoiding punishment, fear of breaking the rules). Competition is generally an extrinsic motivator; the drive to compete is motivated by a desire to win or to beat others.

In 1981, psychologist Susan Harter developed a motivational scale, with extrinsic and intrinsic motivation on opposite poles of a single dimension. Children were asked whether they read books for intrinsic (e.g., because they enjoyed reading) or extrinsic (e.g., to please the teacher) reasons. However, there was no way for children to indicate that both types of motivations might be valid. More recent research seems to indicate that extrinsic and intrinsic motivation may coexist (they are not mutually exclusive); motivation varies depending on individual factors (e.g., age), activity or task, and other factors. Numerous studies have examined the relationship between motivation (primarily intrinsic or extrinsic) and academic achievement. It has been found that higher levels of intrinsic motivation are linked to greater academic achievement. Developmentally, intrinsic motivation appears to decrease significantly (and extrinsic motivation increase) as children progress through the elementary and middle school years. There is speculation that this is related to the heavy use of rewards in American classrooms as well as increased emphasis on grades and test scores, especially as students get older (Lepper, Iyengar, & Henderlong Corpus, 2005).

Emotions motivate behavior, and different emotions have unique functions related to motivation. For example, interest provokes curiosity, wonder, and the urge to explore or discover. Interest is an intrinsic motivator that helps focus attention and provide the energy to promote interaction and engagement with the environment. Happiness follows from achievement of a goal; joy serves as a reward that promotes returning to a reinforcing activity. Sadness (e.g., grief about the death of a loved one) can motivate renewal and strengthening of social bonds with friends and loved ones. Anger can mobilize and sustain energy, with a corresponding increase in motor activity at high levels. Shame acts as a force for social cohesion and conformity; the anticipation of shame (or desire to avoid shame) may motivate an individual to accept responsibility for the welfare of the family or community. Fear motivates escape from dangerous situations (Izard & Ackerman, 2000).

The ability to plan and follow through (related to executive functioning) is not always associated with motivation. Difficulties with organization or planning, together with a high degree of motivation, can lead to frustration and negatively affect one's sense of self-esteem. In bipolar disorder, mania (or hypomania) is characterized by expansive, elevated, or irritable mood, inflated sense of self (feelings of superiority or importance), decreased need for sleep, pressured speech, flight of ideas, increased involvement in goal-directed activities, excessive pleasure seeking, and/or risk-taking behaviors. Mania may be associated with increased energy, motivation, and creativity. However, because of the nature of mania—and the cognitive features of bipolar disorder—this can lead to many ideas, plans, and unfinished projects.

Amotivation means lack of motivation. Amotivation may be a feature of depression. It may also be associated with the use of certain drugs (e.g., marijuana).

See also bipolar disorder, curiosity, depressant drugs, desire, evolutionary psychology (human sociobiology), learned helplessness, libido, locus of control, Abraham Maslow.

Further Readings:

Brewer, M. B., & Hewstone, M. (2004). *Emotion and motivation.* Bodmin, England: Wiley-Blackwell.

Reeve, J. (2009). *Understanding motivation and emotion* (5th ed.). Hoboken, NJ: John Wiley.

References:

Harter, S. (1981). A new self-report scale of intrinsic versus extrinsic orientation in the classroom: Motivational and informational components. *Developmental Psychology, 17*, 300–312.

Izard, C. E., & Ackerman, B. P. (2000). Motivational, organizational, and regulatory functions of discrete emotions. In M. Lewis & J. M. Haviland-Jones (Eds.), *Handbook of emotions* (2nd ed., pp. 253–264). New York: Guilford.

Lepper, M. R., Iyengar, S. S., & Henderlong Corpus, J. (2005). Intrinsic and extrinsic motivational orientations in the classroom: Age differences and academic correlates. *Journal of Educational Psychology, 97*, 184–196.

Multimodal Therapy: BASIC I.D.

Arnold Lazarus developed the multimodal BASIC I.D. model in 1970 as a cognitive-behavioral therapy. BASIC I.D. is an acronym of several dimensions (or modes) of a person's interactions with and perceptions of the world: B (behavior), A (affect), S (sensory), I (imagery), C (cognition), I. (interpersonal), and D. (diet/drugs/biology).

The multimodal model can be used by a psychotherapist or counselor to work with clients on issues such as anxiety, depression, other mood problems, or various psychological disorders. It can also be used as a self-analysis tool as part of a stress reduction program to gain insight into one's style of thinking and interacting with the world. Multimodal therapy has been used in private practice, in conjunction with art therapy, and in working with children in school settings. The multimodal process asks the questions about each letter of the BASIC I.D. acronym given in Table 7.

Table 7: Multimodal Therapy: BASIC I.D.

B: behavior	What self-defeating actions or maladaptive *behaviors* are getting in the way of my personal fulfillment or happiness? What should I do differently?
A: affect	What seems to generate negative *affects* (emotional reactions), including anger, anxiety, or depression? To what degrees are these emotions experienced (e.g., rage or irritation, uneasiness vs. panic)? Do certain thoughts, images, or interpersonal conflicts generate these negative emotions? How do I respond (behave) when I feel a certain way?

(continued)

S: sensory	What *sensations* do I feel in my body (e.g., pain, muscle tension, butter-flies in the stomach)? What thoughts, feelings, and behaviors accompany these sensations?
I: imagery	What kinds of *images* do I tend to experience (e.g., images of failure or success)? How do these images connect with thoughts, feelings, and behaviors? What is my "self-image"?
C: cognition	What are my main *cognitions* (i.e., thoughts, including values, beliefs, attitudes, and opinions)? Are they rational or irrational? Do my thoughts include "I should," "I ought to," or "I must"?
I.: interpersonal	What are my significant *interpersonal* relationships like? What do I expect from and provide to others? Which relationships are satisfactory and which cause problems?
D.: diet/drugs	Regarding biological health (including *diet* and *drugs*), how is my overall health? How do I manage my health, including exercise and nutrition, sleep, and use of drugs and alcohol?

Source: Yvette Malamud Ozer, based on Lazarus (1984) and Lazarus and Abramovitz (2004).

Let's say that Henry wants to reduce the level of stress in his life. Henry describes a typical situation that recently caused him stress:

Last night I had three or four beers in a sports bar while watching the big game with my friends. I got home kind of late, and I didn't sleep well, so I didn't hear the alarm go off this morning. When I woke up, I was kind of hung over and I was afraid I'd be late for work, I could just see my boss chewing me out; so I was rushing, and then this guy cut me off on the freeway. Boy was I pissed! I gunned the engine and laid on the horn. I was passing him at 95 miles per hour when I saw the flashing lights in my rearview mirror. I felt my heart pounding as I pulled the car over and thought about what I'd say to the cop, and to my boss. I was really afraid I'd get fired this time.

We can describe various aspects of Henry's situation using the BASIC I.D. model as follows:

- B (behavior): Stay out late drinking; sleep through alarm; drive recklessly
- A (affect): Anger; worry, anxiety
- S (sensory): Hung over; heart pounding
- I (imagery): I see my boss chewing me out; I imagine what I'll say to the cop, to my boss
- C (cognition): I'll be late; I'll get fired
- I. (interpersonal): I like to spend time with my friends watching sports; I'm upset that I got a speeding ticket; I'm afraid my boss is going to chew me out or fire me; I hate it when other drivers cut me off!
- D. (diet/drugs/biology): Drinking so much alcohol and getting to bed late may have affected how well I slept, and I didn't get enough sleep, so I woke up grouchy and hung over

After breaking the stressful situation into its BASIC I.D. components, Henry can gain additional insight about the relationships between his different modalities by determining his *firing order*, or the sequence in which he responds to stress (Lazarus refers to this as *tracking*). In Henry's example, D. (diet/drugs/biology) is the biggest factor that sets the stage for all the other elements. If Henry consumes too much alcohol and has too little sleep, then S (sensory) kicks in—in the form of a hangover—closely followed by A (affect, e.g., fear), I (imagery, e.g., seeing the boss chewing him out), and C (cognition, "I'll be late," "I'll get fired"). If Henry does not intervene at this point, then self-defeating behaviors (B) follow on the heels of negative feelings, with resultant interpersonal (I.) consequences. So Henry's firing order in this example is DSAIC.

Lazarus pointed out in his decades-long discussions of multimodal approaches to therapy that we experience the world on many different levels, and we react and cope using many different modalities. Using the BASIC I.D. approach can help someone determine the role that outside stressors and ways of viewing and interacting with the world have on her ability to cope with life. Identifying her firing order can help someone figure out which therapeutic or stress management techniques to focus on most and where she has the most challenges.

Someone whose negative feelings, thoughts, or behaviors are often prompted by physical stress may benefit from yoga, meditation, biofeedback, aerobic exercise, or other body-oriented approaches. If diet or drugs appear early in someone's firing order, he might benefit more from a nutritional approach, smoking cessation, or switching from regular coffee to decaf. Someone whose negative thoughts always precede negative feelings or behaviors may benefit more from a cognitive therapy approach.

See also Arnold A. Lazarus, cognitive therapy and cognitive-behavioral therapy, stress.

Further Readings:
Lazarus, A. A. (1984). Multimodal therapy. In L. Grinspoon (Ed.), *Psychiatry update: The American Psychiatric Association annual review* (Vol. 3, pp. 67–76). Washington, DC: American Psychiatric Press.
Lazarus, A. A., & Abramovitz, A. (2004). A multimodal behavioral approach to performance anxiety. *Journal of Clinical Psychology, 60*, 831–840.
Palmer, S. (2009). *A multimodal approach to stress management and counselling.* Retrieved from Centre for Stress Management: http://www.managingstress.com/articles/webpage3.htm

References:
Lazarus, A. A. (1984). Multimodal therapy. In L. Grinspoon (Ed.), *Psychiatry update: The American Psychiatric Association annual review* (Vol. 3, pp. 67–76). Washington, DC: American Psychiatric Press.
Lazarus, A. A., & Abramovitz, A. (2004). A multimodal behavioral approach to performance anxiety. *Journal of Clinical Psychology, 60*, 831–840.

Music

Music is able to influence and evoke emotions. It seems to offer a unique means of communication—rooted in emotion—that can bypass the need for verbal expression. Music conveys certain emotions across cultures. In a study of emotion recognition in music among the Mafa (a culturally isolated people in Cameroon, Africa) and Western (German) listeners, both groups were able to recognize happy, sad, and scared/fearful emotions conveyed by both types of music (Western and Mafa). Neither group had been previously exposed to music from the other culture (Fritz et al., 2009).

Individuals with autism exhibit social and emotional processing deficits, including difficulty identifying others' emotions (e.g., from facial or vocal expression). A study investigating recognition of emotions (anger, fear, love, triumph, and contemplation) in music compared children with autism, Down syndrome (an intellectual disability), and typically developing children. This study found that understanding emotions conveyed by music was more closely linked to chronological age and verbal ability than to diagnosis (e.g., autism, intellectual disability). Findings suggest that social emotional processing deficits in autism do not extend to recognition of emotions in music (Heaton, Allen, Williams, Cummins, & Happé, 2009).

Emotion recognition and processing in music involves several brain structures, including those involved in emotion, cognition (thinking), motor (movement), speech and language (sounds), and spatial processing. *Amusia* is a condition in which ability to perceive and enjoy music is impaired. Amusia can be caused by brain damage (e.g., stroke, epilepsy, or traumatic brain injury) or abnormal development (congenital amusia). Studies of individuals with amusia have provided insight into the brain structures involved with music perception and processing. A study of stroke patients found that patients with amusia had a higher incidence of damage to the frontal lobe and auditory cortex of the brain. It was also found that patients' music perception abilities returned as they recovered their verbal learning, visuospatial processing, and attention abilities, indicating the close link between musical perception and other cognitive processing abilities (Särkämö et al., 2009). Patients with temporal lobe epilepsy showed decreased ability to distinguish happy and sad music, depending on which side of the brain was damaged. This study showed that brain regions on the right and left side were involved in recognizing different emotions in music (Khalfa et al., 2008). Functional magnetic resonance imaging (fMRI) studies have shown that neural systems in the right hemisphere of the brain are necessary to process the pitch, melody, harmony, and structure of music. A study exposing newborn infants (one to three days old) to music found that the same brain regions were activated in infants as in adults, primarily in the right hemisphere of the brain. When dissonant (unpleasant) music was played, brain systems on the left side (inferior frontal cortex and limbic structures) were activated, as in adults. This study showed that the brain structures used to process music are present at birth (Perani et al., 2008).

The brain's responses to music may depend on the experience and training of the listener. Brain studies with musicians have provided evidence of the brain's ability to form new connections in response to musical activities. Musicians (with years of musical training) show increased development of brain regions (e.g., auditory and motor cortices) over the brains of nonmusicians (Weinberger, 2004).

Music therapy has been used to reduce stress, anxiety, and pain. It has also been used as a treatment for specific disorders, including traumatic brain injury. Imaging studies have shown that many different brain areas are used in music processing and that music processing involves collaboration between the right and left hemispheres of the brain. Therapy involving music encourages communication among different brain regions and hemispheres and may help forge new brain connections. Research shows that music therapy stimulates cognitive functions, improves mood, and reduces anxiety, depression, and aggression in some disorders (Guétin, Soua, Voiriot, Picot, & Hérisson, 2009).

See also autistic spectrum disorders, functional magnetic resonance imaging, limbic system, traumatic brain injury.

Further Readings:
Musicophilia videos and links: http://www.musicophilia.com/
Sacks, O. (2007). *Musicophilia: Tales of music and the brain.* New York: Vintage Books.

References:
Fritz, T., Jentschke, S., Gosselin, N., Sammler, D., Peretz, I., Turner, R., et al. (2009). Universal recognition of three basic emotions in music. *Current Biology, 19*, 573–576.
Guétin, S., Soua, B., Voiriot, G., Picot, M.-C., & Hérisson, C. (2009). The effect of music therapy on mood and anxiety–depression: An observational study in institutionalised patients with traumatic brain injury. *Annals of Physical and Rehabilitation Medicine, 52*, 30–40.
Heaton, P., Allen, R., Williams, K., Cummins, O., & Happé, F. (2008). Do social and cognitive deficits curtail musical understanding? Evidence from autism and Down syndrome. *British Journal of Developmental Psychology, 26*(Part 2), 171–182.
Khalfa, S., Guye, M., Peretz, I., Chapon, F., Girard, N., Chauvel, P., et al. (2008). Evidence of lateralized anteromedial temporal structures involvement in musical emotion processing. *Neuropsychologia, 46*, 2485–2493.
Perani, D., Saccuman, M.C., Scifo, P., Spada, D., Andreolli, G., Rovelli, R., et al. (2008, July 23). Music in the first days of life. Retrieved from http://hdl.handle.net/10101/npre.2008.2114.1
Särkämö, T., Tervaniemi, M., Soinila, S., Autti, T., Silvennoinen, H.M., Laine, M., et al. (2009). Cognitive deficits associated with acquired amusia after stroke: A neuropsychological follow-up study. *Neuropsychologia, 47*, 2642–2651.
Weinberger, N.M. (2004). Music and the brain. *Scientific American, 291*, 88–95.

Music as we know it has been around for about 50,000 years. A bone flute made out of the femur bone of a cave bear has been found dating from between 43,000 and 82,000 years ago. For more on the origins of music, see Mithen, S. (2006). *The singing Neanderthals: The origins of music, language, mind, and body.* Cambridge, MA: Harvard University Press.

Source: http://www.greenwych.ca/fl-compl.htm

N

NAADAC (The Association for Addiction Professionals)

The Association for Addiction Professionals (NAADAC) is the world's largest organization of addiction-focused health care professionals. NAADAC was originally founded in 1972 as the National Association of Alcoholism Counselors and Trainers (NAACT). The NAACT was created with the goal of developing a field of professional counselors with professional training and qualifications. In 1982, NAACT professionals collaborated with professionals interested in addictions to other substances and became the National Association of Alcohol and Drug Abuse Counselors. Later the name of the organization was changed to NAADAC, the Association for Addiction Professionals, to recognize the diverse professionals who are members; members include counselors, administrators, social workers, and others.

The services NAADAC offers for addiction professionals include education, reports of research projects and opportunities for involvement in research projects, and opportunities for involvement in advocacy. At the annual convention, numerous talks, symposia, and other programs are presented over several days. Courses on single topics are offered and delivered at several locations in the United States in a given year. For example, courses offered in 2009 were New Innovations in Opioid Treatment: Buprenorphine and New Horizons—Integrating Motivational Styles Strategies and Skills with Pharmacotherapy. NAADAC also publishes a number of books and two regular newsletters. Brochures on specific topics related to drugs and addiction are downloadable on NAADAC's Web site (http://www.naadac.org/).

NAADAC works with academic partners on research projects, including ongoing surveys of members' needs and members' opinions regarding how to sustain and improve their profession. NAADAC is involved in advocacy for prevention, early intervention, and treatment for addictions. NAADAC's Political Action Committee (PAC) advocates with the federal government for improving addiction prevention, treatment, and research. The PAC works to support political candidates who care about addiction issues and improve the chances that they are elected for office.

NAADAC also has a certification program through which individuals may become certified as a National Certified Addiction Counselor, Master Addiction Counselor, or Tobacco Addiction Specialist. Other credentialing and qualification programs are available through the NAADAC.

See also alcohol abuse and alcoholism, substance abuse.

Further Reading:
NAADAC Web site: http://www.naadac.org/

Narcotics Anonymous

Narcotics Anonymous (NA), founded in 1953, was modeled after the first 12-step program, Alcoholics Anonymous (AA, founded 1935). NA is a nonprofit fellowship whose members hold regular 12-step meetings to help each other recover from addiction.

NA meetings started in the Los Angeles, California, area and spread slowly to other North American cities and Australia in the 1970s. Within a few years of the 1983 publication of NA's Basic Text, groups formed in many other countries. Today, NA books and literature are available in 27 languages. In 2005, there were over 21,500 registered NA groups holding over 33,500 weekly meetings in 116 countries. A 2003 voluntary membership survey (about 7,500 responses) revealed that 45 percent of NA members are female, 61 percent are 31 to 50 years of age, 70 percent are Caucasian, 72 percent are employed full-time, and average continuous abstinence/recovery is 7.4 years.

NA utilizes 12 Steps adapted from the 12 Steps of AA. The principles incorporated in NA's 12 Steps include admitting there is a problem, seeking help, thorough self-examination, making amends for harm done, and helping other addicts to recover. NA emphasizes practicing spiritual (not necessarily religious) principles, and each NA member is encouraged to come to his own understanding of a higher power. NA is not affiliated with treatment centers, correctional facilities, or any other organization. NA members are encouraged to practice complete abstinence from all drugs, including alcohol. NA has no official position on outside issues, including the use of prescribed medications. People are not excluded from NA membership because of race, ethnicity, religion, lack of religion, nationality, gender, sexual orientation, or social or economic status.

Because addiction is a family disease, Nar-Anon Family Groups was founded in 1968 to help support family members and friends of addicts. *Codependency* is the term now used to describe the family dynamics that enable the addict to keep using, shield the addict from adverse consequences, and keep the whole family sick.

See also Alcoholics Anonymous, substance abuse, 12-step programs.

Further Readings:
Narcotics Anonymous World Services Web site: http://www.na.org/index.php?ID=home-content-inf
Narcotics Anonymous World Services. (1988). *Narcotics Anonymous* (5th ed.). Chatsworth, CA: Author.

National Alliance on Mental Illness

The National Alliance on Mental Illness (NAMI) is a nationwide advocacy group representing people affected with mental illness and their families. As a nonprofit grassroots organization, NAMI has affiliates in every American state and in over 1,000 local communities. The history of NAMI goes back to 1979, when six independent support groups for parents of adults with severe and persistent mental illnesses from around the country held the first conference in Madison, Wisconsin. Over the decades, the interest and the membership of NAMI has extended to incorporate families and friends of people with mental illness as well as mental health care professionals.

The mission statement of NAMI is to improve the quality of life of all persons affected by mental illness; NAMI maintains that recovery, resiliency, and support are necessary for the wellness and quality of life of mentally ill persons. The main activities of NAMI include providing public education about mental illness, peer education and support groups, raising awareness and fighting stigma, and gaining state and federal support. Examples of specific issues that NAMI works on behalf of the mentally ill include insurance parity, affordable housing, increases in research appropriations, improved work incentives and income assistance, and access to medications. NAMI has emphasized the importance of evidence-based treatment practices and assertive community treatment.

NAMI includes a number of well-organized and well-developed programs that each focus on a specific issue or closely related issues. In Our Own Voice (IOOV), a core program of NAMI, was designed to involve consumers in educating the public and other mentally ill persons about serious mental illness. In this program, people with mental illness share their life experiences. Through the presentations, audience members learn the process of recovery and life with a serious mental illness. IOOV helps presenters build self-esteem and learn new coping skills as well. StigmaBusters, another specific program, was formed to fight against inaccurate and hurtful language and portrayals of mental illness in the media. Its mission is to promote understanding and respect for those who live with mental illness. Individuals involved in StigmaBusters produce general brochures that challenge common stereotypes and timely e-mail alerts when potentially harmful stereotypes are presented in the media. NAMI also has a number of specific advocacy groups and action centers. NAMI Advocacy advocates for state and federal and private-sector policies that will increase support for research, decrease discrimination, and foster efficacious mental health services. Action centers such as the Children and Adolescent Action Center and the Multicultural Action Center play central roles in developing and offering vital information to meet specific needs of specific groups of mentally ill persons. NAMI also provides information about mental illness through its Web site.

Further Reading:
National Alliance on Mental Illness Web site: http://www.nami.org/

National Association of School Psychologists

The National Association of School Psychologists (NASP), founded in 1969, is the largest organization of school psychologists in the world, representing more than 21,000 members. NASP describes its goals in the following words:

- serve the mental health and educational needs of all children and youth
- promote prevention and early intervention, problem-solving approaches and collaboration, and research-based strategies and programs
- encourage and provide opportunities for the professional growth of individual members
- inform the public about the services and practice of psychology in schools
- advance the standards of the profession of school psychology

In its brochure "What Is a School Psychologist?" NASP describes the work of school psychologists in the following terms: "School psychologists help children and youth succeed academically, socially, and emotionally. They collaborate with educators, parents, and other professionals to create safe, healthy, and supportive learning environments for all students that strengthen connections between home and school." School psychologists also develop programs to train teachers and parents about effective teaching and learning strategies, behavior management techniques, working with students with disabilities, crisis prevention and management, and drug and alcohol abuse. School psychologists perform evaluations for special education eligibility, assessments of learning style and academic skills, and social-emotional health. Interventions may include individual or group counseling or training in social skills or anger management. School psychologists use research and evaluation skills to identify evidence-based programs to implement in schools, evaluate the effectiveness of interventions, and monitor progress.

School psychologists are highly trained in both psychology and education. Some school psychologists have doctoral degrees (e.g., PhD, PsyD, EdD), and some are master's-level practitioners. Training includes preparation in data-based decision making, consultation and collaboration, effective instruction, child development, student diversity and development, school organization, prevention, intervention, mental health, learning styles, behavior, research, and program evaluation. School psychologists must be certified or licensed by the state in which they work. They may be nationally certified by the National School Psychology Certification Board as Nationally Certified School Psychologists (NCSP). This credentialing system has elevated national standards and credentialing to align with those of other educational and mental health organizations and created greater continuity in practice and credentialing across states. While the majority of school psychologists work in schools, they may also practice in various public and private settings including school-based health centers, clinics, hospitals, private practice, universities, and community or state agencies.

NASP's advocacy efforts focus on specific issues that support children's learning and development and school psychology. As a nonpartisan professional organization, NASP does not support or endorse political candidates. NASP's comprehensive policy platform, titled "Ready to Learn, Empowered to Teach: Excellence in Education for the 21st Century," can be found on its Web site.

NASP publishes several professional journals, including *Communiqué*, *School Psychology Review*, and *School Psychology Forum*. It also publishes books and resources for school psychologists, parents and families, and teachers addressing various mental health and school-related topics.

Further Readings:

National Association of School Psychologists Web site: http://www.nasponline.org/

National Association of School Psychologists. (2008). *Ready to learn, empowered to teach: Excellence in education for the 21st century.* Retrieved from http://www.nasponline.org/advocacy/Ready_to_learn_Breaking_Ranks.pdf

Silva, A. (2003). *What is a school psychologist?* Retrieved from http://www.nasponline.org/about_sp/whatis.aspx

National Coalition for the Homeless

The National Coalition for the Homeless (NCH) is an organization committed to ending homelessness. Its members are mainly people who are now experiencing or who have formerly experienced homelessness, activists, advocates, and service providers. These individuals share NCH's mission to make a difference in people's attitudes and to create a social system to prevent homelessness. NCH helps those who are currently experiencing or those who are at risk for being homeless. Public education, advocacy, and grassroots organizing are the main activities of NCH. NCH members contribute to material assistance by providing needed items and services such as clothing and job opportunities.

NCH was established in 1982 by Robert Hayes, who filed a lawsuit for a man experiencing homelessness in New York City in 1981. The lawsuit resulted in a victory for people experiencing homelessness; they won the right to shelter in New York City. In 1984, NCH was incorporated and became a nonprofit organization. NCH is primarily funded by support from individuals, foundations, and member organizations. As a community-based coalition, NCH has collaborated with other local and statewide homeless coalitions. There are NCH member organizations in Chicago, San Francisco, Seattle, and Houston and statewide coalitions in Massachusetts and Colorado.

Volunteers play an important role in activities such as working at a shelter, offering professional skills in job training, and inviting others to join the network. Volunteering helps foster people's understanding of homelessness and meets the immediate needs of those who are facing homelessness. The NCH board consists of 32 members, including service providers, academics, and organizers from all major geographic regions in the United States. Some of those members are formerly homeless.

NCH has worked with the federal government to create a systematic change needed to prevent homelessness. The Bring America Home Act (BAHA), initially proposed in 2004 by NCH, underwent revisions. NCH is preparing the bill for re-introduction in the 111th Congress, in an attempt to end mass homelessness in the United States. The purpose of BAHA is to end homelessness by providing for housing, health care, and income security (such as minimum income provisions) for all citizens. A number of specific civil rights provisions are also included such as adding homeless persons as a protected class of people for hate crime reporting and removing a homeless person's impediments to receiving identification. The passage and implementation of this act would greatly improve the living conditions of many homeless persons.

In addition, NCH has been engaged in studies of homelessness. According to NCH, a lack of affordable rental housing and an increase in poverty are the main cause of growing homelessness over the past 20 to 25 years. Low employment opportunities and a decline in the availability of public assistance contribute to rising poverty, while the current housing crisis is aggravated by limited housing assistance programs. Other factors contributing to homelessness include lack of affordable health care, domestic violence, mental illness, and addiction disorders.

Further Reading:
National Coalition for the Homeless Web site: http://www.nationalhomeless.org/

National Eating Disorders Association

The National Eating Disorders Association (NEDA) is the largest nonprofit organization in the United States devoted to providing support and resources to those affected by eating disorders, including individual sufferers, loved ones, and care providers, and to educating concerned individuals and the general public about eating disorders. NEDA was formed in 2001 with the merger of the two largest prevention and advocacy groups for eating disorders in the world: Eating Disorders Awareness and Prevention and the American Anorexia Bulimia Association.

NEDA's goals include improving access to appropriate treatment for eating disorders, providing education about eating disorders, supporting research on eating disorders, and ultimately, preventing eating disorders. NEDA works toward its goals through the efforts of its own employees, through partnerships with other organizations, and with the help of volunteers.

NEDA sponsors the States for Treatment Advocacy and Research (STAR) program. Through STAR, NEDA advocates collaborate with state legislators to improve access to treatments and to support efforts that intervene early and prevent eating disorders. NEDA educates the public, affected individuals, and treatment providers about eating disorders in a variety of ways. NEDA's annual conference allows families and treatment providers to come together to build networks and share stories. Other annual events, a walk and an awareness week, primarily increase public awareness. NEDA publishes educational materials, including the *Healthy Body Image* book by Kathy J. Kater and a program called "Go Girls!" The goals of the program, designed for high school students, are to improve individual body image and to encourage young women and men to advocate for appropriate body image presentations in the media. As part of the program, participants view advertisements with a critical eye, learning to identify those advertisements that are promoting unhealthy body image. Participants are taught to write letters to companies and to legislators, expressing their thoughts and feelings about proper presentation of body image in the media.

NEDA supports research through cosponsoring young investigator grants and in other ways. The NEDA toll-free help line provides information referrals. Many other resources are available to people with eating disorders and those who care about them.

Further Reading:
National Eating Disorders Association Web site: http://www.nationaleatingdisorders.org/

National Institute of Mental Health

The National Institute of Mental Health (NIMH) is the primary institute in the United States to specialize in research on mental illness. NIMH is one of the 27 component organizations of the National Institutes of Health (NIH), a division of the U.S. Department of Health and Human Services. NIMH conducts research at a central campus in Bethesda, Maryland, while also funding research throughout the United States. NIMH aims to improve the lives of mentally ill people through increasing understanding and improving the diagnosis, prevention, and treatment of mental illness through basic and clinical research on mind, brain, and behavior. NIMH has initiated studies of genetics, neuroscience, and clinical trials of psychiatric medication.

The history of NIMH goes back to 1946, with the enforcement of the National Mental Health Act (NMHA). The objective of the NMHA was to support the research, prevention, and treatment of psychiatric illness. The NMHA led to the establishment of a National Advisory Mental Health Council and a National Institute of Mental Health. NIMH was formally established on April 15, 1949. The primary activities of NIMH include supporting research in the United States and throughout the world; collecting, analyzing, and disseminating information on mental illnesses;

supporting the training of scientists to conduct mental health research; and communicating with researchers, patients, the media, and mental health professionals about mental illnesses.

NIMH divisions and programs are designed to provide support for research programs in each area of mental illness. NIMH funds research both by scientists across the country and through NIMH's internal program. In 2009, more than 2,000 research grants and contracts at universities and other institutions across the country and overseas were supported by NIMH through its extramural program. Approximately 500 scientists work in the NIMH intramural research program, ranging from molecular biologists working in laboratories to clinical researchers working with patients at the NIH Clinical Center. Intramural scientists are accorded unique flexibility in rapidly following up research leads and unexpected opportunities. Supplemental government funds further support NIMH such as funding from the American Recovery and Reinvestment Act of 2009 (the Recovery Act).

The American Psychological Association and other organizations have criticized the NIMH for deemphasizing research from behavioral and social sciences perspectives relative to research on the brain and genetics. According to their arguments, solely focusing on brain and genetics does little if anything to help us understand the cognitive, affective, motivational, and social processes lying behind the mental illnesses (Breckler, 2008).

Further Reading:
National Institute of Mental Health Web site: http://www.nimh.nih.gov/

Reference:
Breckler, S. (2008). The strategic plan of NIMH. *Psychological Science Agenda, 22*(1). Retrieved from http://www.apa.org/science/about/psa/2008/01/ed-column.aspx

National Institute of Neurological Disorders and Stroke

The National Institute of Neurological Disorders and Stroke (NINDS) is the leading U.S. institute supporting and conducting research on neurological disorders and stroke. Its mission is to reduce the burden of neurological disease. NINDS promotes the training of researchers in the basic and clinical neurosciences for better understanding, diagnosis, treatment, and prevention of neurological disorders. NINDS is a branch of the U.S. National Institutes of Health, an agency of the U.S. Department of Health and Human Services accountable for biomedical and health-related research.

NINDS was initially created by the U.S. Congress in 1950. Since its establishment, NINDS has retained a leading position in the world of neuroscience. Research conducted by scientists in NINDS laboratories and clinics covers the important areas of neuroscience and neurological disorders, including the healthy and diseased brain, spinal cord, and peripheral nerves, and disorders afflicting the nervous system such as Parkinson's disease, Alzheimer's disease, multiple sclerosis, stroke, epilepsy, and autism. Basic research promotes understanding of the structures and activities of the cells in the nervous system, brain and nervous system development, genetics of the brain, cognition and behavior, neurodegeneration, brain plasticity and repair, neural signaling, and learning and memory. The external program of NINDS supports research project grants and contracts for universities, medical schools, and hospitals, while its institutional training grants and individual fellowships support scientists in training. Extramural scientists in public and private institutions conduct the majority of NINDS-funded research.

NINDS has collaborated with other NIH institutes, federal agencies, and organizations to support neuroscientific research. NINDS is known for its contribution to the development of treatments for formerly intractable problems such as spinal cord injury, acute stroke, multiple sclerosis, and Parkinson's disease. The knowledge gained from NINDS research has helped diagnose disease. NINDS has had some success in building the next generation of neuroscientists through funding research training. Its new strategic plan focuses on combining its vision for the future with a practical approach to help NINDS achieve an ideal balance among basic, clinical, translational (relatively easily applied), and disease-related research in neuroscience.

See also autistic spectrum disorders, Parkinson's disease, right hemisphere syndrome.

Further Reading:
National Institute of Neurological Disorders and Stroke Web site: http://www.ninds.nih.gov/

National Institute on Alcohol Abuse and Alcoholism

The National Institute on Alcohol Abuse and Alcoholism (NIAAA) is part of the National Institutes of Health (NIH), an agency of the U.S. Department of Health and Human Services responsible for biomedical and behavioral research on health-related issues. With an aim to reduce severe problems associated with alcohol use nationwide, NIAAA takes a leading role in conducting and supporting research on the causes, consequences, treatment, and prevention of alcoholism and alcohol-related problems. Its research encompasses a range of areas, including genetics, neuroscience, epidemiology, and the health risks and benefits of alcohol consumption. For example, NIAAA has been involved in research on medication development for alcohol-use disorders, genetic studies of vulnerability to alcohol and markers of alcohol-induced organ damage and organ protection, and behavioral risk factors for alcoholism.

Alcohol use disorders include alcohol abuse and alcohol dependence. NIAAA describes *alcohol dependence* (often referred to as alcoholism) as characterized by craving (a strong need or urge to drink alcohol), a loss of control over drinking, physical dependence (withdrawal symptoms such as nausea, sweating, shakiness, and anxiety after stopping drinking), and tolerance (need to drink increased amounts of alcohol over time to achieve the same effects). *Alcohol abuse* is a pattern of drinking with significant and recurring adverse consequences related to drinking alcohol. A person may drink too much and too often. Some of the problems linked to alcohol abuse include not being able to meet work, school, or family responsibilities; drunk-driving arrests and car crashes; and alcohol-related medical conditions (National Institute on Alcohol Abuse and Alcoholism, 2007). For clinical and research purposes, NIAAA follows formal diagnostic criteria for alcohol use disorders included in the *Diagnostic and Statistical Manual of Mental Disorders* (*DSM-IV-TR*; American Psychiatric Association, 2000). The *DSM-IV-TR* is a diagnostic classification system for mental health disorders used mostly in the United States.

The National Advisory Council (NAC) on Alcohol Abuse and Alcoholism plays an important role in NIAAA. The NAC makes suggestions to the secretary and director of the NIH and the director of NIAAA regarding program and policy matters in the field of alcohol abuse and alcoholism. The council also gives advice about research conducted at NIAAA, reviews applications for grants and cooperative agreements for research and research training, and recommends applications for projects that show promise of making valuable contributions to human knowledge.

NIAAA collaborates with other institutions at international, national, state, and local levels. As a means of disseminating scientific findings and information on alcohol-related issues, NIAAA publishes a number of journals and newsletters aimed at different audiences. Publications for researchers and health professionals include epidemiological data, clinicians' resources such as information about how to assess alcohol abuse and dependence and how alcohol use affects relationships, and teacher resources. The findings through research sponsored by NIAAA have contributed to health care providers' increased understanding of normal and abnormal biological functions and behavior regarding alcohol use, which in turn has improved the diagnosis, prevention, and treatment of alcohol-related problems. NIAAA has also helped to deepen and broaden the understanding of alcohol use and alcohol use disorders in the general public. For the public, NIAAA publishes pamphlets, brochures, fact sheets, posters, and publications in Spanish and provides public service announcements.

See also alcohol abuse and alcoholism.

Further Readings:
National Institute on Alcohol Abuse and Alcoholism Web site: http://www.niaaa.nih.gov/
Rethinking drinking: Alcohol and your health (interactive Web site): http://rethinkingdrinking.niaaa. nih.gov/

References:
American Psychiatric Association. (2000). *Diagnostic and statistical manual of mental disorders* (4th ed., text rev.). Washington, DC: Author.
National Institute on Alcohol Abuse and Alcoholism. (2007). *FAQ for the general public.* Retrieved from http://www.niaaa.nih.gov/FAQs/General-English/

National Institute on Drug Abuse

The National Institute on Drug Abuse (NIDA), part of the National Institutes of Health (NIH), specializes in research on drug abuse and addiction. Founded in 1974, NIDA has addressed its mission to lead the nation in scientific research on drug abuse and addiction and to rapidly and effectively distribute the resulting knowledge. NIDA supports over 85 percent of the world's research on drug abuse and addiction (National Institute on Drug Abuse, n.d.).

NIDA's main activities are centered on research programs in basic and clinical sciences, including genetics, functional neuroimaging, social neuroscience, medication and behavioral therapies, prevention, and health services. By encompassing biological, behavioral, and social components of drug addiction, NIDA aims to confront the complex aspects of drug abuse and addiction and to tackle their underlying causes.

In 2009, NIDA identified four major goal areas that encompass their five-year strategic plan: prevention, treatment, HIV/AIDS, and cross-cutting priorities. NIDA aims to work toward prevention of both the initiation of drug use and the escalation to addiction in those who have already started to use. NIDA has supported a great deal of research on treatments for drug addiction, with its strategic goal to improve accessibility to all groups. Additionally, as part of prevention efforts, NIDA has focused on the issues involving the spread of HIV/AIDS through its connection with other risky behaviors such as needle sharing and unprotected sex. NIDA supports primary prevention research to find the most effective HIV risk-reduction interventions for different populations to diminish the spread of drug abuse–related HIV and minimize the associated health and social consequences of the disease. NIDA goals (called *cross-cutting priorities*) include supporting research on other health conditions that influence drug abuse and addiction, educating diverse groups (e.g., media, legislators, medical groups) about the biology of drug addiction and abuse, attracting new researchers, and supporting international collaboration on research and outreach efforts.

NIDA disseminates information through publications, meetings, and its Web site. Its publications include books, summary research reports, brochures, fact sheets, a serial titled *NIDA Notes* that reports on research studies, and other publications. Regular NIDA meetings, which are open to the public, focus on general NIDA activities or special topics (e.g., specific drugs, particular treatments). NIDA's Web site presents a wealth of information on the organization and on addiction and abuse.

NIDA is headquartered in Rockville, Maryland; its Intramural Research Program (IRP) is located in east Baltimore. NIDA's funding comes through congressional appropriations as well as donations to support its research activities.

See also alcohol abuse and alcoholism, substance abuse.

Further Reading:
National Institute on Drug Abuse Web site: http://www.nida.nih.gov/

Reference:
National Institute on Drug Abuse. (n.d.). *NIDA for teens: Frequently asked questions.* Retrieved from http://teens.drugabuse.gov/drnida/drnida_general1.php

Negative Emotions

Although experiencing negative emotions may be unpleasant, the immediate negative reactions that we have to situations are often functional. For example, when we experience fear at the sound of a rattle at our feet, we jump back to avoid the rattlesnake. When we bring food to our mouths and smell a foul odor, we feel disgust, put down the fork, and push the plate away. According to the leading theories about emotion, the function of negative emotions is to enhance our survival.

The negative emotions and affective states are many and diverse. Examples include fear, anger, disgust, sadness, jealousy, envy, shame, guilt, contempt, anxiety, hate, depression, and hopelessness, to name a few. When perusing this list, it may have occurred to the reader that it is difficult to think of some of these emotional states as functional. For instance, what is the use of feeling hopelessness, or even sadness? Is hate functional? Frijda (1994) addressed this issue in his chapter "Emotions Are Functional, Most of the Time." Frijda compares the functionality of emotions to the functionality of language. The function of language is to communicate, but we often produce sentences that do little to communicate whatever we intended to communicate, and we sometimes even produce sentences that get us in trouble. According to Frijda, it is the same with emotions. In general, emotions serve a function. However, there are many cases in which our experience, expression, or reactions to our emotions can serve us ill rather than serve us well. In fact, in the history of the study of emotion, researchers have focused more on the ways in which negative emotions are dysfunctional than on the ways in which negative emotions are functional. Therefore we have devoted a great deal of research time and effort to disorders of emotions, which include depression; the anxiety disorders such as phobias, generalized anxiety disorder, obsessive-compulsive disorder, panic disorder, and posttraumatic stress disorder; and others. This is understandable; people in disciplines such as psychology are interested in relieving human suffering, and fully understanding the causes and nature of suffering seems more urgent than developing a basic intellectual understanding of emotions.

However, some scholars have devoted their work lives to a more general understanding of negative emotions, and basic knowledge has progressed rapidly. Many emotion theories view negative emotions as each being associated with a specific action tendency (e.g., Frijda, 1986; Tooby & Cosmides, 1990). For example, anger is linked with an urge to attack and fear with an urge to escape. The action tendency does not mean that the organism must engage in the particular behavior in any particular way, but a general urge exists. Some cognitive (thinking) aspects are associated with these action tendencies. According to research findings, negative emotions are linked with a focusing (narrowing) of attention, in contrast with positive emotions, which are associated with an expanding of attention (e.g., Basso, Schefft, Ris, & Dember, 1996). This focusing is functional; the individual can attend specifically to the threat or other relevant stimulus and block out other stimuli, thus being maximally prepared to take the action necessary for survival.

Fredrickson (2001) has developed a theory of positive emotion that has proven helpful for understanding positive emotions and that additionally serves to shed light on the function of negative emotions. Her *broaden-and-build theory* proposes that positive emotions function to broaden our perceptions and cognitions, leading to an openness and flexibility in thinking. The benefit of positive emotions comes in the long run (the *build* part of her theory) because while broadening, the individual also builds physical, intellectual, and social resources that can help him in the future. For instance, while feeling joy and playing (say, a game of softball), the individual may build muscular strength and coordination. Additionally, he may exhibit glee and have a good laugh with others, building social relationships. By contrast, negative emotions are most helpful in the short term; in general, negative emotions have little in the way of building effects. Those negative emotions that are functional arise as a reaction to an immediate stimulus, are linked with a tendency to produce a fairly specific action, and typically dissipate at the conclusion of the event.

See also ambivalence, anger, anxiety, contempt, depression, disgust, dysphoria, fear, grief, guilt, hate, hopelessness, jealousy, Positive and Negative Affect (Activation) Schedule, positive emotions, sadness, shame.

Further Reading:
Fredrickson, B. L., & Cohn, M. A. (2008). Positive emotions. In M. Lewis, J. M. Haviland-Jones, & L. F. Barrett (Eds.), *Handbook of emotions* (3rd ed., pp. 777–796). New York: Guilford.

References:
Basso, M. R., Schefft, B. K., Ris, M. D., & Dember, W. N. (1996). Mood and global-local visual processing. *Journal of the International Neuropsychological Society, 2*, 249–255.
Fredrickson, B. L. (2001). The role of positive emotions in positive psychology: The broaden-and-build theory of positive emotions. *American Psychologist, 56*, 218–226.

Frijda, N. H. (1986). *The emotions.* Cambridge, England: Cambridge University Press.

Frijda, N. H. (1994). Emotions are functional, most of the time. In P. Ekman & R. Davidson (Eds.), *The nature of emotion: Fundamental questions* (pp. 112–122). New York: Oxford University Press.

Tooby, J., & Cosmides, L. (1990). The past explains the present: Emotional adaptations and the structure of ancestral environments. *Ethology and Sociobiology, 11*, 375–424.

Neuroticism

Among the most significant and well-researched traits in personality psychology is neuroticism, a constellation of attributes that are primarily negative emotions. The most central emotions are fear/anxiety, depression/sadness, and anger/hostility. Neuroticism is a trait continuum such that each individual possesses anywhere from very low to very high levels of neuroticism. The low end of this trait is also called *emotional stability*; high neuroticism is *low emotional stability* and low neuroticism is *high emotional stability*.

The person who is extremely high in neuroticism is not only fearful, depressed, and angry but also moody, nervous, high strung, temperamental, and insecure. An individual who is low in neuroticism (high in emotional stability) is not necessarily high in positive emotions, such as happiness, but experiences low levels of negative emotions. This individual could be described as stable, secure, self-assured, relaxed, and contented.

Ozer and Benet-Martínez (2006) discuss several traits, including neuroticism, and how they are related to "individual outcomes," "interpersonal outcomes," and "institutional outcomes." Not surprisingly, high neuroticism is generally associated with negative outcomes in each of these arenas. For example, those high in neuroticism have higher rates of physical symptoms, psychiatric illness, stress, and loneliness and lower satisfaction with both interpersonal relationships and work life.

Some researchers have hypothesized that neuroticism may have a biological basis. The British psychologist Hans Eysenck proposed that neuroticism may be associated with activity of the limbic system, a set of structures in the brain theoretically involved in the experience and regulation of emotion. His and other general theories have failed to find much support. However, one brain structure, the amygdala, is implicated in the experience of a specific emotion: fear. LeDoux (1996) argues that when danger is perceived, the amygdala activates different responses (endocrine, autonomic, behavioral) to contend with the danger. Nonetheless, the direct connection between the amygdala and the trait of neuroticism, should it exist, has not yet been demonstrated. Since neuroticism is linked to significant suffering, and since much about it is still unknown, it will likely remain a popular topic of study in psychology and related fields.

See also affective personality traits, amygdala, fear, lability (emotional), limbic system, negative emotions, PEN model of personality, personality, regulation of emotion, temperament.

Further Reading:

Harary, K., & Robinson, E. D. (2005). *Who do you think you are?* London: Penguin Group.

References:

LeDoux, J. (1996). *The emotional brain: The mysterious underpinnings of emotional life.* New York: Touchstone.

Ozer, D.J., & Benet-Martínez, V. (2006). Personality and the prediction of consequential outcomes. *Annual Review of Psychology, 57*, 401–421.

Neurotransmitter

Neurotransmitters (also referred to as *neuromodulators*) are chemicals in the body that convey messages between neurons (nerve cells). Types of neurotransmitters include monoamines, amino acids, and peptides. The major monoamines include dopamine, serotonin (5-HT), norepinephrine (noradrenaline), epinephrine (adrenaline), acetylcholine, and melatonin. Amino acids include gamma-aminobutyric acid (GABA), glutamate, aspartate, and glycine. Other neurotransmitters are adenosine and histamine.

In 1904, British scientist T.R. Elliott found that the substance extracted from the adrenal glands (adrenaline) mimicked actions of the sympathetic nervous system (SNS). The SNS is responsible for regulating the fight-or-flight response, including increased heartbeat, blood pressure, and perspiration. In 1914, British physiologist Sir Henry Halett Dale (1865–1968) investigated the active substance in ergot, a fungal infection of wheat or rye. Ergot has strong effects on the central nervous system, including death. Dale found that the active substance in ergot (later chemically identified as acetylcholine) would reverse the effects of adrenaline (Sabbatini, 2003). In the 1920s, Otto Loewi, a professor of physiology in Vienna, Austria, did an experiment with two frog hearts. Stimulating a nerve on one frog heart resulted in inhibition of the heartbeat. When he infused the second frog heart with material from the first, the second heart showed a similar effect. He was able to demonstrate that a substance (later identified as acetylcholine) was responsible for the inhibiting effects on the heartbeat. He used a similar technique to demonstrate the effects of adrenaline as an excitatory (stimulating) substance. In research conducted in the 1920s and 1930s, Sir Henry Dale demonstrated that neurotransmitters could also act in the voluntary nervous system. For their work clarifying the role of neurotransmitters, Loewi and Dale shared the Nobel Prize in 1936 (Sabbatini, 2003). The catecholamines (dopamine, norepinephrine, and epinephrine) were studied in the 1950s and 1960s. Swedish researcher Ulf Von Euler and American researcher Julius Axelrod received the 1970 Nobel Prize for their work identifying and studying the metabolism of norepinephrine (Sabbatini, 2003). Amino acids have been studied since the 1960s (Gordon, 2000). Several peptides studied in the 1970s—Substance P, leucine, and methionine-enkephalin—were all found to be involved in the sensation of pain (Gordon, 2000).

Neurotransmitter receptors alter cellular excitability. Some neurotransmitters are primarily *inhibitory* (e.g., GABA and glycine), others are primarily *excitatory* (e.g., L-glutamate), and others may serve multiple functions (both inhibitory and excitatory). An *excitatory* neurotransmitter increases the probability that a target receptor cell (neuron) will activate (fire), while an *inhibitory* one decreases this probability. Neurotransmitters transmit signals by binding to specific *receptor* cells. For example, the neurotransmitter dopamine (DA) only binds to DA receptors. After a neurotransmitter is released into the *synapse* (a tiny space between cells), it may bind to a receptor, be destroyed by enzymes, or be reabsorbed by the neuron. The reabsorption mechanism is known as a *reuptake transporter pump*. Through reabsorption, some neurotransmitters are recycled so that they can be used over and over (Preston, O'Neal, & Talaga,

2008). Neurons continuously manufacture new neurotransmitters to replenish those lost through enzymatic degradation.

Some neurotransmitters have been linked with certain functions. For example, acetylcholine has been implicated with memory. Dopamine is associated with reward and addiction. Addictive drugs (e.g., cocaine, heroin, methamphetamine) primarily affect the dopamine system. Endorphins are associated with pain, norepinephrine with memory and the fight-or-flight response, melatonin with circadian rhythms and the body's biological clock, and serotonin with mood and aggression. Some psychiatric medications make use of the reuptake transporter system to block specific neurotransmitter receptors. Drugs that block reuptake make more of the neurotransmitter available for use in the synapse. Antidepressant medications such as selective serotonin reuptake inhibitors (SSRIs) block serotonin reuptake. Antipsychotic medications that block dopamine receptors are used to treat schizophrenia. Benzodiazepines (such as Valium) prescribed to treat anxiety bind to specific sites in GABA receptors. The functions and effects of neurotransmitters depend on the location of receptor neurons, interconnections with other neurons, and interactions among brain and body regions. Factors and relationships are often complex; often several neurotransmitters and interactions among multiple brain regions influence human behavior, cognition, and emotion. As research continues to shed light on these relationships, new medications are being developed to increase treatment effectiveness and decrease side effects.

See also antidepressant, antipsychotic, anxiety, anxiolytic, atypical antidepressants, benzodiazepine, depression, schizophrenia, selective serotonin reuptake inhibitor, serotonin.

Further Reading:
National Institute of Mental Health, *The brain's inner workings* (five-minute video hosted by Leonard Nimoy that lead viewers deep into the brain, introducing the physical, chemical, and electrical events that occur in the normal brain): http://mentalhealth.about.com/library/rs/brain/blcd.htm

References:
Gordon, E. (2000). *Integrative neuroscience: Bringing together biological, psychological and clinical models of the human brain.* Boca Raton, FL: CRC Press.
Preston, J. D., O'Neal, J. H., & Talaga, M. C. (2008). *Handbook of clinical psychopharmacology for therapists* (5th ed.). Oakland, CA: New Harbinger.
Sabbatini, R.M.E. (2003, April–July). Neurons and synapses: The history of discovery. *Revista Cérebro & Mente* [Brain & Mind], *17*, 1–6. Retrieved from http://www.cerebromente.org.br/n17/history/neurons5_i.htm

Nonverbal Expression

Humans have many different ways of expressing their emotions nonverbally. These include facial expression, body posture, body movements, vocal expression, touch, use of space (e.g., how closely one sits or stands to another person), appearance (e.g., clothing, grooming, hair style, etc.), and others. In the late 1800s, after having developed his theory of evolution by natural selection, Charles Darwin became interested in studying the nonverbal expression of emotion. He wrote a now classic book, *The Expression of the Emotions in Man and Animals*, originally published in 1872. Darwin's book includes descriptions, drawings, and photographs of facial, body posture, and other types of emotional expressions in several species, including domestic dogs, domestic cats, several monkey species, several bird species, and humans. Darwin described expressions associated with several emotions, including sadness, anger, high spirits, contempt, disgust, fear, and surprise. For example, he described and graphically represented that a threatened dog or cat displays a snarling expression that looks similar to the angry expression of a human. Darwin argued that the existence of these similarities demonstrates that emotional expression must have evolved through natural selection in the same way that other characteristics evolved. He further contended that the expressions must serve a function; they enhance survival of the organism. His observations also suggested that emotions exist as distinct categories (e.g., happiness, anger, sadness, fear) because specific facial and other expressions are associated with specific emotional states.

More recently, individual researchers have tended to focus on modes of nonverbal expression such as facial expression or vocal expression. The most well known of the modern researchers on nonverbal expression of emotion is American psychologist Paul Ekman, who began researching facial expression with his colleagues in the 1960s. Ekman and Friesen's 1975 book *Unmasking the Face* describes in detail the movements of facial muscles that are associated with specific emotions. The book is also filled with photographs illustrating the descriptions. In the 1970s, Ekman and Friesen also developed the Facial Action Coding System (FACS) for categorizing and classifying facial expressions based on how muscular action in the face affects the appearance of the face. The system is used by psychologists and other behavioral scientists, computer scientists, animators, and others.

Other researchers have specialized on other modes of expression. For instance, Bachorowski and Owren (2008) and colleagues and Sherer and colleagues (e.g., Johnstone & Sherer, 2000) have studied vocal expression of emotion extensively. The study of nonverbal expression of emotion has produced applicable findings, such as Ekman's research on facial expression, and thus nonverbal emotional expression remains a popular research topic.

See also animals, body language, Charles Darwin, deimatic, display rules, Paul Ekman, Facial Action Coding System, facial expression, universal signals, vocal expression.

Further Readings:

Darwin, C. (1998). *The expression of the emotions in man and animals* (3rd ed.). New York: Oxford University Press. (Original work published 1872)

Ekman, P. (2007). *Emotions revealed: Recognizing faces and feelings to improve communication and emotional life* (2nd ed.). New York: Holt Paperbacks.

Ekman, P., & Friesen, W. V. (1975). *Unmasking the face.* Englewood Cliffs, NJ: Prentice Hall.

References:

Bachorowski, J., & Owren, M. J. (2008). Vocal expressions of emotion. In M. Lewis, J. M. Haviland-Jones, & J. F. Barrett (Eds.), *Handbook of emotions* (3rd ed., pp. 196–210). New York: Guilford.

Darwin, C. (1998). *The expression of the emotions in man and animals* (3rd ed.). New York: Oxford University Press. (Original work published 1872)

Ekman, P., & Friesen, W. V. (1975). *Unmasking the face.* Englewood Cliffs, NJ: Prentice Hall.

Johnstone, T., & Scherer, K. R. (2000). Vocal communication of emotion. In M. Lewis & J. M. Haviland-Jones (Eds.), *Handbook of emotions* (2nd ed., pp. 220–235). New York: Guilford.

Nucleus Accumbens

The nucleus accumbens (NAc; also known as the *nucleus accumbens septi*) is part of the ventral striatum, which is part of the basal ganglia of the brain. The NAc serves as an interface between the limbic system and the motor system of the brain. The NAc, sometimes referred to as the brain's pleasure center, is believed to play a role in reward, pleasure, addiction, laughter, fear, and the placebo effect. Neuroimaging studies—such as functional magnetic resonance imaging (fMRI) and positron emission tomography (PET)—have helped shed light on the function of the NAc.

Two neurotransmitters (chemical messengers), dopamine and serotonin, are instrumental in the functioning of the NAc. Dopamine release in the NAc seems to promote desire, while serotonin affects inhibition and feelings of satiation. Addictive drugs—including cocaine, amphetamines, alcohol, opiates, cannabis, and nicotine—seem to affect the NAc. NAc activation and dopamine release in the NAc have been found when listening to music. Together, the brain's ventral tegmental area (VTA) and the NAc are involved in the experiencing of pleasure and reward (Menon & Levitin, 2005). The NAc also seems to be involved in the experience of humor: research participants exposed to funny cartoons demonstrated activation of the NAc, ventral striatum, VTA, and amygdala, all implicated in dopamine-related reward processing and all components of the brain's limbic system (Mobbs, Greicius, Abdel-Azim, Menon, & Reiss, 2003).

The *placebo effect* is based on expectations. For example, if an individual is given a pill and told that it will relieve pain, and if that person expects or anticipates pain relief, she may experience pain relief, even if the pill contains no actual medicine (a placebo). The placebo effect can be observed by the expectation of pain, pain relief, or other rewarding or aversive experiences. Research has observed (through PET scans) dopamine release in the NAc during placebo tests. The magnitude of the dopamine release was proportional to the anticipated effectiveness of the placebo (Scott et al., 2007).

A study of children and adolescents at risk for major depressive disorder showed greater activation of the NAc and amygdala when viewing fearful faces, and lower activation when shown happy faces, than adolescents with low depression risk (Monk et al., 2008). Deep brain stimulation (a type of psychosurgery) of the NAc is being investigated as a promising therapy to treat severe, treatment-resistant depression and obsessive-compulsive disorder (Dumitriu, Collins, Alterman, & Mathew, 2008).

See also amusement, depression, limbic system, major depressive disorder, neurotransmitter, obsessive-compulsive disorder, pleasure, psychosurgery, serotonin, substance abuse.

Further Reading:

The pleasure centres affected by drugs: http://thebrain.mcgill.ca/flash/a/a_03/a_03_cr/a_03_cr_par/a_03_cr_par.html

References:

Dumitriu, D., Collins, K., Alterman, R., & Mathew, S.J. (2008). Neurostimulatory therapeutics in management of treatment-resistant depression with focus on deep brain stimulation. *Mount Sinai Journal of Medicine, 75*, 263–275.

Menon, V., & Levitin, D.J. (2005). The rewards of music listening: Response and physiological connectivity of the mesolimbic system. *NeuroImage, 28*, 175–184.

Mobbs, D., Greicius, M.D., Abdel-Azim, E., Menon, V., & Reiss, A.L. (2003). Humor modulates the mesolimbic reward centers. *Neuron, 40*, 1041–1048.

Monk, C. S., Klein, R.G., Telzer, E.H., Schroth, E.A., Mannuzza, S., Moulton, J.L., et al. (2008). Amygdala and nucleus accumbens activation to emotional facial expressions in children and adolescents at risk for major depression. *American Journal of Psychiatry, 165*, 90–98.

Scott, D. J., Stohler, C. S., Egnatuk, C. M., Wang, H., Koeppe, R. A., & Zubieta, J.-K. (2007). Individual differences in reward responding explain placebo-induced expectations and effects. *Neuron, 55,* 325–336.

Nutritional Therapies

Nutritional therapies involve using dietary regimens or supplements to treat various conditions, including mental health disorders. Dietary supplements may include vitamins, fish oils, minerals, amino acids, herbs, or other botanicals. Dietary regimens may include functional foods, such as chocolate, cranberries, soy, or nuts, for their specific properties or functions. Whole diet therapy may involve restricting or eliminating certain foods (e.g., saturated fats, carbohydrates, gluten, sugar, caffeine) or increasing intake of other foods (e.g., protein). Nutritional therapies may be employed instead of, or in addition to, standard pharmaceutical treatments. Mental health disorders that have been treated nutritionally include major depressive disorder (MDD), bipolar disorder, obsessive-compulsive disorder (OCD), anxiety disorders, insomnia, fatigue, and schizophrenia. Nutritional therapies have also been used to treat conditions such as autistic spectrum disorders and attention-deficit hyperactivity disorder (ADHD) and to improve cognitive function (e.g., memory).

In 1968, renowned chemist Linus Pauling published a controversial article about orthomolecular psychiatry, a biochemical model that explored nutritional therapies for mental diseases (Hoffer, 2008). Pauling's theories led to the popular megavitamin therapies of the 1970s. While orthomolecular psychiatry was dismissed by mainstream mental health professional organizations (e.g., American Psychiatric Association), the theory sparked interest and further exploration into nutritional therapies for mental health disorders. Some of these therapies include supplemental vitamins or glycine for schizophrenia, kava kava (*Piper methysticum*) for anxiety, valerian (an herb) and melatonin (a pineal hormone) for insomnia, ginseng and ephedra for fatigue, and ginkgo bilboa to improve memory (Elkins, Marcus, Rajab, & Durgam, 2005).

The neurotransmitters (chemical messengers in the brain) serotonin, dopamine, noradrenaline, and gamma-aminobutyric acid have been implicated in depression, bipolar disorder, and schizophrenia. Some individuals with mood disorders (e.g., depression, bipolar disorder) have been shown to have deficiencies of some of these neurotransmitters (Lakhan & Vieira, 2008). Chemicals or substances that the body converts into other substances (e.g., neurotransmitters) are known as *precursors.* The amino acid tryptophan is a precursor to the neurotransmitter serotonin. Tryptophan is found naturally in foods such as milk and turkey. Tyrosine (and sometimes its precursor, phenylalanine) is converted into dopamine and noradrenaline. Dietary supplements containing tyrosine and phenylalanine increase arousal and alertness. Methionine is a precursor of S-adenosylmethionine (SAMe), which facilitates the production of neurotransmitters in the brain (Lakhan & Vieira, 2008). Utilizing dietary supplements with the goal of increasing neurotransmitter production is known as *neurotransmitter precursor therapy.* For some neurotransmitters, use of dietary supplements may influence neurotransmitter synthesis, affecting mood and behavior (Young, 1996).

Some studies have found that omega-3 fatty acids, which naturally occur in fish, may alleviate symptoms of MDD, bipolar disorder, and schizophrenia (Freeman et al., 2006). Omega-3 fatty acids can cause some side effects (e.g., gastrointestinal distress) and may not be suitable for individuals taking anti–blood clotting medications.

Individuals with bipolar disorder or depression have been found to have deficiencies in vitamins C and B (folate), magnesium, taurine, and omega-3 fatty acids (Lakhan & Vieira, 2008). Increasing tryptophan intake has been suggested as a means to treat symptoms of depression and OCD (Lakhan & Vieira, 2008).

St. John's wort (*Hypericum perforatum*) is an herb that has been much studied for the treatment of depression. It has been found to be useful in the treatment of mild to moderate depression but not for severe depression. St. John's wort has also been used to treat fatigue and increase energy. St. John's wort has been associated with exacerbation of psychosis in individuals with schizophrenia and onset of manic episodes in individuals with bipolar disorder. Symptoms of mania may include abnormally high levels of excitement and energy, racing thoughts, and inappropriate or impulsive behavior (Lal & Iskandar, 2000). When combining St. John's wort (or other substances that increase serotonin) with standard antidepressant medications (e.g., selective serotonin reuptake inhibitors), there is a risk of causing a potentially severe reaction known as *serotonin syndrome* (Natural Standard Research Collaboration, 2009). Several herbs and dietary supplements have been found to interfere or interact with prescription medications, including St. John's wort, garlic, glucosamine, ginseng, saw palmetto, soy, and yohimbe (National Center for Complementary and Alternative Medicine, 2007).

Food allergies and food sensitivities have been implicated in emotional, behavioral, and developmental disorders including learning disabilities, ADHD, depression, and autism. Some diets used to treat these conditions include eliminating sugar, caffeine, processed foods, food additives, food colorings, or fruits and vegetables. A gluten-free, casein-free (GFCF) diet—sometimes used to treat individuals with autism—eliminates all dairy products (which contain casein) and wheat products that contain gluten. Studies of the effectiveness of nutritional therapies show mixed results (Shaw, 2008).

Claims about natural treatments or miracle cures for certain conditions may be appealing to people who are seeking relief or are disenchanted with the mainstream medical establishment. Some people try nutritional interventions because they do not like the side effects associated with pharmaceutical medications. Others may use nutritional interventions because they are perceived as more natural, because they may cost less than pharmaceutical medications, or because of lack of access to health care services. There is considerable controversy about the risks and benefits of nutritional therapies. The U.S. Food and Drug Administration (FDA) classifies herbs (such as St. John's wort) as dietary supplements. FDA requirements for testing dietary supplements differ from those of pharmaceutical drugs. Dietary supplements can be sold without requiring studies on dosage, safety, or effectiveness. Possible risks of utilizing nutritional therapies include difficulty regulating dosage, lack of supervision by a health care professional, side effects, or interaction with other medications. In an attempt to treat symptoms, an individual may not be pursuing treatment for the correct diagnosis or may neglect to consider using established treatments. While more medical and mental health practitioners are being trained in integrative approaches—combining standard medical and pharmaceutical treatment with complementary and alternative treatments (CAM)—not all health practitioners are familiar with CAM. This may make it difficult to recommend effective dosages of nutritional supplements. It may be difficult to avoid dangerous drug interactions when combining CAM (including nutritional supplements) with standard pharmaceutical treatments.

See also antidepressant, antimanic, antipsychotic, anxiety, anxiolytic, autistic spectrum disorders, bipolar disorder, complementary and alternative medicine, depression, major depressive disorder, neurotransmitter, obsessive-compulsive disorder, schizophrenia, serotonin, St. John's wort.

Further Readings:

National Center for Complementary and Alternative Medicine Web site: http://nccam.nih.gov/

Pauling, L. (1968). Orthomolecular psychiatry: Varying the concentrations of substances normally present in the human body may control mental disease. *Science, 160*, 265–271.

References:

Elkins, G., Marcus, J., Rajab, M. H., & Durgam, S. (2005). Complementary and alternative therapy use by psychotherapy clients. *Psychotherapy: Theory, Research, Practice, Training, 42*, 232–235.

Freeman, M. P., Hibbeln, J. R., Wisner, K. L., Davis, J. M., Mischoulon, D., Peet, M., et al. (2006). Omega-3 fatty acids: Evidence basis for treatment and future research in psychiatry. *Journal of Clinical Psychiatry, 67*, 1954–1967.

Hoffer, L. J. (2008). Vitamin therapy in schizophrenia. *Israel Journal of Psychiatry and Related Sciences, 45*, 3–10.

Lakhan, S. E., & Vieira, K. F. (2008). Nutritional therapies for mental disorders. *Nutritional Journal, 7*(2), doi:10.1186/1475-2891-7-2.

Lal, S., & Iskandar, H. (2000). St. John's wort and schizophrenia. *Canadian Medical Association Journal, 163*, 262–263.

National Center for Complementary and Alternative Medicine. (2007). Biologically based practices: An overview. *NCCAM Backgrounder.* Retrieved from http://nccam.nih.gov/health/whatiscam/overview.htm

Natural Standard Research Collaboration. (2009, August 26). *St. John's wort (Hypericum perforatum L.).* Retrieved from http://www.nlm.nih.gov/medlineplus/druginfo/natural/patient-stjohnswort.html

Pauling, L. (1968). Orthomolecular psychiatry: Varying the concentrations of substances normally present in the human body may control mental disease. *Science, 160*, 265–271.

Shaw, S. R. (2008). Complementary and alternative therapies: An evidence-based framework. *NASP Communiqué, 37*(3), 1, 27–30.

Young, S. N. (1996). Behavioral effects of dietary neurotransmitter precursors: Basic and clinical aspects. *Neuroscience and Biobehavioral Reviews, 20*, 313–323.

O

Obsessive-Compulsive Disorder

Obsessive-compulsive disorder (OCD) is an anxiety disorder characterized by obsessions and related compulsions. Obsessions are intrusive, repetitive thoughts and images that appear uncontrollable. For instance, one might repeatedly experience an idea of germs lurking everywhere. The forms of obsessions include wishes, impulses, images, and ideas. Common themes of obsessions are dirt or contamination, orderliness, violence, aggression, and sexuality. Because obsessions are persistent and upsetting, people with OCD commonly experience distress and anxiety that impairs their daily functions. One's efforts to ignore or reduce these thoughts frequently results in increased anxiety. Despite their failure to ignore their repetitive thoughts, people with OCD are usually aware of the unreasonable and excessive characteristics of their obsessions.

Compulsions are irresistible impulses to repeat a ritualistic act or acts. Though minor compulsions like washing one's hands regularly are common in many people's lives, people with OCD spend a great amount of time engaging in compulsive behaviors. The recurring and rigid behaviors are performed to prevent or reduce anxiety caused by obsessions, and anxiety does typically decrease after performing the acts. However, the activity may not be a realistic manifestation of its apparent purpose. For instance, a person may feel it is necessary to count to 50 to purify her food before eating it. Compulsions take various forms. Some examples of compulsions are cleaning, checking (checking items over and over to make sure they are right such as checking that the doors are locked), touching (touching or avoiding the touching of certain objects), and counting.

Most people with OCD experience both obsessions and compulsions, though some experience only one of these symptoms. It is estimated that about 1 to 2 percent of adults in the United States have OCD (Kessler, Berglund, Demler, Jin, & Walters, 2005). OCD is equally common in men and women. The onset of OCD usually happens in young adulthood.

Explanations for OCD are varied. Abnormally low activity of serotonin (a chemical messenger in the brain) may be associated with OCD. The finding by researchers (e.g., Julien, 2007) that antidepressants such as clomipramine and fluoxetine

(Anafranil and Prozac) reduce the symptoms of OCD supports this view because these antidepressants increase serotonin activity. Another promising line of research from the biological perspective focuses on two areas of the brain, the orbitofrontal cortex (above each eye) and the caudate nuclei, part of the basal ganglia. The theory that these regions are too active in people with OCD is supported by research indicating that symptoms of OCD either originate or diminish after damage to one of these areas (e.g., Coetzer, 2004). Another perspective on causal explanation comes from cognitive theorists. Their view is that while most people have obsessive thoughts, people with OCD interpret them in maladaptive ways; they may believe that their recurring thoughts are somehow "bad"—perhaps morally wrong or dangerous (e.g., Salkovskis, 1985). To alleviate the obsessive thoughts, they perform compulsive behaviors. The compulsions reduce the anxiety and are therefore reinforced. Eventually, a pattern develops.

OCD is commonly treated with some antidepressant medications, particularly ones that increase serotonin activity and that regularize activity in the orbitofrontal cortex and caudate nuclei (Baxter et al., 2000). The success of these medications is moderate or better. Another helpful treatment is exposure with response prevention (a behavioral technique), in which clients are exposed to anxiety-producing situations related to their obsessions (such as engaging in dirty yard work) and prevented from engaging in compulsions (in this case, washing). Effective cognitive approaches guide clients in tracing the origins of their OCD. Clients are taught to challenge possibly irrational beliefs that may be contributing to their obsessions and compulsions. Some research suggests that combinations of effective treatment lead to better success than does using a single treatment.

See also antidepressant, anxiety, cognitive therapy and cognitive-behavioral therapy, exposure with response prevention, serotonin.

Further Readings:

Bell, J. (2007). *Rewind, replay, repeat: A memoir of obsessive-compulsive disorder.* Center City, MN: Hazelden.

Colas, E. (1999). *Just checking: Scenes from the life of an obsessive-compulsive.* New York: Washington Square Press.

National Institute of Mental Health. (2009). *Obsessive-compulsive disorder.* Retrieved from http://www. nimh.nih.gov/health/publications/anxiety-disorders/complete-index.shtml#pub3

References:

Baxter, L. R., Jr., Ackermann, R. F., Swerdlow, N. R., Brody, A., Saxena, S., Schwartz, J. M., et al. (2000). Specific brain system mediation of obsessive-compulsive disorder responsive to either medication or behavior therapy. In W. K. Goodman, M. V. Rudorfer, & J. D. Maser (Eds.), *Obsessive-compulsive disorder: Contemporary issues in treatment* (pp. 573–609). Mahwah, NJ: Lawrence Erlbaum Associates.

Bell, J. (2007). *Rewind, replay, repeat: A memoir of obsessive-compulsive disorder.* Center City, MN: Hazelden.

Coetzer, B. R. (2004). Obsessive-compulsive disorder following brain injury: A review. *International Journal of Psychiatric Medicine, 34*, 363–377.

Julien, R. M. (2007). *A primer of drug action* (11th ed.). New York: Worth.

Kessler, R. C., Berglund, P., Demler, O., Jin, R., & Walters, E. E. (2005). Lifetime prevalence and age-of-onset distributions of DSM-IV disorders in the National Comorbidity Survey Replication (NCS-R). *Archives of General Psychiatry, 62*, 593–602.

Kessler, R. C., Chiu, W. T., Demler, O., & Walters, E. E. (2005). Prevalence, severity, and comorbidity of 12-month DSM-IV disorders in the National Comorbidity Survey Replication (NCS-R). *Archives of General Psychiatry, 62*, 617–627.

Salkovskis, P. M. (1985). Obsessional-compulsive problems: A cognitive-behavioral analysis. *Behavioral Research and Therapy, 23*, 571–584.

- Radio news anchor Jeff Bell (2007) describes his struggles with, and attempts to overcome, OCD in his memoir *Rewind, Replay, Repeat*.
- Approximately 2.2 million American adults aged 18 and older, or about 1.0 percent of people in this age group in a given year, have OCD (Kessler, Chiu, Demler, & Walters, 2005).
- The first symptoms of OCD often begin during childhood or adolescence; however, the median age of onset is 19.5 (Kessler, Berglund, Demler, Jin, & Walters, 2005).

Optimism

A typical description of optimism is that it is a stable and general tendency to expect the best. Based on more careful thinking and research, psychologists and other scientists have come up with two distinct but related ways to think about optimism. Scheier and Carver's view of optimism was introduced in a 1985 article in the journal *Health Psychology*. More in accordance with the typical conception of optimism, Scheier and Carver (1985) have defined optimism as a stable tendency to "believe that good rather than bad things will happen" (p. 219). This definition focuses on expectancies for the future. Martin Seligman and colleagues (e.g., Seligman, 1991) identified *learned optimism*, which is centered on an individual's attribution process (process of attributing cause) of events that have already occurred. The optimist consistently uses healthy or adaptive causal attributions to account for events and experiences that have happened to him.

Scheier and Carver's concept emphasizes expectancies of good or bad events or experiences (outcomes). In this concept, optimism is optimism regardless of the reason *why* the person expects good things. The person could be optimistic for various reasons, including a strong belief in her own abilities, a belief that other people like her and will help make good things happen, or a belief that she has good luck. The important defining feature is a belief in good outcomes and low likelihood of negative outcomes.

The learned optimism concept was introduced by Martin Seligman and colleagues (e.g., Seligman, 1991). When addressing the question, why did this bad thing happen to me? the learned optimist makes particular types of attributions (beliefs about causes of events). The attributions the optimist makes are external, variable, and specific, contrasted with the internal, stable, and global attributions that the pessimist makes. For example, in answering the questions, why did my boyfriend break up with me? the optimist would look for reasons outside of the self—"He is immature"—whereas the pessimist would look internally: "I am unloveable." The optimist would see the situation as variable (unlikely to repeat)—"I have had other, positive relationships in the past, and I can in the future"—rather than stable: "I always get dumped in this way in all relationships." The optimist would make a specific attribution—"I am not doing well in the relationship arena right now, but my friendships are great and so is work"—whereas the pessimist would make a global attribution: "My whole life is going downhill." Learned optimism tends to focus more on attributions for negative events than attributions for positive events. Thus learned optimism is more about distancing oneself from negative outcomes than about linking oneself to positive outcomes (Snyder & Lopez, 2007).

Optimism is believed to have bases in both genetics and socialization in childhood. Researchers have found associations between an individual's level of optimism/pessimism and the quality of family life in childhood (i.e., safety of the environment, degree of affection in parental relationship), experience of childhood trauma, divorce of parents, parents' levels of optimism/pessimism, and other environmental factors (for a review, see Gillham & Reivich, 2004). Compared to pessimism, optimism is related to many positive outcomes, including positive work performance, effectively coping with illnesses such as cancer and AIDS, superior athletic performance, and coping well with starting college, to name just a few. See Carr (2004) and Carver and Scheier (2002) for reviews.

A number of programs have been developed to foster optimism in both adults and children. The Penn Resiliency Program was created to increase optimism and prevent depression and anxiety in early adolescence. The techniques can be used by psychological professionals in outpatient treatment and by teachers or counselors in a school setting. The program begins by adapting the ABC model developed by Albert Ellis. The idea behind this model is that when an activating event (A) occurs, the emotional consequence (C) is caused by both the event itself and beliefs (Bs) that are produced by the individual experiencing the event. So, for example, if an individual fails an exam, the emotional reaction is a result of both the failing of the exam and the ideas or beliefs that the individual has. Individuals can modify their beliefs and thus modify their emotional reactions.

In the Penn program, children are shown cartoons with three panels. The "A" and "C" panels are presented and children are to fill in the "B" panel (a "thought bubble") that would fit in the context of the "A" and "C" panels. For example, in one cartoon, the "A" panel shows a student receiving an exam that has many answers marked incorrect. The "C" panel shows the student looking very sad. Children then complete a thought bubble. They may write, for instance, "I am stupid" or "I keep failing." After mastering this exercise, children are taught to identify their typical attributions as *me* versus *not me*, *always* versus *not always*, and *everything* versus *not everything* (this corresponds to internal versus external, stable versus unstable, and global versus specific). Once they can identify their attribution tendencies, they are taught to dispute those tendencies that are pessimistic.

The Penn program includes other techniques for fostering optimism, including assertiveness training, negotiation training, goal setting, including the one-step-at-a-time technique, and others (Penn Positive Psychology Center, 2007).

See also ABC model of emotional reaction, cognitive therapy and cognitive-behavioral therapy, depression, hope, learned helplessness, locus of control, positive psychology, rational emotive behavior therapy.

Further Readings:
Carr, A. (2004). *Positive psychology: The science of happiness and human strengths.* New York: Brunner-Routledge.
Penn Positive Psychology Center. (2007). *Resilience research in children.* Retrieved from http://www.ppc.sas.upenn.edu/prpsum.htm
Seligman, M.E.P. (1991). *Learned optimism.* New York: Knopf.

References:
Carr, A. (2004). *Positive psychology: The science of happiness and human strengths.* New York: Brunner-Routledge.

Carver, C., & Scheier, M. (2002). Optimism. In C. R. Snyder & S. J. Lopez (Eds.), *The handbook of positive psychology* (pp. 231–243). New York: Oxford University Press.

Gillham, J., & Reivich, K. (2004, January). Cultivating optimism in childhood and adolescence. *Annals of the American Academy of Political and Social Science, 591,* 146–163.

Penn Positive Psychology Center. (2007). Resilience research in children. Retrieved from http://www.ppc.sas.upenn.edu/prpsum.htm

Scheier, M. F., & Carver, C. S. (1985). Optimism, coping, and health: Assessment and implications of generalized outcome expectancies. *Health Psychology, 4,* 219–247.

Seligman, M.E.P. (1991). *Learned optimism.* New York: Knopf.

Snyder, C. R., & Lopez, S. J. (2007). *Positive psychology: The scientific and practical explorations of human strengths.* Thousand Oaks, CA: Sage.

Overeaters Anonymous

Overeaters Anonymous (OA) is a worldwide fellowship of people who share a desire to stop eating compulsively. As a self-supporting association, there are no dues or fees for its members, and it has no affiliation with other organizations. OA was founded by Rozanne S. and two other women in 1960 and is headquartered in Rio Rancho, New Mexico. The development of OA was based on Rozanne S.'s observation that the 12-step program founded by Alcoholics Anonymous could be applied to abstaining from overeating. OA helps people to recover from problems related to food such as compulsive overeating, binge eating disorder, bulimia, and anorexia. Members are encouraged to share their experiences with other members to improve their relationship with food. Anyone who wishes to stop compulsive overeating is accepted to its membership.

OA recognizes that overeating is a progressive illness that requires intervention. OA uses the 12-step recovery program, which promotes a change in people's attitude toward food. The 12-step recovery program is believed to be effective for the recovery of compulsive eating at physical, emotional, and spiritual levels. Members of OA vary from those who are extremely overweight to those who are average weight or underweight. The degree of control over eating behavior also differs among members. The symptoms of problems related to overeating include obsession with body weight, size and shape, constant preoccupation with food, and inability to stop eating certain foods after taking the first bite.

A philosophy of OA is that people's acceptance of their inability to control compulsive eating is the most effective way to recover from the illness. Accordingly, OA does not promote traditional dieting. Instead, OA centers its primary activities on meetings where members talk about their experiences related to compulsive eating and follow the 12-step recovery program as a solution. To accelerate the recovery process, OA encourages members to keep a personal plan of eating that guides them in their dietary decisions, use telephone services to reach out and ask for help, write thoughts and feelings down on paper, and offer any services to fellow sufferers. Since anonymity is a principle of OA, shared experience is held in confidentiality. Mutual understanding and acceptance of their problems help members live their lives without the need to eat compulsively. The average size of a meeting is nine people. About 6,500 meetings are held each week in over 75 countries with approximately 54,000 members worldwide. OA also promotes pamphlets and books, including *Overeaters Anonymous*, *The Twelve Steps and Twelve Traditions of Overeaters Anonymous*, *For Today*, *Lifeline*, and *Alcoholics Anonymous*.

See also Alcoholics Anonymous, 12-step programs.

Further Reading:
Overeaters Anonymous Web site: http://www.oa.org/

P

Panic Disorder

Panic disorder is an anxiety disorder characterized by recurring and unpredictable panic attacks. A panic attack is a sudden attack of intense physical and psychological symptoms of anxiety that reaches a peak within minutes and gradually goes away. Panic attacks are accompanied by at least four of the following symptoms: heart palpitations, tingling in the hands or feet, shortness of breath, sweating, hot and cold flashes, trembling, chest pains, sensation of choking, faintness, dizziness, and dearealization (perception that one's environment is strange or unreal) or depersonalization (feeling detached or disconnected from oneself). People can have panic attacks at any time, even during sleep. People with panic disorder experience panic attacks without any clear provocation. They believe that they are having a serious and dramatic experience such as a heart attack or complete loss of control, or even that they are dying. It is common that they go to the emergency room believing that they need treatment for their symptoms. Since they cannot predict when the next attack will take place, their unexplained physical symptoms provoke persistent fear about having another attack. In an attempt to prevent panic attacks, some people restrict their lives by avoiding normal activities. For instance, if an individual experiences a panic attack while on the stairs, he may become so fearful of stairs in any place that he might change his apartment or workplace to avoid stairs. In addition to recurrent unexpected panic attacks, one must have a month or more of one of the following symptoms for a diagnosis of panic disorder: consistent worry about having additional attacks, concern about the consequences or implications of the attack, and significant behavior change due to the attacks.

Panic disorder affects 2 to 3 percent of the U.S. adult population per year (Kessler, Chiu, Demler, & Walters, 2005). Women are twice as likely to be diagnosed with panic disorder as men. Although many people first experience panic attacks in late adolescence or early adulthood, not everyone who experiences panic attacks develops panic disorder. About one-third of people with panic disorder also have agoraphobia (fear of leaving the house). Panic disorder may also be comorbid with depression and substance abuse (including alcoholism; Preston, O'Neal, & Talaga, 2008).

Several biological factors have been linked with panic disorder. Research suggests that people with panic disorder have problems with norepinephrine (a chemical messenger in the brain), possibly in a part of the brain stem called the *locus ceruleus* (an area in the brain in which much norepinephrine is present). Research has shown that when the locus ceruleus of monkeys is electrically stimulated, monkeys have symptoms of panic (Redmond, 1977). The neurotransmitters serotonin and GABA (gamma-aminobutyric acid) may also play a role in panic disorder since medications that operate on these substances relieve symptoms (Preston et al., 2008). The degree of potential genetic contribution to panic disorder has not been studied extensively.

Cognitive-behavioral theorists suggest that people with panic disorder are highly sensitive to bodily sensations and interpret them in a dramatic fashion (Casey, Oei, & Newcombe, 2004). All people sometimes experience bodily sensations that may seem out of the ordinary such as the heart racing slightly or an unexplained sensation of pain. People with panic disorder may literally panic when experiencing these sensations, believing that some catastrophe, such as a medical emergency, is occurring.

Panic disorder is very responsive to a combination of medication and psychotherapy (Preston et al., 2008). In the initial phase of treatment, it is necessary to eliminate or greatly reduce panic attacks. While cognitive and behavioral techniques may help, anxiolytic medications (e.g., benzodiazepines such as Valium) take effect more quickly. Other medications useful in treatment include antidepressants that affect norepinephrine and serotonin (e.g., selective serotonin reuptake inhibitors and monoamine oxidase [MAO] inhibitors) and anxiolytics that affect GABA and reduce panic symptoms (e.g., benzodiazepines). About 80 percent of panic disorder sufferers experience improvement in symptoms after taking antidepressants that operate on norepinephrine. About half are dramatically improved, some cured, as long as they continue taking the medications (McNally, 2001). After reducing initial symptoms with medication, behavioral techniques (such as systematic desensitization) may be useful to reduce anxiety, phobias, and avoidance of anxiety-producing situations. Cognitive therapy has been found to be highly effective (Hollon, Stewart, & Strunk, 2006). First, therapists educate clients about their bodily sensations, about healthy interpretations of the sensations, and about the nature of panic attacks. Next, clients are trained to make appropriate interpretations even during stressful situations.

Chronic cases of panic disorder may be comorbid with major depression or substance abuse (including alcohol abuse or dependence; Preston et al., 2008).

See also antidepressant, anxiety, anxiolytic, behavior therapy, benzodiazepine, cognitive therapy and cognitive-behavioral therapy, neurotransmitter, serotonin.

Further Readings:
National Institute of Mental Health. (2009). *Panic disorder.* Retrieved from http://www.nimh.nih.gov/health/topics/panic-disorder/index.shtml
Rand, R. (2004). *Dancing away an anxious mind: A memoir about overcoming panic disorder.* Madison: University of Wisconsin Press.

References:
Casey, L. M., Oei, T.P.S., & Newcombe, P. A. (2004). An integrated cognitive model of panic disorder: The role of positive and negative cognitions. *Clinical Psychology Review, 24,* 529–555.
Hollon, S. D., Stewart, M. O., & Strunk, D. (2006, January). Enduring effects for cognitive behavior therapy in the treatment of depression and anxiety. *Annual Review of Psychology, 57,* 285–315.
Kessler, R. C., Chiu, W. T., Demler, O., & Walters, E. E. (2005). Prevalence, severity, and comorbidity of 12-month DSM-IV disorders in the National Comorbidity Survey Replication (NCS-R). *Archives of General Psychiatry, 62,* 617–627.

McNally, R. J. (2001). Vulnerability to anxiety disorders in adulthood. In R. E. Ingram & J. M. Price (Eds.), *Vulnerability to psychopathology: Risk across the lifespan* (pp. 304–321). New York: Guilford.

National Institute of Mental Health. (2009). *The numbers count: Mental disorders in America.* Retrieved from http://www.nimh.nih.gov/health/publications/the-numbers-count-mental-disorders-in-america/index.shtml#Panic

Preston, J. D., O'Neal, J. H., & Talaga, M. C. (2008). *Handbook of clinical psychopharmacology for therapists* (5th ed.). Oakland, CA: New Harbinger.

Redmond, D. E. (1977). Alterations in the function of the nucleus locus coeruleus: A possible model for studies of anxiety. In I. Hanin & E. Usdin (Eds.), *Animal models in psychiatry and neurology* (pp. 293–305). New York: Pergamon Press.

- Approximately six million American adults aged 18 and older, or about 2.7 percent of people in this age group, have panic disorder in any given year.
- Panic disorder typically develops in early adulthood (median age of onset is 24), but the age of onset extends throughout adulthood.
- About one in three people with panic disorder develops agoraphobia, a condition in which the individual becomes afraid of being in any place or situation where escape might be difficult or help unavailable in the event of a panic attack.
- Individuals with panic disorder are 18 times more likely to attempt suicide as people without any mental health disorder.
- It is estimated that only 30 percent of individuals with panic disorder receive treatment. Treatment is effective in 70 to 90 percent of those who do receive treatment.

Source: National Institute of Mental Health, 2009.

Parasympathetic Nervous System

The parasympathetic nervous system (PNS) is a division of the autonomic nervous system (ANS). Neurons in the ANS monitor the organs and internal activities such as heart rate, digestion, breathing, energy mobilization, and glandular activity. The ANS regulates these internal body functions to maintain the body's homeostasis (regulation of the internal body to maintain a stable state). The PNS and the other primary division of the ANS, the sympathetic nervous system (SNS), immediately respond to environmental circumstances and work together to achieve homeostasis. The PNS and SNS have different yet complementary functions; the former is involved in the functioning of the body at rest, whereas the latter is involved in the functioning of the active body. Both systems operate automatically without the involvement of human consciousness.

The PNS originates in the cranial (neck) and sacral (lower) regions of the spinal cord. Most PNS neurons are part of the peripheral nervous system. The peripheral nervous system mainly controls the functioning of internal organs and muscles in the periphery of the body. Through chains of sympathetic ganglia (nerve complexes), PNS neurons of the spinal cord connect to peripheral PNS neurons. This connection leads to the physiological reactions throughout the body.

The primary function of the PNS is to facilitate development and growth and to conserve energy to be used later. The PNS increases digestive processes, involving secretion of digestive acids and enzymes, secretion of insulin, and movement of the intestinal tract. Other actions include decreased heart rate, decreased blood pressure, constriction of pupils, contraction of the bladder, and others. Parasympathetic activation is necessary for the sexual response; when parasympathetic nerves are active, blood flow is increased to the penis and clitoris.

Results of some studies indicate a link between PNS activity and compassion and related emotions. In one study, participants were shown slides that were intended to evoke either compassion (e.g., slides of crying babies) or pride (slides of positive symbols of one's university; Oveis, Horberg, & Keltner, 2005). The compassion slides were associated with increased parasympathetic activity in participants while the pride slides were not. The researchers interpreted this finding to mean that parasympathetic activity is associated with the positive emotions related to pro-sociality but not to pride (and possibly not to other positive emotions). In other research, participants who reported that they wished to help a suffering woman experienced a decrease in heart rate while they were learning about the tragic circumstances of the woman (Eisenberg et al., 1989). Steven Porges (1995, 1998) has described a theory that a large portion of the PNS, which is present only in mammals, is crucial for social interaction and attachment. According to Porges, this part of the nervous system facilitates adaptation to fluctuating social circumstances and allows the individual to feel relaxed while in the company of others.

The PNS may be active when an individual is experiencing disgust. Levenson (1992) found that heart rate decreases when an individual feels disgust.

See also autonomic nervous system, disgust, physiology of emotion, positive emotions, stress, sympathetic nervous system.

References:

Eisenberg, N., Fabes, R. A., Miller, P. A., Fultz, J., Shell, R., Mathy, R. M., et al. (1989). Relation of sympathy and personal distress to prosocial behavior: A multimethod study. *Journal of Personality and Social Psychology, 57*, 55–66.

Levenson, R. W. (1992). Autonomic nervous system differences among emotions. *Psychological Science, 3*, 23–27.

Oveis, C., Horberg, L., & Keltner, D. (2005). *Compassion, similarity of self to other, and vagal tone.* Unpublished manuscript, University of California, Berkeley.

Porges, S. W. (1995). Orienting in a defensive world: Mammalian modifications of our evolutionary heritage. A polyvagal theory. *Psychophysiology, 32*, 301–318.

Porges, S. W. (1998). Love: An emergent property of the mammalian autonomic nervous system. *Psychoendocrinology, 23*, 837–861.

Parkinson's Disease

Parkinson's disease (PD) was first described by British physician James Parkinson in 1817. PD is a degenerative brain disorder that results from destruction of neurons (nerve cells) in the substantia nigra of the brain. The substantia nigra (which means "black substance"), part of the basal ganglia, is located in the midbrain (mesencephalon). The substantia nigra has many neurons that produce and utilize dopamine, a neurotransmitter (chemical messenger). Dopamine helps with coordination of muscles and movement. PD symptoms manifest after about 80 percent of the dopamine-producing cells in the substantia nigra have been damaged or destroyed (National Parkinson Foundation [NPF], n.d.). The primary symptoms of PD are tremor (shaking of a limb at rest), bradykinesia (slowness of movement), rigidity (stiffness), and postural instability (balance difficulties). Not all symptoms occur in all individuals; symptoms may only occur (or be more noticeable) on one side of the body. Some individuals with PD have micrographia (small, cramped, handwriting), facial fixity (a blank expression showing little emotion), staring (due to reduced frequency of eye blinking), a shuffling gait, muffled (low volume) speech, or a stooped posture. Symptoms may be a source of embarrassment or anxiety for individuals with PD; depression may accompany PD.

PD usually occurs after age 65, although 15 percent of individuals with PD are diagnosed before the age of 50. Young-onset PD (starting before the age of 40) occurs in 5 to 10 percent of individuals with PD. PD affects 1 in 100 people over the age of 60. PD affects more men than women, and age of onset tends to be later for women (Van Den Eeden et al., 2003). A diagnosis of PD is usually made by a neurologist, sometimes after blood tests and magnetic resonance imaging (MRI) have ruled out other causes. PD is probably caused by a combination of genetic and environmental factors (e.g., exposure to toxins). The characteristic complex of symptoms (tremor, rigidity, bradykinesia, and postural instability) is called *parkinsonism*. Not everyone with parkinsonism has PD. Parkinsonism may be drug induced, vascular (due to obstruction of small blood vessels feeding the brain), or atypical. Medications that can cause parkinsonism include antipsychotics, tetrabenazine (Xenazine, a medication for Huntington's Chorea), reserpine (Harmonyl, used to treat high blood pressure), metoclopramide (Reglan, used to treat nausea and vomiting), and calcium channel blockers (for high blood pressure). Vascular parkinsonism can be caused by multiple small strokes and may result in more gait difficulty (especially in the lower limbs) than tremor. Atypical parkinsonism is considered if an individual has no tremor, an early loss of balance, rapid onset or progression, dementia, low blood pressure when rising from a seated position (postural hypotension), or a poor response to dopaminergic medications.

Treatment for PD usually involves medications that increase the level of dopamine in the brain—either by adding more or inhibiting its breakdown. These medications improve symptoms (tremor, rigidity, and brakykinesia) but do not slow the progression of the disease. Other treatments may include speech therapy, physical therapy, botulin toxin (botox) for dystonia (muscle spasms causing abnormal postures), and antidepressants (to treat depression accompanying PD). Surgery is another option to treat PD symptoms; however, surgery does not slow disease progression. Brain-lesioning surgeries (which destroy small regions of brain tissue) may improve tremor. Deep brain stimulation (DBS) involves implanting an electrode in part of the brain and linking it to a pulse generator (similar to a heart pacemaker). Different types of DBS have benefits for different groups of PD symptoms. New medications are being explored to treat PD symptoms and to slow its progression. Selegiline (an inhibitor of monoamine-oxidase B) has some mild antidepressant effects, but there is no evidence that it slows the progression of PD (NPF, n.d.). Coenzyme Q_{10} (an antioxidant that plays a role in mitochondrial function) appears to improve motor function and slow functional decline in PD (Shults, 2005). Current clinical tests are exploring whether coenzyme Q_{10} has neuroprotective properties. It is found in fish and meat; lesser concentrations are found in eggs, spinach, broccoli, peanuts, wheat germ, and whole grains.

See also depression, functional magnetic resonance imaging, neurotransmitter.

Further Readings:
Fox, M. J. (2002). *Lucky man: A memoir.* New York: Hyperion.
National Institute of Neurological Disorders and Stroke Web site: http://www.ninds.nih.gov/disorders/parkinsons_disease/parkinsons_disease.htm
Parkinson's Disease Foundation Web site: http://www.pdf.org/

References:
National Parkinson Foundation. (n.d.). *About Parkinson's disease.* Retrieved from http://www.parkinson.org/Page.aspx?pid=225
Shults, C. W. (2005). Therapeutic role of coenzyme Q_{10} in Parkinson's disease. *Pharmacology & Therapeutics, 107*, 120–130.
Van Den Eeden, S. K., Tanner, C. M., Bernstein, A. L., Fross, R. D., Leimpeter, A., Bloch, D. A., et al. (2003). Incidence of Parkinson's disease: Variation by age, gender, and race/ethnicity. *American Journal of Epidemiology, 157*, 1015–1022.

- American television actor Michael J. Fox developed young-onset Parkinson's at the age of 30. He established the Michael J. Fox Foundation for Parkinson's Research to raise awareness and research funding for Parkinson's. He has detailed his experiences in his best-selling memoir, *Lucky Man* (2002).
- Other famous people with PD include the following:

  - former U.S. Attorney General Janet Reno
  - evangelist Billy Graham
  - former boxer Muhammad Ali
  - former Alabama Governor George Wallace
  - Chinese leader Deng Xiaoping

Source: http://parkinsons-disease.emedtv.com/parkinson's-disease/famous-people-with-parkinson's-disease.html

PEN Model of Personality

The PEN model of personality was proposed by Hans Eysenck, a prominent psychologist who contributed to the development of modern scientific theories of personality in the 1900s. In developing his model, Eysenck sought personality characteristics that were clearly distinct from one another (nonoverlapping), heritable, and rooted in biology. Additionally, the model he developed would be a comprehensive taxonomy of personality; all significant traits would be included in the model, and traits would be arranged in a hierarchical fashion. Eysenck's resultant PEN model of personality suggests that personality is made up of three distinct dimensions or *supertraits*: psychoticism–impulse control, extraversion-introversion, and neuroticism–emotional stability (or PEN). As a hierarchal model of personality, the PEN model of personality includes a large number of narrower traits that are subsumed under each of the supertraits. These narrower traits then encompass a number of habitual acts that are characteristic of these traits. Accordingly, the PEN model of personality proposes an organization of personality traits based on a hierarchal structure.

Although heritability is difficult and complex to determine, several researchers have reported that the two traits most studied, extraversion and neuroticism, are moderately heritable (e.g., Birley et al., 2006; Floderus-Myrhed, Pedersen, & Rasmuson, 1980). Eysenck demonstrated that these supertraits are not correlated with each other (and therefore truly distinct; Eysenck & Eysenck, 1985) and that each supertrait is composed of different traits and habits.

Extraversion consists of narrower traits such as being outgoing, talkative, sociable, lively, and sensation-seeking. An extravert is also likely to be carefree, dominant, and venturesome. These narrower traits are accompanied by such habitual acts as going to parties and having many friends. These habitual acts constitute the third level of the PEN model of personality (the first being the three supertraits and the second being the narrower traits just mentioned). Introversion, on the other hand, is marked by personality traits including being quiet and withdrawn. An introvert tends to spend time alone and tends to dislike being in a large crowd. Extraversion and introversion are at the opposite ends on the continuum.

The second supertrait, neuroticism, covers more specific traits. People who score high in neuroticism tend to be anxious, irritable, tense, and moody. On average, people who score high experience high levels of negative emotions in response to stressful events in everyday life. Highly anxious people are found at the one end on this scale. In contrast, people who score low in neuroticism are emotionally stable, carefree, sometimes stoic, and react calmly to stressful events. The third supertrait, psychoticism, represents personality traits including aggressive, cold, egocentric, impulsive, antisocial, creative, and tough-minded. People who score high in psychoticism are often described as loners and tend to be verbally and physically aggressive. They may also be cruel to other people and animals. Though it is easy to describe the ends of each dimension, we need to keep in mind that most people fall somewhere in the middle; extreme cases are rare. An extreme extravert, for instance, craves excitement and needs to have someone to talk to most of the time.

To clarify the causal aspects of personality, Eysenck further provided biological explanations for personality traits. According to his theory, introverts are more easily aroused by activation in parts of the brain than are extraverts. He suggested that the changeability of the autonomic nervous system—which produces the stress (fight-or-flight) response—is associated with neuroticism. He also posited that high testosterone levels and low monoamine oxidase (MAO) inhibitor (a chemical messenger in the brain) activity are linked with high levels of psychoticism. In general, research has not yet clearly supported Eysenck's hypotheses about the relationships between the supertraits and biological aspects (for a review, see McAdams, 2008). However, research in this area is ongoing.

The PEN model of personality has held a prominent place in the history of personality psychology. Several personality inventories (questionnaires) have been developed that measure the three supertraits (and possibly a few additional traits); these inventories are widely used in research in personality psychology and related areas of psychology such as social, abnormal, and health psychology.

See also affective personality traits, extraversion, introversion, neuroticism, personality, temperament.

Further Reading:
Jang, K. M. (1998, August). *Eysenck's PEN model: Its contribution to personality psychology*. Retrieved from http://www.personalityresearch.org/papers/jang.html

References:
Birley, A. J., Gillespie, N. A., Heath, A. C., Sullivan, P. F., Boomsma, D. I., & Martin, N. G. (2006). Heritability and nineteen-year stability of long and short EPQ-R Neuroticism scales. *Personality and Individual Differences, 40*, 737–747.

Eysenck, H. J., & Eysenck, M. W. (1985). *Personality and individual differences: A natural science approach.* New York: Plenum.

Floderus-Myrhed, B., Pederson, N., & Rasmuson, I. (1980). Assessment of heritability for personality based on a short form of the Eysenck Personality Inventory: A study of 12,898 twin pairs. *Behavior Genetics, 10*, 153–162.

McAdams, D. P. (2008). *The person: An introduction to the science of personality psychology* (4th ed.). New York: John Wiley.

Personality

Emotions are of great concern to personality psychologists. This interest centers around the nature of particular emotions and emotion in general, individual differences in experiencing emotion, and the association between emotion and other personality-related processes such as motivation, mental health, physical health, and physiology.

Each of the four major approaches to personality psychology—psychodynamic, humanistic/existential, trait, and social cognitive—addresses emotion. When Sigmund Freud originated his version of the psychodynamic perspective in the late 1800s, *psychoanalysis*, his earliest writings established emotion as a centerpiece of his theory. In Freudian theory, the emotion anxiety is pervasive and powerful, affecting nearly all emotional experience, much of one's personality functioning, and much of one's general life functioning. According to Freudian theory, many of one's impulses, particularly aggressive and sexual ones, have the potential to produce anxiety in the adult because they are considered taboo by society. (These drives did not originally produce anxiety as a child; the child had to learn that such impulses are forbidden.) When a person learns that many of his thoughts and desires are "unacceptable" to society, he tends to repress these mental products. Repression does not eliminate these desires and thoughts; they remain in the unconscious mind, continuing to push for expression. Parts of the mind protect the conscious self from having full knowledge of the forbidden desires. Anxiety arises to keep oneself from knowing the shameful truth (and therefore protecting one's self-esteem), to keep oneself from engaging in socially unacceptable behavior, and to warn the individual about possible physical dangers. For instance, an individual may be sexually attracted to his sister-in-law. Engaging in a sexual relationship with her would be *bad* behavior; it would conflict with the family values that he holds most dear, resulting in feelings of shame and guilt; it would threaten to destroy his relationships with family members, and it could be physically dangerous—a baby could result, creating a new responsibility for the man. Anxiety, though painful and unpleasant, thus serves the function of encouraging constructive behavior and discouraging harmful behavior. As mentioned earlier, anxiety is also often interrelated with other emotions. Consciously, in addition to feeling anxious about the sister-in-law without knowing exactly why, the individual may begin to hate his sister-in-law; this decreases the likelihood of making a sexual pass. Sigmund Freud and his daughter Anna wrote about anxiety and the ways that people protect themselves from inappropriate or dangerous behavior through Freudian defense mechanisms (A. Freud, 1936; S. Freud, 1926). Since people have so many forbidden impulses, anxiety is very common. Other emotions that Freudian theory emphasized were guilt and depression.

The humanistic/existential approach is most often associated with American psychologist Carl Rogers, who began to publish his theories in the 1940s. Rogers's theory, like Freud's, emphasizes anxiety over all other emotions. From Rogers's perspective, anxiety arises when one's view of self (self-concept) conflicts with ongoing experiences or with one's emotions (Rogers, 1951, 1959). For instance, if an individual thinks of himself as patient and kind, whereas people regularly react to him as if he is behaving in an impatient, hostile manner, this incongruity causes anxiety. Additionally, if he believes that he is patient and kind but has been feeling impatient and mean for several weeks, he experiences anxiety. Rogers wrote about the development of the tendency toward anxiety. In short, anxiety is more common in people whose self-concepts are too narrow or are distorted. The child's self-concept develops as she interacts with her parents. If parents apply "conditions of worth" to her behavior, meaning that they communicate that they will love and accept her only under certain conditions (e.g., only when she is sweet and quiet), she begins to view herself as possessing only those qualities that are rewarded by her parents. Other characteristics that she naturally possesses are denied awareness because they become associated with painful disapproval by the parents. For instance, a little girl may have many natural tendencies to behave as a tomboy, but her parents disapprove of these behaviors and accept only her feminine behaviors. She thus comes to view herself as feminine only, and consciously denies the tomboy aspects of herself. According to Rogers, the tomboy aspects still exist and will creep into awareness on a regular basis, creating anxiety. She may find herself envious of and angry with women who engage in masculine activities. Conversely, some children grow up with parents who are accepting of most of their natural qualities (communicating what Rogers calls *unconditional positive regard*). Under this circumstance, a child develops a self-concept that is quite accurate, does not have to deny many aspects of the self, and will be relatively free of anxiety.

Trait approaches, which date to the 1930s, have long recognized emotional qualities as central to personality. Early trait theorists were British-American psychologist Raymond B. Cattell and British psychologist Hans J. Eysenck. Cattell (1965) identified three broad categories of traits: ability traits, temperament traits, and dynamic (motive) traits. Temperament traits are emotional. Some examples of temperament traits on which individuals differ are emotionally stable versus emotionally unstable, outgoing versus reserved, trusting versus suspicious, and relaxed versus tense. Eysenck (1990) proposed three broad trait dimensions that he claimed were the most significant personality characteristics on which people differ: neuroticism–emotional stability, extraversion-introversion, and psychoticism–ego strength. Neuroticism is fundamentally a negative emotion dimension, encompassing anxiety, depression, and anger/hostility. Positive emotions are a large component of extraversion. The most prominent trait model, the five-factor model or the "Big Five," focuses on five main personality dimensions: neuroticism, extraversion, conscientiousness, agreeableness, and openness to experience. All five contain some emotional aspects; however, as in Eysenck's model, neuroticism and extraversion are the primary emotional traits.

Social cognitive approaches dating to the 1940s focus on how individuals take in, process and store, and retrieve information. These cognitive functions are interrelated with emotions, although cognitions are seen as primary. Emotions thus arise from cognitions. For instance, from this perspective, people feel depressed because they have sad thoughts and feel angry because they have hostile thoughts. American psychotherapist Aaron T. Beck (1976) proposed this intimate relationship between cognitions and emotions and was fundamental in creating a modern approach to psychotherapy, *cognitive therapy*, which has proven to be effective in treating a variety of psychiatric conditions, especially depression. American psychologist George Kelly (1955) theorized that our personality is a set of ideas. These ideas, which he called *constructs*, serve as filters through which people perceive the world; people view other people through their own constructs. In attempting to understand other people, one person may utilize the constructs nice–not nice, intelligent-unintelligent, and humorous–not humorous. A second person has different constructs, evaluating people on attractive-unattractive, rich-poor, and so on. In Kelly's theory, anxiety can result when one's constructs begin to do a poor job of aiding in the understanding of the world. In other words, through applying one's constructs, the individual finds that people behave differently than expected, react to him in disturbing ways, and so forth. In Kelly's theory, like other social cognitive theories, emotions arise from cognitive sources.

Personality psychologists have also studied individual differences in emotions and emotion processes without adhering to any of the preceding theoretical perspectives. Topics of interest have included individual differences in intensity of emotion, variability of emotional states, degree to which people experience either positive or negative emotions or both, ability to regulate (modulate) one's emotions in functional ways, and others. For instance, Eaton and Funder (2001) found that individuals with rapidly changing emotions tended to be described by others as generally hostile and fearful.

See also affective personality traits, anxiety, defense mechanisms, PEN model of personality, psychoanalytic perspective, self-image, sensation-seeking and risk-taking, temperament, Type A behavior pattern.

Further Readings:

Funder, D. C. (2010). *The personality puzzle* (5th ed.). New York: W. W. Norton.

Pervin, L. A. (1999). Personality. In D. Levinson, J. J. Ponzetti, & P. F. Jorgensen (Eds.), *Encyclopedia of human emotions* (2nd ed., pp. 500–504). New York: Macmillan Reference USA.

References:

Beck, A. T. (1976). *Cognitive therapy and the emotional disorders.* New York: International Universities Press.

Cattell, R. B. (1965). *The scientific analysis of personality.* Baltimore, MD: Penguin.

Eaton, L. G., & Funder, D. C. (2001). Emotional experiences in daily life: Valence, variability and rate of change. *Emotion, 1,* 413–421.

Eysenck, H. J. (1990). Biological dimensions of personality. In L. A. Pervin (Ed.), *Handbook of personality: Theory and research* (pp. 244–270). New York: Guilford.

Freud, A. (1936). *The writings of Anna Freud: Vol. 2. The ego and the mechanisms of defense.* New York: International Universities Press.

Freud, S. (1959). Inhibitions, symptoms, and anxiety. In J. Strachey (Ed. & Trans.), *The standard edition of the complete psychological works of Sigmund Freud* (Vol. 20). London: Hogarth Press. (Original work published 1926)

Kelly, G. A. (1955). *The psychology of personal constructs.* New York: W. W. Norton.

Rogers, C. R. (1951). *Client-centered therapy, its current practice, implications, and theory.* Boston: Houghton Mifflin.

Rogers, C. R. (1959). A theory of therapy, personality, and interpersonal relationships as developed in the client-centered framework. In S. Koch (Ed.), *Psychology: A study of a science: Vol. 3. Formulations of the person in the social context.* New York: McGraw-Hill.

Personality Disorder

Personality is a long-standing pattern of behavior and inner experience, including characteristic thoughts and emotions. A personality disorder may be present when the following criteria are met: the personality pattern differs significantly from the expectations of the individual's culture in at least two of the following four areas: cognition, emotional response, interpersonal functioning, and impulse control. The pattern is inflexible and generalizes across a variety of personal and social situations. Impairment in social or occupational functioning or significant distress, or both, are present. The pattern is long-lasting, persistent, and originated in early adulthood or earlier.

The *Diagnostic and Statistical Manual of Mental Disorders* (*DSM-IV-TR*; American Psychiatric Association, 2000), which lists and describes mental disorders, identifies 10 personality disorders that are separated into three groups. The first group, characterized by eccentric or odd behaviors, includes the paranoid, schizoid, and schizotypal personality disorders. The second group, marked by dramatic, emotional, or erratic behavior, consists of antisocial, borderline, histrionic, and narcissistic personality disorders. The third group features disorders characterized by high anxiety, the avoidant, dependent, and obsessive-compulsive personality disorders (note that obsessive-compulsive *personality* disorder is different from obsessive-compulsive disorder [OCD]). According to Phillips, Yen, and Gunderson (2004), about 9 to 13 percent of adults may be diagnosable with a personality disorder.

In 2009, when the final writing of this book was occurring, diagnosticians were proposing that the current conception of personality disorders be reconsidered. The degree to which diagnosticians can agree on a particular personality disorder diagnosis for an individual is low enough to cause concern (e.g., Jablensky, 2002). Some have complained that is it difficult to distinguish the personality disorders from one another (e.g., Gunderson & Ronningstam, 2001). One proposed solution has been to abandon the 10 personality disorders and instead view personality disorders in a dimensional fashion. According to this point of view, the personality disorders should be identified by the intensity or severity of key traits rather than by the mere presence or absence of traits (dimensional view rather than all-or-none view). See Widiger and Simonsen (2005) for an example of such a proposed alternative model.

See also borderline personality disorder, histrionic, personality.

References:

American Psychiatric Association. (2000). *Diagnostic and statistical manual of mental disorders* (4th ed., text rev.). Washington, DC: Author.

Gunderson, J.G., & Ronningstam, E. (2001). Differentiating narcissistic and antisocial personality disorders. *Journal of Personality Disorders, 15*, 103–109.

Jablensky, A. (2002). The classification of personality disorders: Critical review and need for rethinking. *Psychopathology, 35*, 112–116.

Phillips, K. A., Yen, S., & Gunderson, J.G. (2004). Personality disorders. In R.E. Hales & S.C. Yudofsky (Eds.), *Essentials of clinical psychiatry* (2nd ed., pp. 567–589). Washington, DC: American Psychiatric.

Widiger, T.A., & Simonsen, E. (2005). Alternative dimensional models of personality disorder: Finding a common ground. *Journal of Personality Disorders, 19*, 110–130.

- A 2001–2002 survey conducted by the National Institutes of Health (NIH) and National Institute on Alcohol Abuse and Alcoholism (NIAAA) survey of 43,000 American adults found that the most common personality disorder is obsessive-compulsive personality disorder (which differs from obsessive-compulsive disorder), at about 7.9 percent, or 16.4 million people. Next most common were paranoid (4.4%; 9.2 million), antisocial (3.6%; 7.6 million), and schizoid (3.1%; 6.5 million) personality disorders. Least common personality disorders were avoidant, histrionic, and dependent personality disorders. The study did not look at incidence of borderline, schizotypal, or narcissistic personality disorders. (*Source:* http://pn.psychiatryonline.org/content/39/17/12.full)
- Some well-known movies that depict *narcissistic personality disorder* include *Alfie* (1966), *American Gigolo* (1980), *Citizen Kane* (1941), *Lawrence of Arabia* (1962), and *Jerry Maguire* (1996). The 1982 movie *Sophie's Choice* depicted *dependent personality disorder.*

Pet Therapy

Pet therapy, also called *pet psychology* or *animal behavior consulting*, is a field devoted to changing the behavior problems of pets. Pet therapy has its origins in dog training and the practice of veterinary medicine (Overall, 1997) and has been growing in demand in recent years. Among the most common reasons for turning over a cat or dog to an animal shelter are issues of behavior. Every year, millions of cats and dogs in the United States are euthanized because of problematical behavior (Hetts, 1999).

Certified pet therapists come from different educational and experiential backgrounds. Veterinarians may become certified by the American College of Veterinary Behaviorists by receiving supplementary education in animal behavior. Veterinary technicians may become certified by their professional group, the National Association of Veterinary Technicians. Certified Applied Animal Behaviorists (CAAB) are certified by the Animal Behavior Society and possess a master's or doctoral degree in a behavioral science or a doctorate of veterinary medicine with additional training in animal behavior. Other organizations certify individuals who do not necessarily have a veterinary, master's, or doctoral degree, and some individuals provide behavioral consulting without any credentials or certification.

Pets can present a wide variety of behavior problems. The most common ones reported by dog owners are aggression toward people or other animals, excessive barking, destructive chewing, and begging. The most common behavior issues for cats are soiling and aggression (Overall, 1997). Causes of behavior problems vary; they include lack of stimulation for the pet, which may be exacerbated by keeping the pet indoors, and conflict between animals in homes with more than one pet.

The goals of pet therapy are to help clients understand their pets' behavior and ultimately to change pets' behavior. Typically, as consulting begins, a medical screening of the pet is recommended to eliminate medical issues as sources of the problem. Additionally, the consultant will obtain a history of the problem behavior, eliciting as much detail as possible (what behavior, how often, when, where). Common techniques that are used to change behavior are two forms of behavior therapy: operant conditioning and classical conditioning. Operant conditioning involves providing rewards, such as food, for desirable behaviors. Punishment is another form of operant conditioning but is not recommended; if possible, the pet's situation should be viewed creatively so that undesirable behaviors are ignored rather than punished, and desirable behaviors that could, in the future, take the place of the undesirable behavior are reinforced. For instance, if one cat is aggressive with another cat, rather than punishing the cat when he aggresses, the owner could spend more time playing with both cats. If two people live in the household, it may be helpful if one person plays with one cat while another person plays with the other cat (so that the dominant cat does not try to completely dominate the play) in the same room. The play time is stimulation and attention for both cats, and the aggressive cat may associate the pleasure he experiences during playtime with the entire situation, which even includes the other cat. He may thus develop a positive feeling toward the other cat (although this is speculation—we cannot really know what an animals "feels"). This association of stimuli (the play situation, presence of the other cat, etc.) is classical conditioning. After the consultant determines a diagnosis, he provides the client with an appropriate behavior modification plan, which may include operant conditioning, classical conditioning, modifying the home environment, stimulating (play) activities for the animal, educating the client about normal and problematic pet behavior, and other solutions (Landsberg, Hunthausen, & Ackerman, 1997).

See also animal-assisted therapy, Animal Behavior Society, behavior therapy, behaviorism.

Further Reading:
Overall, K. L. (1997). *Clinical behavioral medicine for small animals*. Portland, OR: Mosby.

References:

Hetts, S. (1999). *Pet behavior protocols.* Lakewood, CO: AAHA Press.

Landsberg, G., Hunthausen, W., & Ackerman, L. (1997). *Handbook of behavior problems of the dog or cat.* Oxford, England: Butterworth Heinemann.

Overall, K. L. (1997). *Clinical behavioral medicine for small animals.* Portland, OR: Mosby.

Phobia

A person suffering from a phobia is persistently afraid of a particular object or situation. Phobias are extreme and out of proportion to the danger presented by the object or situation, and the sufferer recognizes the irrationality of the fear. The individual can remain calm as long as he can avoid the feared object, but if not, the phobia can be quite disrupting. For instance, if any individual develops a car phobia, many aspects of his life can become more difficult. Phobias are more common in women than in men.

The *Diagnostic and Statistical Manual of Mental Disorders* (*DSM-IV-TR*; American Psychiatric Association 2000) describes three categories of phobias: specific phobia, social phobia, and agoraphobia. The most common is a *specific phobia*, a persistent and unreasonable fear of a specific object, activity, or situation. Examples of common specific phobias include fears of particular animals, blood, heights, enclosed spaces, and flying in an airplane. Up to 9 percent of the population experiences a specific phobia in any given year (Kessler, Chiu, Demler, & Walters, 2005). When exposed to the dreaded object or situation, the individual immediately exhibits intense fear. Many people with a specific phobia experience more than one phobia simultaneously. The most common effective treatments for specific phobias are behavioral treatments called *exposure treatments*. These involve being exposed to the feared object or situation. For instance, in systematic desensitization, the individual is taught a relaxation technique and, while relaxed, is exposed to a mild stimulus of the fear (e.g., if the person fears spiders, she may be placed in a room with an aquarium in which a spider is present). The idea is to associate the feared object with relaxation. When success is achieved with the mild stimulus, the person will be taught to relax while experiencing a more intense version of the feared object, and so on. Other exposure treatments are modeling, flooding, and implosive therapy. Exposure treatments are very effective for simple phobias (Wolfe, 2005).

A *social phobia* is a persistent, irrational fear linked to the presence of other people, which includes public speaking, meeting people, or speaking in groups. Some social phobias are quite specific, such as a fear of eating in public. Up to 7 percent of the U.S. population experiences a social phobia each year (Kessler et al., 2005). People with social phobias are tremendously anxious about embarrassing themselves in social situations. Some sufferers become reclusive, and this avoidance may lead them to seek treatment. Social phobias are commonly accompanied by such physical symptoms as blushing, trembling, and nausea. The individual's fears persist for days and weeks before the feared situation.

Effective treatment for social phobias is more complex than treatment for simple phobias. First, a psychological approach is recommended. This could be an exposure therapy of the sort used for simple phobias or cognitive therapy such as rational emotive therapy, in which a clinician or counselor encourages the individual with the phobia to question her irrational and self-defeating beliefs. As an adjunct to the psychological approach, social skills training is utilized. Techniques include the therapist modeling appropriate behavior, role-playing between phobic person and therapist, and honest feedback from the therapist. A final treatment is antidepressant or anxiolytic medications, which function to reduce social anxiety in some individuals. Each of these treatments is at least somewhat helpful, and combinations of treatments may be more effective than utilizing a single approach (Heimberg, 2002).

Agoraphobia refers to fear of leaving one's house. Sufferers have sometimes experienced panic attacks and begun to worry that an attack could occur in a public place. Overall, it is the most debilitating phobia; individuals may lose their jobs or friendships or be unable to properly care for their children. Around 2.7 percent of the population suffers from agoraphobia per year (Kessler et al., 2005). Exposure therapy, in which the individual is instructed to go outside the house and remain for a certain period of time, even if fear occurs, is a common treatment for agoraphobia (e.g., Emmelkamp, 1982). This treatment is used over a number of sessions with moderate success.

Although the cause of phobias is unknown, the behavioral theories—classical conditioning and modeling—receive the most support. Classical conditioning occurs when an individual associates two events that occur close together in time and reacts similarly to these events. For instance, if a person falls down the stairs and break her legs, the fear that she naturally experiences with the broken legs might lead to a fear of stairs. Another way of developing a phobia is through modeling. By observing other people who are afraid of a certain object, people may develop fear of the same object. Although research has clearly shown that phobias can be caused through classical conditioning or modeling (Bandura & Rosenthal, 1966; Wolfe, 2005), phobias do not always develop under these circumstances. Thus a more complex causal model for phobias is suggested.

See also behaviorism, cognitive therapy and cognitive-behavioral therapy, fear, rational emotive behavior therapy, systematic desensitization.

Further Readings:
Bourne, E.J. (2005). *The anxiety and phobia workbook.* Oakland, CA: New Harbinger Press.
National Institute of Mental Health. (n.d.). *Social phobia (social anxiety disorder).* Retrieved from http://www.nimh.nih.gov/health/topics/social-phobia-social-anxiety-disorder/index.shtml

References:
American Psychiatric Association. (2000). *Diagnostic and statistical manual of mental disorders* (4th ed., text rev.). Washington, DC: Author.
Bandura, A., & Rosenthal, T.L. (1966). Vicarious classical conditioning as a function of arousal level. *Journal of Personality and Social Psychology, 3,* 54–62.
Dittmann, M. (2005). Hughes's germ phobia revealed in psychological autopsy. *Monitor on Psychology, 36,* 102.
Emmelkamp, P.M.G. (1982). *Phobic and obsessive-compulsive disorders.* New York: Plenum Press.
Heimberg, R.G. (2002). Cognitive-behavioral therapy for social anxiety disorder. *Current Status and Future Directions in Biological Psychiatry, 51,* 101–108.
Kessler, R.C., Chiu, W.T., Demler, O., & Walters, E.E. (2005). Prevalence, severity, and comorbidity of 12-month DSM-IV disorders in the National Comorbidity Survey Replication. *Archives of General Psychiatry, 62,* 617–627.
Wolfe, B.E. (2005). The application of the integrative model to specific anxiety disorders. In B.E. Wolfe (Ed.), *Understanding and treating anxiety disorders: An integrative approach to healing the wounded self* (pp. 125–153). Washington, DC: American Psychological Association.

- Well-known billionaire aviator, movie producer, and business tycoon Howard Hughes had a phobia so extreme that he went to great lengths to avoid germs. He spent the last years of his life lying naked in bed in a darkened hotel room (a place he considered a germ-free zone), with tissue boxes on his feet to protect them from contamination. After Hughes's death, a psychological autopsy conducted by Dr. Raymond D. Fowler determined that Hughes's fears for his health probably emerged during childhood. His mother, afraid Hughes would contract polio, checked him every day for diseases and was cautious about what he ate. Later in his life, Hughes went to great lengths to protect himself, developing obsessions and compulsions. He wrote an instruction manual for his staff on how to open a can of peaches. However obsessed Hughes was about contamination from the outside, Hughes neglected his own hygiene, rarely bathing or brushing his teeth (Dittmann, 2005).
- According to the "Phobia List" (http://www.phobialist.com/reverse.html), some lesser-known names of phobias include *triskadekaphobia* (fear of the number 13), *myrmecophobia* (ants), *pogonophobia* (beards), *alektorophobia* (chickens), *leukophobia* (the color white), *ichthyophobia* (fish), *xenoglossophobia* (foreign languages), *genuphobia* (knees), *geliophobia* (laughter), *selenophobia* (the moon), *melophobia* (music), *lutraphobia* (otters), *papyrophobia* (paper), *arachibutyrophobia* (peanut butter sticking to the roof of the mouth), *herpetophobia* (reptiles), *scoleciphobia* (worms), and *hippopotomonstrosesquipedaliophobia* (long words).

Phrenology

Phrenology—the theory that personality traits can be ascertained from the shape of a person's skull—comes from a combination of the Greek roots *phrenos* (mind) and *logos* (knowledge). Incorporating elements of philosophy, physiology, and early neuroscience, phrenology is now considered a pseudoscience. Phrenology was popular in the 19th century and influenced developments in psychiatry, psychology, and neuroscience.

Phrenology was developed in 1796 by Austrian physician Franz Josef Gall (1758–1828). It is based on the concept that the brain is the organ of the mind and that certain brain areas have particular functions—each function is located in a different area of the brain. The size of these areas (or prominences on the surface of the skull) were said to relate to the degree to which a person manifested that mental faculty or character trait. It was believed that the cranial bone (skull) conformed to the convolutions of the brain and that measuring the skull would indicate an individual's personality characteristics. Gall's theories were based on examinations of the heads of his friends and family members as well as studies of the heads of inmates in prisons and asylums. In 1819 Gall published his principles of phrenology in *The Anatomy and Physiology*

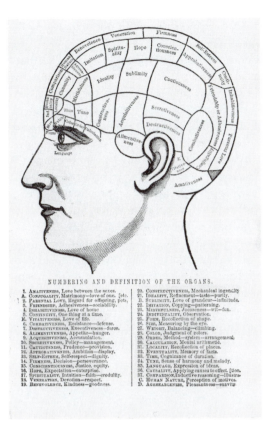

19th century etching of phrenological diagram with definitions of the various areas of the human skull. (iStockPhoto)

of the Nervous System in General, and of the Brain in Particular, with Observations upon the Possibility of Ascertaining the Several Intellectual and Moral Dispositions of Man and Animal, by the Configuration of Their Heads. Johann Gaspar Spurzheim (1776–1832), a German physician and a collaborator of Gall, helped to disseminate ideas about phrenology in the United Kingdom and United States. George Combes (1788–1858), a Scottish collaborator of Spurzheim, established the Phrenological Society of Edinburgh with his brother Andrew. American brothers Lorenzo Niles Fowler (1811–1896) and Orson Squire Fowler (1809–1887) were leading phrenologists in the United States. Orson Fowler, Nelson Sizer, and Samuel Wells established a phrenological publishing house in New York City, Fowler and Wells, which published books and journals about phrenology, including the *American Phrenological Journal.* Lorenzo Fowler spent his time in England, where he established a phrenology publishing house (L. N. Fowler and Company). Lorenzo is best known for a china head depicting phrenology regions, which became a symbol of phrenology. Phrenologists were consulted to make hiring decisions, find suitable marriage partners, and predict an individual's future. Phrenology influenced Victorian era literature and became the popular psychology of the day. It was most popular from the 1820s through the 1840s.

Phrenologists would run their hands over the head to feel for bumps and indentations and used calipers to take measurements of the head. This information was used to describe the character and temperament of an individual and address each of the "brain organs." Gall originally identified 26 brain organs; 19 were common in other animal species, and the rest were unique to humans. Later, Spurzheim and Combes divided the scalp into 35 distinct regions, with names such as amativeness, philoprogenitiveness, concentrativeness, love of approbation, imitativeness, wit, and metaphysical spirit. There were separate regions for different types of perception (form, size, weight, color, locality, number, order, time, tune, and linguistics). Many of the brain organs or regions were associated with religious or moral values. As enthusiasm grew for phrenology in the United States, some people began conducting their own research and identifying new phrenological organs such as for love of Bologna sausage, the propensity to kiss women, the tendency to swindle the public out of money, or the urge to enjoy strong drink (Rothenberg, 2000).

Phrenology was used as an explanation in the case of Phineas P. Gage, a Vermont railroad worker who was injured in an explosion in 1848 that drove a large iron bar through his head. Gage survived the injury with language and motor functions apparently intact. However, he exhibited significant behavior and personality changes, including impaired decision-making and planning abilities, impulsive behavior, use of profanity, and impaired social functioning. In his 1884 book about phrenology, Nelson Sizer explains that the personality changes observed in Gage were due to the iron passing "in the neighborhood of Benevolence and the front part of Veneration" (Damasio, 1994, p. 17). The Benevolence and Veneration brain organs purportedly controlled proper behavior, kindness, and respect for others. Sizer surmised that profanity was the result of damage to Gage's organ of Veneration (Damasio, 1994).

Phrenology was distinct from *craniometry* (the study of skull size, weight, and shape) and *physiognomy* (the study of facial and body characteristics), which also claimed to be able to discern moral character or intelligence. All three theories—phrenology, craniometry, and physiognomy—were used to justify and support racism, eugenics, and theories about differing abilities of males and females. In the 19th and early 20th centuries, anthropology (especially physical anthropology) and ethnology (the branch of science that studies racial differences) utilized these theories to justify segregation.

See also Phineas P. Gage.

Further Readings:

Fowler, L. F. (1847). *Familiar lessons on phrenology: Designed for the use of children and youth in schools and families.* New York: Fowler and Wells. Available from http://www.archive.org/details/familiarlessons01fowlgoog

Sizer, N. (1884). *Forty years in phrenology: Embracing recollections of history, anecdote, and experience.* New York: Fowler and Wells.

Sizer, N., & Drayton, H. S. (1885). *Heads and faces and how to study them, a manual of phrenology and physiognomy for the people.* New York: Fowler and Wells. Available from http://www.archive.org/stream/headsfaceshowtos00sizeuoft#page/n5/mode/2up

References:

Damasio, A. R. (1994). *Descartes' error: Emotion, reason and the human brain.* New York: Putnam.

Rothenberg, M. (2000). *History of science in the United States: An encyclopedia.* London: Garland Science.

Sizer, N. (1884). *Forty years in phrenology: Embracing recollections of history, anecdote, and experience.* New York: Fowler and Wells.

Physical Activity (Exercise) for Depression

Aerobic exercise is an effective treatment for clinical depression. Research on this topic began in full force in the 1980s, utilizing exercise by itself and observing changes in depression over time or comparing exercise and psychotherapy as treatments for depression. In the past 10 years, Blumenthal and Babyak and their colleagues (e.g., Babyak et al., 2000; Blumenthal et al., 1999) have studied exercise in well-controlled experiments, comparing exercise and sertraline (Zoloft, an atypical antidepressant) as treatments for depression. In their studies, they found that exercise was better than or equal to Zoloft as a treatment for mild to moderate depression.

Exercise may also be used to augment antidepressant medication as a treatment, given that antidepressants are generally effective in reducing, but not eliminating, depression. The experimental investigation of the most effective "dose" of exercise (amount of total exercise per week and frequency of exercise) has not been resolved (e.g., see Dunn, Trivedi, Kampert, Clark, & Chambliss, 2005). Although exercise is beginning to look quite good as a depression treatment, researchers such as Seime and Vickers (2006) have pointed out that special challenges exist regarding implementing exercise as a treatment. Specifically, some depressed patients are highly resistant to initiating an exercise program and are less likely than other people to reinitiate exercise if their exercise routine has been disrupted (e.g., due to sickness such as a cold or the flu). Reluctance to exercise may be related to a relatively low rate of physical activity prior to the onset of depressive symptoms, a high level of pessimism, or a low sense of self-effectiveness associated with depression. Figuring out how to encourage depressed individuals to exercise is a current and exciting topic of study. Some evidence exists that exercise may be an effective treatment for other emotional conditions, including general anxiety, obsessive-compulsive disorder, posttraumatic stress disorder, and substance (drug and alcohol) abuse.

See also atypical antidepressants, depression.

References:
Babyak, M. A., Blumenthal, J. A., Herman, S., Khatri, P., Doraiswamy, M., Moore, K., et al. (2000). Exercise treatment for major depression: Maintenance of therapeutic benefit at ten months. *Psychosomatic Medicine, 62*, 633–638.
Blumenthal, J. A., Babyak, M. A., Moore, K. A., Craighead, W. E., Herman, S., Khatri, P., et al. (1999). Effects of exercise training on older patients with major depression. *Archives of Internal Medicine, 159*, 2349–2356.
Dunn, A. L., Trivedi, M. H., Kampert, J. P., Clark, C. G., & Chambliss, H. O. (2005). Exercise treatment for depression: Efficacy and dose response. *American Journal of Preventive Medicine, 28*, 1–8.
Seime, R. J., & Vickers, K. S. (2006). The challenges of treating depression with exercise: From evidence to practice. *Clinical Psychology: Science and Practice, 13*, 194–197.

Physiology of Emotion

An emotion is a complex phenomenon consisting of a number of components, including appraisals (cognitions or thoughts), feelings, and physiological reactions. Two physiological aspects that have been examined extensively have been activity of the autonomic nervous system (ANS) and brain physiology.

American psychologist William James (1884) was instrumental in introducing the idea that emotions involve physiological changes. James argued that when encountering a stimulus that produces an emotion, physiological changes occur before subjective feelings occur. His work and the work of others inspired people to study the ANS to determine its relation to emotion. The ANS is responsible for maintaining homeostasis (a balanced state) and for making energy available for the body's requirements. The ANS has two branches, the sympathetic nervous system (SNS), which is active when the body is aroused or activated, and the parasympathetic nervous system (PNS), which is active when the body is not in an emergency or highly active situation but rather is taking care of vegetative, ordinary function. (In actuality, both the SNS and PNS are active at all times, but the ratio of activity is related to the current demands of the body.) SNS activation is associated with many bodily changes, including increased heart rate, blood pressure, respiration rate, perspiration, and release of hormones (including adrenaline and noradrenaline). When the PNS is active, in general, opposite bodily responses occur (e.g., decreases in heart rate and blood pressure).

Because emotional experience typically means some degree of arousal or excitement, the SNS was initially the main branch of the ANS that was of interest to researchers. William James's (1884) writings had led others to speculate that specific patterns of SNS activity may be associated with specific emotions. In general, research does indicate that SNS activity is greater (e.g., heart rate increase) when an individual is experiencing one of the primary negative emotions (i.e., fear, anger, or sadness) than when he is experiencing positive emotions or no emotion (for a review, see Larsen, Berntson, Poehmann, Ito, & Cacioppo, 2008). Disgust looks different than the other negative emotions; it may involve a deceleration of heart rate rather than acceleration (Levenson, 1992). As Larsen et al. (2008) point out, however, evidence that specific ANS activity is associated with specific emotions is mixed and inconclusive; they state that ongoing research is likely to shed light on whether a relationship exists between specific emotions and specific ANS activity. Also, the association between specific emotions and specific ANS patterns is likely to be more complex than originally theorized. For instance, as Lang, Bradley, and Cuthbert (1990) have pointed out, behaviors linked to fear include freezing, vigilance, and flight, each of which requires different metabolic responses. Thus emotion-specific ANS patterns may exist only in a limited fashion.

Positive and negative emotions are also associated with activity in the two hemispheres of the brain. In general, the right hemisphere is linked with negative affect and the left hemisphere with positive affect. For example, people with more activity in the left frontal lobe (relative to the right) report more subjective well-being (Urry et al., 2004). Additionally, in a study of separation between infants and their mothers, infants who cried when their mothers left the room had relatively high activity in the right hemisphere immediately before the separation (Davidson & Fox, 1989). Research in this area may be helpful in understanding some emotional disorders such as depression. For instance, Henriques and Davidson (1990) found that people with a history of depression had less activity in the left anterior (front) of the brain than people with no history of depression.

See also amygdala, autonomic nervous system, Cannon-Bard theory of emotion, William James, James-Lange theory of emotion, negative emotions, parasympathetic nervous system, positive emotions, sympathetic nervous system.

References:

Davidson, R. J., & Fox, N. A. (1989). Frontal brain asymmetry predicts infants' response to maternal separation. *Journal of Abnormal Psychology, 98,* 127–131.

Henriques, J. B., & Davidson, R. J. (1990). Regional brain electrical asymmetries discriminate between previously depressed and healthy control subjects. *Journal of Abnormal Psychology, 99,* 22–31.

James, W. (1884). What is an emotion? *Mind, 9,* 188–205.

Lang, P. J., Bradley, M. M., & Cuthbert, B. N. (1990). Emotion, attention, and the startle reflex. *Psychological Review, 97,* 377–395.

Larsen, J. T., Berntson, G. G., Poehmann, K. M., Ito, T. A., & Cacioppo, J. T. (2008). The psychophysiology of emotion. In M. Lewis, J. M. Haviland-Jones, & L. F. Barrett (Eds.), *Handbook of emotions* (3rd ed., pp. 180–195). New York: Guilford.

Levenson, R. W. (1992). Autonomic nervous system differences among emotions. *Psychological Science, 3*, 23–27.

Urry, H. L., Nitschke, J. B., Dolski, I., Jackson, D. C., Dalton, K. M., Mueller, C. J., et al. (2004). Making a life worth living: Neural correlates of well-being. *Psychological Science, 15*, 367–372.

Plato (427–347 BC)

Aristocles was nicknamed "Plato" (*platon* in Greek meaning "broad") because of his broad shoulders. He was born in Athens to upper-class parents. As a teenager and young adult, he was a good student, a wrestler, and an aspiring poet. When he was 20, he heard Socrates speak, was taken with his philosophy and style, and became his student for eight years. Much of what we know about Socrates' thinking comes from Plato's writing, as Socrates himself did no writing.

When Plato was in his late twenties and following some political upheaval in Athens, Socrates was tried and convicted of treason for statements he made during the years of turmoil. He was condemned to death by drinking hemlock and died in 399 BC. Plato was appalled and disgusted and left Athens for a time, traveling to various Mediterranean locations. When Plato was 40, he challenged the ruler of Syracuse, Dionysius, and was apprehended and sold into slavery. Anniceris bought and freed him, and Plato moved back to Athens. There, Plato's friends raised money to repay Anniceris. However, Anniceris refused the money; instead it was used to found Plato's influential school, the Academy, in 387 BC.

The Academy was a center of higher learning in Greece for nine centuries. In AD 529, the school was shut down, reputedly because the teachings there conflicted with teachings of Christianity. The Academy focused on the Socratic way of thinking, which used reason to obtain knowledge. Both Socrates and Plato believed that humans possess immortal souls and that souls are born with knowledge. In the Socratic and Platonic views, reasoning and introspecting led to recollection of knowledge that already exists. This belief interfered with the development of the scientific approach to knowledge, which is dependent on observation rather than recollection of preexisting knowledge. By contrast, Plato's pupil, Aristotle, is credited with hastening and encouraging the development of science because he focused on observation—information derived from one's own sense organs as the source of knowledge—rather than recollection.

No evidence exists that Plato married. He was handsome and had romantic affairs with both women and men. Plato died at age 80 or 81.

Plato's primary contribution to thinking about emotion was his model of the soul or mind. According to Plato, the soul exists in a body and functions on three levels: thought or reason, spirit or will, and appetite or desire. Each component of the soul is important, and none should overwhelm either of the others. Reason, however, is supposed to be the center of the soul. He compared the soul to a charioteer who is running two steeds or horses. The charioteer is reason and has the reigns. One steed is appetite, which he said was disorderly and wayward, and potentially violent.

The other steed, spirit, is energetic and dynamic but obedient. Numerous scholars have noticed the similarity between this model and Freud's (1923/1953) model of the mind, which consists of the reality-based ego, the pleasure-seeking id, and the morality-oriented superego.

See also Aristotle, Sigmund Freud, psychoanalytic perspective.

Further Readings:
Neeson, L., & Harrison, C. (2005). *Empires—The Greeks: Crucible of civilization.* Arlington, VA: PBS Paramount.
Stevenson, J. (2005). *The complete idiot's guide to philosophy* (3rd ed.). New York: Alpha.

Reference:
Freud, S. (1953). The ego and the id. In J. Strachey (Ed. & Trans.), *The standard edition of the complete psychological works of Sigmund Freud* (Vol. 19). London: Hogarth Press. (Original work published 1923)

Play Therapy

The Association for Play Therapy (APT) defines play therapy as "the systematic use of a theoretical model to establish an interpersonal process wherein trained play therapists use the therapeutic powers of play to help clients prevent or resolve psychosocial difficulties and achieve optimal growth and development" (Association for Play Therapy, n.d.). Play therapy is a counseling approach that utilizes toys and play as the primary vehicle for communication. The rationale for this is that young children often lack the language or ability to verbally communicate what is going on with them. Even older children and adolescents with well-developed verbal skills may benefit from play therapy since they may be better able to act out their issues or communicate their feelings through play rather than through traditional talk therapy.

Play therapy is considered especially appropriate for children between the ages of 3 and 12 years who have difficulty with verbal reasoning but may also be suitable for very young (1-1/2 to 2 years) or older (ages 11–15) children who have experienced trauma. Play therapy may be appropriate for children who are experiencing behavioral or emotional difficulties, including (but not limited to) aggression or acting-out behavior, attachment difficulties, attention-deficit hyperactivity disorder, conduct disorders, phobias, separation anxiety, and selective mutism. Play therapy may also be suitable for children who are contending with grief, adoption, divorce, abuse or neglect, hospitalization, chronic or terminal illness, or traumas such as war, natural disasters, kidnapping, or automobile accidents.

Play therapy approaches range on a continuum from *nondirective* (meaning the child rather than the therapist generally directs what transpires, as in *child-centered play therapy*) to *directive* (e.g., Theraplay, in which the therapist directs the course of therapy). Approaches that combine both directive and nondirective elements include Adlerian and cognitive-behavioral play therapy. In play therapy, children choose from a variety of play materials, including toys, games, and art supplies, which they use to express themselves in the language of play. Toys and play materials offered for therapy cover a range of developmental stages (toys for both younger and older children) and include family/nurturing toys, aggressive toys, scary toys, expressive toys, and pretend/fantasy toys (Kottman, 1999).

The play therapist works with a child's family and/or teacher to formulate goals for the play therapy. Whenever possible, the child is included in the formulation of treatment goals. Play therapy goals vary depending on the child's issues and presenting problems as well as the child's age and developmental stage. General play therapy treatment goals may include enhancing self-confidence and self-reliance, helping the child explore and express feelings, practicing self-control and self-responsibility, developing problem-solving and relationship-building skills, and exploring behavioral alternatives.

Basic play therapy techniques include tracking (describing the child's behavior to the child), restating content (paraphrasing the child's verbalizations), reflecting the child's feelings, returning responsibility (for behaviors or decisions) to the child, and using the child's metaphor (adopting the child's story without imposing one's own meaning or interpretation). Setting appropriate limits with the child and maintaining a consistent structure for play therapy sessions can provide the child with a sense of predictability and self-control and provide a safe space for the child to explore and do therapeutic work. Limits and structure include things such as leaving toys and play materials in the room, starting and stopping sessions on time, and agreements that the child not harm itself or others during the session. Approaches to setting limits in play therapy include stating the limit in a nonjudgmental way, reflecting the child's feelings, engaging the child in redirecting its own inappropriate behavior, and setting up logical consequences that the child can enforce (Kottman, 1999).

The APT emphasizes that the practice of play therapy by licensed or certified mental health professionals requires specialized training and supervised clinical experience.

See also Anna Freud.

Further Readings:
Association for Play Therapy Web site: http://www.a4pt.org/
Webb, N. B. (Ed.). (1999). *Play therapy with children in crisis: Individual, group, and family treatment* (2nd ed.). New York: Guilford.

References:
Association for Play Therapy. (n.d.). About play therapy: Overview. Retrieved from http://www.a4pt. org/ps.playtherapy.cfm
Kottman, T. (1999). Play therapy. In A. Vernon (Ed.), *Counseling children and adolescents* (2nd ed., pp. 98–119). Denver, CO: Love.

Pleasant-Unpleasant

Among the most basic questions that an emotion theorist may address is how to categorize the variety of experiences of emotion or affect. One approach, called the *basic emotions approach*, is to view emotions as separate categories (e.g., sadness, happiness, fear, anger; Ekman, 1994; Panksepp, 1994). This approach assumes that the emotion categories are qualitatively different; that distinct boundaries exist between the different emotions.

An alternative viewpoint is that there are no distinct boundaries; rather, emotions are best understood by first identifying the underlying continuous dimensions on which they differ. The most well-known modern models identify two different dimensions. In these models, each emotion is mapped onto the space created by these two dimensions. All these well-known models have identified the same two dimensions or variants of these dimensions: pleasant-unpleasant and activated-unactivated (or high arousal–low arousal; e.g., Russell, 1980; Watson & Tellegen, 1985).

For example, in Russell's (1980) model, for which he labeled one dimension pleasure-misery and the second dimension arousal-sleepiness, examples of how emotional states are mapped onto the two-dimensional space are as follows: excited, delighted, happy, and glad all fit within the pleasure-arousal quadrant; satisfied, content, calm, and relaxed fit within the pleasure-sleepiness quadrant; afraid, angry, distressed, and annoyed fit within the misery-arousal quadrant; and depressed, gloomy, bored, and droopy fit within the misery-sleepiness quadrant.

See also basic emotions.

References:
Ekman, P. (1994). All emotions are basic. In P. Ekman & R. J. Davidson (Eds.), *The nature of emotion: Fundamental questions* (pp. 15–19). New York: Oxford University Press.
Panksepp, J. (1994). The basics of basic emotion. In P. Ekman & R. J. Davidson (Eds.), *The nature of emotion: Fundamental questions* (pp. 20–24). New York: Oxford University Press.
Russell, J. A. (1980). A circumplex model of affect. *Journal of Personality and Social Psychology, 39,* 1161–1178.
Watson, D., & Tellegen, A. (1985). Toward a consensual structure of mood. *Psychological Bulletin, 98,* 219–235.

Pleasure. *See* Joy.

Polygraph

Often called a *lie detector*, the polygraph is an electronic instrument that measures signs of physical arousal. During the test, electrodes are attached to different parts of a person's body. These electrodes collect physiological changes in breathing, perspiration, heart rate, and other signs of arousal. For instance, blood pressure cuffs placed around the person's upper arm record blood pressure, and electrodes placed on the fingertips measure perspiration. The collected signals are transformed and projected into a visual display.

The examiner first measures the baseline of physiological arousal. Then the subject's physiological responses are monitored while she answers a series of yes-no questions. These yes-no questions are either control questions or test questions. Control questions are questions that are irrelevant to the issue at hand. When used in court cases, control questions are not related to the crime. They include such a question as "Do you live in South Dakota?" or one that may be more emotionally arousing such as "In your lifetime, have you ever stolen anything?" Test questions that are related to crimes may be emotionally arousing. This includes questions like "Did you commit this murder?" The examiner compares the subject's physical responses to these two kinds of questions. If there is an increase in breathing, perspiration, heart rate, or other indicators in response to test questions, but little or no increase in response to control questions, the supposition is that the individual may be (or is) lying. The use of the polygraph is based on the assumption that physiological responses indicate underlying psychological issues. Particularly, it assumes that when people lie, they become anxious and will produce physiological signs of anxiety.

In the mid-1890s, Italian criminologist and psychiatrist Cesare Lombroso used the technique of measuring a suspect's heart rate and blood pressure in an attempt to reveal deception. He speculated that changes in heart rate and blood pressure could indicate an emotional response connected with deception. In 1907, Carl G. Jung used a galvanometer (to measure skin resistance) and pneumograph (to measure breathing) as indications of emotional arousal. In 1914, Vittorio Benussi looked to breathing patterns to discern deceit in suspects. These ideas were brought from Europe to the United States by Hugo Münsterburg, whom psychologist William James had invited from Germany to take charge of a laboratory at Harvard. In 1908, Münsterburg proposed that the courts could use physiological indicators such as heart rate and breathing to detect deception. Münsterburg's student William Marston conducted research and developed what came to be known as the Marston Deception Test (based on blood pressure) in 1917 (Alder, 2002). Marston is often credited as the inventor of the polygraph. While Marston started out as a dedicated psychological researcher, he became a promoter of the lie detector technique and device, often using it as a stage prop in demonstrations. In 1928 Marston used his technique to examine blonde, brunette, and redheaded showgirls at the Embassy Theatre in New York in an attempt to demonstrate a connection between hair color and personality type (Kelly, 2004). In 1921, Berkeley police psychologist John Larson refined Marston's technique, with an adaptation of Benussi's respiration detection device, and a means to continually record readings on paper. Larson called his device the ink polygraph, as it was similar to a device introduced by Scottish cardiologist James Mackenzie in 1902 to record blood flow (Kelly, 2004). While Larson was able to use the ink polygraph to find a shoplifting suspect among a group of coeds living together in a University of California dormitory, Larson believed his results came more from intimidation than from the machine itself. Larson did not believe polygraph results should be introduced in court without supporting evidence. Leonarde Keeler, who had worked with Larson at University of California, advanced the technology with the addition of galvanic skin response to measure changes in skin conductance (caused by perspiration). The Keeler polygraph became the basis of most modern polygraphs (Kelly, 2004). For several decades, William Marston advocated the use of the polygraph in the courts. His reasoning and suggestions for use of the polygraph appear in his 1938 book *The Lie Detector Test.*

The use of the polygraph has been controversial almost since its inception. In the mid-1980s. when the American Psychological Association reported its inaccuracy, the U.S. Congress decided to restrict its use in criminal prosecutions and in hiring (Krapohl, 2002). Numerous studies have pointed out the imprecision of the polygraph as a lie detector. Some critics insist that people can fake the test, for example, appearing innocent of a crime when they are in fact guilty. Other studies have shown that people frequently appear to be lying when they are not. Studies have shown that on average, 8 percent of truths were determined by the polygraph to be lies (MacLaren, 2001; Raskin & Honts, 2002). Today, the polygraph is still widely used by prosecutors, defense attorneys, and law enforcement agencies, although various federal and state laws restrict its use. For instance, in several states it is illegal to use the polygraph in employment decisions, and federal law states that defendants and witnesses cannot be forced to take a polygraph test. Despite the controversy surrounding the test, use of the polygraph increased in legal and law enforcement settings in the 1990s and the following decade.

See also fabrication of emotion, galvanic skin response.

Further Readings:

American Psychological Association. (2004). The truth about lie detectors (*aka* polygraph tests). *Psychology Matters*. Retrieved from http://www.psychologymatters.org/polygraphs.html

Hirstein, W. (2006). *Brain fiction: Self-deception and the riddle of confabulation.* Cambridge, MA: MIT Press.

References:

Alder, K. (2002, Autumn). A social history of untruth: Lie detection and trust in twentieth-century America. *Representations, 80,* 1–33.

Kelly, J. (2004). The truth about the lie detector. *American Heritage of Invention & Technology, 19,* 14–20.

Krapohl, D. J. (2002). The polygraph in personnel screening. In M. Kleiner (Ed.), *The handbook of polygraph testing* (pp. 217–236). San Diego, CA: Academic Press.

MacLaren, V. V. (2001). A qualitative review of the Guilty Knowledge Test. *Journal of Applied Psychology, 86,* 674–683.

Marston, W. M. (1938). *The lie detector test.* New York.

Richard R. Smith; Raskin, D. C., & Honts, C. R. (2002). The comparison question test. In M. Kleiner (Ed.), *The handbook of polygraph testing* (pp. 1–47). San Diego, CA: Academic Press.

- Early polygraph research and promoter William Moulton Marston (1893–1947) also authored the *Wonder Woman* comic book under the nom de plume Charles Moulton.
- From the Greek *polygraphos* (writing copiously), *polygraph* literally means writing down many things or writing many copies. Thomas Jefferson used a polygraph machine starting in 1806 to make multiple copies of documents. In the modern context (an instrument for recording several pulsations of the body at the same time), the word *polygraph* was first used in 1871.

Positive and Negative Affect (Activation) Schedule

The Positive and Negative Affect Schedule (PANAS; renamed the Positive and Negative Activation Schedule in 1999) was developed in 1988 by American psychologist David Watson. His research focused primarily on positive emotions, which, compared to negative emotions, had been relatively neglected in psychology before about the 1980s. His instrument was designed to measure emotions for both research and clinical purposes.

The PANAS consists of 20 items, each a single word describing an affect. The 10 positive affect items are enthusiastic, interested, determined, excited, inspired, alert, active, strong, proud, and attentive. The 10 negative affect items are scared, upset, distressed, ashamed, guilty, hostile, irritable, nervous, jittery, and afraid. Participants rate each word on a scale from 1 to 5, indicating the degree to which the word describes their feelings during a certain time (e.g., "in general," a day, a week, a month, etc.).

The PANAS is widely used in research on emotions and mood. An example of a question that has been of primary interest to researchers who use the PANAS is, "Can an individual experience both positive and negative affects at the same time?" For instance, can we have a conversation with a loved friend and experience both pleasure and sadness, or pleasure and anger? Results of research (e.g., see Watson, 2002) have generally indicated that positive and negative affects are independent of one another and that people can experience these divergent types of emotions simultaneously.

See also affect, affective personality traits, mood, negative emotions, pleasant-unpleasant, positive emotions.

References:

Watson, D. (1988). The vicissitudes of mood measurement: Effects of varying descriptors, time frames, and response formats on measures of positive and negative affect. *Journal of Personality and Social Psychology, 55*, 128–141.

Watson, D. (2002). Positive affectivity. In C. R. Snyder & S. J. Lopez (Eds.), *Handbook of positive psychology* (pp. 106–119). New York: Oxford University Press.

Positive Emotions

The interest in positive emotions has increased dramatically in the past two decades. Since much of the history of clinical psychology and related fields has been concerned with curing ills, the focus of research on emotion has traditionally been on negative emotions. However, at least two developments have led to the increased attention on positive emotions. One has been a concern with the good life, a focus associated with a field called *positive psychology*. A second, related development has been the discovery of the benefits that positive emotions provide. For example, positive emotions have been linked with better health, better interpersonal relationships, a superior ability to cope with stress, and other favorable outcomes (e.g., Lyubomirsky, King, & Diener, 2005).

Humans experience a wide variety of positive emotions or affective states, including happiness, joy, ecstasy, satisfaction, interest, excitement, contentment, pride, awe, love, hope, and relief, to name a few. These states differ on a number of dimensions. One dimension is arousal, with some emotions characterized by high arousal (e.g., excitement), others demonstrating low arousal (e.g., contentment), and many falling somewhere in between. Positive emotions may be other-directed (interpersonal) or self-directed (intrapersonal). Whereas most emotions are self-directed, love is an example of an other-directed emotion. Positive emotions are less distinct than negative ones (e.g., Smith & Ellsworth, 1985; Fredrickson & Branigan, 2001); individuals experiencing a positive emotion are less likely to be able to identify exactly what they are feeling than are individuals experiencing a negative emotion. Related to this, people are likely to experience more than one positive emotion at a time, whereas people often experience only one negative emotion at a time (e.g., Barrett, Gross, Christensen, & Benvenuto, 2001). There is a functional explanation for these facts. Negative emotions typically arise when an individual is threatened in some way and a fairly specific type of behavior is required. For instance, fear occurs when one should flee, anger occurs when one should fight, and disgust occurs when one should expel (e.g., spit out food that is tainted). However, positive emotions are usually not associated with threats. And positive emotions do, in fact, generate a wider range of thoughts and behaviors, opening oneself up to a greater number of possibilities.

Positive emotions are often associated with a desire to approach or to continue with behavior that has already been initiated (rather than a desire to avoid, which is linked to many of the negative emotions; e.g., Frijda, 1994). This is likely one of the ways that positive emotions are evolutionarily adaptive; positive emotions encourage us to interact with our environments, and without them, we may be passive to the degree that we jeopardize our survival.

A contemporary theory that has received significant support in explaining the function of positive emotions is Fredrickson's (2001) broaden-and-build theory. Fredrickson argues that positive emotions produce their best benefits for the individual over the long term. As previously described, the negative emotions tend to be most functional for emergency situations. However, the positive ones help one to broaden and build for the future.

Fredrickson and Cohn (2008) review research that supports the idea that positive emotions tend to produce a broadening of one's attention and cognition. Several studies show that when presented with a visual stimulus, people who are experiencing positive emotions attend more to global or broader aspects of the stimulus, whereas people experiencing negative emotions pay more attention to the detail of the stimulus. A large body of evidence also shows a broadening of cognition when one is in a positive emotional state. For instance, in one study, Fredrickson and Branigan (2005) induced positive, negative, or no emotions in participants, then requested that the participants list all the things that they felt they wanted to do. Those who had a positive emotion induction listed *more* activities and *more varied* activities than those with either a neutral or negative emotion induction. Furthermore, those with the negative emotion induction listed the fewest behaviors of all. This research indicates that positive emotion is associated with thinking characterized by more openness and flexibility. Additionally, as Fredrickson and Cohn (2008) describe, positive emotions are associated with broadening in the social cognition area, meaning in particular that people become more attentive of others, see fewer differences between themselves and others, and see fewer differences between different groups of people.

The second part of Fredrickson's theory is building. Positive emotions are linked with building enduring resources over time. The resources are, for example, physical, social, and intellectual. Both Fredrickson and Cohn (2008) and Lyubomirsky et al. (2005) review relevant studies. Play, associated with the emotion joy, can lead to physical development that can be helpful for survival. For instance, when a lion cub plays by attacking his sibling, he is practicing hunting skills. Play also can build social resources. When laughing together, people often create a bond of loyalty. As another example, positive emotions can build intellectual resources. For instance, children who are securely attached—those who are most secure in their feelings of love from parents—explore their environments more than do children who are less securely attached. Their explorations lead to intellectual improvements, for instance, they develop excellent cognitive maps (well-developed spatial memories) of the places they explore (Hazen & Durrett, 1982). In sum, the broadening of attention and cognition that occurs while experiencing positive emotions creates attitudes and propensities toward openness and flexibility. The positive emotions also tend to lead to development of physical or intellectual skills or social bonds, each of which may come in handy in the future.

Fredrickson and Cohn (2008) suggest a number of areas in which researchers could focus to further expand our understanding of positive emotions. One is to continue to study the relationship between physiology and positive emotions. Important topics to research include brain regions, brain chemicals (such as neurotransmitters, chemical messengers in the brain), and hormones linked with positive emotion. A second is to investigate how to use positive emotions as interventions, or ways to improve people's lives. For example, positive emotions could be induced to affect physical health, influence psychological health, or improve relationships. Another area of study is to look very closely at the specific positive emotions—rather than studying them as a general class—to see how each emotion relates to important life outcomes. The investigation of positive emotions is rife with possibility.

See also amusement, ecstasy, empathy, euphoria, happiness, hope, joy, love, negative emotions, optimism, pleasure, Positive and Negative Affect (Activation) Schedule, positive psychology, pride, relief, satisfaction, sympathy, temperament, trust.

Further Reading:
Fredrickson, B. L., & Cohn, M. A. (2008). Positive emotions. In M. Lewis, J. M. Haviland-Jones, & L. F. Barrett (Eds.), *Handbook of emotions* (3rd ed., pp. 777–796). New York: Guilford.

References:
Barrett, L. F., Gross, J., Christensen, T. C., & Benvenuto, M. (2001). Knowing what you're feeling and knowing what to do about it: Mapping the relation between emotion differentiation and emotion regulation. *Cognition and Emotion, 15*, 713–724.

Fredrickson, B. L. (2001). The role of positive emotions in positive psychology: The broaden-and-build theory of positive emotions. *American Psychologist, 56*, 218–226.

Fredrickson, B. L., & Branigan, C. (2001). Positive emotions. In T. J. Mayne & G. A. Bonnano (Eds.), *Emotions: Current issues and future directions* (pp. 123–151). New York: Guilford.

Fredrickson, B. L., & Branigan, C. (2005). Positive emotions broaden the scope of attention and thought-action repertoires. *Cognition and Emotion, 19*, 313–332.

Fredrickson, B. L., & Cohn, M. A. (2008). Positive emotions. In M. Lewis, J. M. Haviland-Jones, & L. F. Barrett (Eds.), *Handbook of emotions* (3rd ed., pp. 777–796). New York: Guilford.

Frijda, N. H. (1994). Emotions are functional, most of the time. In P. Ekman & R. Davidson (Eds.), *The nature of emotion: Fundamental questions* (pp. 112–122). New York: Oxford University Press.

Hazen, N. L., & Durrett, M. E. (1982). Relationship of security of attachment and cognitive mapping abilities in 2-year-olds. *Developmental Psychology, 18*, 751–759.

Lyubomirsky, S., King, L., & Diener, E. (2005). The benefits of frequent positive affect: Does happiness lead to success? *Psychological Bulletin, 131*, 803–855.

Smith, C. A., & Ellsworth, P. C. (1985). Patterns of cognitive appraisal in emotion. *Journal of Personality and Social Psychology, 48*, 813–838.

Positive Psychology

Positive psychology is a recent development in the field, founded by a group of psychologists and spearheaded by University of Pennsylvania professor Martin Seligman. Positive psychology is concerned with three primary areas of study: positive emotion (such as happiness, love, and contentment; *the pleasant life*), positive character or traits (such as resilience, wisdom, and spirituality; *the engaged life*), and positive institutions (such as positive work environments and positive communities; *the meaningful life*). According to proponents of positive psychology, all three of these aspects are related to life satisfaction, with the latter two (character traits and institutions) holding a stronger relationship than the first (positive emotion).

Positive psychology endeavors to understand the good life and the best in people primarily through application of the scientific method. According to some positive psychologists, this is what distinguishes positive psychology from related approaches such as humanistic psychology, which was founded several decades ago and which also focuses on positive attributes and experiences of humans. Positive psychologists, such as Seligman and Csikszentmihalyi (2000), argue that the research methods of humanists tended to be more qualitative, for example, using case studies, whereas positive psychologists use the types of research methods that are closer to what hard scientists such as physicists or biologists utilize. Some psychologists, for example, Robbins (2008), have challenged this characterization, arguing that humanists have always used both case studies and more rigorous research methods and that positive psychology is essentially "old wine in a new bottle." Debates about both the connections and the distinctions between humanistic psychology and positive psychology are likely to continue. Positive psychology is rapidly gaining in popularity, and some humanists appear to feel that they are not given enough credit for their contributions to understanding the best in people and the best in life.

In the short history of the field, positive psychologists have already produced research findings that help us to understand aspects of human nature. For example, evidence indicates that it is healthier to have a generally optimistic attitude in life than to have a pessimistic one, or even a realistic one. Compared to pessimists, optimists have better outcomes in a variety of domains, including better academic performance, greater satisfaction in interpersonal relationships, more productive work records, and even superior physical health (Snyder & Lopez, 2007). Additionally, positive psychologists have already developed a number of applied programs that train people in positive traits such as optimism, resiliency, and forgiveness. An example of such a program is the Penn Resiliency Program, in which psychologists work with preteens and teenagers to prevent depression. The goal is to teach the children to interpret events in alternative ways from their typical ones; the new interpretations are ones that foster optimism and a greater sense of control over one's reactions to life circumstances.

The first undergraduate course in positive psychology was taught in 1999 at the University of Pennsylvania. By 2007, over 200 courses existed worldwide. Now master's degrees are offered (the master's of applied positive psychology) as well as doctoral degrees. The first PhD program was offered at Claremont Graduate University in Southern California, established by Mihaly Csikszentmihalyi in 2007. Whether positive psychology is a fad or an approach that will continue to remain influential remains to be seen. However, with its resonance with positive American values such as happiness and meaning, its scientific grounding, and its success in real-life applications, the field is off to a good start.

See also affective personality traits, Aristotle, flow, happiness, hope, humanistic psychotherapy, learned helplessness, optimism, positive emotions.

Further Readings:
Compton, W. C. (2005). *An introduction to positive psychology.* Belmont, CA: Thomson Wadsworth.
Ehrenreich, B. (2009). *Bright-sided: How the relentless promotion of positive thinking has undermined America.* New York: Metropolitan Books.
Haidt, J. (2006). *The happiness hypothesis: Finding modern truth in ancient wisdom.* New York: Basic Books.

References:

Robbins, B. D. (2008). What is the good life? Positive psychology and the renaissance of humanistic psychology. *The Humanistic Psychologist, 36*, 96–112.

Seligman, M., & Csikszentmihalyi, M. (2000). Positive psychology: An introduction. *American Psychologist, 55*, 5–14.

Snyder, C. R., & Lopez, S. J. (2007). *Positive psychology: The scientific and practical explorations of human strengths.* Thousand Oaks, CA: Sage.

Positron Emission Tomography

Positron emission tomography (PET) is a body-imaging technique that involves taking a series of two-dimensional pictures of body processes and producing a "movie"—a three-dimensional reconstruction of the progression of the body process or processes on a computer screen. In preparation for the scan, a radioactive substance is administered to the subject, usually through injection into the bloodstream. Fluorodeoxyglucose (FDG)—a radioactive substance that behaves similarly to glucose in the body—is commonly used. Parts of the body that are active use relatively high amounts of FDG; thus PET scans can indicate which parts of the body are active. During the scan, the subject lies down in a machine.

In studying psychological processes, PET generally involves scanning the brain. Mosconi (2005) and colleagues conducted a longitudinal study using PET scans that contributed to our understanding of Alzheimer's disease and general dementia (dementia often develops in an individual prior to expression of Alzheimer's disease). In a sample of 53 elderly research participants, Mosconi studied activity in a particular brain structure, the hippocampus. She conducted PET scans at the beginning of the study, then follow-up PET scans 10 to 24 years after the initial scan. Over the course of the study, 19 participants developed dementia, and an additional 6 developed Alzheimer's disease. Mosconi found that participants who developed either dementia or Alzheimer's disease had less hippocampus activity at the beginning of the study than those who did not develop either form of cognitive impairment. This study, along with many others, has led researchers to conclude that the hippocampus is an important brain structure that is responsible for the formation of new memories.

PET scans are helpful for understanding emotion. Wong, Grunder, and Brasic (2007) reviewed imaging techniques and concluded that both PET and single photon emission computed tomography (SPECT) are beneficial tools in the diagnosis, treatment, and prevention of a number of psychiatric disorders. Thus far, these techniques have been helpful in understanding schizophrenia, alcoholism and other drug abuse, attention-deficit hyperactivity disorder, depression, and other disorders.

SPECT and PET technology are similar to one another but differ in a few significant ways. PET scans can produce images of a wider variety of brain activity than SPECT scans. However, SPECT produces longer-lasting images and therefore can monitor longer-lasting brain activity; the radioactivity used in PET scanning decays too rapidly for viewing of long-lasting activity. Additionally, SPECT is much less expensive to use. Resolution is better with PET (than SPECT); however, both PET and SPECT provide only limited visualization of brain structures, so sometimes functional magnetic resonance imaging (fMRI) is a better option (Hales, Yudofsky, & Gabbard, 2008). Both PET and SPECT scans have a decades-long and distinguished history in the study of the brain, with new applications of the techniques being discovered on a regular basis.

See also functional magnetic resonance imaging, hippocampus, single photon emission computed tomography.

References:
Hales, R. E., Yudofsky, S. C., & Gabbard, G. O. (2008). *The American Psychiatric Publishing textbook of psychiatry.* Arlington, VA: American Psychiatric Publishing.
Mosconi, L. (2005, June 18). *Hippocampal metabolism in the longitudinal prediction of decline from normal cognition to MCI and AD.* Paper presented at the Alzheimer's Association International Conference on Prevention of Dementia, Washington, DC.
Wong, D. F., Grunder, G., & Brasic, J. R. (2007). Brain imaging research: Does the science serve clinical practice? *International Review of Psychiatry, 19*, 541–558.

Postal

"Going postal" is an American slang expression meaning to become uncontrollably livid, often turning violent. The term typically means that the rage occurs in the workplace, although it can also apply outside the workplace. It commonly means that extreme violence occurs, particularly, murder or attempted murder, but it can also mean rage without physical violence.

The term originated following a number of workplace occurrences in which employees of the U.S. Postal Service (USPS) shot supervisors, coworkers, police officers, or members of the public. Between 1983 and 1997, there were at least 21 such incidents in the United States (Musacco, 2009). What was perhaps the most deadly event occurred in Edmond, Oklahoma, in 1986. On August 20, postman Patrick Sherrill killed 14 employees and wounded 6 at the Edmond Post Office, then committed suicide. Another significant event occurred in 2006 in Goleta, California. Jennifer San Marco, who had been forced to retire from the post office in 2003 due to mental health issues, traveled to a postal processing plant on January 30. She killed six employees, then killed herself. Later, the police found a seventh person murdered at a condominium in Goleta and attributed this killing to San Marco. According to Strauther (2007), this was likely the most deadly workplace shooting in the United States perpetrated by a woman.

The occupation that involves the highest homicide rate is taxi driving, in which 17.9 per 100,000 workers are killed on the job—a risk 36 times greater than for all other employed persons (Sygnatur & Toscano, 2000). However, taxi drivers are much more often murdered by passengers than by coworkers. According to Musacco (2009), data support the idea that the expression "going postal" as applied in its original sense—employees killing others in the workplace—is apt; during the 1980s, 13 percent of workplace homicides occurred at postal facilities and were perpetrated by current or past USPS employees. To put that in perspective, less than 1 percent of the total full-time civilian workforce was in the USPS. Musacco (2009) discusses reasons why such acts of violence occur disproportionately in the USPS.

See also aggression, road rage.

Further Readings:
Lasseter, D. (1997). *Going postal.* New York: Pinnacle.
Musacco, S. (2009). *Beyond going postal.* Charleston, SC: BookSurge.

References:

Musacco, S. (2009). *Beyond going postal.* Charleston, SC: BookSurge.

Strauther, L. (2007). *The mail carrier: Things customers need to know, from inside the mind of a mailman.* Bloomington, IN: AuthorHouse.

Sygnatur, E. F., & Toscano, G. A. (2000, Spring). Work-related homicides: The facts. In *Compensation and Working Conditions.* Retrieved from http://www.bls.gov/opub/cwc/archive/spring2000art1.pdf

Postpartum Depression

While having children is generally considered to be a happy event, some women undergo periods of clinical depression following the birth of a child. Postpartum depression is a depressive mood disorder that occurs after childbirth. It typically starts within four weeks following the birth of a child. Many women experience some symptoms of depression or blues after having a baby. Symptoms may include sleepless nights, crying spells, anxiety, fatigue, and sadness; generally, these symptoms disappear within a few days or weeks. Postpartum depression (also referred to as *perinatal depression*) is a severe and long-lasting type of clinical depression; it is different than the commonly experienced "baby blues."

Postpartum depression is estimated to affect 10 to 15 percent of new mothers (Duckworth, 2009) and may last up to a year. Typical symptoms include insomnia, depressed mood, tearfulness, changes in appetite, difficulty coping, loss of interest or pleasure, feelings of inadequacy as a parent, suicidal thoughts, and panic attacks. As a result of this disorder, some women have problems maintaining a healthy relationship with their children and the health of their children can be at risk. In severe cases, postpartum depression can lead to suicide. In rare cases, postpartum psychosis develops, involving intrusive harmful thoughts or actions toward the baby.

Various risk factors have been identified for postpartum depression. Many researchers suggest that changes in hormonal levels during and after childbirth trigger postpartum depression. Levels of hormones such as estrogen and progesterone dramatically drop after childbirth. Since the levels of these hormones may rise up to 50 times above the normal levels during pregnancy, some say that this withdrawal of hormones may trigger postpartum depression in some individuals (e.g., Bloch, Daly, & Rubinow, 2003). In addition to estrogen, thyroid hormones change dramatically after pregnancy, which may leave the mother feeling tired, sluggish, and depressed.

A past personal or family history of mood disorder increases a woman's likelihood of developing postpartum depression (American Psychiatric Association, 2000). A new mother might be overwhelmed by emotional factors that come with a newborn (especially a first-born child) or may be sleep-deprived, anxious, or feel she has no control over her life. Lifestyle changes can influence the risk of depression, including dealing with a demanding baby or older sibling, financial stresses, or lack of support from a partner. Researchers (e.g., Gjerdingen & Center, 2005) point out that family and sociocultural factors may play important roles in postpartum depression. For instance, intimate relationships, friendships, and family relationships may all change. Having a baby produces a financial challenge, yet the new mother may stop or significantly decrease her paid work. Women who have experienced stressful life events (e.g., divorce, death in the family, moving, change in employment) within 12 months preceding delivery have an increased risk of depression. No significant links have been found between ethnicity or educational level and risk of postpartum depression (Duckworth, 2009).

Treatments for postpartum depression usually depend on the severity of the symptoms. Self-help support groups may be very effective for sufferers with mild symptoms. Those with more severe symptoms require medical treatment. Most benefit from treatments used for other forms of depression such as cognitive therapy or cognitive-behavioral therapy, interpersonal psychotherapy, and antidepressant medication (e.g., Cuijpers, Brännmark, & van Straten, 2008). Nursing mothers will want to consult with their physicians regarding the safety of specific medications on the developing infant.

See also antidepressant, cognitive therapy and cognitive-behavioral therapy, depression, hormones, interpersonal psychotherapy, major depressive disorder.

Further Reading:

Duckworth, K. (2009, October). *Depression and pregnancy*. Retrieved from http://www.nami.org/Content/NavigationMenu/Mental_Illnesses/Depression/Women_and_Depression/pregnancy.pdf

References:

American Psychiatric Association. (2000). *Diagnostic and statistical manual of mental disorders* (4th ed., text rev.). Washington, DC: Author.

Bloch, M., Daly, R., & Rubinow, D. (2003). Endocrine factors in the etiology of postpartum depression. *Comprehensive Psychiatry, 44*, 234–246.

Cuijpers, P., Brännmark, J., & van Straten, A. (2008). Psychological treatment of postpartum depression: A meta-analysis. *Journal of Clinical Psychology, 64*, 103–118.

Duckworth, K. (2009, October). Depression and pregnancy. Retrieved from http://www.nami.org/Content/NavigationMenu/Mental_Illnesses/Depression/Women_and_Depression/pregnancy.pdf

Gaynes, B. N., Gavin, N., Meltzer-Brody, S., Lohr, K. N., Swinson, T., Gartlehner, G., et al. (2005, February). *Perinatal depression: Prevalence, screening accuracy, and screening outcomes* (Evidence Report/Technology Assessment No. 119, AHRQ Publication No. 05-E006-2). Rockville, MD: Agency for Healthcare Research and Quality.

Gjerdingen, D. K., & Center, B. A. (2005). First-time parents' postpartum changes in employment, childcare, and housework responsibility. *Social Science Research, 34*, 103–116.

- The precise prevalence and incidence of postpartum depression is uncertain. Published estimates range widely: from 5 percent to more than 25 percent of new mothers, depending on the assessment method, the timing of the assessment, and population characteristics. Although many screening instruments have been developed or modified to detect major and minor depression in pregnant and newly delivered women, the evidence on their screening accuracy has yet to be systematically reviewed and assessed (Gaynes et al., 2005).
- Left untreated, postpartum depression can interfere with mother-child bonding and cause family distress. Children of mothers who have untreated post-

partum depression are more likely to have behavioral problems (e.g., sleeping and eating difficulties, temper tantrums, hyperactivity) and delays in language development.

Source: http://www.mayoclinic.com/health/postpartum-depression/DS00546/DSECTION=complications

Posttraumatic Stress Disorder

People's reactions after exposure to traumatic events have been observed since ancient times. In the mid-19th century, names for somatic (physically based) reactions to extreme stress included *soldier's heart, effort syndrome, shell shock,* and *neurocirculatory asthenia.* Psychological explanations of stress reactions included nostalgia, combat fatigue, and traumatic neurosis (Friedman, Keane, & Resick, 2007). In 1896, German psychiatrist Emil Kraepelin used the term *fright neurosis* to describe anxiety symptoms following injury or accidents (Friedman et al., 2007). *Gross stress reaction* was included in the first edition of the *Diagnostic and Statistical Manual of Mental Disorders* (*DSM-I*; American Psychiatric Association, 1952). The *DSM* lists symptoms and criteria of mental health disorders and is used to aid diagnosis in the United States. *Gross stress reaction* was used to describe individuals who experienced symptoms after exposure to extreme stressors such as catastrophes or combat (*DSM-I*). At the height of the Vietnam War, this category was eliminated in the second edition (*DSM-II*; American Psychiatric Association, 1968). John Talbott, a psychiatrist who had served in Vietnam and later became president of the American Psychiatric Association, advocated for this diagnostic category to be put back into the *DSM* as no other *DSM* diagnosis could account for the symptoms he had seen observed in Vietnam (Friedman et al., 2007). During the 1970s, social movements in the United States and elsewhere drew attention to the reactions people exhibited after experiencing interpersonal violence and combat. Mandatory child abuse reporting in the United States, along with rape shield laws and marital rape laws, raised awareness and changed attitudes and treatment approaches. This led to descriptions of child abuse syndrome, rape trauma syndrome, and battered woman syndrome, all of which presented with similar symptoms as those observed in Vietnam veterans and Holocaust survivors. In the next revision of the *DSM*, reactions to all traumatic events were pooled into a single category (Friedman et al., 2007). Posttraumatic stress disorder (PTSD) was included in *DSM-III* (American Psychiatric Association, 1980) and was classified as an anxiety disorder. PTSD criteria have been refined somewhat in subsequent editions of the *DSM*. Current criteria in the *DSM-IV-TR* (American Psychiatric Association, 2000) include the presence of symptoms following exposure to an extreme, traumatic stressor—actual or threatened death or serious injury, or a threat to the physical integrity of self or others—with a response involving intense fear, helplessness, or horror (in children, the response involves disorganized or agitated behavior). Symptoms include persistent reexperiencing of the traumatic event, avoidance of stimuli associated with the traumatic event, and emotional numbing. Symptoms must have been present for at least one month and must cause clinically significant distress or impairment in social or occupational functioning. When symptoms occur and resolve within four weeks following exposure to a trauma and resolve, acute stress disorder is diagnosed. If symptoms persist beyond four weeks, a diagnosis of PTSD may be considered (American Psychiatric Association, 2000).

While many people are exposed to traumatic events, most of them do not develop PTSD. There is a relationship between the severity of the trauma exposure and the onset of PTSD; this is known as a *dose-response relationship*. In the United States, where 50 to 60 percent of adults have been exposed to trauma during their lifetimes, the incidence of PTSD is about 8 percent. In Algeria (a war-torn country) where trauma exposure is 92 percent, PTSD prevalence is about 37 percent (Friedman et al., 2007). The type of trauma and social climate are relevant to rates of PTSD. In the United States, trauma from interpersonal violence (e.g., rape) appears to be much more toxic than accidents. While about 46 percent of female rape victims in the United States develop PTSD, only 9 percent of female accident victims do. In developing countries, natural disasters (with associated loss of resources) may be more likely to result in PTSD (Friedman et al., 2007). More women than men develop PTSD, and women tend to respond better to treatment. It appears that social support may protect individuals exposed to trauma from developing PTSD (Friedman et al., 2007). Individuals who have been exposed to traumatic events may attempt to self-medicate with alcohol or other drugs, leading to substance abuse or dependence.

Treatments utilized for PTSD include cognitive-behavioral therapy (CBT; with and without exposure), cognitive restructuring, eye movement desensitization and reprocessing therapy (EMDR), coping skills training modality (e.g., relaxation, biofeedback), group therapy, family therapy, and medications. The most successful psychotherapeutic treatments for PTSD are CBT approaches, most notably prolonged exposure, and cognitive therapy (Friedman et al., 2007). Exposure therapies encourage trauma survivors to visualize and cope with distressing trauma-related memories. There are still questions about the effectiveness of EMDR, cognitive restructuring, and coping skills training for PTSD (Committee on Treatment of Post-traumatic Stress Disorder [CTPSD], 2008). Medications that have been studied to treat PTSD include mood stabilizers, novel antipsychotics, benzodiazepines (antianxiety medications), antidepressants, and other drugs (e.g., inositol, cycloserine, and naltrexone). Antidepressants used for PTSD include selective serotonin reuptake inhibitors (SSRIs), monoamine oxidase inhibitors, tricyclic antidepressants, and atypical antidepressants. Some medications have been shown to be effective at treating some symptoms of PTSD. However, because much of the research has been conducted or sponsored by pharmaceutical companies and there are questions about the quality of the research, questions remain about the effectiveness of specific drugs in the treatment of PTSD (CTPSD, 2008; Henigsberg, 2006). Some novel approaches to the treatment of PTSD show promise; these include virtual reality therapy and Internet- or e-mail-based therapy (e.g., Henigsberg, 2006; Knaevelsrud & Maercker, 2007).

Freidman et al. (2007) have reviewed criticisms of the PTSD construct. They maintain that PTSD is a legitimate diagnosis as PTSD has a different presentation from other anxiety disorders, depression, or other psychiatric diagnoses. Regarding the validity of traumatic memories, which have been publicized by the media as "false memory syndrome," external verification has confirmed accurate recall and representation of most traumatic events. Other criticisms of the PTSD construct are that it needlessly pathologizes normal reactions to abusive violence and that PTSD is a syndrome bound to European-American cultures. Responses to these criticisms include pointing out the usefulness of PTSD as a diagnostic label to inform treatment decisions and the need for culturally competent treatment of all stress and trauma (Friedman et al., 2007).

See also acute stress disorder, antidepressant, anxiety, anxiolytic, cognitive therapy and cognitive-behavioral therapy, *Diagnostic and Statistical Manual of Mental Disorders*, eye movement desensitization and reprocessing, stress.

Further Readings:

Gateway to posttraumatic stress disorder information: http://www.ptsdinfo.org/

McFall, E. E. (2007). *I can still hear their cries, even in my sleep: A journey into PTSD.* Parker, CO: Outskirts Press.

Tick, E. (2005). *War and the soul: Healing our nation's veterans from post-traumatic stress disorder.* Wheaton, IL: Quest Books.

References:

American Psychiatric Association. (1952). *Diagnostic and statistical manual: Mental disorders.* Washington, DC: Author.

American Psychiatric Association. (1968). *Diagnostic and statistical manual of mental disorders* (2nd ed.). Washington, DC: Author.

American Psychiatric Association. (1980). *Diagnostic and statistical manual of mental disorders* (3rd ed.). Washington, DC: Author.

American Psychiatric Association. (2000). *Diagnostic and statistical manual of mental disorders* (4th ed., text rev.). Washington, DC: Author.

Committee on Treatment of Post-traumatic Stress Disorder, Institute of Medicine. (2008). *Treatment of post-traumatic stress disorder: An assessment of the evidence.* Washington, DC: National Academy Press.

Friedman, M. J., Keane, T. M., & Resick, P. A. (2007). *Handbook of PTSD: Science and practice.* New York: Guilford.

Henigsberg, N. (2006). Pharmacotherapy research in posttraumatic stress disorder. In M. J. Roy (Ed.), *Novel approaches to the diagnosis and treatment of posttraumatic stress disorder* (pp. 101–110). Amsterdam, NL: IOS Press.

Knaevelsrud, C., & Maercker, A. (2007). Internet-based treatment for PTSD reduces distress and facilitates the development of a strong therapeutic alliance: A randomized controlled clinical trial. *BMC Psychiatry,* 7, 1–10.

National Institute of Mental Health. (2009). *The numbers count: Mental disorders in America.* Retrieved from http://www.nimh.nih.gov/health/publications/the-numbers-count-mental-disorders-in-america/index.shtml#PTSD

- Approximately 7.7 million American adults aged 18 and older, or about 3.5 percent of people over 18, have PTSD in any given year.
- PTSD can develop at any age, including childhood; the median age of onset is 23 years.
- About 19 percent of Vietnam veterans experienced PTSD at some point after the war.

- PTSD frequently occurs after violent personal assaults such as rape, mugging, or domestic violence; terrorism; natural or human-caused disasters; and accidents.

Source: National Institute on Mental Health, 2009.

Prefrontal Cortex

The prefrontal cortex (PFC) is situated in the anterior (front) part of the frontal lobe in the brain. The PFC is instrumental in attention and executive function, which includes integrating information from diverse sources, planning, making deliberate decisions, and following through with plans. This includes the ability to reflect on behaviors that occurred in the past and to think about the potential emotional consequences of actions before engaging in behavior. The PFC is also important to *working memory*, which is necessary for the temporary storage and manipulation of information. The PFC plays a part in rational decision making, the ability to engage in socially appropriate behavior, and emotional regulation.

The 1848 accident of Phineas P. Gage, a railroad worker in Vermont, lent some insight into the links between the PFC, emotions, and behavior. Gage survived an explosion that drove a railroad spike through his skull. The injury damaged his frontal lobes, more the left hemisphere than the right, with more damage in the anterior portion than in the back (posterior). There was damage to the ventromedial prefrontal region (middle underside of the frontal lobe), which is critical for normal decision making. While attention, memory, language, and motor functions appeared to remain intact, Gage experienced profound changes in his personality, social functioning, ability to act in his own best interest, and ability to anticipate and plan for the future. Emotionally, he displayed disinhibition (e.g., impulsiveness, using profanity, not following social conventions), emotional lability (unpredictable mood changes), and irritability (Damasio, 1994). Gage's case is illustrative of the impairment associated with his pattern of traumatic brain injury.

In the 1930s, American physiologists John F. Fulton and Carlyle Jacobsen found that creating lesions (wounds) in part of the frontal lobes of chimpanzees (Becky and Lucy) produced behavioral changes. After the surgery, Becky no longer became agitated. However, Lucy (who had previously been docile) became violent (Damasio, 1994). Fulton and Jacobsen presented their findings at the 1935 Second World Congress of Neurology. Portuguese neurologist António Egas Moniz, intrigued by Fulton and Jacobsen's findings, developed a type of brain surgery to treat anxiety, agitation, depression, obsessive-compulsive disorder (OCD), and schizophrenia. In this procedure, known as a prefrontal leucotomy, Moniz severed nerve fibers in the frontal lobes of the brain. The prefrontal lobotomy—a more destructive version of the leucotomy—gained popularity in the 1940s and 1950s to treat patients with depression, anxiety disorders, OCD, schizophrenia, and violent behavior. However, it was found that prefrontal lobotomy caused many side effects, including apathy, decreased attention span, personality change, seizures, infections, and death (Mashour, Walker, &

Martuza, 2005). Prefrontal lobotomy declined after the introduction of the antipsy-chotic medication chlorpromazine (Thorazine) in the 1950s and with the increasing popularity of psychoanalysis. Nevertheless, prefrontal lobotomy gave researchers op-portunities to examine the link between the PFC and emotions.

Modern imaging techniques, such as functional magnetic resonance imaging (fMRI), positron emission tomography (PET) scans, and diffusion tensor imaging (DTI), have contributed significantly to research that explores the workings of the PFC. PFC damage may result in perseveration, which involves repeating the same be-havior over and over. This is seen in conditions such as autism as well as in compulsive disorders such as OCD. Some research has demonstrated that activation of the left PFC is more associated with positive emotions and reward, while activation of the right PFC is associated with negative emotions and punishment (Davidson, Scherer, & Goldsmith, 2002). Left PFC lesions have been associated with crying and depressed behaviors, while right PFC lesions have been associated with laughter, euphoria, or indifference (Hale & Fiorello, 2004). Left hemisphere PFC regions may be implicated in depressive disorders (e.g., major depressive disorder). The orbital prefrontal cortex (a region of the PFC) is thought to be involved in emotional regulation. Damage to this area has been associated with irritability, lability, poor judgment, distractibility, antisocial behavior, and socially inappropriate behavior. The orbital PFC is thought to be underactive in individuals with attention-deficit hyperactivity disorder and overac-tive in people with OCD (Hale & Fiorello, 2004).

See also depression, diffusion tensor imaging, functional magnetic resonance imag-ing, Phineas P. Gage, Egas Moniz, negative emotions, obsessive-compulsive disorder, positive emotions, positron emission tomography, prefrontal lobotomy, psychosur-gery, regulation of emotion, traumatic brain injury.

Further Readings:

Explore the brain and spinal cord (a visual and descriptive Web site that illustrates and explains the di-vided brain, the functional areas within the brain, and brain development): http://faculty.washing ton.edu/chudler/introb.html

LeDoux, J. (1996). *The emotional brain: The mysterious underpinnings of emotional life.* New York: Touchstone.

References:

Damasio, A. (1994). *Descartes' error: Emotion, reason and the human brain.* New York: Putnam.

Davidson, Richard J., Scherer, K. R., & Goldsmith, H. H. (2002). *Handbook of affective sciences.* Cary, NC: Oxford University Press.

Hale, J. B., & Fiorello, C. A. (2004). *School neuropsychology.* New York: Guilford.

Mashour, G. A., Walker, E. E., & Martuza, R. L. (2005). Psychosurgery: Past, present, and future. *Brain Research Reviews, 48,* 409–419.

Prefrontal Lobotomy

Prefrontal lobotomy is a type of neurosurgery that involves destroying tissue in the frontal lobe of the brain. It has been used to treat various psychiatric disorders, in-cluding depression, anxiety disorders, obsessive-compulsive disorder, schizophrenia, and violent behavior. It was popularized in the United States by American neurolo-gist Walter Freeman (1895–1972). Over 40,000 procedures were performed, and it remained in use through the 1970s (Persaud, 2005).

In the 1930s, American physiologists John F. Fulton and Carlyle Jacobsen found that creating lesions (wounds) in part of the frontal lobes of chimpanzees (Becky and Lucy) produced behavioral changes. After the surgery, Becky no longer became agitated. However, Lucy (who had previously been docile) became violent (Weiss, Rauch, & Price, 2006). Fulton and Jacobsen presented their findings at the 1935 Second World Congress of Neurology. Portuguese neurologist and dean of medicine at the University of Lisbon Egas Moniz was intrigued by these findings. Moniz and neurosurgeon Almeida Lima began testing the prefrontal leucotomy on patients with psychoses. In 1936 (after Moniz's initial reports), Americans Walter Freeman and neurosurgeon James Watts started performing the treatment in the United States, which they modified and renamed *prefrontal lobotomy*. Their first 200 cases were deemed successful, although adverse effects such as seizures and apathy were noted. Freeman, enthusiastic about the procedure and seeking ways to make it more efficient, devised a method to avoid drilling through the skull, using a tool similar to an ice pick to break through the orbital bone and sever the nearby prefrontal cortex. Watts broke off relations with Freeman when he learned that Freeman was performing ice-pick lobotomies in his private office, using electroconvulsive therapy (shock treatments) as the only form of anesthesia (Weiss et al., 2006). However, the prefrontal lobotomy became increasingly popular and was often performed by practitioners who were neither surgeons nor physicians (Mashour, Walker, & Martuza, 2005).

Rosemary Kennedy, eldest sister of U.S. President John F. Kennedy, had a mild intellectual disability and learning disabilities. She started exhibiting extreme mood swings and outbursts around the age of 23. Her father, Joseph Kennedy Sr., consulted with Freeman and Watts in 1941. Watts diagnosed her with "agitated depression" (although others have said she had schizophrenia). Freeman performed a frontal lobotomy, which affected Rosemary's cognitive abilities and left her unable to speak more than a few words; she was unable to care for herself or live independently (El-Hai, 2007). She was cared for in a private institution in Wisconsin until her death in 2005, at the age of 86 (Weil, 2005). A great deal of controversy surrounded Freeman's lobotomies of children. His first child patient was a nine-year-old whose brutal tantrums and symptoms of schizophrenia did not abate after his lobotomy in 1939. In 1943, Freeman and Watts lobotomized a four-year-old boy. Lobotomy on a 12-year-old boy in 1945 resulted in the boy's death the night after the operation (El-Hai, 2007). Lobotomy was used as an attempt to eliminate criminal behavior in some individuals. For example, 37-year-old habitual burglar Millard Wright was facing a prison sentence in Pennsylvania. In jail, he refused to eat and threatened to take his life, so he was moved to a state hospital for observation. After a year, he was pronounced recovered and sent back to court to face charges. His attorney requested a postponement so that Wright could undergo a prefrontal lobotomy to treat his "personality disorders." The judge consented to the postponement. However, when Wright returned to court two months later, the original judge had died, and the new judge convicted Wright of burglary and sentenced him to 2 to 12 years in prison. Wright committed suicide (El-Hai, 2007). Popular views of lobotomies performed in state hospitals were reinforced by the film based on Ken Kesey's 1962 book *One Flew Over the Cuckoo's Nest*.

In the early part of the 20th century, somatic (biological) therapies for mental illness included convulsive therapy, insulin shock therapy, hydrotherapy (water therapy), and psychosurgery. The prefrontal lobotomy was embraced in part because of overcrowded asylums, the costs and burden of mental illness on society, media reports of positive outcomes from prefrontal lobotomy, and a lack of effective alternative treatments. The 1949 Nobel Prize in Physiology or Medicine, awarded to Egas Moniz for his work in psychosurgery, lent validation to the procedure (Mashour et al., 2005). The lobotomy started to fall out of favor after reports of lobotomies being performed in unsterile conditions by unqualified practitioners. Scientific and medical reports questioned the efficacy of the lobotomy and brought to light serious side effects, including seizures, infections, apathy, decreased attention span, personality change, and death (Mashour et al., 2005). Use of the lobotomy declined after the introduction of the antipsychotic medication chlorpromazine (Thorazine) in the 1950s and with the increasing popularity of psychoanalysis. Controversy about psychosurgery was sparked again in the 1970s with the publication of Mark and Ervin's *Violence and the Brain*, which suggested that neurosurgical procedures could treat aberrant limbic system function responsible for much of the violent behavior afflicting society. The landmark case *Kaimowitz vs. Department of Mental Health* (1973), in which a prisoner was offered psychosurgery to temper his aggressive behavior, spurred ethical debate about government use of neurosurgery as a tool of suppression and control. This resulted in guidelines about ethical use and regulation of psychosurgery. Prefrontal lobotomy is illegal in some countries and states (Mashour et al., 2005).

Currently psychosurgery utilizes imaging techniques—such as magnetic resonance imaging (MRI) and computed tomography (CT) scans—to create more accurate, targeted lesions (wounds) that destroy less brain tissue, resulting in fewer side effects. Modern psychosurgery may be used to treat psychiatric disorders such as severe, chronic treatment-resistant obsessive-compulsive disorder or severe mood disorders such as major depressive disorder or bipolar disorder. It is usually a treatment of last resort. Alternatives to psychosurgery include medication, behavior therapy, psychotherapy, and electroconvulsive therapy. Transcranial magnetic stimulation and vagal nerve stimulation are being explored as nonsurgical alternative treatments for depression. Deep brain stimulation—implanting a stimulating probe at targeted brain sites—is being explored as a means to increase efficacy and reduce adverse outcomes of psychosurgery.

See also bipolar disorder, electroconvulsive therapy, functional magnetic resonance imaging, major depressive disorder, Egas Moniz, mood disorder, obsessive-compulsive disorder, prefrontal cortex, psychosurgery, schizophrenia.

Further Readings:
Dully, H., & Fleming, C. (2007). *My lobotomy.* New York: Crown.
El-Hai, J. (2007). *The lobotomist: A maverick medical genius and his tragic quest to rid the world of mental illness.* Hoboken, NJ: John Wiley.
Kesey, K. (1962). *One flew over the cuckoo's nest.* New York: Viking.
Mark, V. H., & Ervin, F. R. (1970). *Violence and the brain.* New York: Harper and Row.

References:
Berenda, C. W. (1965). *World visions and the image of man: Cosmologies as reflections of man.* New York: Vantage Press.
El-Hai, J. (2007). *The lobotomist: A maverick medical genius and his tragic quest to rid the world of mental illness.* Hoboken, NJ: John Wiley.
Freeman, D. (1976, November 26). Deep down in his heart Steve Allen is silly. *Danville (VA) Bee*, p. 19.
Kesey, K. (1962). *One flew over the cuckoo's nest.* New York: Viking.

Mashour, G. A., Walker, E. E., & Martuza, R. L. (2005). Psychosurgery: Past, present, and future. *Brain Research Reviews, 48*, 409–419.

Persaud, R. (2005). The lobotomist: A maverick medical genius and his tragic quest to rid the world of mental illness. *British Medical Journal, 330*, 1275.

Weil, M. (2005, January 8). Rosemary Kennedy, 86; President's disabled sister. *The Washington Post*. Retrieved from http://www.washingtonpost.com/wp-dyn/articles/A58134–2005Jan8.html

Weiss, A. P., Rauch, S. L., & Price, B. H. (2006). Neurosurgical intervention for psychiatric illness. In B. L. Miller & J. L. Cummings (Eds.), *Human frontal lobes: Functions and disorders* (2nd ed., pp. 505–517). New York: Guilford.

- Notorious American lobotomist Walter Freeman used electroconvulsive therapy as the sole form of anesthesia during prefrontal lobotomies (Weiss, Rauch, & Price, 2006).
- The prefrontal lobotomy was very much a part of popular culture, as illustrated by the quip, "I'd rather have a bottle in front of me than a prefrontal lobotomy." This has been attributed to various sources, including Carlton W. Berenda (1965, p. 196) and an interview with comedian Steve Allen (Freeman, 1976).

Prejudice

In 1954, American psychologist Gordon Allport published his classic book on prejudice, *The Nature of Prejudice*. He described ethnic prejudice as an antipathy toward the other, based on a faulty and rigid stereotype of the other. His definition emphasized both emotional and cognitive (thinking) aspects, as do modern prejudice scholars. Allport said that there can be many emotions involved in prejudice: anger, aggression, hate, resentment, jealousy, and others.

The magnitude of prejudice and probability of acting on prejudice are related to a number of social and personal factors. A primary factor is threat, which may be either personal or societal. Stephan and Stephan (1996) identified three types of threat: realistic threat, symbolic threat, and intergroup anxiety. Realistic threat occurs when the out-group (group that is the object of prejudice) is perceived to threaten the in-group (one's own group) financially or physically. For instance, the out-group may be perceived as taking employment opportunities away from the in-group. Symbolic threat is when the out-group is perceived as a challenge to the in-group's values and view of the world. Intergroup anxiety is the discomfort and stress that occurs when in-group and out-group members interact directly.

Both realistic and symbolic threat, and general threat in society (e.g., war or a declining economy), may increase authoritarianism—a favoring of obedience to authority and devaluing of individual freedom. Authoritarian individuals are rigid, strict, and punitive and prone to prejudice. Prosperity is relatively protective against authoritarianism, and therefore against hostility and prejudice, because realistic and general societal threats do not exist. Symbolic threat can lead to prejudice even when realistic and general societal threats do not exist. According to theory (e.g., Greenberg,

Solomon, & Pyszczynski, 1997), one's worldview typically acts as a barrier against one's awareness of fear of death. When the worldview is threatened by the differing values of an out-group, anxiety (representing fear of death) increases, and hostility and prejudice may follow.

Both the cognitive and emotional aspects of prejudice contribute to the feelings of hostility and related hostile actions that may occur. If people believe that an out-group is gaining in power or status relative to the in-group (a cognitive aspect), to be prejudiced, they must also experience emotion (e.g., anger; Pettigrew, 1999). In a large study, Pettigrew (1997) reported results that suggest a way to combat prejudice. In his study, Pettigrew found that having a friend or friends from another culture leads to decreased prejudice, and he showed that it is often the case that the intergroup friendship occurs first, followed by reduced prejudice, rather than the other way around.

See also aggression, attitude, culture, ethnocentrism, hate, hate crimes.

Further Readings:

Allport, G. W. (1954). *The nature of prejudice.* Reading, MA: Addison-Wesley.

Dovidio, J. F., Glick, P., & Rudman, L. (2005). *On the nature of prejudice: Fifty years after Allport.* Malden, MA: Blackwell.

Pettigrew, T. F. (1999). Prejudice. In D. Levinson, J. J. Ponzetti, & P. F. Jorgensen (Eds.), *Encyclopedia of human emotions* (2nd ed., pp. 532–536). New York: Macmillan Reference USA.

Wills, G. (2006). *Lincoln at Gettysburg: The words that remade America.* New York: Simon and Schuster.

References:

Allport, G. W. (1954). *The nature of prejudice.* Reading, MA: Addison-Wesley.

Greenberg, J., Solomon, S., & Pyszczynski, T. (1997). Terror management theory of self-esteem and cultural worldviews: Empirical assessments and conceptual refinements. In M. P. Zanna (Ed.), *Advances in experimental social psychology* (Vol. 29, pp. 61–139), San Diego, CA: Academic Press.

Pettigrew, T. F. (1997). Generalized intergroup contact effects on prejudice. *Personality and Social Psychology Bulletin, 23*, 173–185.

Pettigrew, T. F. (1999). Prejudice. In D. Levinson, J. J. Ponzetti, & P. F. Jorgensen (Eds.), *Encyclopedia of human emotions* (2nd ed., pp. 532–536). New York: Macmillan Reference USA.

Stephan, W. G., & Stephan, C. W. (1996). Predicting prejudice. *International Journal of Intercultural Relations, 20*, 409–426.

Pride

In their textbook on emotion, psychologists James Kalat and Michelle Shiota (2007) define pride as "the emotion felt when someone takes credit for causing a positive outcome that supports a positive aspect of his or her self-concept" (p. 239). As is clear from this description, pride is a positive emotion. It is different from the other positive emotions because (1) the individual experiencing pride feels that he is responsible for the favorable event or outcome and (2) the favorable event supports the person's positive view of himself.

If an individual wins a contest, he would not experience pride if the winner were chosen by a random drawing of names. If the contest were won based on merit, however, the individual would be much more likely to feel proud. The amount of pride would be related to how much the individual values what the contest is about. A struggling artist who puts his heart, soul, blood, and tears into his work would feel very proud about winning a highly competitive art contest. He would feel less proud about taking first place in an athletic contest at a local fair if athletic performance is not central to his sense of self.

A few emotion researchers, including Jessica Tracy and Richard Robins (2004, 2008), have identified the facial and bodily expression characteristic of pride. When proud, an individual tilts the head back slightly, stands or sits tall and erect, with the arms placed on the hips or raised above the head, and smiles slightly. Tracy and Robins (2008) have studied the expression of pride in three different cultures: the United States, Italy, and the Burkina Faso of West Africa, a tribe of people who, due to their isolation, are unlikely to have learned the expression of pride through exposure to other cultures. Their results suggested that the pride expression is highly similar across these cultures and recognizable between cultures. Tracy and Robins use this evidence and other evidence to argue that pride (in addition to other emotions) is a universal emotion.

Although pride may exist universally, there are some cultural differences associated with aspects of pride such as expression of pride or events that are sources (elicitors) of pride. Since pride has been studied most in the United States, which is an individualistic culture, there is more understanding of pride from this perspective. Most world cultures are more communal (group oriented) than the United States, and pride may manifest somewhat differently in these cultures. For instance, in one study of cross-cultural comparisons, Stipek (1998) asked Chinese and American research participants how proud they would be if they were accepted to attend an elite university and how proud they would feel if their child was accepted into the same university. The American participants projected more pride if they themselves were accepted, whereas the Chinese predicted more pride if their children were accepted. Thus, although it appears that pride is considerably similar across cultures, differences between cultures do exist.

See also basic emotions, body language, culture, embarrassment, guilt, positive emotions, shame, universal signals.

References:
Kalat, J. W., & Shiota, M. N. (2007). *Emotion.* Belmont, CA: Thomson Wadsworth.
Stipek, D. (1998). Differences between Americans and Chinese in the circumstances evoking pride, shame, and guilt. *Journal of Cross-cultural Psychology, 29,* 616–629.
Tracy, J. L., & Robins, R. W. (2004). Show your pride: Evidence for a discrete emotion expression. *Psychological Science, 15,* 194–197.
Tracy, J. L., & Robins, R. W. (2008). The non-verbal expression of pride: Evidence for cross-cultural recognition. *Journal of Personality and Social Psychology, 94,* 516–530.

- The expression "pride goeth before a fall" is paraphrased from Proverbs 16:18–19 (King James version): "Pride goeth before destruction, and an haughty spirit before a fall. Better it is to be of an humble spirit with the lowly, than to divide the spoil with the proud." This expression is a warning to not overstep one's bounds or offend the wrong people, as it might lead to one's downfall.

- The Greek goddess Nemesis exacted retribution on people who thought themselves too god-like. The Greek legend of Icarus (son of Daedalus) is often used as a parable of pridefulness. Icarus fashioned wings out of feathers and wax but flew too close to the sun, which melted the wax; he crashed into Icarian Sea and died.

Primal Therapy

In the 1960s, the psychoanalytic model of therapy (based on Sigmund Freud's theories) started to lose popularity as patients demanded better and quicker results. Arthur Janov developed primal therapy—a process involving reexperiencing repressed psychological trauma—as a means to effect lasting therapeutic change. Primal therapy has been used to treat various conditions, including depression, anxiety, bipolar disorder, substance abuse, and eating disorders.

Arthur Janov was born in 1924. His father drove a meat truck. His mother had a nervous breakdown when he was five years old, which may have influenced his decision to go into psychology. He earned a PhD in psychology from Claremont Graduate School and worked as a conventional psychotherapist for 17 years (Miller & Dodd, 1998). He developed the basis of primal therapy in the late 1960s. In 1968, Arthur Janov and his first wife, Vivian, established the Primal Institute in Los Angeles, California. He has since dissociated himself from the institute, which is still run by Vivian Janov. Arthur Janov now runs the Primal Center in Venice, California, with his current wife, France (a former Primal Institute patient). In 1970, Arthur Janov published *The Primal Scream*, which sold over two million copies.

While some have referred to primal therapy as *scream therapy*, Janov says that this is a misnomer. Screaming is a by-product of pain from early trauma; it is the experiencing of the pain that is essential to primal therapy (not the screaming itself). Primal therapy does not claim to teach coping strategies; its main purpose is to teach people to feel their pain. Primal therapy depends on affective (emotional) release while in an altered state of consciousness to bring about significant emotional change quickly and dramatically (Yassky, 1979). It is designed to be a powerful means to access repressed material. In repression, the conscious mind does not integrate painful memories but stores the experience in the unconscious. Repressed material could include memories and feelings about physical trauma, physical or sexual abuse, or neglect. Deeply felt repressed childhood pain is known as *primal pain*. Primal therapy is a *cathartic* approach; that is, it depends on a dramatic emotional release. Catharsis may also be experienced in other types of therapy (e.g., traditional psychodynamic psychotherapy).

Janov's theories about primal pain are based in part on studies of pain inhibition (Eisner, 2000). Janov proposes that emotional pain is blocked in a similar manner as physical pain. He also claims that reliving a painful event will result in physical changes such as lowering blood pressure. Janov links many adult emotional disorders to birth trauma. For example, he claims that bipolar disorder results from the birth struggle, and migraine headaches are a result of oxygen deprivation during birth. He claims that reliving birth trauma could cause forceps marks to show on the head of a patient (Eisner, 2000). Janov claims that because all neurosis has its origins in trauma, diagnosis and gaining insight are irrelevant to the treatment and healing process. The primal therapist's role is to get to the early trauma.

The three-week intensive required at the beginning of primal therapy can be very expensive. In addition to the cost ($6,000; Miller & Dodd, 1998), clients are instructed to take a leave of absence from work or school for three weeks. During that time, the client stays alone in a hotel room and is told to abstain from all drugs, alcohol, smoking, sex, TV, radio, and phone calls. The client meets with the therapist daily for long sessions (sometimes many hours) during the three-week intensive. Janov has claimed that the three-week intensive followed by six months of group therapy would result in a cure. However, many therapists and patients were still working together after six or seven years, suggesting that treatment is much more extensive than previously thought (Yassky, 1979). The Primal Center Web site states that "although the length of the therapy varies widely, our recommendation is that all applicants should be prepared to stay an average of one year at Dr Janov's Primal Center. . . . One must have the financial means that will allow for continuing therapy, particularly more individual sessions during the year."

Primal therapy, a dramatic, bold, and different approach in the early 1970s, was initially popular. It was hailed as a universal cure for neurosis with virtually unlimited success. Janov provides case studies and testimonials by celebrities who have undergone primal therapy, such as John Lennon of the Beatles and actor James Earl Jones, to back up his claims that primal therapy can reduce or eliminate many physical and psychological ailments. However, primal therapy has been criticized by mainstream psychologists as lacking a scientific basis, there is little research demonstrating effectiveness (other than anecdotal evidence from case studies), and it has the potential to cause harm. In *The New Primal Scream: Primal Therapy 20 Years On* (Janov, 1991), Janov claims his theories have been validated by scientific studies in the fields of immunology, cancer, and brain science. Unfortunately, references that can be validated are conspicuously lacking in the book; the studies that can be found do not support his claims (Eisner, 2000).

Critics claim that because primal therapy is unimodal (e.g., it utilizes only one method), it has limited success. As there is little or no focus on cognitive approaches, certain issues are not worked through. Current real-life problems and circumstances are ignored. This, combined with a lack of diagnosis, may result in inappropriate treatment for some individuals. People not only might undertake a treatment that is possibly ineffective (or harmful) but may neglect to initiate treatments that have been shown to be effective for their condition (e.g., medication or traditional psychotherapy). Primal therapy may be inappropriate for people with certain diagnoses (e.g., schizophrenia, personality disorders). In primal therapy, there is an inherent power differential: the therapist directs the therapy process with a patient who has been regressed to an infantile state that leaves the client vulnerable and powerless. This creates great potential for abuse (Eisner, 2000). Many practitioners claim to be doing primal therapy but have not been properly trained. Janov himself warns of the dangers and abuses perpetrated by unqualified, untrained practitioners.

See also altered states of consciousness, birth trauma, catharsis, psychodynamic psychotherapy and psychoanalysis, the unconscious mind.

Further Readings:
Janov, A. (1970). *The primal scream.* New York: Putnam.
Primal Center, Venice, California, Web site: http://www.primaltherapy.com/
Rossman, M. (1979). The I-scream man cometh. In M. Rossman (Ed.), *New age blues: On the politics of consciousness* (pp. 26–29). New York: Dutton.

References:
Eisner, D. A. (2000). *Death of psychotherapy: From Freud to alien abductions.* Westport, CT: Greenwood.
Janov, A. (1970). *The primal scream.* New York: Putnam.
Janov, A. (1991). *The new primal scream: Primal therapy 20 years on.* Boston: Little, Brown.
Miller, S., & Dodd, J. (1998, November 23). Scream on. *People, 50*(19), 97.
Yassky, A. D. (1979). Critique on primal therapy. *American Journal of Psychotherapy, 33,* 119–127.

Primary Emotions

Many philosophers, sociologists, and psychologists have attempted to define and classify emotions. Charles Darwin suggested that there are several *basic emotions:* they are innate, can be distinguished from each other, and are characterized by similar facial expressions across different cultures. In 1896, Darwin suggested that emotional expressions are universal responses, tied evolutionarily to humans by the facial expressions of animals. In addition to basic or universal emotions, emotions have been described as primary and secondary. The terms *primary emotions* and *basic emotions* are sometimes used interchangeably. Some emotion researchers define primary emotions as belonging to all animals (including humans), while secondary emotions are those experienced only by humans (Rodríguez-Torres et al., 2005). Other researchers define secondary emotions as blends of primary emotions, combinations of primary and nonprimary emotions, or any emotion that is not considered primary. Some theories describe primary emotions as simple, basic, or universal and secondary emotions as complex.

Biological (or deterministic) theories, such as those of Darwin and Paul Ekman, see emotions as involuntary, hardwired, patterned responses. Other types of emotions theories—such as social interactionism and social constructionism—take the position that emotions may be voluntary (Smith & Schneider, 2009). American sociologist Theodore David Kemper's social interactionist theory suggests that emotions help maintain and alter social relationships. Social constructionist theories suggest that human emotions result from real, anticipated, imagined, or recalled outcomes of social relationships (Smith & Schneider, 2009). Portuguese neurologist Antonio Damasio describes primary emotions as those that are hardwired and affect brain circuitry in the limbic system. Secondary emotions occur when we experience feelings and form systematic connections between primary emotions and categories of situations that evoke them. Secondary emotions involve functions in the prefrontal and somatosensory cortexes of the brain, in addition to the limbic system (Damasio, 1994).

The number of primary and secondary emotions vary according to the theory. L. Alan Sroufe's 1979 theory lists only three primary emotions—pleasure, fear, and anger—while Carroll E. Izard's 1994 theory purports that there are 11: enjoyment, fear, anger, contempt, surprise, disgust, shame, shyness, distress, guilt, and interest (Smith & Schneider, 2009). Michael Lewis's human development theory (2000) lists six primary emotions, natural, internal mental processes that emerge in infants by six months of age: happiness, sadness, disgust, anger, fear, and surprise. Other (nonprimary) emotions—such as embarrassment, envy, pride, shame, and guilt—appear later in a child's development. Kemper's social interactionist theory proposes that there are four primary emotions—fear, anger, depression, and satisfaction—that are physiologically based, evolutionarily important, universal across cultures, and linked to important outcomes of social relations. Secondary emotions—acquired through social interactions—include guilt, shame, pride, gratitude, love, nostalgia, and ennui (Kemper, 1987).

In 1971, American psychologist Paul Ekman pursued the idea of primary emotions by looking at the universality of facial expressions across cultures (Smith & Schneider, 2009). Ekman proposed six primary emotions with universal facial expressions: surprise, happiness, anger, fear, disgust, and sadness. Ekman made a distinction between universal emotional expressions (especially facial expressions) common to all cultures and other bodily movements (i.e., emblems and illustrators) that vary among cultures. *Emblems* are body movements that have specific meanings such as nodding the head side to side to indicate no or nodding up and down to indicate yes. *Illustrators* punctuate speech, fill in when searching for words, or help explain what is being said (LeDoux, 1996).

Robert Plutchik's 1962 emotions theory utilizes a wheel or palette approach, whereby eight primary emotions (acceptance, surprise, fear, sorrow, disgust, expectancy, anger, and joy) are arranged on a circle. Primary emotions combine in dyads to make first-order, second-order, or third-order emotions. Two adjacent primary emotions combine to form first-order dyads (e.g., joy + acceptance = love). Emotions that are separated by one other emotion on the wheel (e.g., joy and fear) form second-order dyads (e.g., joy + fear = guilt; LeDoux, 1996).

Emotions researchers have looked at the commonalities between emotions and emotional expressions among different cultures and languages. While this has generated much controversy about what constitutes primary (and secondary) emotions, there is agreement among many cross-cultural researchers that there are four universal primary emotions: happiness, fear, anger, and sadness (Smith & Schneider, 2009).

See also basic emotions, culture, Charles Darwin, Paul Ekman, facial expression, human development, limbic system, prefrontal cortex, universal signals.

Further Reading:
Ekman, P. (2007). *Emotions revealed: Recognizing faces and feelings to improve communication and emotional life* (2nd ed.). New York: Holt Paperbacks.

References:
Damasio, A. (1994). *Descartes' error: Emotion, reason and the human brain*. New York: Putnam.
Kemper, T.D. (1987). How many emotions are there? Wedding the social and autonomic components. *American Journal of Sociology, 93*, 263–289.
LeDoux, J. (1996). *The emotional brain: The mysterious underpinnings of emotional life*. New York: Touchstone.
Lewis, M. (2000). The emergence of human emotions. In M. Lewis & J.M. Haviland-Jones (Eds.), *Handbook of emotions* (2nd ed., pp. 265–280). New York: Guilford.
Rodríguez-Torres, R., Leyens, J.P., Rodríguez Pérez, A., Betancor Rodríguez, V., Quiles del Castillo, M.N., Demoulin, S., et al. (2005). The lay distinction between primary and secondary emotions: A spontaneous categorization? *International Journal of Psychology, 40*, 100–107.

Smith, H., & Schneider, A. (2009). Critiquing models of emotions. *Sociological Methods & Research, 37*, 560–589.

Primates

Primates comprise several human and nonhuman mammals, including lemurs, lorsids, tarsiers, galagos, monkeys, and great apes (chimps, gorillas, orangutans, and humans). Charles Darwin was one of the first scientists to systematically study emotions in animals. Darwin published his ideas about similarities between human and nonhuman emotions in his 1872 book *The Expression of the Emotions in Man and Animals*. Some people consider the idea of animal emotions to be anthropomorphizing— ascribing human attributes (e.g., emotions, motives) to nonhumans. Some emotional expressions that may look similar in humans and nonhumans may actually reflect different emotions. For example, in a human, an open-mouthed, bared-teeth display looks like a smile; in a chimpanzee, it is a gesture of submission. Proponents of the idea that nonhuman animals have emotions point out that emotions are an adaptive way to meet basic challenges (e.g., finding food, finding mates, defending against aggression)— both for human and nonhuman animals. One can get information about animal emotions by observing animals' body posture, eyes, facial expressions, sounds, and social interactions (Hess & Thibault, 2009).

A study that compared emotions between human infants and several nonhuman primates (adult chimpanzees, gorillas, orangutans, several species of monkeys, and lemurs) found that the primate species most closely related to humans exhibited the most similar emotional reactions elicited by tastes. For example, the emotional reactions of great apes (chimpanzees, gorillas, orangutans) were more similar to those of human infants than the reactions of monkeys. Sweet flavors tended to elicit positive emotional reactions, while sour or bitter tastes tended to elicit negative reactions. The valence (positive or negative) and intensity of emotional reactions were evaluated by observing facial expressions (Steiner, Glaser, Hawilo, & Berridge, 2001).

Nonhuman primates have been observed to exhibit empathy, a sense of fairness, and compassion. For example, after one chimpanzee has been attacked by another, a bystander (another chimpanzee) will embrace the victim. Chimpanzees exhibit reciprocity and a sense of fair play. Chimpanzees will be more likely to share food with chimpanzees who have previously groomed them (de Waal, 2006). Nonhuman primates exhibit similar responses to situations that produce fear and anxiety in humans (Barros & Tomaz, 2002). Similar outcomes of early social deprivation or maternal neglect have been found for humans and other primates (e.g., monkeys). Social deprivation, neglect, or abuse early in life may result in altered response to stress, changes in immune function, repetitive behaviors (as in obsessive-compulsive disorder), aggression, addictive behaviors, inappropriate sexual or parenting behaviors, and depression (Gilmer & McKinney, 2003).

Similar brain regions appear to be involved in the processing of some emotions among human and nonhuman primates. For example, in the brain's limbic system, damage to the amygdala or orbitofrontal cortex (part of the prefrontal cortex) leaves monkeys unable to produce appropriate emotional responses to communicate and interact socially with other monkeys. Likewise, in humans, damage to the amygdala or orbitofrontal cortex interferes with the ability to correctly interpret others' emotional facial expressions and can cause personality changes and inappropriate social inter-actions (Barbas, 2000). When humans, chimpanzees, and rhesus monkeys produce emotional facial expressions, the left side of the face is involved more than the right. Among other nonhuman primates, in marmoset monkeys, the left side of the face is more involved in silent fear expressions and fear vocalizations, but the right side is more involved in producing calls for social contact (Fernández-Carriba, Loeches, Morcillo, & Hopkins, 2002).

See also animals, anthropomorphism, body language, Charles Darwin, empathy, facial expression, limbic system.

Further Reading:
Oatley, K., Keltner, D., & Jenkins, J. M. (2006). *Understanding emotions.* Malden, MA: Blackwell.

References:
Barbas, H. (2000). Connections underlying the synthesis of cognition, memory, and emotion in primate prefrontal cortices. *Brain Research Bulletin, 52,* 319–330.
Barros, M., & Tomaz, C. (2002). Non-human primate models for investigating fear and anxiety. *Neuroscience and Biobehavioral Reviews, 26,* 187–201.
Darwin, C. (1872). *The expression of the emotions in man and animals.* London: John Murray. Available from http://darwin-online.org.uk/pdf/1872_Expression_F1142.pdf
de Waal, F. (2006). The animal roots of human morality. *New Scientist, 192*(2573), 60–61.
Fernández-Carriba, S., Loeches, A., Morcillo, A., & Hopkins, W. D. (2002). Functional asymmetry of emotions in primates: New findings in chimpanzees. *Brain Research Bulletin, 57,* 561–564.
Gilmer, W. S., & McKinney, W. T. (2003). Early experience and depressive disorders: Human and non-human primate studies. *Journal of Affective Disorders, 75*(2), 97–113.
Hess, U., & Thibault, P. (2009). Darwin and emotion expression. *American Psychologist, 64,* 120–128.
Steiner, J. E., Glaser, D., Hawilo, M. E., & Berridge, K. C. (2001). Comparative expression of hedonic impact: Affective reactions to taste by human infants and other primates. *Neuroscience and Biobehavioral Reviews, 25,* 53–74.

Progressive Muscle Relaxation

Progressive muscle relaxation involves tensing and relaxing muscles, one at a time or in muscle groups, to induce a state of relaxation. Another objective of the technique is for the participant to learn to feel the difference between muscle tension and muscle relaxation; often people are unaware that they may be holding tension in particular muscles.

The technique was developed by American physician Edmund Jacobson, who published his book *Progressive Relaxation* in 1929. As Jacobson described, stress and anxiety are associated with muscle tension. The physical tension, in cyclical fashion, produces further stress and anxiety. This cycle can be broken by deep muscle relaxation.

To practice progressive muscle relaxation, one may sit in a chair or lie down. Individuals are instructed to tense each muscle group for several seconds, then relax the same muscles for 20 to 30 seconds. The procedure starts with the extremities (usually the hands and arms first), then moves to the interior of the body. Davis, Eshelman, and McKay (2008) provide precise instructions. They also describe a shorthand procedure that can be utilized for quick relaxation (it generally works best with experience and practice) and some cautions and general tips about the procedure.

Regular practice of progressive muscle relaxation is helpful for treating many psychological and physical conditions, including depression (Pawlow, O'Neil, & Malcolm, 2003), anxiety (Cheung, Molassiotis, & Chang, 2003), alcoholism (Greeff & Conradie, 1998), headaches (Devineni & Blanchard, 2005), and high blood pressure (Schneider et al., 2005). See Greenberg (2008) for a more comprehensive review of the benefits of progressive muscle relaxation and the conditions that are effectively treated by this technique.

See also autogenic training, deep breathing, meditation, stress.

Further Readings:

Davis, M., Eshelman, E. R., & McKay, M. (2008). *The relaxation and stress reduction workbook* (6th ed.). Oakland, CA: New Harbinger.

McKay, M., & Fanning, P. (2008). *Progressive relaxation and breathing* [Audio CD]. Oakland, CA: New Harbinger.

References:

Cheung, Y. L., Molassiotis, A., & Chang, A. M. (2003). The effect of progressive muscle relaxation training on anxiety and quality of life after stoma surgery in colorectal cancer patients. *Psychooncology, 12,* 254–266.

Davis, M., Eshelman, E. R., & McKay, M. (2008). *The relaxation and stress reduction workbook* (6th ed.). Oakland, CA: New Harbinger.

Devineni, T., & Blanchard, E. B. (2005). A randomized controlled trial of an Internet-based treatment for chronic headache. *Behaviour Research and Therapy, 43,* 277–292.

Gessel, A. H. (1989). Edmund Jacobson, M.D., Ph.D.: The founder of scientific relaxation. *International Journal of Psychosomatics, 36,* 5–14.

Greeff, A. P., & Conradie, W. S. (1998). Use of progressive relaxation training for chronic alcoholics with insomnia. *Psychological Reports, 82,* 407–412.

Greenberg, J. S. (2008). *Comprehensive stress management.* San Francisco: McGraw-Hill.

Jacobson, E. (1974). *Progressive relaxation.* Chicago: University of Chicago Press. (Original work published 1929)

Pawlow, L. A., O'Neil, P. M., & Malcolm, R. J. (2003). Night eating syndrome: Effects of brief relaxation training on stress, mood, hunger, and eating patterns. *International Journal of Obesity and Related Metabolic Disorders, 27,* 970–978.

Schneider, R. H., Alexander, C. N., Staggers, F., Orme-Johnson, D. W., Rainforth, M., Salerno, J. W., et al. (2005). A randomized controlled trial of stress reduction in African Americans treated for hypertension for over one year. *American Journal of Hypertension, 18,* 88–98.

Edmund Jacobson, originator of progressive relaxation techniques, dates his interest in nervous excitability to the age of 10, when a serious hotel fire broke out in Chicago. He observed people's frightened behavior and recalled being curious about the way people showed their fear. He decided that when he was old enough to go to college, he would study the treatment of nervous excitability (Gessel, 1989).

Projective Tests

A projective test is a type of personality test that utilizes "ambiguous," unstructured stimuli or tasks such as inkblots, pictures of people and scenes, incomplete sentences, and requests for drawings. During the test, the assessor (person administering the test) presents stimuli to the assessee (person taking the test) and requests an open-ended response to each stimulus. For instance, the assessor may present inkblots, one at a time, to the assessee, with the instructions, "Tell me what you see" (in each ink-blot). When the test is complete, the assessor scores the results, usually according to predetermined scoring guidelines. In the fields of psychiatry and psychology, these tests may be used to measure general personality traits, needs, motives, or unconscious characteristics, to aid in diagnosis, or for other purposes.

The other main form of personality test is an objective test, also called a *personality questionnaire* or *personality inventory*. The objective tests use structured stimuli, such as sentences or short phrases, to which the assessees will respond with structured re-sponses, for instance, true and false or a five-point rating on each test item. Scoring these tests is typically more straightforward than scoring projective tests; assessees receive scores on all scales on the test (i.e., separate scores indicating degrees of de-pression, paranoia, schizophrenia, and any other personality characteristics that the test measures). For many objective tests, these scale scores are the only possible scores produced by the test.

Projective techniques have existed in psychology since at least the late 1800s. It was Swiss psychiatrist and psychoanalyst Hermann Rorschach's inkblot test, the Ror-schach Psychodiagnostic Technique, that ushered in a new tradition of projective test-ing in psychology and psychiatry. Rorschach published his test and an accompanying manuscript in 1921, and it was exported to the United States several years later. A rapid succession of projective techniques were published in the decades that fol-lowed by both American and European authors. Two famous projective techniques that came after Rorschach's were Morgan and Murray's Thematic Apperception Test in 1938 and Machover's Draw-A-Person test in 1949. Most projective techniques are based in psychoanalytic theory, which emphasizes the unconscious mind.

Given the diversity of projective tests, some researchers have attempted to identify the qualities that these tests have in common. Rotter (1954) published a well-known book in which he describes typical characteristics of projective techniques:

- Assessees impose their own structure onto ambiguous stimuli. In the practice of doing this, it is assumed that they reveal aspects of themselves (personality char-acteristics, needs, conflicts, etc.).
- Test stimuli (items) are unstructured and ambiguous. They include stimuli such as inkblots, pictures of people or scenes, requests for drawings, incomplete sen-tences, and words to which one must associate (word association tests).
- The testing method is indirect. Assessors do not directly ask about the assessees' characteristics (general personality traits, needs, wishes, etc.). For this reason, as-sessees are unlikely to know the purposes of the test. They may know the very general purpose, for example, the test is being used for diagnosis, but the specific qualities that are being measured are assessed inexplicitly (indirectly).
- There is freedom of response. Structured personality tests (inventories) allow for "true" or "false," ratings on a scale of 1 to 5, and so on, but with projective tests, the response range is completely open. For instance, in responding to an inkblot, one person may provide one short response, "I see a wolf's head," whereas another person may say, "I see a bat . . . ," providing enormous detail about why what he sees is a bat. He may continue to say, "Also, it could be a rug . . ." Responses

to projective tests vary greatly from assessee to assessee in quality, length, and detail.

- Scoring of responses, compared to structured tests, is more complex and potentially flexible. With projective tests, assessors may interpret responses based on a variety of criteria such as psychiatric diagnoses, needs, unconscious conflicts, or unconscious defense mechanisms.

Use of projective tests in psychology and psychiatry has been controversial. These tests have been criticized for low reliability (consistency of measurement) and low validity (accuracy of measurement, meaning, whether the test measures what it is intended to measure). An article by Lilienfeld, Wood, and Garb (2001), published in the magazine *Scientific American*, describes studies and criticizes projective tests on these and other grounds. In an article in the journal *Psychological Assessment*, Meyer and Archer (2001), focusing on the Rorschach as a projective technique, respond to the types of criticisms Lilienfeld and colleagues raised. They conclude that the validity of the Rorschach is equivalent to that of the most widely used personality test (the Minnesota Multiphasic Personality Inventory) and of IQ tests. Regardless of the controversy, projective tests are still very popular. Three projective tests, the Rorschach, the Thematic Apperception Test, and the House-Person-Tree Test, are among the 10 psychological tests most frequently used by clinical psychologists (Camara, Nathan, & Puente, 2000).

Projective tests have been used in fields outside psychology, including anthropology and sociology, for research purposes. They have been used in many business areas, including advertising, management, and marketing research. In the marketing research field, they aid in establishing how people respond emotionally to products. In their book *Projective Techniques for Social Science and Business Research*, Soley and Smith (2008) discuss uses of projective tests in diverse fields.

See also Children's Apperception Test, defense mechanisms, Machover Draw-A-Person Test, psychoanalytic perspective, psychodynamic psychotherapy and psychoanalysis, Rorschach Psychodiagnostic Technique, Thematic Apperception Test, the unconscious mind.

Further Readings:

Lilienfeld, S. O., Wood, J. M., & Garb, H. N. (2001). What's wrong with this picture? *Scientific American, 284*, 80–87.

Soley, L., & Smith, A. L. (2008). *Projective techniques for social science and business research.* Milwaukee, WI: Southshore Press.

References:

Camara, W. J., Nathan, J. S., & Puente, A. E. (2000). Psychological test usage: Implications in professional psychology. *Professional Psychology: Research and Practice, 31*, 141–154.

Lilienfeld, S. O., Wood, J. M., & Garb, H. N. (2001). What's wrong with this picture? *Scientific American, 284*(5), 80–87.

Machover, K. (1949). *Personality projection in the drawing of the human figure.* Springfield, IL: C. C. Thomas.

Meyer, G. J., & Archer, R. P. (2001). The hard science of Rorschach research: What do we know and where do we go? *Psychological Assessment, 13*, 486–502.

Morgan, C. D., & Murray, H. H. (1935). A method for investigating fantasies: The thematic apperception test. *Archives of Neurology & Psychiatry, 34*, 289–306.

Rorschach, H. (1998). *Psychodiagnostics: A diagnostic test based on perception.* Berne: H. Huber. (Original work published 1921)

Rotter, J. B. (1954). *Social learning and clinical psychology.* Englewood Cliffs, NJ: Prentice Hall.

Soley, L., & Smith, A. L. (2008). *Projective techniques for social science and business research.* Milwaukee, WI: Southshore Press.

Prosody

Prosody is a quality of speech that helps communicate feeling or intent. *Linguistic* prosody refers to the pitch, stress, duration, and changes in frequency, intensity, and timing of speech. Linguistic prosody is thought to be primarily related to mechanisms in the left hemisphere of the brain. *Emotional* (*affective*) prosody refers to the inflection and tone in language and the use of gestures and other nonverbal signals (such as body language) to communicate emotion and feeling.

Aprosodia means lack of prosody. Aprosodia can result from lesions (wounds) in the right hemisphere of the brain, as may occur in individuals affected by right hemisphere stroke or traumatic brain injury. People with schizophrenia or autistic spectrum disorders (ASD) may have difficulty understanding the emotional prosody of others (receptive emotional aprosodia). Aprosodia may also affect individuals with Parkinson's disease.

See also aprosodia, autistic spectrum disorders, body language, facial expression, Parkinson's disease, schizophrenia, traumatic brain injury.

Prozac (Fluoxetine)

Prozac, the most common trade name for the drug fluoxetine hydrochloride, is a selective serotonin reuptake inhibitor (SSRI), an example of one of several classes of antidepressants. Fluoxetine is approved by the U.S. Food and Drug Administration (FDA) for treatment of major depression, obsessive-compulsive disorder, panic disorder, and bulimia nervosa. It is widely prescribed in the United States and other parts of the world.

The discovery of fluoxetine began in 1970, when Bryan Molloy and Robert Rathbun of Eli Lilly Laboratories began work with a compound, 3-phenoxy-3-phenylpropylamine, which is molecularly similar to an antihistamine (diphenhydramine) known to have some antidepressant effects (Wong, Bymaster, & Engleman, 1995). Molloy and Rathbun produced a drug that was a selective norepinephrine reuptake inhibitor (SNRI). Norepinephrine is a chemical messenger in the brain that sometimes malfunctions in cases of depression. Reuptake involves reabsorption of the neurotransmitter; the medication inhibits reuptake, recycling, and making more norepinephrine available for use.

David Wong of Eli Lilly worked to find a similar chemical which would operate as an SSRI because serotonin is often implicated as a neurotransmitter that malfunctions in depression. By 1972, fluoxetine was developed. Although it was not the first SSRI created and released on the market, it had fewer side effects than earlier SSRIs; two early SSRIs were withdrawn from the market because of their side effects. Eli Lilly implemented highly effective marketing, and therefore fluoxetine is often perceived as the first SSRI. Fluoxetine was sold in Belgium in 1986 and was approved in the United States by the FDA in 1987.

Use of fluoxetine may be associated with side effects, most commonly nausea, insomnia, drowsiness, anxiety, nervousness, weight gain or loss, and tremor (Preston, O'Neal, & Talaga, 2008). Patients have reported that another side effect, akathisia (restlessness and an inability to remain motionless), caused them to feel suicidal (Rothschild & Locke, 1991). Sexual side effects may occur. Taking fluoxetine during pregnancy may increase the risk of prenatal complications and could have adverse effects on newborns (Preston et al., 2008). It is also known that fluoxetine passes into breast milk, but research is lacking into its effects on nursing infants. All potential risks should be discussed with a doctor.

Serotonin syndrome is a potentially lethal condition that results from toxic levels of serotonin in the central nervous system. Serotonin syndrome can be caused by combining antidepressants with each other or with some opioids, antimigraine medications, stimulants (e.g., amphetamines, cocaine), empathogens (e.g., MDMA or Ecstasy), some herbs (e.g., St. John's wort), and various other medications and over-the-counter products. Symptoms of serotonin syndrome may include rapid heart rate, sweating, shivering, dilated pupils, tremor or twitching, muscular rigidity, elevated temperature, confusion, agitation, delirium, hallucinations, coma, or death. Combining antidepressants and alcohol is not advisable; alcohol, a depressant, can worsen clinical depression and increase the toxicity of some SSRIs.

In 2004, the FDA announced that use of Prozac may increase the risk of suicide attempts in children. This official statement followed years of discussion regarding potential suicidality or homicidality associated with taking antidepressants such as Prozac. The FDA's statement, however, is controversial. Mental health practitioners and scientists such as psychiatrist Peter Kramer, author of *Listening to Prozac* (1997), heralded the benefits of Prozac and argued that side effects are minimal. Conversely, others, such as psychiatrist Peter Breggin—author of *The Anti-depressant Fact Book* (2001)—agree with the FDA and make even stronger claims, arguing that psychiatric medications are used much too frequently, with disastrous results. For some people, this controversy brings up questions about what it means to be a human being: are we solely biological creatures? Does the effectiveness of antidepressants and other psychoactive drugs imply that we lack free will or a soul? This controversy is likely to continue for years to come.

See also antidepressant, depression, major depressive disorder, neurotransmitter, selective serotonin reuptake inhibitor, serotonin.

Further Readings:

Breggin, P. R. (2001). *The anti-depressant fact book: What your doctor won't tell you about Prozac, Zoloft, Paxil, Celexa, and Luvox.* Cambridge, MA: De Capo Press.

Kramer, P. D. (1997). *Listening to Prozac: The landmark book about antidepressants and the remaking of the self.* New York: Penguin.

References:

Breggin, P. R. (2001). *The anti-depressant fact book: What your doctor won't tell you about Prozac, Zoloft, Paxil, Celexa, and Luvox.* Cambridge, MA: De Capo Press.

Kramer, P. D. (1997). *Listening to Prozac: The landmark book about antidepressants and the remaking of the self.* New York: Penguin.

Preston, J. D., O'Neal, J. H., & Talaga, M. C. (2008). *Handbook of clinical psychopharmacology for therapists* (5th ed.). Oakland, CA: New Harbinger.

Rothschild, A. J., & Locke, C. A. (1991). Reexposure to fluoxetine after serious suicide attempts by three patients: The role of akathisia. *Journal of Clinical Psychiatry, 52*, 491–493.

Wong, D. T., Bymaster, F. P., & Engleman, E. A. (1995). Prozac (fluoxetine, Lilly 110140), the first selective serotonin uptake inhibitor and an antidepressant drug: Twenty years since its first publication. *Life Sciences, 57*, 411–441.

- The book *Prozac Nation (Young and Depressed in America: A Memoir)*, an autobiography by Elizabeth Wurtzel published in 1994, details the author's experience with major depression. The book was adapted into a movie of the same name.
- Several musicians and musical groups are named after Prozac, including Prozac+ (an Italian punk band), Prozak (an independent rapper from Michigan whose actual name is Steven T. Shippy), and Prozzäk (a Canadian pop band).

Psychoanalytic Perspective

In 1895, Sigmund Freud and Josef Breuer introduced a new perspective on the relationship between emotion and mental illness when they published several case studies in their classic book *Studies on Hysteria* (Breuer & Freud, 1895/1955). A conversion disorder (formerly known as hysteria) is a psychiatric condition in which the sufferer experiences physical symptoms with no known physical cause (and therefore the cause is assumed to be psychological). Symptoms can be quite dramatic, for instance, blindness, paralysis of limbs, lack of sensation in some part of the body, and even false pregnancy. In the classic case of Anna O, Freud and Breuer reported on "the talking cure," in which the patient's symptoms disappeared when she spoke about their origin. For example, under hypnosis, Anna was able to recall the origin of her arm paralysis. After telling her doctor, Breuer, about the origin, the symptom went away. According to Freud and Breuer, when the patient discusses the origin of the symptom, the retelling is accompanied by an emotional release called *catharsis*. It is because of the catharsis that the symptom disappears. Freud and Breuer had elevated emotional expression as a key to cure of psychological disturbance and argued that it was a lack of emotional expression at the time when the symptom originated, called *strangulation*, that caused the symptom in the first place.

An emotion central to psychoanalytic theory is anxiety. In one of his later writings, Freud (1936/1959) stated that anxiety was a warning sign that forbidden, unconscious impulses may seep out or break out into consciousness. In Freudian theory, people experience many impulses, often sexual or aggressive, that they repress because the impulses are socially unacceptable. For instance, an individual may have a strong hostility and murderous feelings toward his sister, and feeling these consciously would be associated with shame, guilt, and other painful emotions. Therefore the feeling is repressed. Anxiety arises in consciousness when such impulses are likely to break through to consciousness, with the possibility of acting out those impulses in some form (not necessarily murder). In healthy functioning, such impulses are kept unconscious through psychological defense mechanisms such as denial, projection, displacement, and intellectualization. Sigmund Freud introduced such defense mechanisms, and his daughter Anna Freud elaborated on them, discussing them thoroughly in her book *The Ego and the Mechanisms of Defense* (1936).

Another emotion prominent in psychoanalytic writings is guilt (Freud, 1905/1953, 1923/1961). In Freud's famous theory of the mind—the id, ego, superego model—the superego operates according to the morality principle, acting as an "internalized parent," warning the center of the mind (the ego) that some of one's thoughts and feelings arising out of the id (which is purely pleasure centered) are immoral and unacceptable. According to Freud, guilt is at the root of some mental illness, for example, obsessive-compulsive disorder. In Freudian theory, the obsessive thoughts and compulsive behaviors of this disorder occur because an individual feels guilty about his strong impulses—usually hostile ones. The hostile impulses are not experienced consciously, but the person can achieve some satisfaction by expressing both the id and the superego impulses in the symptoms of the disorder. For example, one of Freud's patients, the Rat Man, suffered from obsessive-compulsive disorder, experiencing intrusive, obsessive images that his father and his girlfriend were devoured by rats. When these images arose, he performed compulsive behaviors (e.g., counting to 100 as quickly as possible, saying certain phrases) designed to prevent his father or girlfriend from being devoured. Freud interpreted these symptoms as symbolically representing the overwhelming ambiguous feelings—love and hate—that the Rat Man felt for both individuals. Consciously the Rat Man felt only love and repressed the strong hatred out of guilt.

Freud also wrote famously about depression (which he called *melancholia*; Freud, 1917), presenting the theory that this state may occur when an individual loses a loved one to death or abandonment. With loss, Freud said, people "internalize" the loved one, adopting his characteristics to keep a part of the person with himself. Depression is an expression of anger directed toward this internalized loved one. Freud believed that by explaining depression in this way, he was accounting for the self-punishing, reproachful qualities of depression.

Psychoanalysis was developed and modified by numerous theorists who followed Freud, and several contributed new ideas about emotion and psychoanalysis. For example, John Bowlby discussed the attachment relationship between mother and infant and how this relationship affects emotional development. Charles Brenner questioned Freud's emphasis on anxiety as the primary emotion involved in psychological conflict. Mitchell and Black (1996) have provided an historical overview of major developments in psychoanalysis since Freud's time.

Freud's theory experienced a resurgence in the 1990s, when neuroscientists acknowledged that his structural model of the mind (id, ego, superego) may accurately describe different aspects of brain function. As briefly discussed, in Freud's theory, each part of the mind has its own motivational drives, which conflict with one another. The id is pleasure seeking, the superego is motivated by morality, and the ego is centered in reality, motivated by self-preservation. Furthermore, in Freudian theory, much of one's psychological experience is unconscious. Many neuroscientists now agree that different parts of the brain may motivate different behaviors that may conflict with one another. Additionally, they agree that some emotional processing is unconscious. Joseph LeDoux (1996) discusses these issues in his book *The Emotional Brain.*

See also ambivalence, anxiety, catharsis, defense mechanisms, Anna Freud, Sigmund Freud, guilt, obsessive-compulsive disorder, personality, psychodynamic psychotherapy and psychoanalysis, the unconscious mind.

Further Readings:

Mitchell, S. A., & Black, M. J. (1996). *Freud and beyond: A history of modern psychoanalytic thought.* New York: Basic Books.

Murphy, R. A. (1999). Psychoanalytic perspective. In D. Levinson, J. J. Ponzetti, & P. F. Jorgensen (Eds.), *Encyclopedia of human emotions* (2nd ed., pp. 538–545). New York: Macmillan Reference USA.

Solms, M. (2004). Freud returns. *Scientific American, 290,* 82–88.

References:

Breuer, J., & Freud, S. (1955). Studies on hysteria. (A. Strachey & J. Strachey, Trans.). In J. Strachey (Ed.), *The standard edition of the complete psychological works of Sigmund Freud* (Vol. 2). London: Hogarth Press. (Original work published 1895)

Freud, A. (1936). *The writings of Anna Freud: Vol. 2. The ego and the mechanisms of defense.* New York: International Universities Press.

Freud, S. (1953). Mourning and melancholia. In J. Strachey (Ed. & Trans.), *The standard edition of the complete psychological works of Sigmund Freud* (Vol. 14). London: Hogarth Press. (Original work published 1917)

Freud, S. (1953). Three essays on the theory of sexuality. In J. Strachey (Ed. & Trans.), *The standard edition of the complete psychological works of Sigmund Freud* (Vol. 7, pp. 123–213). London: Hogarth Press. (Original work published 1905)

Freud, S. (1959). Inhibitions, symptoms, and anxiety. In J. Strachey (Ed.), *The standard edition of the complete psychological works of Sigmund Freud* (Vol. 20). London: Hogarth Press. (Original work published 1936)

Freud, S. (1961). The ego and the id. In J. Strachey (Ed. & Trans.), *The standard edition of the complete psychological works of Sigmund Freud* (Vol. 19). London: Hogarth Press. (Original work published 1923)

LeDoux, J. (1996). *The emotional brain: The mysterious underpinnings of emotional life.* New York: Touchstone.

Mitchell, S. A., & Black, M. J. (1996). *Freud and beyond: A history of modern psychoanalytic thought.* New York: Basic Books.

Psychodrama

Psychodrama was developed by Jacob L. Moreno, a Viennese psychiatrist in the 1920s. While the existing psychotherapies of the day (Freudian, Jungian, and Adlerian) focused mostly on talking between one therapist and one patient and analysis or interpretation by the therapist, psychodrama techniques involved acting out situations as well as talking about them. Psychodrama could involve individuals or groups and depended less on interpretation by the therapist than on insight gleaned from feedback and the group process (Moreno, 1948).

Psychodrama uses guided dramatic action to examine problems or explore issues. Psychodrama is used to facilitate insight, clarify issues, and enhance learning and development of new skills, personal growth, and emotional and physical well-being. Psychodrama is used in various types of therapy, including behavioral, Gestalt, family, and affective (emotion)-oriented group therapies. As a therapeutic tool, psychodrama is a way to help clients experience the emotional qualities of an event. It provides a safe and supportive environment in which to explore new ways of behaving and interacting with others.

Psychodrama may refer to both group and individual experiences, although the term *sociodrama* is sometimes used to refer to the group experience. As a group experience, psychodrama involves spontaneous (unscripted and unrehearsed) role-plays. Group members serve as the actors, and the group facilitator (or therapist) serves as the director. Generally, one person is given the role of the protagonist (the main character); other group members are actors in the protagonist's play or serve as the audience. Audience members give feedback to the protagonist.

The classical model of psychodrama occurs in three phases: the warm-up, the action, and closure (Kipper & Hundal, 2003). During the warm-up, the protagonist is selected, the theme or issue is identified, and the stage is set. The protagonist selects other group members to play auxiliary roles. The stage is the physical space in which the psychodrama occurs. Props may be utilized during the dramatization. In the action stage, the protagonist (and auxiliaries) act out the theme or issue. The protagonist may explore new methods of resolving a problem during this phase. During closure (sharing and processing), other group members (including audience members and auxiliary actors) give feedback to the protagonist. Group members are also invited to share ways in which they felt personally connected to the protagonist's work (how the action affected them).

There are a variety of psychodrama techniques, including doubling, role reversal, and future projection. In doubling, another group member or the therapist plays the part of (and gives voice to) the protagonist's inner voice. Doubling is useful to elicit emotions, is used to offer support to the protagonist during rehearsals of new behaviors, and is used to offer more effective suggestions and interpretations of situations. In role reversal, the protagonist switches places with major figures in her life and tries to enter their shoes, offering practical and emotional insight into others' situations as well as into her own responses to other people and situations. Future projection helps identify future goals, fears, or anxiety-provoking situations; identify the steps needed to reach goals; or provide a perspective on situations (Royce-Davis, 1999).

With its focus on interpersonal action, psychodrama is a powerful vehicle for exploring relationships and resolving family problems. The family sculpture is a type of psychodrama utilized in family therapy. In the family sculpture, the therapist asks one family member to arrange the other members of the family in a tableau (arrangement). This is a way to graphically portray family members' perceptions of their roles within the family. Family therapy pioneer Virginia Satir utilized the family sculpture, often incorporating blindfolds and ropes to dramatize the roles in which family members trap each other (Nichols, 2008). Family sculpture can be used to illuminate scenes from the past to focus awareness and heighten sensitivity, either with actual family members or in a group therapy setting.

Psychodrama has been conducted in a variety of settings, including schools, hospitals, mental health clinics, detention centers, private practice, churches, and training centers. It can be performed with adults, children, adolescents, individuals with developmental disabilities, and trauma survivors. Psychodrama has been incorporated into treatment for many issues, including social skills training, substance abuse treatment, and rehabilitation from stroke or traumatic brain injury (Royce-Davis, 1999). Research has yielded several attributes of psychodrama, including self-understanding, reenactment of family dynamics, group cohesiveness, insight, catharsis (emotional release), and the instillation of hope. Group psychodrama has been shown to be helpful in solving problems, anger control, resolution of emotional conflict, and decreasing levels of anxiety and depression (Kim, 2003).

See also anxiety, catharsis, depression, family therapy, Gestalt therapy, group therapy, traumatic brain injury.

Further Reading:
American Society of Group Psychotherapy and Psychodrama Web site: http://www.asgpp.org/

References:
Kim, K. W. (2003). The effects of being the protagonist in psychodrama. *Journal of Group Psychotherapy, Psychodrama, and Sociometry, 55*, 115–127.
Kipper, D. A., & Hundal, J. (2003). A survey of clinical reports on the application of psychodrama. *Journal of Group Psychotherapy, Psychodrama, and Sociometry, 55*, 141–157.
Moreno, J. L. (1948, October). Psychodrama and group psychotherapy. *Annals of the New York Academy of Sciences, 49*, 902–903.
Nichols, M. P. (2008). *Family therapy: Concepts and methods* (8th ed.). Boston: Allyn and Bacon.
Royce-Davis, J. C. (1999). Psychodrama: An approach to addressing psychosocial issues associated with the experience of a traumatic brain injury in adolescence. *Guidance and Counseling, 14*, 29–33.

Psychodynamic Psychotherapy and Psychoanalysis

Psychodynamic psychotherapy has its origins in psychoanalysis, the form of psychotherapy developed by Sigmund Freud in the late 1800s and early 1900s. Psychodynamic therapy and psychoanalysis involve similar techniques and goals. However, psychoanalysis typically involves more sessions and is more intensive; the patient usually attends three to five sessions per week while undergoing psychoanalysis, whereas in psychodynamic psychotherapy, clients generally attend sessions once per week. According to Levy (2009), central tenets of psychodynamic therapy and psychoanalysis include unconscious mental functioning, defense mechanisms, a developmental perspective, and the centrality of individual and personal meaning of events.

A primary idea associated with the therapy of Freud and his followers is the importance of the unconscious mind. According to this perspective, many of our mental contents—motives, memories, wishes, even emotions—are outside conscious awareness. These unconscious mental factors, can, however, cause us great suffering and serve as impetuses for behavior. The reason that many memories, wishes, impulses, and so forth are unconscious is because of the intense negative emotions aroused by them such as fear, shame, guilt, and self-loathing. For instance, a person may have strong feelings of hostility toward a loved one, and since this feeling causes so much shame and guilt, he represses those feelings. However, according to psychodynamic and psychoanalytic theorists, unconscious factors push for expression in much the same way that all mental content does. The expression of these unconscious elements is outside the control of the conscious mind and may involve the creation of neurotic symptoms such as phobias, obsessions, depression, and so on. A primary goal of psychodynamic psychotherapy and psychoanalysis is to bring the unconscious mind into consciousness. When an individual is more fully aware of aspects of himself, he can make conscious choices regarding which impulses or motives to express and which ones not to express. This is psychological maturity and, essentially, mental health.

Defense mechanisms are also central in psychodynamic and psychoanalytic theory. Defense mechanisms are the means through which individuals keep mental processes and content outside awareness. Defense mechanisms also usually serve as ways to express the unconscious factors. Each person tends to have favorite defense mechanisms, ones that he uses with regularity. Some examples are projection (attributing one's own qualities, often negative qualities, to someone else), denial (pretending that an event, reality, or one's own impulse does not exist), and reaction formation (behaving in a way opposite to the way one actually feels unconsciously, for instance, expressing love when one feels unconscious hatred). When bringing the unconscious mind into consciousness, theoretically, the need for defense mechanisms will decrease.

The psychodynamic and psychoanalytic perspectives take a developmental approach to personality and emphasize the importance of childhood experiences. Childhood relationships, especially with parents, are presumed to influence the dynamics present in adult relationships. This is not to say that other influences on present relationships are completely ignored, such as biological factors or current social circumstances, but rather that childhood experiences tend to be the focus.

Psychodynamic and psychoanalytic psychologists are also interested in an individual's subjective and phenomenological experience—how he experiences himself, other people, and the world in general. Other approaches in psychology, such as cognitive and phenomenological approaches, also have this emphasis. Psychodynamic and psychoanalytic psychologists differ, however, in weighting unconscious experience at least as highly as conscious experience. Additionally, in the psychodynamic and psychoanalytic approaches, emotions are emphasized over cognitions.

Given these fundamental principles and emphases, psychodynamic and psychoanalytic psychotherapists utilize specific psychotherapy techniques. One such technique is analyzing transference. *Transference* is an emotional experience that occurs in therapy for the client: the transfer of emotions from an important relationship (such as one's relationship with a parent) onto the therapist. Psychodynamic and psychoanalytic therapists interpret the transference to help the client reach the goal of bringing the unconscious mind into consciousness. For instance, a client may transfer strong feelings of both love and hatred that he had for his father onto the therapist. The hatred in particular may be largely unconscious. By transferring the feelings onto the therapist (i.e., the client feels that he hates the therapist), he is continuing to deny his hatred of his father but is making movements toward recognizing and eventually accepting this painful feeling, beginning with the recognition that he is capable of having such a strong feeling at all (although it is initially directed toward a different object, or person). Transference is a type of *catharsis*, or emotional release, which psychodynamic therapists believe helps the client to become well. Psychodynamic therapy involves many other techniques, including *free association*, in which the client says whatever comes to mind without censorship; *clarification*, in which the therapist makes sure that she understands what the client is saying by restating it to the client; and *confrontation*, in which the therapist, at appropriate times, gently points out inconsistencies in the client's behaviors and thoughts or values.

Blagys and Hilsenroth (2000) conducted a literature review of empirical studies that compared psychodynamic psychotherapy to cognitive-behavioral therapy in regard to psychotherapy process and technique. On the basis of the review, they identified core characteristics of both types of therapy. They concluded that psychodynamic psychotherapy has seven specific characteristics: (1) emphasis on emotion and emotional expression; (2) a probing of efforts to avoid or deny experience; (3) recognition of patterns of behavior, perception, and experience; (4) focus on past experience; (5) emphasis on interpersonal relationships; (6) importance of the therapy relationship; and (7) discussion of wishes, dreams, and fantasies.

Levy (2009) reviews research on the effectiveness of psychodynamic psychotherapy for a variety of psychiatric conditions. He concludes that one or more variants of psychodynamic therapy are helpful for depression, anxiety, personality disorders, and eating disorders. Particular types of psychodynamic psychotherapy are also helpful for borderline personality disorder.

See also ambivalence, catharsis, defense mechanisms, Anna Freud, Sigmund Freud, human development, motivation, psychoanalytic perspective, transference, the unconscious mind.

Further Readings:
Freud, S. (1989). Part 3: Therapy and technique. In P. Gay (Ed.), *The Freud reader* (pp. 307–426). New York: W. W. Norton.
Levy, K. N. (2009). Psychodynamic and psychoanalytic psychotherapy. In D.C.S. Richard & S. K. Huprich (Eds.), *Clinical psychology: Assessment, treatment, and research* (pp. 181–214). San Francisco: Elsevier.

References:
Blagys, M. D., & Hilsenroth, M. J. (2000). Distinctive feature of short-term psychodynamic-interpersonal psychotherapy: A review of the comparative psychotherapy process literature. *Clinical Psychology: Science and Practice, 7*, 167–188.
Levy, K. N. (2009). Psychodynamic and psychoanalytic psychotherapy. In D.C.S. Richard & S. K. Huprich (Eds.), *Clinical psychology: Assessment, treatment, and research* (pp. 181–214). San Francisco: Elsevier.
Silvio, J. R. (1994). Woody Allen's *The Purple Rose of Cairo*: A psychoanalytic allegory. *Journal of the American Academy of Psychoanalysis, 22*, 545–553.

Many Woody Allen films depict the conflict, torment, and pain of neurotic suffering, or the experience of psychoanalysis. Woody Allen's film *The Purple Rose of Cairo* is considered an allegory for the psychoanalytic experience. A female character in the film is having two different relationships with the same man at the same time. This type of relationship parallels the psychoanalytic experience in the sense that a patient relates to the psychoanalyst both as a transference figure from the past and as a helpful professional in the present (Silvio, 1994).

Psychosurgery

Psychosurgery is a type of neurosurgery (brain surgery) used to alleviate mental distress. It has also been referred to as *psychiatric neurosurgery* and *limbic system surgery*. Trephination (or *trepanning*, now referred to as *craniotomy*), an ancient form of psychosurgery, involved drilling or sawing holes in the skull. A trephined skull has been found at Eisisheim, France; carbon dating places it in the Neolithic period (about 5100 BC). Literature describing trephination for relief of psychotic and affective (mood) symptoms dates back to 1500 BC (Mashour, Walker, & Martuza, 2005).

In the modern era, the unusual accident in 1848 of Phineas P. Gage, a railroad worker in Vermont, lent some insight into the links between the brain and behavior. Gage survived an explosion that drove a railroad spike through his skull. While his language and cognitive functions were apparently intact, his personality and social reasoning were affected (Damasio, 1994). Swiss psychiatrist Gottlieb Burckhardt is considered the founder of modern psychosurgery. Burckhardt's 1888 *topectomy* involved excising (cutting) multiple points in the frontal, parietal, and temporal cortices of the brain. The topectomy resulted in some successes and some failures (including fatalities); it was not well received in Switzerland (Mashour et al., 2005). In the 1930s,

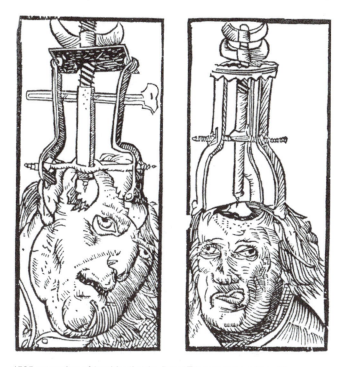

1525 engraving of trephination by Peter Treveris (taken from Hieronymus Braunschweig's *Buch der Cirurgia Hantwirckung der Wundartzny*, 1497. Trephination (or trepanning, now referred to as craniotomy), an ancient form of psychosurgery, involved drilling or sawing holes in the skull. Literature describing trephination for relief of psychotic and affective (mood) symptoms dates back to 1500 BC. (National Library of Medicine)

American physiologists John F. Fulton and Carlyle Jacobsen found that creating lesions (wounds) in part of the frontal lobes of chimpanzees (Becky and Lucy) produced behavioral changes. After the surgery, Becky no longer became agitated. However, Lucy (who had previously been docile) became violent (Weiss, Rauch, & Price, 2006). Fulton and Jacobsen presented their findings at the 1935 Second World Congress of Neurology.

Portuguese neurologist and dean of medicine at the University of Lisbon Egas Moniz was intrigued by these findings. Moniz and neurosurgeon Almeida Lima began testing the prefrontal leucotomy on patients with psychoses. Moniz coined the term *psychosurgery*. In 1936 (after Moniz's initial reports), American neurologist Walter Freeman and American neurosurgeon James Watts started performing the treatment in the United States, which they modified and renamed *prefrontal lobotomy*. Their first 200 cases were deemed successful, although adverse effects such as seizures and apathy were noted (Freeman & Watts, 1942). Freeman, enthusiastic about the procedure and seeking ways to make it more efficient, devised a method to avoid drilling through the skull, using a tool similar to an ice pick to break through the orbital bone and sever the nearby prefrontal cortex. Watts broke off relations with Freeman when he learned that Freeman was performing ice-pick lobotomies in his private office, using electroconvulsive therapy (shock treatments) as the only form of anesthesia (Weiss et al., 2006). However, the prefrontal lobotomy became increasingly popular and was often performed by practitioners who were neither surgeons nor physicians (Mashour et al., 2005). In the early part of the 20th century, somatic (biological) therapies for mental illness included convulsive therapy, insulin shock therapy, hydrotherapy (water therapy), and psychosurgery. The prefrontal lobotomy was embraced in part because of overcrowded asylums, the costs and burden of mental illness on society, media reports of positive outcomes from prefrontal lobotomy, and a lack of effective alternative treatments. The 1949 Nobel Prize in Physiology or Medicine, awarded to Egas Moniz for his work in psychosurgery, lent validation to the procedure (Mashour et al., 2005). The lobotomy started to fall out of favor after reports of lobotomies being performed in unsterile conditions by unqualified practitioners. Scientific and medical reports questioned the efficacy of the lobotomy and brought to light serious side effects, including seizures, infections, apathy, decreased attention span, personality change, and death (Mashour et al., 2005). Use of the lobotomy declined after the introduction of the antipsychotic medication chlorpromazine (Thorazine) in the 1950s, and with the increasing popularity of psychoanalysis. Prefrontal lobotomy became illegal in some countries and states (Mashour et al., 2005).

Controversy about psychosurgery was sparked again in the 1970s with the publication of Mark and Ervin's *Violence and the Brain*, which suggested that neurosurgical procedures could treat aberrant limbic system function responsible for much of the violent behavior afflicting society. The landmark case *Kaimowitz vs. Department of Mental Health* (1973), in which a prisoner was offered a psychosurgical procedure to temper his aggressive behavior, spurred ethical debate about government use of neurosurgery as a tool of suppression and control. This resulted in guidelines about ethical use and regulation of psychosurgery (Mashour et al., 2005).

Psychosurgical techniques became more accurate (reducing side effects) with the development of stereotactic devices in the 1940s. The sterotactic frame allows the neurosurgeon to create lesions in precise target areas. Adverse outcomes have been reduced using surgical techniques guided by modern imaging techniques such as magnetic resonance imaging (MRI) or computed tomography (CT) scans. Modern psychosurgery includes anterior cingulotomy, subcaudate tractotomy, limbic leucotomy, and anterior capsulotomy. Psychosurgery may be used to treat psychiatric disorders such as severe, chronic treatment-resistant obsessive-compulsive disorder (OCD) or severe mood disorders such as major depressive disorder (MDD) or bipolar disorder. The anterior cingulate is an important circuit in the frontal lobe of the brain. Anterior cingulotomy, first performed in the 1950s, has been shown to be effective in 25 to 30 percent of OCD patients treated and 53 to 57 percent of patients with affective disorders (MDD or bipolar disorder). The most common adverse effects of cingulotomy are seizures, urinary difficulties, and mild cognitive impairments. While many patients have demonstrated overall cognitive improvements after the procedure, some have shown deficits in attention and visual processing (Weiss et al., 2006). Subcaudate tractotomy, designed by Knight in London in 1964, creates lesions that interrupt fibers going from the frontal lobes to subcortical structures such as the amygdala. Subcaudate tractotomy has been shown to be effective in about 34 percent of patients treated for MDD or OCD. Side effects occur at a higher rate with subcaudate tractotomy than with anterior cingulotomy. Adverse effects include seizures and personality changes (Weiss et al., 2006). Limbic leucotomy is a combination of the lesions created in anterior cingulotomy and subcaudate tractotomy. It has been shown to be effective in treating 36 to 50 percent of patients with OCD or MDD (Weiss et al., 2006). Limbic leucotomy has been effective in treating some patients with severe OCD accompanied by self-mutilating behaviors (Mashour et al., 2005). Anterior capsulotomy, developed by French neurosurgeon Talairach in the late 1940s, has demonstrated greater effectiveness (about 70%) in treating severe OCD than anterior cingulotomy. However, anterior capsulotomy also has greater potential for adverse effects, including confusion, weight gain, depression, nocturnal incontinence, cognitive and affective (mood) changes, and decreased initiative (Mashour et al., 2005).

Psychosurgery is usually a treatment of last resort, when treatments such as psychotherapy and medications have failed (Glannon, 2006). Psychosurgery is not usually considered an effective intervention for individuals with schizophrenia, personality disorders, or substance abuse disorders (including alcoholism). Rarely, individuals with severe violent outbursts, with the potential for injury to themselves or others, may be considered for psychosurgery involving the amygdala, thalamus, or hypothalamus (Cosgrove & Rauch, 2005).

Electroconvulsive therapy is a nonsurgical alternative to psychosurgery. Transcranial magnetic stimulation and vagal nerve stimulation are being explored as nonsurgical alternative treatments for depression. Deep brain stimulation—implanting a stimulating probe at targeted brain sites—is being explored as a means to increase efficacy and reduce adverse outcomes of psychosurgery. Some consider endoscopic sympathetic block—a surgical intervention involving cauterizing or clamping ganglions (nerve bundles) on the sympathetic nerve trunk as a treatment for social phobia—to be a type of psychosurgery.

See also anterior cingulate cortex, bipolar disorder, electroconvulsive therapy, endoscopic sympathetic block, Phineas P. Gage, major depressive disorder, Egas Moniz, mood disorder, obsessive-compulsive disorder, prefrontal cortex, prefrontal lobotomy.

Further Reading:

Mark, V. H., & Ervin, F. R. (1970). *Violence and the brain*. New York: Harper and Row.

References:

Cosgrove, G. R., & Rauch, S. L. (2005). *Psychosurgery*. Retrieved from http://neurosurgery.mgh.har vard.edu/Functional/psysurg.htm

Costandi, M. (2008). An interview with Heather Perry. *Neurophilosophy weblog*. Retrieved from http:// scienceblogs.com/neurophilosophy/2008/08/lunch_with_heather_perry.php

Damasio, A. (1994). *Descartes' error: Emotion, reason and the human brain*. New York: Putnam.

Freeman, W., & Watts, J. W. (1942). *Psychosurgery: Intelligence, emotion and social behavior following prefrontal lobotomy for mental disorders*. Springfield, IL: Charles C. Thomas.

Glannon, W. (2006). *Bioethics and the brain*. Cary, NC: Oxford University Press.

Mashour, G. A., Walker, E. E., & Martuza, R. L. (2005). Psychosurgery: Past, present, and future. *Brain Research Reviews, 48*, 409–419.

Michell, J. (1999). *Eccentric lives and peculiar notions*. Kempton, IL: Adventures Unlimited Press.

Reporters Committee for Freedom of the Press. (2000). *ABC ordered to hand over unedited head-drilling tapes*. Retrieved from http://www.rcfp.org/news/2000/1016trepan.html

Weiss, A. P., Rauch, S. L., & Price, B. H. (2006). Neurosurgical intervention for psychiatric illness. In B. L. Miller & J. L. Cummings (Eds.), *Human frontal lobes: Functions and disorders* (2nd ed., pp. 505–517). New York: Guilford.

Some people advocate self-trepanation (drilling holes in their own skulls) for health reasons or to achieve a higher state of consciousness. *Eccentric Lives and Peculiar Notions* (Michell, 1999) describes a British group that promotes self-trepanation to purportedly allow the brain access to more space and oxygen. In 2000, two men were prosecuted in Utah for practicing medicine without a license when they trepanned a British woman in an attempt to treat her depression and chronic fatigue syndrome (Costandi, 2008; Reporters Committee for Freedom of the Press, 2000). An ABC news reporter who witnessed and videotaped the home brain surgery was ordered to turn over the videotapes and testify in court.

R

Rational Emotive Behavior Therapy

Rational emotive behavior therapy (REBT) was developed by Albert Ellis in 1955 to highlight the power of reframing one's irrational beliefs into more rational perspectives. Ellis provided an alternative to the then-prevalent model of cause of emotional disturbance, which was viewed as a disease with a genesis outside of the self such as a biological agent or traumatic childhood experience. Ellis believed this model was incomplete and argued that the source of many emotional problems is often what one tells oneself. He emphasized that people have many choices in how they perceive events and do not have to be batted around by circumstances; many aspects of our lives, and the ways we feel about our lives, are self-created. Furthermore, people do not necessarily need an outside force (such as a therapist or a medication) to cure themselves. Rather, people can become better by retraining themselves, by changing the way they think.

People often say things to themselves that are self-defeating. In cases of disappointment, individuals may react with extreme self-statements such as "I never get what I want" or "I am always rejected by people." Ellis states that if we examine these statements, we realize that they are untrue and that alternative statements are both more accurate and help one to feel better. "I never get what I want" may be changed to "I sometimes don't get what I want." "I am always rejected by people" may be changed to "Lately, I have been rejected by some people." Training in REBT involves learning to recognize whether a belief is more rational or more irrational. Irrational beliefs tend to emphasize polar extremes, are characterized by black-and-white thinking (without recognizing shades of gray), overgeneralize to other situations, and are rooted in a desire for perfection. As Ellis states, "The road to hell . . . is paved with unrealistic expectations!" (Ellis & Harper, 1975, p. 4). Rational beliefs are more tentative and conditional, acknowledge gray areas in life, and recognize that perfection is not possible.

REBT can be practiced in both individual and group therapy contexts. Techniques include disputing irrational beliefs, social skills training, and reinforcement for successfully applying REBT. The therapy includes homework assignments that may involve the preceding techniques and others such as risk-taking and rational-emotive imagery (e.g., vividly imagining having a rational reaction to a "horrible" event). A favorable aspect of REBT is that it can also be done as self-help. However, Ellis states that since one's self-defeating patterns tend to develop over long periods of time and may be difficult to recognize or identify, many people would benefit from applying these techniques under the supervision of a therapist. REBT therapy is widely used today. It and other forms of cognitive therapy are among the most successful treatments for clinical depression, some anxiety problems, and other disorders.

See also ABC model of emotional reaction, cognitive therapy and cognitive-behavioral therapy, Albert Ellis.

Further Reading:
Albert Ellis Institute Web site: http://www.albertellisinstitute.org/

Reference:
Ellis, A., & Harper, R. A. (1975). *A guide to rational living.* Chatsworth, CA: Wilshire.

Recovery International

Recovery International (formerly Recovery Inc.) is a mental health self-help organization that uses cognitive-behavioral self-help techniques to help people lead more peaceful and productive lives. It especially intends to prevent relapses in people with a history of psychiatric problems. Recovery International was founded at the Neuropsychiatric Institute of the University of Illinois Research and Education Hospitals in 1937 by neuropsychiatrist Abraham A. Low. It is one of the earliest organizations to use cognitive techniques for changing behavior and problematic emotions such as irrational fears, excessive anger, and depression. The development of the organization was based on Low's theories of will-training, temper control, and symptom analysis. In the book *Mental Health through Will-Training*, Low (1950) gave details about techniques for managing fear, anger, and the symptoms of depression, which are now referred to as behavior modification and cognitive therapy. In opposition to the prevailing psychoanalytic (Freudian) theory, Low believed that mental disease has biological causes and that people's behavior is driven by will-power, namely, people's ability to control their behavior through their own will and determination. Accordingly, Recovery Inc. has focused on the self-control aspect of managing mental illnesses.

Low observed that a structured organization and therapeutic group setting are needed to provide support to former psychiatric patients. As the organization became independent, Recovery Inc. expanded outside of Illinois and later overseas, while it turned completely into a self-help organization, in which instruction and training similar to cognitive or behavioral therapy are given to the patient to help herself. Recognized by the American Psychiatric Association for its contribution to the field of psychiatric rehabilitation, Recovery Inc. won the Arnold L. van Amerigen Award in Psychiatric Rehabilitation in 2000.

In 2008, Recovery Inc. announced its merger with the Abraham Low Institute and changed its name to Recovery International/The Abraham Low Institute (RI/TALI), headquartered in Chicago. As a self-help organization, RI/TALI holds hundreds of support group meetings in the United States, Canada, Ireland, Puerto Rico, Spain, Israel, and the United Kingdom. Recovery International's support group meetings offer training in their self-help methods. Objectives of self-help methods are to assist people in changing their behaviors and attitudes in response to disturbing thoughts, impulses, and symptoms accompanied by such mental problems as depression, stress, anger, anxiety, obsessive-compulsive disorder, bipolar disorder (formerly called manic depression), schizophrenia, posttraumatic stress disorder, and suicidal thoughts. At the meetings, members talk about a specific situation in which they had psychological or emotional symptoms. They also share their thoughts before the symptom, how they recognized their symptoms, and how they reacted to their symptoms. In return, other members suggest different ways of looking at the situation and better ways to manage their symptoms. Through the support meetings, members seek and obtain the help of fellow members and learn effective ways to practice the self-help methods. For the long run, members are expected to develop skills in taking control of damaging thoughts and behaviors.

To help students in grades 6 through 12 manage anger and increase self-control, RI/TALI has developed the Power to Change program, which uses Dr. Low's tools and techniques. Since its introduction in Chicago public schools in 2005, more than 700 students have benefited from the program (Weller, 2008).

See also cognitive therapy and cognitive-behavioral therapy.

Further Reading:
Recovery International Web site: http://www.lowselfhelpsystems.org/index.asp

References:
Low, A. A. (1950). *Mental health through will-training.* West Hanover, MA: Christopher.
Weller, F. (2008). Recovery International merges with the Abraham Low Institute. *Lakewood Observer,* 4(7). Retrieved from: http://www.webcitation.org/5eLxDb1qE

Regulation of Emotion

An emotion unfolds over a short period of time in reaction to a stimulus or event (either external or internal) and involves a number of components: physiological, experiential (feeling), cognitive (thinking), and behavioral, which includes an expressive component. Given the complexity of an emotion, there is much that can be regulated (modulated), and the regulation can occur in a variety of ways; that is, emotion regulation can involve changing the strength or duration of the emotion, or the expressive components (facial expression, gestures, etc.), physiological response, behavioral response, or other aspects of the emotion.

For example, an individual could go to work, walk into the office of her boss, and be told that she is being laid off. In this instance, she will likely react (internally) with a variety of emotions, including anger and fear. Hopefully (if she wants a higher probability of finding another job), she will engage in some regulation of her emotions. In general, it may be acceptable to express some disappointment, a little sadness, or some surprise, but a very strong reaction of anger or fear (smashing things, having a panic attack) will serve her less well. So although she may, in the moment, internally be experiencing strong anger and fear, she will hopefully regulate at least the expressive component of the emotion. A few days later, after she thinks again about having lost her job, the emotions of anger and fear may arise again. At this point, it would serve her well to modulate more aspects of her emotion—physiological response, cognitive, experiential (feeling)—so that she may focus on engaging in some action that will increase her probability of getting a job (sitting down and working on her résumé, calling people for references, getting out of the house and applying for jobs, etc.).

Although the preceding example demonstrates functional behavior, emotion regulation need not be functional; it merely involves attempts at modulating emotions. Additionally, emotion regulation need not be conscious; it could be unconscious. In the preceding example, for instance, the individual may, in the few days after losing her job, consciously suppress her anxiety, but later, her anxiety becomes suppressed in an automatic and unconscious fashion. As Gross and Thompson (2007) point out, emotion regulation may even occur before an emotion occurs in that people can select situations (e.g., approach or avoid them) in such a way as to affect their emotions. They can also attempt to behaviorally modify a situation once they are in it, for instance, if the woman looking for a job goes to a job interview and sees that all people in the waiting room are dressed much more professionally than she is, she can choose to leave the situation before the job interview occurs. Or if she chooses to be interviewed, she can use various strategies to regulate emotions that may arise while being interviewed such as manipulating her attention toward or away from the well-dressed competitors, modifying the way she thinks about the fact that others are well dressed, and/or attempting to modulate her physiological or expressive responses to the anxiety she feels (e.g., maintaining a relaxed facial expression despite her anxiety).

Other concepts in the emotion field and related fields bear some similarity to or overlap with emotion regulation (Gross & Thompson, 2007). A related concept is coping. One way coping differs from emotion regulation is that coping tends to apply to longer periods of time; that is, coping often refers to a process that can take place over weeks, months, or years such as coping with a cancer diagnosis. Second, coping generally focuses on decreasing negative emotions and affects, whereas emotion regulation may involve increasing or decreasing either positive or negative emotions. Defenses are similar to emotion regulation also, except that defenses are most often automatic and unconscious and are typically viewed as stable characteristics, akin to personality traits (Cramer, 2000).

Emotion regulation can take a different form in children than it does in adults. Central to the adult-child distinction is the issue of whether emotion regulation has to involve *intrinsic* processes (an individual regulates her own emotions) or whether it can also involve *extrinsic* processes (one person's emotions are regulated by another person such as an adult regulating a child's emotions). Emotion experts Gross and Thompson (2007) state that emotion regulation can occur both intrinsically and extrinsically. Although research on adults has generally revealed intrinsic regulation and research on children has often focused on extrinsic regulation, both children and adults may regulate their emotions (or have their emotions regulated) in either way. Family environment and parental modeling influence how children learn to regulate their emotions (Charles & Carstensen, 2006; Sheffield Morris, Silk, Steinberg, Myers, & Robinson, 2007). A feature of some mental health disorders (e.g., mood disorders, traumatic brain injury) is difficulty with emotional regulation.

See also defense mechanisms, family, human development, human life span.

Further Reading:
Gross, J. J., & Thompson, R. A. (2007). Emotion regulation: Conceptual foundations. In J. J. Gross (Ed.), *Handbook of emotion regulation* (pp. 3–24). New York: Guilford.

References:

Charles, S. T., & Carstensen, L. L. (2006). Emotion regulation and aging. In J. J. Gross (Ed.), *Handbook of emotion regulation* (pp. 307–327). New York: Guilford.

Cramer, P. (2000). Defense mechanisms in psychology today: Further processes for adaptation. *American Psychologist, 55*, 637–646.

Gross, J. J., & Thompson, R. A. (2007). Emotion regulation: Conceptual foundations. In J. J. Gross (Ed.), *Handbook of emotion regulation* (pp. 3–24). New York: Guilford.

Sheffield Morris, A., Silk, J. S., Steinberg, L., Myers, S. S., & Robinson, L. R. (2007). The role of the family context in the development of emotion regulation. *Social Development, 16*, 361–388.

Relationships

A relationship is an association or connection between two or more people. It may be brief or long term and may be based on kinship, affinity (e.g., love or liking), business, or social commitment. There are many types of interpersonal relationships, including family (e.g., parents, siblings, children), romantic or intimate (e.g., marriage), roommates, employer-employee, student-teacher, social, friends, and acquaintances. People in relationships influence each other, sharing thoughts, feelings, and rituals. Interdependence in relationships is shaped by individual experience and temperament, family background, culture, gender, and role expectations. For example, one man's ideas about roles (e.g., husband and father, wife and mother) will influence his behaviors, feelings, and expectations within a relationship with his spouse and children. While primarily individualistic societies (as in the United States) may focus on independence and individual autonomy, many cultures (e.g., some Asian and Hispanic cultures) are more collectivist, stressing interdependence of family members and responsibility to the family. Lack of understanding about culture may lead to inappropriate judgments about dynamics within a family (or other relationships) being overly dependent.

Many theories about interpersonal relationships cite the importance of early childhood experiences, including behaviors and dynamics modeled within one's family of origin. British psychiatrist John Bowlby proposed that attachment—the early bond between a baby and its primary caregiver (parents and others who care for the baby)—sets the stage for future emotional relationships, especially intimate relationships (Fraley & Shaver, 2000). People raised in families with patterns of detrimental behavioral interactions may repeat these behaviors in future relationships.

People may experience negative emotions when a relationship is threatened by interpersonal conflict. Emotions enable humans to respond to basic challenges in living in several ways: emotions produce adaptive physiological changes, the experience of emotion guides behavior, and emotional expression facilitates social communication and interaction. Psychologist Keith Sanford of Baylor University (Waco, Texas) has researched emotions and interpersonal conflict (2007). Emotions can be classified as selfish or pro-social. *Selfish* emotions, which focus on self-preservation, conflict, competition, and fighting, appear to be associated with activation of the right hemisphere of the brain and the amygdala (a brain structure associated with emotion, especially fear). In contrast, *pro-social* emotions, which focus on interpersonal relationships, cooperation, and attachment, appear to be associated with the left hemisphere of the brain (Sanford, 2007). Negative emotions have been described as "hard" (e.g., selfish emotions such as feeling angry or aggravated) or "soft" (e.g., pro-social emotions such as feeling sad or hurt). Hard (selfish) emotions are associated with exerting power and control, while soft (pro-social) emotions are associated with experiencing or expressing vulnerability. The type of negative emotion expressed during conflict may predict communication and conflict resolution in the relationship. Hard emotions (e.g., anger) may signal a potential attack, putting the recipient of the anger on the defensive. Expression of hard emotions may be destructive to a relationship. The expression of soft emotion (e.g., sadness) may indicate a need for social support, elicit helping or comforting behaviors, or facilitate resolution of conflict. A study examining hard and soft emotion expression during conflict in different types of relationships (peers and married couples) found that the expression of hard emotions was predictive of increased negative communication, decreased positive communication, and less relationship satisfaction (Sanford, 2007).

Emotional expression in intimate (romantic) relationships changes across the life span of the relationship and is influenced by cultural display rules. *Display rules*, learned by an individual within the context of culture and family, dictate appropriate ways to express emotions. When the relationship is new, it may be considered more appropriate to express mostly positive emotions and emotions that produce harmony. As a relationship evolves toward increasing intimacy, it may be considered more acceptable to express intense or negative emotions. This may explain why some people put more effort into controlling or suppressing the expression of negative emotions early on in a romantic relationship (Strzyzewski Aune, Aune, & Buller, 1994).

Features of some mental health disorders include difficulties with interpersonal dynamics. Individuals with borderline personality disorder often experience a fear of abandonment. They have very unstable (*roller coaster*) interpersonal relationships, often alternating between extremes of expressing positive and negative emotions toward (and about) others. Individuals with schizoid personality disorder tend to be aloof and are uninterested in and unresponsive to interpersonal relationships.

See also attachment, borderline personality disorder, culture, display rules, family, family therapy, gender and emotions, interpersonal psychotherapy, intimacy, loneliness, loss, personality disorder, social support, transference, trust.

Further Reading:
Ryff, C. D., & Singer, B. H. (2001). *Emotion, social relationships, and health.* New York: Oxford University Press.

References:
Fraley, R. C., & Shaver, P. R. (2000). Adult romantic attachment: Theoretical developments, emerging controversies, and unanswered questions. *Review of General Psychology, 4*, 132–154.
Sanford, K. (2007). Hard and soft emotion during conflict: Investigating married couples and other relationships. *Personal Relationships, 14*, 65–90.
Strzyzewski Aune, K., Aune, R. K., & Buller, D. B. (1994). The experience, expression, and perceived appropriateness of emotions across levels of relationship development. *Journal of Social Psychology, 134*, 141–150.

Relief

Relief is a type of pleasure that arises following the cessation of an aversive stimulus or in the event that an unpleasant stimulus is expected but does not occur. Scholars disagree regarding at least one aspect of relief. Schopenhauer (1994) argued that relief is simply a temporary decrease in unhappiness. However, Frijda (2001) contends that it is often more than that; joy often follows relief, expressed as smiling, sighing, laughter, and in other ways.

One type of relief that follows the termination of something unpleasant is bodily relief pleasures, as identified by Kubovy (1999). They include sneezing, spitting, coughing, belching, orgasm, urination, defecation, and passing gas. Relief following the ending of something unpleasant has also been studied in other species such as rats. Over many decades, behaviorists (psychologists who study behavior only, without considering inner processes such as thought and emotions) investigated reinforcement in the form of cessation of electric shock. If an animal is subjected to a shock and must perform a behavior for the shock to cease, the behavior it performs is reinforced by the termination of the shock. Reinforcement means that in the future, the animal is likely to repeat that behavior that produced the termination of shock since it led to agreeable consequences. Often, the purpose of these studies was to learn more about the nature of reinforcement, but researchers at the same time observed relief in the animals, and some studies produced the added benefit of increasing our understanding of relief as an emotion. In a study specifically designed to investigate relief in rats, researchers found that after an unpleasant stimulus ceases, rats produce a vocalization that is apparently a sigh (Soltysik & Jelen, 2005).

Relief that involves a comparison between what *has* happened (something good) and what *could have* happened (something bad) engages higher-order thinking and has been studied in humans. For instance, Kray and Gelfand (2009) studied relief that occurs in salary negotiations with a new employer. People experienced relief when their offer was accepted. In particular, Kray and Gelfand (2009) found that women experienced more relief when their first offer was accepted than did men, which they interpreted as being related to the higher social cost that women face from negotiating salaries—that women are more concerned than men that salary negotiation will harm relationships with people in the workplace.

See also positive emotions.

References:

Frijda, N. H. (2001). The nature of pleasure. In J. A. Bargh & D. K. Apsley (Eds.), *Unraveling the complexities of social life: A festschrift in honor of Robert B. Zajonc* (pp. 71–94). Washington, DC: American Psychological Association.

Kray, L., & Gelfand, M. (2009). Relief versus regret: The effect of gender and negotiating norm ambiguity on reactions to having one's first offer accepted. *Social Cognition, 27*, 418–436.

Kubovy, M. (1999). On the pleasures of the mind. In D. Kahneman, E. Diener, & N. Schwarz (Eds.), *Well-being: The foundations of hedonic psychology* (pp. 134–154). New York: Russell Sage Foundation.

Schopenhauer, A., & Schirmacher, W. (1994). *Philosophical writings.* New York: Continuum International.

Soltysik, S., & Jelen, P. (2005). In rats, sighs correlate with relief. *Physiology & Behavior, 85*, 598–602.

Revised Children's Manifest Anxiety Scale

The Revised Children's Manifest Anxiety Scale: Second Edition (RCMAS-2) is a self-report scale that measures the level and nature of anxiety as experienced by children using a simple yes-or-no response format. It is designed for children and youth aged 6 to 19 years. Published by Western Psychological Services, it was created in 2008 by Cecil R. Reynolds and Bert O. Richmond. An individual's responses are compared to those of similarly aged children or teens in a sample of more than 2,300 children and teens. The RCMAS-2 consists of 49 items that look at several dimensions, including physiological anxiety, worry, social anxiety, and defensiveness. It also yields an overall anxiety score. It looks at issues such as stress, test anxiety, school avoidance, peer and family conflicts, and drug use. The RCMAS-2 can be completed in 10 to 15 minutes; a short form is available with only 10 items. Items are written at a second-grade reading level. The RCMAS-2 is available in English and Spanish.

See also anxiety, Beck Anxiety Inventory, Depression Anxiety and Stress Scales, generalized anxiety disorder, panic disorder, phobia, State-Trait Anxiety Inventory.

Further Reading:
Western Psychological Services Web site: http://portal.wpspublish.com/

Right Hemisphere Syndrome

In right-handed individuals, the *right* hemisphere of the brain (RH) is usually associated with prosody (controlling the emotional tone of speech), understanding facial expressions, sustaining attention, and visual-spatial control; the *left* hemisphere is usually associated with language and motor control. In addition, the RH controls motor functions and perceptions on the left side of the body, while the left hemisphere controls them on the opposite side. Stroke, brain trauma (e.g., traumatic brain injury), or disease (e.g., brain tumor) that damages regions of the RH may result in a condition called right hemisphere syndrome (RHS). Symptoms of RHS may include attention difficulties, visual-perception and motor problems, cognitive or emotional impairment, and alterations of body perception. Motor and visual-spatial perception difficulties may include problems with topographic memory (memory of familiar surroundings), dressing and constructional apraxia (inability to perform coordinated movements), motor impersistence (inability to sustain purposeful movement), prosopagnosia (inability to recognize faces), and poor comprehension of facial expression. Communication and perceptual difficulties may result in aprosodia (inability to control the emotional tone of speech) or amusia (loss of musical ability). Cognitive and emotional difficulties may include anosognosia (lack of awareness that one is sick or has a disability), confusion, apathy, flattened expression or affect (displaying little emotion), reduplication (belief that two versions of a person or place exist simultaneously), impaired judgment or decision making, or socially inappropriate behavior. RHS can result in misidentification of people, including the delusion that someone has a double (a doppelgänger); this is known as Capgras syndrome. RHS may cause significant problems on the left side of the body, including hemiplegia (paralysis) and hemispatial neglect (lack of attention or awareness of one side of the body). Congenital or developmental RHS in children is characterized by difficulties with attention, slow performance (processing) speed, emotional and interpersonal difficulties, visual-spatial problems, and nonverbal learning disabilities (especially difficulty with math).

Anosognosia is a condition in which an individual is unaware that he has been affected by illness or disability (e.g., when paralyzed following a stroke). The term anosognosia, from the Greek (*a*, "without"; *noso*, "disease"; *gnosia*, "knowledge"), was first described in 1914 by French neurologist Joseph Jules François Félix Babinski

(Heilman, Barrett, & Adair, 1998). Anosognosia is accompanied by a lack of concern about one's condition, with little or no display of emotion (Damasio, 1994). If an individual is unaware that there is something wrong, he may delay in seeking medical care, which could seriously impact outcomes (prognosis) or impede rehabilitation efforts. Anosognosia can be accompanied by an inability to make appropriate personal or social decisions, socially inappropriate behavior, or dangerous behavior. While some researchers have posited that anosognosia is a psychological defense mechanism (i.e., denial or repression), clinical evidence suggests that anosognosia is a cognitive result of neurological impairment (Damasio, 1994; Heilman et al., 1998). Anosognosia is caused by damage to the right somatosensory cerebral cortices, which are responsible for external and internal senses and perception of the body (body image), and to the white matter in the right hemisphere, which transmits signals between various body regions and the motor and prefrontal cortices (Damasio, 1994). Disruptions of body perception and awareness (body image or schema) combined with left-side paralysis or neglect may result in *somatoparaphrenia*, in which an individual does not believe that one of his body parts (or an entire side of his body) belongs to him. For example, an individual with RHS may believe that his paralyzed left arm belongs to the therapist who is working with him or that it belongs to his son (who is in another location).

When typical symptoms of RHS are observed in a right-handed individual with damage in the left hemisphere of the brain, this is known as crossed right hemisphere syndrome (Marchetti, Carey, & Della Sala, 2005). Genetic, hormonal, or developmental factors may lead to atypical patterns of brain lateralization (functions in different brain regions or hemispheres than the majority of the population). Aphasia (loss of language abilities) usually occurs with strokes affecting the left hemisphere. In crossed aphasia, damage to the right hemisphere (in a right-handed person) causes aphasia. Early cases of crossed aphasia were noted by Farge (1877) and Bramwell (1899; Marchetti et al., 2005). Data from crossed aphasia and crossed RHS indicate that rules of cerebral dominance are not always the case; that is, there is not always strict division (lateralization) of brain functions (e.g., language in one hemisphere, visual spatial in the other). Reports of exceptions, such as in crossed RHS, help neuroscientists learn more about how the brain functions.

RHS is diagnosed by clinical examination, neuropsychological testing, and imaging studies, most often functional magnetic resonance imaging (fMRI) or computed tomography (CT) scans. Other types of imaging, such as SPECT (single photon emission computed tomography), PET (positron emission tomography), or DTI (diffusion tensor imaging), may yield useful information about blood flow or neuron activity in specific brain regions. Treatments for RHS may include speech and language therapy, physical therapy, occupational therapy, cognitive rehabilitation, and psychotherapy.

See also aprosodia, Cotard's syndrome, diffusion tensor imaging, functional magnetic resonance imaging, Phineas P. Gage, positron emission tomography, prefrontal cortex, prosody, psychosurgery, traumatic brain injury.

Further Reading:
National Institute of Neurological Disorders and Stroke Web site: http://www.ninds.nih.gov/disorders/stroke/stroke.htm

References:

Damasio, A. (1994). *Descartes' error: Emotion, reason and the human brain.* New York: Putnam.

Heilman, K. M., Barrett, A. M., & Adair, J. C. (1998). Possible mechanisms of anosognosia: A defect in self-awareness. *Philosophical Transactions of the Royal Society of London, Series B, 353,* 1903–1909.

Marchetti, C., Carey, D., & Della Sala, S. (2005). Crossed right hemisphere syndrome following left thalamic stroke. *Journal of Neurology, 252,* 403–411.

Robertson, I. H., & Halligan, P. W. (1999). *Spatial neglect: A clinical handbook.* Hove, England: Psychology Press/Taylor and Francis.

> Notable cases of anosognosia after right hemisphere stroke include U.S. President Woodrow Wilson (in 1919) and Supreme Court justice William O. Douglas (in 1975). In addition to left-side paralysis, President Wilson showed signs of hemineglect—he ignored or was unaware of people and things positioned to his left. (His aides made sure all his guests were ushered in on the president's right side.) He denied any physical effects from the stroke and even sought reelection to a third term after his second stroke (Robertson & Halligan, 1999). Supreme Court Justice Douglas not only denied any physical effects of his stroke (he was paralyzed on the left) but he attributed his hospitalization to a fall, checked himself out of the hospital against medical advice, told reporters that he was kicking 40-yard field goals, and invited them to go hiking with him. He failed to observe social conventions, another symptom of his right-hemisphere syndrome. Although he was unable to perform his job, he refused to resign (Damasio, 1994).

Road Rage

Motor vehicle accidents (MVAs) are the number one cause of accidental death and injury in the United States (National Vital Statistics System, 2009). A primary factor contributing to MVAs is aggressive driving or *road rage.* Aggressive driving involves verbal and gestural aggression (e.g., yelling and cursing at other drivers, honking, and making obscene gestures), vehicular aggression (e.g., tailgating and blocking other drivers), and extreme forms of aggression (e.g., assault such as throwing objects, punching, or shooting other drivers).

Prevalence of aggressive driving has been studied in both general populations and among individuals in court-approved programs for traffic violators. Among the general public, research indicates that in a one-year period, between 7 and 34 percent of U.S. drivers report at least one instance of verbal or gestural driving aggression, between 16 and 28 percent report at least one example of vehicular aggression, and fewer than 1 percent report extreme vehicular aggression (Miller, Azrael, Hemenway, & Solop, 2002; Wells-Parker et al., 2002). Among individuals who enroll in programs for traffic violators, aggressive driving is much more frequent; for instance, 31 percent of these drivers reported chasing other vehicles with their car at some point in their lifetimes (Novaco, 1991), whereas fewer than 1 percent in the general population state that they engage in this behavior over their lifetimes.

A number of studies have confirmed that aggressive driving is associated with MVAs (for a review, see Galovski, Malta, & Blanchard, 2006). Aggressive driving is also correlated with assaults and other violent crimes and thus is a social problem worthy of study and a target for interventive treatments (Galovski et al., 2006).

Aggressive driving has multiple causes. Personal characteristics contribute to aggressive driving. For instance, individuals diagnosed with attention-deficit hyperactivity disorder (ADHD) are at higher risk (e.g., see Barkley, Guevremont, Anastopoulos, DuPaul, & Shelton, 1993). ADHD involves inattention, hyperactivity, and impulsivity. Additionally, individuals who do not have ADHD but are high in impulsiveness (low in self-control) are more likely to engage in aggressive driving. Social factors such as cultural norms and traffic congestion are also related to aggressive driving (Galovski et al., 2006).

Galovski, Malta, and Blanchard (2006) recommend a cognitive-behavioral approach to treatment. At the Albany Center for Stress and Anxiety Disorders, Galovski and Blanchard (2004) developed a program with the following components: education about the harmfulness of aggressive driving and of anger in general, teaching the aggressive driver to acknowledge that he is an aggressive driver, relaxation training, development of new coping techniques, and training in alternative (less angry) ways to view events. This treatment regimen is similar to anger management programs in general, such as have been created by Novaco (1975). Additionally, some self-help resources exist, for instance, the American Automobile Association (AAA) Foundation for Traffic Safety describes anger management tips on its Web site, and self-help manuals are available.

Aggressive driving is a dangerous problem that is likely to persist in the United States. Research on origins and treatment is relatively recent and is likely to advance in coming years.

See also aggression, anger, anger management, postal.

Further Readings:

AAA Foundation for Traffic Safety. (1997). *Road rage: How to avoid aggressive driving.* Retrieved from http://www.aaafoundation.org/pdf/roadrage.pdf

Galovski, T. E., Malta, L. S., & Blanchard, E. B. (2006). *Road rage: Assessment and treatment of the angry, aggressive driver.* Washington, DC: American Psychological Association.

References:

Barkley, R. A., Guevremont, D. C., Anastopoulos, A. D., DuPaul, G. J., & Shelton, T. L. (1993). Driving-related risks and outcomes of attention deficit hyperactivity disorder in adolescents and young adults. *Pediatrics, 92,* 212–218.

Galovski, T. E., & Blanchard, E. B. (2004). Road rage: A domain for psychological intervention? *Aggression and Violent Behavior, 9,* 105–127.

Galovski, T. E., Malta, L. S., & Blanchard, E. B. (2006). *Road rage: Assessment and treatment of the angry, aggressive driver.* Washington, DC: American Psychological Association.

Miller, M., Azrael, D., Hemenway, D., & Solop, F. I. (2002). "Road rage" in Arizona: Armed and dangerous. *Accident Analysis and Prevention, 34,* 807–814.

National Vital Statistics System. (2009). *Deaths: Final data for 2006* (National Vital Statistics Report No. 57(14), DHHS Publication No. (PHS) 2009-1120). Washington, DC: U.S. Department of Health and Human Services. Retrieved from http://www.cdc.gov/nchs/data/nvsr57/nvsr 57_14.pdf

Novaco, R. (1975). *Anger control: The development and evaluation of an experimental treatment.* Lexington, MA: D. C. Health.

Novaco, R. W. (1991). Aggression on roadways. In R. Baenninger (Ed.), *Targets of violence and aggression: Advances in psychology* (pp. 253–326). Oxford, England: North Holland.

Smart, R. G., Mann, R. E., & Stoduto, G. (2003). The prevalence of road rage: Estimates from Ontario. *Canadian Journal of Public Health, 94,* 247–250.

Wells-Parker, E., Ceminsky, J., Hallberg, V., Snow, R. W., Dunaway, G., Guiling, S., et al. (2002). An exploratory study of the relationship between road rage and crash experience in a representative sample of U.S. drivers. *Accident Analysis and Prevention, 34,* 271–278.

- A Canadian study found that about half of 1,395 adult survey respondents (46.6%) in Ontario, Canada, were shouted at, cursed at, or had rude gestures directed at them in the past year, and 7.2 percent were threatened with personal injury or car damage. Studies have found that road rage is more common among men and younger drivers. It is more common for drivers who often drive on busy roads and those who drive high-performance cars to perpetrate road rage (Smart, Mann, & Stoduto, 2003).

- Wells-Parker et al. (2002) conducted a survey of 1,382 adult drivers in the United States and found that 30 percent complained about other drivers; 17 percent had yelled at other drivers; 3 percent had chased other drivers or prevented others from passing; and 1 to 2 percent had gotten out of their cars to hurt or argue with other drivers, had deliberately hit other cars, or had carried a weapon.

- In Arizona, 34 percent of 790 drivers surveyed had made obscene gestures or cursed angrily, and 28 percent had aggressively followed or blocked other vehicles. About 11 percent carried guns in their cars; hostile behavior while driving was much more common among drivers who had guns (Miller, Azrael, Hemenway, & Solop, 2002).

Carl Rogers (1902–1987)

Carl Ransom Rogers was born in Oak Park, Illinois, a suburb of Chicago. He had five siblings, an engineer as a father, and a housewife mother. Both parents were deeply religious Protestants and hard workers. Rogers reported that his parents were kind and loving, but strict. They disapproved of drinking, smoking, dancing, playing cards, movies, and any demonstrations of sexual interest. Although Rogers's childhood was pleasant, his social life was limited.

He attended college at the University of Wisconsin, initially majoring in agriculture. In his junior year he was selected as one of 10 U.S. students to go to China, representing the World Student Christian Federation Conference. While in China, he began to doubt some of the literal teachings of the Bible. Around the same time, he fell in love with a young woman from his hometown, and they became engaged. He graduated with a degree in religion, married fiancée Helen Elliot, and enrolled in Union Theological Seminary in New York City.

In seminary, he developed further religious doubts and began to take courses at Columbia University, where he eventually earned a PhD in psychotherapy. While still a graduate student at Columbia, he took a job working as a psychologist in the Child Study Department of the Society for Prevention of Cruelty to Children in Rochester, New York. It was there, working with underprivileged and "delinquent" children for 12 years, that he developed much of his philosophy of psychotherapy.

Rogers had two children and a happy family life. He held academic jobs at Ohio State University, the University of Chicago, and the University of Wisconsin. At Wisconsin he became disenchanted with academia and in 1964 began working at the Western Behavioral Studies Institute in La Jolla, California. He continued in research positions into his eighties. Throughout his career he maintained an active psychotherapy practice. He wrote several books, including the classics *Client-Centered Therapy* (1951), *On Becoming a Person* (1961), and *A Way of Being* (1980). His honors include the American Psychological Association presidency in 1946, awards from the American Psychological Association, and a nomination for the Nobel Peace Prize in 1987. He died of a heart attack in 1987.

Rogers's primary contribution was his approach to psychotherapy, "the new psychotherapy" called *client-centered therapy*, which he also argued was an approach to life. Rogers, one of the founders of the humanist movement, contended that humans and other organisms naturally seek to "grow" and "actualize." This natural actualizing tendency will emerge as long as the individual is in an environment that provides the correct context—a relationship with another person who is warm, empathic, and genuine. Another focus of Rogers's therapy is that it is experiential and feeling oriented. Both client and therapist are to focus on the client's current experience, emotional and otherwise. Rogers presented a true alternative to the approaches to psychotherapy that existed in the 1950s, many of which still strongly resembled Freudian approaches. Rogers's humanism bears some similarity to a modern movement in psychology: positive psychology.

See also client-centered therapy, experiential therapy, humanistic psychotherapy, Abraham Maslow, positive psychology.

Further Readings:
Kirschenbaum, H., & Henderson, V. L. (1989). *The Carl Rogers reader.* Boston: Houghton Mifflin.
Rogers, C. R. (1951). *Client-centered therapy, , its current practice, implications, and theory.* Boston: Houghton Mifflin.
Rogers, C. R. (1961). *On becoming a person: A therapist's view of psychotherapy.* Boston: Houghton Mifflin.
Rogers, C. R. (1980). *A way of being.* Boston: Houghton Mifflin.

References:
Rogers, C. R. (1951). *Client-centered therapy, its current practice, implications, and theory.* Boston: Houghton Mifflin.
Rogers, C. R. (1961). *On becoming a person: A therapist's view of psychotherapy.* Boston: Houghton Mifflin.
Rogers, C. R. (1980). *A way of being.* Boston: Houghton Mifflin.

Rorschach Psychodiagnostic Technique

The Rorschach Psychodiagnostic Technique, also known as the Rorschach Inkblot Test or simply as the Rorschach, is the best known of the projective personality tests. A projective personality test is one in which people are presented with ambiguous, unstructured stimuli or situations and are asked to respond in some way, for example, by telling a story, completing a sentence, or drawing a picture. Projective tests are presumed to assess a variety of psychological attributes, including general personality traits, unconscious conflicts, needs, general adjustment level, and psychiatric conditions.

The Rorschach has a long and colorful history. It was developed by Swiss psychiatrist and psychoanalyst Hermann Rorschach. He published the test and an accompanying manuscript in 1921. The Rorschach was initially introduced in Europe and was poorly received, although a small and loyal following developed. Rorschach died suddenly of peritonitis in 1923 at age 38. He had not yet published most of his recommendations for scoring the test, and it appeared the Rorschach might fade into obscurity.

The test received a second life in America, when Bruno Klopfer, a German Jewish psychologist, left Germany as the Nazis rose to power there in the 1930s. He was hired as a researcher at Columbia University and began teaching a course on the Rorschach. Klopfer, who was a charismatic man, developed a sort of guru status and helped to create the mystique of the Rorschach. Other champions of the Rorschach followed Klopfer, including American psychologist Samuel Beck. By the 1950s and 1960s, the Rorschach was widely used by clinical psychologists. During this time, more dissertations and articles were written about the Rorschach than about any other clinical test.

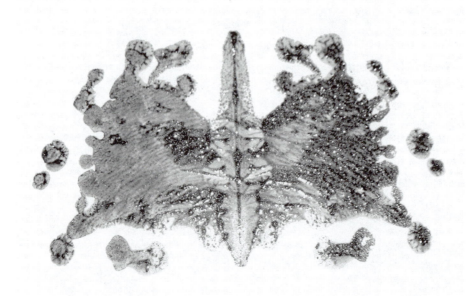

An imitation of a Rorschach inkblot. Developed by Swiss psychiatrist and psychoanalyst Hermann Rorschach, the Rorschach test is one of the most widely used psychological tests by clinical psychologists. (morgueFile.com)

The Rorschach consists of 10 cards on which symmetrical inkblots are printed. Five are black, gray, and white; the remaining five include color. During test administration, the assessor, who is usually sitting next to or across from the assessee, presents the first inkblot to the assessee, with an instruction such as, "Tell me what you see. There are no right or wrong answers. Just tell me what it looks like to you." The assessor writes down everything that the assessee says verbatim and may make note of other behaviors such as whether and how the assessee turns the card, length of time to respond, evidence of nervousness (e.g., foot shaking), and so on. Cards are presented one at a time to the assessee, with the same instructions.

Since Rorschach did not complete a scoring system before his death, others took on the task. Bruno Klopfer and Samuel Beck, both mentioned earlier, developed separate and competitive scoring guidelines, and each had his own group of followers who adhered to the leader's system. Klopfer took a more impressionistic, artistic approach to scoring, and Beck strove to create scoring principles based in empirical science. The two men were passionate rivals who eventually no longer spoke to one another, and therefore a unified scoring system was not created for many years. In fact, three additional groups of people broke off from either man, and three additional scoring approaches arose.

In the 1970s, American psychologist John Exner, who was Beck's student and who admired both men, developed the Comprehensive System, which attempted to integrate the five competing ones, with an emphasis in the empirical science approach. The Comprehensive System greatly improved interrater reliability among people administering the test. This means different assessors are more likely to interpret test results in the same way. The Comprehensive System is now the standard system for interpreting the Rorschach (Exner, 2002). Many agree that Exner's efforts paid off, and he was awarded the prestigious Award for Distinguished Professional Contribution by the American Psychological Association in 1998. Exner's scoring system is complex, with scorers interpreting over 100 characteristics. These characteristics include whether the assessee mentions movement, responds to color, tends to see blots holistically or in parts, whether responses focus on the colored parts of blots or the white spaces, and themes in the responses (e.g., people, animals, food, clothing, clouds, blood, etc.).

Despite the success of Exner's system and improved interrater reliability, use of the Rorschach is controversial. Several reviews have questioned its validity (e.g., Lilienfield, Wood, & Garb, 2000, 2001). Critics claim that the Rorschach is not helpful for diagnosis in general, with a few exceptions (e.g., to identify schizophrenia and other psychotic or thought disorders). In general, critics say, the Rorschach tends to overpathologize. In other words, the Rorschach tends to interpret many more responses as abnormal or indicative of a mental illness than would be expected in the general population. A particular area in which the Rorschach has been criticized is in legal proceedings (see Paul, 2004). It is regularly used in both criminal and civil cases where psychological evaluations are required (e.g., insanity pleas, child custody cases, claims regarding sexual abuse). Meyer and Archer (2001) have disputed these criticisms, arguing that the Rorschach is as valid as any other commonly used psychological test, including IQ tests and the Minnesota Multiphasic Personality Inventory (the personality test that is most commonly used by clinical psychologists).

The Rorschach is one of the most widely used psychological tests by clinical psychologists, ranking fourth in a poll from the year 2000 (Camara, Nathan, & Puente, 2000). Its use will likely remain controversial. Regardless of its future, the Rorschach has a prominent place in the history of psychology.

See also defense mechanisms, projective tests, psychoanalytic perspective, the unconscious mind.

Further Readings:

Lilienfeld, S. O., Wood, J. M., & Garb, H. N. (2001). What's wrong with this picture? *Scientific American, 284*(5), 80–87.

Paul, A. M. (2004). *The cult of personality: How personality tests are leading us to miseducate our children, mismanage our companies, and misunderstand ourselves.* New York: Free Press.

Wood, J. M., Nezworski, T., & Stejskal, J. (1996). The comprehensive system for the Rorschach: A critical examination. *Psychological Science, 7,* 3–10.

References:

Camara, W. J., Nathan, J. S., & Puente, A. E. (2000). Psychological test usage: Implications in professional psychology. *Professional Psychology: Research and Practice, 31,* 141–154.

Exner, J. E. (2002). *The Rorschach, basic foundations and principles of interpretation* (Vol. 1). New York: John Wiley.

Lilienfeld, S. O., Wood, J. M., & Garb, H. N. (2000). The scientific status of projective techniques. *Psychological Science in the Public Interest, 1,* 27–66.

Lilienfeld, S. O., Wood, J. M., & Garb, H. N. (2001). What's wrong with this picture? *Scientific American, 284,* 80–87.

Meyer, G. J., & Archer, R. P. (2001). The hard science of Rorschach research: What do we know and where do we go? *Psychological Assessment, 13,* 486–502.

Paul, A. M. (2004). *The cult of personality: How personality tests are leading us to miseducate our children, mismanage our companies, and misunderstand ourselves.* New York: Free Press.

Rorschach, H. (1998). *Psychodiagnostics: A diagnostic test based on perception.* Berne, Switzerland: H. Huber. (Original work published 1921)

Wolf-Fédida, M. (2006). La correspondance d'Hermann Rorschach de 1902 à 1922. [Correspondence of Hermann Rorschach between 1902 and 1922]. *Psychologie Clinique et Projective, 12,* 277–299.

- The Rorschach inkblot test was first known as Klecksography, named for the game Swiss children would play with inkblots (Wolf-Fédida, 2006).
- Douglas M. Kelley conducted a Rorschach study of the Nazis, published in his book *22 Cells in Nuremberg: A psychiatrist examines the Nazi criminals.*

Rosenberg Self-Esteem Scale

The Rosenberg Self-Esteem Scale (SES) was developed by Morris Rosenberg in 1965 to measure global self-esteem. Originally written to assess adolescents, it is now used with both adolescents and adults in both general and clinical populations. According to Hogan and Rengert (2008), the SES has maintained popularity over the years; it is a widely used measure in counseling research, ranking second of all tests used in research in four leading counseling journals that were surveyed from 2002 to 2005.

The SES is a brief (10 item) questionnaire that can be completed in a few minutes. A strength of the SES is that it has been used in research in a wide variety of populations, including the elderly (Classen, Velozo, & Mann, 2007), Canadian high school students (Bagley, Bolitho, & Bertrand, 1997), crack cocaine drug users (Wang, Siegal, Falck, & Carlson, 2001), and individuals with hearing loss (Crowe, 2002). It has been translated into many different languages, including German, Spanish, French, Japanese, Portuguese, American Sign Language, and Estonian. It is available on the Internet for self-assessment.

Self-esteem—a general feeling of self-worth and self-acceptance—is an important general mental health and well-being concept. It is relevant to both clinical and nonclinical populations. Improving self-esteem can be a helpful aspect of treating mental illnesses.

See also self-esteem.

Further Readings:

Rosenberg, M. (1965). *Society and the adolescent self-image.* Princeton, NJ: Princeton University Press.

Rosenberg Self-Esteem Scale available from York University, Ontario: http://www.yorku.ca/rokada/psyctest/rosenbrg.pdf/

References:

Bagley, C., Bolitho, F., & Bertrand, L. (1997). Norms and construct validity of the Rosenberg Self Esteem Scale in Canadian high school populations: Implications for counseling. *Canadian Journal of Counselling, 31*, 82–92.

Classen, S., Velozo, C., & Mann, W. (2007). The Rosenberg Self-Esteem Scale as a measure of self-esteem for the noninstitutionalized elderly. *Clinical Gerontologist, 31*, 77–93.

Crowe, T. V. (2002). Translation of the Rosenberg Self-Esteem Scale into American Sign Language: A principal components analysis. *Social Work Research, 26*, 57–63.

Hogan, T. P., & Rengert, C. (2008). Test usage in published research and the practice of counseling: A comparative review. *Measurement and Evaluation in Counseling and Development, 41*, 51–56.

Rosenberg, M. (1965). *Rosenberg Self Esteem Scale (RSES).* Princeton, NJ: Princeton University Press.

Wang, J., Siegal, H. A., Falck, R. S., & Carlson, R. G. (2001). Factorial structure of Rosenberg's Self-Esteem Scale among crack-cocaine drug users. *Structural Equation Modeling, 8*, 275–286.

S

Sadness

Sadness is an emotional reaction to a perceived loss, lasting anywhere from a few seconds to several hours. The sad individual may have suffered the death of a loved one, lost a relationship, a job, or a home, or received a low score on an exam. Whether a loss will lead to sadness is a matter of individual interpretation and experience. Scherer's (1997) cross-cultural study of emotions produced results that led to a better understanding of sadness. When research participants were asked to describe circumstances under which they felt sadness, participants mentioned that the situations were unpleasant, they conflicted with personal goals, and the losses that occurred were perceived as irrevocable. Thus sadness is associated with some level of hopelessness.

Sadness is related to other experiences, such as depression and grief, with sadness being the less complicated reaction. Depression includes sadness but also a variety of other symptoms and is longer-lasting than sadness. Grief, like sadness, is a reaction to loss but is longer lasting and includes both sadness and other emotions.

Many emotional reactions, such as fear and sexual desire, are clearly functional, leading to self-protective or self-promoting behaviors such as escape from danger or mating. Sadness is also presumed to have one or more purposes, although researchers have not agreed on what these may be. One theory is that sadness, which is associated with low activity level and social withdrawal, allows for self-reflection in the aftermath of loss of an object or person of central importance to the self (Lazarus, 1991). This reflective period allows the individual to change her plans and goals in a way that integrates the loss (e.g., Bonanno & Keltner, 1997). A second theory is that sad behavior (facial expression, posture of sadness, etc.) evokes empathy in others and encourages others to provide help (e.g., Keltner & Kring, 1998). Therefore an individual becomes sad when he needs assistance, and the signs of sadness may elicit help from others. Bonanno, Goorin, and Coifman (2008) describe other theories of the function of sadness.

Sadness has reliable physiological components. Perhaps counterintuitive, sadness is associated with activation of the sympathetic nervous system, which involves the stress response. For example, with sadness, heart and respiration rates increase (Levenson, Ekman, & Friesen, 1990) and cortisol (a stress hormone) is released (Buss et al., 2003). Additionally, release of beta endorphin (the body's natural painkiller) is decreased when an individual experiences sadness (e.g., Zubieta et al., 2003). Although ordinary people may feel that they know much about this everyday emotion, it is one of the emotions about which we have the least scientific knowledge.

See also basic emotions, crying, depression, dysphoria, grief, loss, negative emotions, sympathetic nervous system.

References:

Bonanno, G. A., Goorin, L., & Coifman, K. G. (2008). Sadness and grief. In M. Lewis, J. M. Haviland-Jones, & L. F. Barret (Eds.), *Handbook of emotions* (3rd ed., pp. 797–810). New York: Guilford.

Bonanno, G. A., & Keltner, D. (1997). Facial expressions of emotion and the course of conjugal bereavement. *Journal of Abnormal Psychology, 106*, 126–137.

Buss, K. A., Schumacher, J.R.M., Dolski, I., Kalin, N. H., Goldsmith, H. H., & Davidson, R. J. (2003). Right frontal brain activity, cortisol, and withdrawal behavior in 6-month-old infants. *Behavioral Neuroscience, 117*, 11–20.

Keltner, D., & Kring, A. (1998). Emotion, social function, and psychopathology. *Review of General Psychology, 2*, 320–342.

Lazarus, R. S. (1991). *Emotion and adaptation.* New York: Oxford University Press.

Levenson, R. W., Ekman, P., & Friesen, W. V. (1990). Voluntary facial action generates emotion-specific autonomic nervous system activity. *Psychophysiology, 27*, 363–384.

Scherer, K. (1997). The role of culture in emotion-antecedent appraisal. *Journal of Personality and Social Psychology, 73*, 902–922.

Zubieta, J.-K., Ketter, T. A., Bueller, J. A., Xu, Y., Kilbourn, M. R., Young, E. A., et al. (2003). Regulation of human affective responses by anterior cingulate and limbic µ-opioid neurotransmission. *Archives of General Psychiatry, 60*, 1145–1153.

San Francisco Bay Area Center for Cognitive Therapy

Founded in 1995, the San Francisco Bay Area Center for Cognitive Therapy (the Center) provides care to people to enhance the quality of their lives. Located in the Rockridge district of North Oakland, it is led by a group of six clinical psychologists who specialize in cognitive-behavioral therapy (CBT). They are committed to providing high-quality CBT, conducting CBT research and training, and disseminating information about CBT to professionals and the public. The Center provides individual and couples therapy for adults, adolescents, and children. They provide treatment for a variety of issues including mood disorders, anxiety, substance abuse, impulse control, sexual dysfunction, eating disorders, and personality disorders.

According to the Center's Web site, CBT is a practical, present-focused approach to treatment in which therapists help people improve functioning by teaching people skills to manage the thoughts (cognitions) and behaviors that contribute to their problems. CBT is based on empirical evidence and is goal oriented, practical and concrete, active (the therapist serves as teacher and coach), and collaborative (patient and therapist work together as a team).

At an initial consultation, patient and therapist discuss presenting issues and explore whether CBT is an appropriate treatment. When the patient is a child or adolescent, the parents or primary caretakers meet with therapists for the initial consultation. Since psychologists at the Center cannot prescribe medications, referrals can be made to local psychiatrists.

Setting concrete goals is an important process in the early stages of the therapy. Treatment goals may focus on reducing unpleasant symptoms (e.g., depression, anxiety, panic attacks, substance abuse) or improving functioning (e.g., ability to function at work, increased work satisfaction, reduced fights with spouse). The therapist may help the patient identify any distorted beliefs contributing to distress and obstacles preventing the patient from taking actions that might accelerate progress. By suggesting new ways to look at the situation, the therapist can teach the patient better ways to handle situations. The patient practices newly learned skills in therapy and as homework; the therapist plays a role as coach. Together, patient and therapist monitor the patient's progress.

The Center's Web site lists publications authored by Center psychologists. It also has a list of resources, including referrals to other treatment professionals, self-help books, a list of current research studies and clinical trials, and professional resources.

See also cognitive therapy and cognitive-behavioral therapy.

Further Reading:
San Francisco Bay Area Center for Cognitive Therapy Web site: http://www.sfbacct.com/.

Satisfaction

Satisfaction is one of a number of positive emotions or affective states. The term *satisfaction* comes from the Latin *facere* (to do or make) and *satis* (enough). True to the meanings of the root words, feeling satisfaction means that one has judged or assessed that a situation is adequate; the situation or circumstance meets some standard or expectation that one has established. In psychology, a type of satisfaction that is frequently considered and studied is overall life satisfaction.

Evaluating one's satisfaction involves making a comparison. A number of researchers have discussed the types of comparisons that an individual makes to determine her satisfaction level. Sirgy et al. (1995) identified several, including comparing what one has to what

- one deserves
- others have
- one has had in the past
- is ideal
- is minimally tolerable
- one has predicted for oneself
- one would expect given one's evaluation of one's personal strengths and weaknesses

An individual may make one comparison or a number of comparisons to evaluate satisfaction in any particular circumstance.

Since satisfaction is relative, it often does not correspond directly to objective conditions. For example, people who are poor often report higher life satisfaction than some people who are rich. Olson and Schober (1993) have dubbed this phenomenon the *satisfaction paradox.*

An affective concept that is similar to satisfaction is happiness. Some scholars argue that the two concepts are identical (e.g., Veenhoven, 1984). However, others have made some distinctions. According to some researchers (e.g., Campbell, Converse, & Rodgers, 1976), satisfaction and happiness are the two primary components of well-being. Satisfaction is the more cognitive (thinking) component, and happiness is the feeling component. According to Schumm (1999), happiness is more often related to the quality of one's interpersonal relationships than is satisfaction. Supporting these theoretical ideas that satisfaction and happiness are distinct, some researchers have found that the same individuals may report high levels of one and low levels of the other. For instance, Adams (1997) found that between 1980 and 1992, African Americans reported that their level of satisfaction increased while their overall happiness decreased.

As Michalos (1980) discussed, satisfaction may occur in two ways. An individual has either achieved one's aspirations, through meeting some absolute standard, doing better than others, doing better than one has done in the past, and so on, or one has lowered or given up on one's aspirations, becoming resigned (in which case aspirations match achievements because the aspirations have now been lowered). With achievement, one is both satisfied and happy with the situation. With resignation, one is satisfied—there is no gap between aspiration and achievement—but is not happy with the circumstance.

See also happiness, positive emotions, positive psychology, Satisfaction with Life Scale.

Further Reading:
Schumm, W. R. (1999). Satisfaction. In D. Levinson, J. J. Ponzetti, & P. F. Jorgensen (Eds.), *Encyclopedia of human emotions* (2nd ed., pp. 583–590). New York: Macmillan Reference USA.

References:
Adams, V. H., III. (1997). A paradox in African American quality of life. *Social Indicators Research, 42,* 205–219.
Campbell, A., Converse, P. E., & Rodgers, W. L. (1976). *The quality of American life: Perceptions, evaluations, and satisfactions.* New York: Russell Sage Foundation.
Michalos, A. C. (1980). Satisfaction and happiness. *Social Indicators Research, 8,* 385–422.
Olson, G. I., & Schober, B. I. (1993). The satisfied poor: Development of an intervention-oriented theoretical framework to explain satisfaction with a life in poverty. *Social Indicators Research, 28,* 173–193.
Schumm, W. R. (1999). Satisfaction. In D. Levinson, J. J. Ponzetti, & P. F. Jorgensen (Eds.), *Encyclopedia of human emotions* (2nd ed., pp. 583–590). New York: Macmillan Reference USA.
Sirgy, M. J., Cole, D., Kosenko, R., Meadow, H. L., Rahtz, D., Cicic, M., et al. (1995). A life satisfaction measure: Additional validation data for the Congruity Life Satisfaction Measure. *Social Indicators Research, 34,* 237–259.
Veenhoven, R. (1984). *Conditions of happiness.* Dordrecht, Netherlands: D. Reidel.

Satisfaction with Life Scale

The Satisfaction with Life Scale (SWLS) was developed by American psychologist Ed Diener and colleagues (Diener, Emmons, Larson, & Griffin, 1985) as a measure of overall life satisfaction. The SWLS is one of relatively few assessment tools of positive emotional states; the majority of assessment tools measuring emotion focus on negative emotional states. The SWLS is one of the most widely used measures of life satisfaction or general well-being and is primarily utilized in research (rather than as a clinical or diagnostic test).

The SWLS consists of only five items that the assessee (person taking the test) rates on a scale from 1 (strongly disagree) to 7 (strongly agree). Examples of items are "In most ways, my life is close to ideal" and "If I could live my life over, I would change almost nothing." Completing the SWLS takes one to two minutes.

A number of research questions can be addressed through use of the SWLS. In addition to measuring general life satisfaction, it can also be used to measure stability or changes in life satisfaction over time. Another potential topic of study is the relationship between people's objective circumstances (e.g., socioeconomic status, level of education, age) and one's general life satisfaction. Researchers have also utilized the SWLS to assess life satisfaction in specific populations such as the elderly (Richeson & Thorson, 2002), people suffering from traumatic injury (Corrigan, Bogner, Mysiw, Clinchot, & Fugate, 2001), and university students (Paolini, Yanez, & Kelly, 2006). With the increasing popularity of the positive psychology movement in psychology, this measure is likely to continue to be widely used.

See also positive emotions, positive psychology, satisfaction.

References:
Corrigan, J. D., Bogner, J. A., Mysiw, W. J., Clinchot, D., & Fugate, L. (2001). Life satisfaction after traumatic brain injury. *Journal of Head Trauma Rehabilitation, 16,* 543–555.
Diener, E., Emmons, R. A., Larsen, R. J., & Griffin, S. (1985). The Satisfaction with Life Scale. *Journal of Personality Assessment, 49,* 71–75.
Paolini, L., Yanez, A. P., & Kelly, W. E. (2006). An examination of worry and life satisfaction among college students. *Individual Differences Research, 4,* 331–339.
Richeson, N., & Thorson, J. A. (2002). The effect of autobiographical writing on the subjective well-being of older adults. *North American Journal of Psychology, 4,* 395–404.

Schizoaffective Disorder

Schizoaffective disorder has elements of both schizophrenia and a mood (affective) disorder. It is generally considered to be a form of schizophrenia, lying on the *schizophrenia spectrum*. There are two subtypes of schizoaffective disorder: the depressive subtype is characterized by major depressive episodes, while the bipolar subtype is characterized by manic episodes with or without depressive symptoms.

Schizoaffective disorder presents with symptoms of a major mood disorder (manic, depressive, or mixed) concurrent with symptoms of schizophrenia. Mood symptoms are prominent throughout the course of the illness, except for minimum two-week period during which there are positive psychotic symptoms (hallucinations or delusions) without prominent mood symptoms. It can be difficult to distinguish schizoaffective disorder from schizophrenia and from bipolar disorder.

Characteristic symptoms of schizoaffective disorder generally fall into four categories: positive symptoms, negative symptoms, symptoms of mania, and depression:

- *Positive symptoms* are the *presence* of thoughts, perceptions, and behaviors that are usually absent in people without schizoaffective disorder. These include hallucinations (seeing and hearing things that are not there), delusions (false beliefs), and thought disturbances (e.g., jumping from topic to topic, making up new words, speech that does not make sense).
- *Negative symptoms* are an *absence* of behaviors, thoughts, or perceptions that would normally be present in people without schizoaffective disorder. These include blunted affect (lack of expression), apathy, anhedonia (inability to experience pleasure), poverty of speech (not saying much), and inattention. Residual and

negative symptoms are usually less severe and less chronic with schizoaffective disorder than those seen in schizophrenia.

- *Symptoms of mania* involve an *excess* of behavior, activity, or mood. These may include euphoric or expansive mood, irritability, inflated self-esteem or grandiosity, decreased need for sleep, rapid or pressured speech, racing thoughts, distractibility, increased goal-directed activity (a great deal of time spent pursuing specific goals, at work, school, or sexually), and excessive involvement in pleasurable activities with high potential for negative consequences (e.g., increased substance use, spending sprees, sexual indiscretions, risky business ventures).
- *Depressive symptoms* involve a *deficit* of activity and mood. Symptoms include depressed mood, sadness, diminished interest or pleasure (anhedonia), changes in appetite or sleeping patterns, decreased activity level, fatigue, loss of energy, feelings of worthlessness, inappropriate guilt, decreased concentration, inability to make decisions, and preoccupation with thoughts of death.

Schizoaffective disorder usually starts in late adolescence or early adulthood, most often between the ages of 16 and 30. Because it is difficult to differentiate schizoaffective disorder from schizophrenia and bipolar disorder, detailed information on the prevalence and demographics of schizoaffective disorder is lacking. Estimates suggest that there is a higher incidence of schizoaffective disorder in women than in men. The bipolar subtype of schizoaffective disorder is more common in young adults, while the depressive subtype is more common in older adults (American Psychiatric Association, 2000). The disorder lasts a lifetime, although symptoms and functioning can improve with time and treatment. Symptom severity also varies over time, sometimes requiring hospitalization. The cause of schizoaffective disorder is not known, although current theories suggest that an imbalance of the neurotransmitter dopamine (a chemical messenger) is at the root of both schizophrenia and schizoaffective disorder.

Features associated with schizoaffective disorder include poor occupational functioning, a restricted range of social contact, difficulties with self-care, increased risk of suicide, increased risk for later developing episodes of pure mood disorder, schizophrenia, or schizophreniform disorder (similar to schizophrenia). Schizoaffective disorder is also associated with alcohol and other substance-related disorders (resulting from attempts to self-medicate). Anosognosia (i.e., poor insight that one is ill) is also common in schizoaffective disorder, but the deficits in insight may be less severe and pervasive than in schizophrenia.

A combination of medication and psychosocial interventions is generally used to treat schizoaffective disorder. Medications include antipsychotics, mood stabilizers, and antidepressants. The effectiveness of psychosocial interventions has been researched less for schizoaffective disorder than for schizophrenia or mood disorders. However, the evidence suggests that beneficial treatments include cognitive-behavioral therapy, social skills training, vocational rehabilitation, family therapy, and case management.

The bipolar subtype of schizoaffective disorder has a better prognosis than the depressive subtype. Everyone responds to treatment differently. While a brief period of treatment can provide effective relief with a return to normal functioning for one person, another person may require ongoing long-term treatment.

See also anhedonia, antidepressant, antimanic, antipsychotic, bipolar disorder, cognitive therapy and cognitive-behavioral therapy, depression, family therapy, mood disorder, mood stabilizer, schizophrenia.

Further Readings:
Dodds, M. (2007). *Schizoaffective: A happier and healthier life.* Frederick, MD: PublishAmerica.
Medline Plus. (2006). *Schizoaffective disorder.* Retrieved from http://www.nlm.nih.gov/medlineplus/ency/article/000930.htm
National Alliance on Mental Illness. (2003). *Schizoaffective disorder.* Retrieved from http://www.nami.org/Template.cfm?Section=By_Illness&Template=/TaggedPage/TaggedPageDisplay.cfm&TPLID=54&ContentID=23043

References:
American Psychiatric Association. (2000). *Diagnostic and statistical manual of mental disorders* (4th ed., text rev.). Washington, DC: Author.
National Alliance on Mental Illness. (2003). *Schizoaffective disorder.* Retrieved from http://www.nami.org/Template.cfm?Section=By_Illness&Template=/TaggedPage/TaggedPageDisplay.cfm&TPLID=54&ContentID=23043

Schizoaffective disorder is one of the more common, chronic, and disabling mental illnesses. Although its exact prevalence is not clear, it may range from 2 to 5 in 1,000 people (0.2% to 0.5%). Schizoaffective disorder may account for one-quarter to one-third of all people diagnosed with schizophrenia (National Alliance on Mental Illness, 2003).

Schizophrenia

Schizophrenia is a mental disorder characterized by abnormal perceptions and expressions of reality. It is marked by positive and negative symptoms. Positive symptoms indicate the *presence* of behaviors, perceptions, or thoughts that people without schizophrenia do not exhibit or experience. These may include hallucinations (hearing or seeing things that are not there), delusions (fixed or bizarre beliefs not necessarily grounded in reality), disorganized speech, and disorganized or catatonic behavior. Negative symptoms indicate the *absence* of behaviors or thoughts experienced or exhibited by individuals without the disorder. These may include flat affect (lack of emotional expression or reactivity), alogia (poverty of speech), and avolition (lack of drive or motivation). Schizophrenia also causes significant social, interpersonal, and occupational (vocational and/or academic) dysfunction.

In 1896, German psychiatrist Emil Kraepelin grouped together paranoid psychosis, hebephrenia (now known as *disorganized type schizophrenia*), and catatonia into a single entity known as *dementia praecox* (which literally means "early dementia"). Swiss psychiatrist Paul Eugen Bleuler changed the name to schizophrenia in 1908. The word *schizophrenia* comes from the Greek roots *schiz* (to split) and *phren* (soul, spirit, or mind). Bleuler believed that the splitting of different psychological functions results in a loss of unity of the personality (Fusar-Poli & Politi, 2008). In the current version of the *Diagnostic and Statistical Manual of Mental Disorders* (*DSM-IV-TR*; American

Rosemary Kennedy (depicted in this 1938 family photograph) was born with mild mental retardation; she developed schizophrenia at the age of 21. After undergoing a lobotomy, she lived most of her life in an institution. From left to right: Bobby, Eunice, Jean, Patricia, Rosemary, and Teddy. (AP/Wide World Photos)

Psychiatric Association, 2000), there are five schizophrenia subtypes: catatonic, disorganized, paranoid, undifferentiated, and residual. Individuals presenting with schizophrenia rarely fall entirely into one subtype; a diagnosis is assigned based on the most prominent symptoms. An individual with schizophrenia may be diagnosed with different subtypes at different points in time. To be diagnosed with schizophrenia, symptoms must have been present for a continuous period of time: at least six months according to the *DSM-IV-TR*, and one month according to the *International Statistical Classification of Diseases and Related Health Problems* (*ICD-10*; World Health Organization, 1990). The *DSM-IV-TR* is a classification system for mental health disorders used more often in the United States; the *ICD-10* is used more often in Europe and the United Kingdom (Stirling, 1999).

The course of schizophrenia falls into phases. The *prodromal* phase is a period of deteriorating function and symptoms including a general loss of interest, avoidance of social interactions, avoidance of work or study, irritability, oversensitivity, odd beliefs (e.g., superstitions), and odd behaviors (e.g., talking to oneself in public). The *acute* (or active) phase is characterized by positive psychotic symptoms (i.e., hallucinations, delusions, disordered thoughts, bizarre behavior) and functional deterioration. In the *recovery* phase, active psychosis begins to remit; there may be some ongoing psychotic symptoms as well as confusion, disorganization, or dysphoria. The *residual* phase is characterized by negative symptoms such as lack of motivation, apathy, social withdrawal, and flat affect with continued (but less severe) impairment. If symptoms persist and do not respond to medication, some individuals remain chronically impaired. There may be overlap between phases. Some phases respond better to different treatments.

It is important to distinguish between schizophrenia and other disorders, for example, bipolar disorder, schizoaffective disorder, personality disorders, other psychotic disorders, or psychosis caused by general medical conditions or substance use. While schizophrenia has some affective (mood-related) symptoms, affective features are less prominent than in bipolar or schizoaffective disorders. Schizotypal, schizoid, paranoid, and borderline personality disorders can be mistaken for schizophrenia. Other psychotic disorders include delusional disorders (e.g., Cotard's or Capgras syndrome), brief psychotic disorder, and shared psychotic disorder (folie à deux). Physiological conditions that can cause symptoms similar to schizophrenia include brain tumors, viral encephalitis, temporal lobe epilepsy, cerebral syphilis, multiple sclerosis, Huntington's disease, and AIDS. Head injury (especially if it damages the left temporal lobe) may cause schizophrenia-like symptoms (Torrey, 2006). Substance-induced psychosis can be caused by drugs of abuse (e.g., amphetamines, psychedelics, PCP) and by some medications; it is usually transient (it passes), whereas schizophrenia does not. An individual's culture must be taken into account when considering a diagnosis of schizophrenia. Individuals who participate in certain religious or spiritual rituals, or belong to a culture with a history of shamanism, may speak in tongues, report hallucinations or visions, or behave in an excited or seemingly irrational manner. If linguistic and cultural differences exist, mental health practitioners should be cautious when interpreting speech as disorganized or behavior as bizarre, and be sensitive to cultural differences in eye contact, emotional expression, and body language. There is some evidence of overdiagnosis of schizophrenia in African Americans and Asian Americans by American clinicians (American Psychiatric Association, 2000).

Schizophrenia has a relatively narrow age of onset. In the United States, 75 percent of individuals who develop schizophrenia do so between 17 and 25 years of age. It can occur in childhood (rarely before age five) or later in life. Schizophrenia tends to affect more men than women (Torrey, 2006). Individuals with better prognoses (positive outcomes and response to treatment) tend to have sudden (rather than gradual) onset, later (adult) onset, be women, have no relatives with a history of schizophrenia, or have predominantly positive (rather than negative) symptoms. Individuals with schizophrenia have a lower life expectancy; this is thought to be related to increased accidents, disease, unhealthy lifestyles (including smoking and substance abuse), inadequate medical care, and homelessness (Torrey, 2006). There is a higher rate of unemployment and suicide among individuals with schizophrenia.

Obsolete theories for causes of schizophrenia include bad mothering, masturbation, demons, parenting styles, poor family relationships, early childhood trauma, and attachment difficulties. Schizophrenia was attributed to "bad cultures" by Margaret Mead in the 1930s; Christopher Lasch revisited this concept in 1979 with his idea that schizophrenia is the characteristic expression of a narcissistic society, and Ronald Laing (in the 1960s) promoted the idea that schizophrenia was a sane response to an insane world. Thomas Szasz purported that schizophrenia and other mental disorders do not actually exist; they are simply semantic artifacts (Torry, 2006). Other theories that have been discredited (but continue to be explored) include the idea that schizophrenia is caused by vitamin deficiencies or food allergies. It is now understood that causes of schizophrenia relate to genetics (it runs in families), neurochemistry, brain structure, neurology, immunology, prenatal factors, and environment. There is an increased incidence of schizophrenia with prenatal exposure to flu, famine, obstetric complications, and central nervous system infection in early childhood (American Psychiatric Association, 2000). The major neurotransmitters (chemical messengers in the brain) implicated in schizophrenia include dopamine, serotonin, norepinephrine, glutamate, and GABA (gamma-aminobutyric acid); (Torrey, 2006). Neuroimaging studies have consistently found enlargement of the lateral ventricles (part of the telencephelon of the brain). Schizophrenia affects a range of neuropsychological abilities, including memory, psychomotor abilities (e.g., coordination), attention, perception, and reaction time. This accounts for much of the disordered thinking and functional impairment experienced by individuals with schizophrenia. Schizophrenia may be associated with aprosodia, or a difficulty in appropriately transmitting and interpreting language-based and nonverbal cues (e.g., tone of voice, body language). It may be accompanied by anhedonia (manifested by a loss of interest or pleasure), dysphoric mood (e.g., depression), anxiety, anger, sleep disturbance, lack of interest in food or eating, abnormal psychomotor activity (e.g., pacing, rocking, grimacing, posturing), odd mannerisms, and ritualistic or stereotyped behavior. Schizophrenia often co-occurs with obsessive-compulsive disorder, panic disorder, and phobias.

Before antipsychotics were developed in the 1950s, treatment for psychosis consisted of shock therapy (e.g., electroconvulsive shock and induced insulin coma), barbiturates, psychosurgery (e.g., prefrontal lobotomy), physical restraint, and institutionalization (Patterson, 2006). Current effective treatment of schizophrenia starts with a thorough diagnostic work-up and combines several treatment modalities. Treatments may include antipsychotic and other medications, family therapy (including psychoeducation), individual supportive therapy (e.g., psychoeducation, cognitive-behavioral therapy), social skills and vocational training, hospitalization (if necessary), and case management (coordination of services and communication between treatment providers). Some practitioners advocate the use of electroconvulsive therapy for the treatment of schizophrenia (Torrey, 2006). Alternatives to antipsychotics such as glycine, vitamin B_3 (niacin), *Rauwolfia serpentina*, and betel nut (*Areca catechu*) have yielded inconclusive results (Javitt et al., 2001; Sullivan, Andres, Otto, Miles, & Kydd, 2007; Werneke, Turner, & Priebe, 2006). More research is needed to determine the safety and effectiveness of these approaches for treating schizophrenia.

See also anhedonia, antipsychotics, anxiety, aprosodia, bipolar disorder, cognitive therapy and cognitive-behavioral therapy, complementary and alternative medicine, Cotard's syndrome, culture-related specific syndromes, depression, dysphoria, electroconvulsive therapy, family therapy, neurotransmitter, obsessive-compulsive disorder, phobia, prefrontal lobotomy, psychosurgery, schizoaffective disorder, serotonin, traumatic brain injury.

Further Readings:

National Alliance on Mental Illness Web site: http://www.nami.org/

National Center for Complementary and Alternative Medicine Web site: http://nccam.nih.gov/health/

Snyder, K. (2007). *Me, myself, and them: A firsthand account of one young person's experience with schizophrenia.* New York: Oxford University Press.

Torrey, E. F. (2006). *Surviving schizophrenia: A manual for families, patients, and providers* (5th ed.). New York: HarperCollins.

References:
American Psychiatric Association. (2000). *Diagnostic and statistical manual of mental disorders* (4th ed., text rev.). Washington, DC: Author.
Fusar-Poli, P., & Politi, P. (2008). Paul Eugen Bleuler and the birth of schizophrenia (1908). *American Journal of Psychiatry, 165*, 1407.
Javitt, D. C., Silipo, G., Cienfuegos, A., Shelley, A. M., Bark, N., Park, M., et al. (2001). Adjunctive high-dose glycine in the treatment of schizophrenia. *International Journal of Neuropsychopharmacology, 4*, 385–391.
National Institute of Mental Health. (2009). *The numbers count: Mental disorders in America*. Retrieved from http://www.nimh.nih.gov/health/publications/the-numbers-count-mental-disorders-in-america/index.shtml#Schizophrenia
Patterson, J. (2006). *Therapist's guide to psychopharmacology: Working with patients, families, and physicians to optimize care.* New York: Guilford.
Stirling, J. D. (1999). *Psychopathology*. London: Routledge.
Sullivan, R. J., Andres, S., Otto, C., Miles, W., & Kydd, R. (2007). The effects of an indigenous muscarinic drug, betel nut (*Areca catechu*), on the symptoms of schizophrenia: A longitudinal study in Palau, Micronesia. *American Journal of Psychiatry, 164*, 670–673.
Torrey, E. F. (2006). *Surviving schizophrenia: A manual for families, patients, and providers* (5th ed.). New York: HarperCollins.
Werneke, U., Turner, T., & Priebe, S. (2006). Complementary medicines in psychiatry: Review of effectiveness and safety. *British Journal of Psychiatry, 188*, 109–121.
World Health Organization. (1990). *International statistical classification of diseases and related health problems* (10th rev.). Geneva, Switzerland: Author.

- Rosemary Kennedy (sister of John, Robert, and Edward Kennedy) was born with mild mental retardation; she developed schizophrenia at the age of 21. Because antipsychotic medications did not exist in 1941, Rosemary was given a lobotomy. This caused severe mental retardation and brain damage. She was confined to a private nursing home until her death in 2005, at the age of 86.
- The 2001 film *A Beautiful Mind* depicted the life of Nobel Prize winner John Forbes Nash as he developed paranoid schizophrenia.
- Approximately 2.4 million American adults, or about 1.1 percent of the population aged 18 and older in a given year, have schizophrenia. Schizophrenia often first appears in men in their late teens or early twenties. In contrast, women are generally affected in their twenties or early thirties (National Institute of Mental Health, 2009).

Seasonal Affective Disorder

Seasonal affective disorder (SAD) is a type of depressive disorder characterized by episodes of depression at certain times of the year. SAD should not be confused with SADS (sudden arrhythmia death syndrome), a genetic heart condition that can cause sudden death in apparently healthy young people. SAD diagnoses are usually made by qualified health professionals using criteria from the *Diagnostic and Statistical Manual of Mental Disorder* (*DSM-IV-TR*; American Psychiatric Association, 2000). Most episodes begin in fall or winter and remit (go away) in the spring. According to the *DSM-IV-TR*, SAD involves a pattern of seasonal onset of at least two depressive episodes with remissions, and no nonseasonal depressive episodes, that have occurred during the past two years. Also, seasonal depressive episodes must outnumber nonseasonal episodes over the person's lifetime. With SAD, seasonal depression cannot be better explained by psychosocial stressors such as unemployment during the winter months or a seasonal school schedule (American Psychiatric Association, 2000). SAD can range from mild dysphoria (feeling unwell or unhappy) to severe depression. In addition to sadness or depressed mood, SAD symptoms include lack of energy, hypersomnia (sleeping a lot), overeating, weight gain, and carbohydrate cravings. Major depressive disorder or bipolar episodes (usually bipolar II) may be seasonal in nature. There are high rates of SAD among adults with attention-deficit hyperactivity disorder (ADHD; Rybak, McNeely, Mackenzie, Jain, & Levitan, 2007). If an individual has seasonal bipolar disorder, full-spectrum light therapy (phototherapy) may cause switching to manic or hypomanic episodes.

SAD occurs more frequently in women and at higher latitudes (closer to the North Pole). Winter depressive episodes occur more in younger people. SAD is also seen in individuals who work at night or do shift work, and in areas with significant cloud cover or pollution that blocks out sunlight (Preston, O'Neal, & Talaga, 2008). SAD is thought to occur by lack of exposure to bright light, and because of deficits of the neurotransmitter (chemical messenger) serotonin.

Effective treatments include full-spectrum intensive light therapy (phototherapy) and medications. Light therapy involves exposure to light of a specified intensity and type for a prescribed duration (dosage), often at a specific time of day. Since the serotonin system is thought to be involved, antidepressant medications prescribed are usually selective serotonin reuptake inhibitors (SSRIs, e.g., Prozac) or monoamine oxidase inhibitors (e.g., Marplan, Nardil; Preston et al., 2008). Melatonin (N-acetyl-5-methoxytryptamine, a hormone extracted from the pineal gland) has been tried as an alternative (complementary) treatment for SAD but has not been found to be effective in relieving depressive symptoms (Putilov & Danilenko, 2005).

See also bipolar disorder, depression, dysphoria, light therapy, major depressive disorder, monoamine oxidase inhibitor, neurotransmitter, selective serotonin reuptake inhibitor, serotonin.

Further Reading:
National Alliance on Mental Illness Web site: http://www.nami.org/.

References:
American Psychiatric Association. (2000). *Diagnostic and statistical manual of mental disorders* (4th ed., text rev.). Washington, DC: Author.
Preston, J. D., O'Neal, J. H., & Talaga, M. C. (2008). *Handbook of clinical psychopharmacology for therapists* (5th ed.). Oakland, CA: New Harbinger.
Putilov, A. A., & Danilenko, K. V. (2005). Antidepressant effects of combination of sleep deprivation and early evening treatment with melatonin or placebo for winter depression. *Biological Rhythm Research, 36*, 389–403.

Rybak, Y. E., McNeely, H. E., Mackenzie, B. E., Jain, U. R., & Levitan, R. D. (2007). Seasonality and circadian preference in adult attention-deficit/hyperactivity disorder: Clinical and neuropsychological correlates. *Comprehensive Psychiatry, 48*, 562–571.

Selective Serotonin Reuptake Inhibitor

Selective serotonin reuptake inhibitors (SSRIs) are used to treat clinical depression, obsessive-compulsive disorder, generalized anxiety disorder, social anxiety disorder, and posttraumatic stress disorder. Some SSRIs are also used to suppress cocaine cravings. SSRIs include alaproclate, citalopram (Celexa, Cirpam, Cirpamil, Elopram), escitalopram (Lexapro), etoperidone (Etonin), fluoxetine (Prozac, Sarafem), fluvoxamine (Luvox), paroxetine (Paxil, Pexeva), sertraline (Zoloft), and zimelidine (Normud, Zel).

The first generation of antidepressants included monoamine oxidase inhibitors (MAOIs), introduced in the 1950s, and tricyclics (TCAs) and tetracyclics, introduced in the 1960s. SSRIs are known as second-generation antidepressants and were first introduced in the 1980s (Patterson, 2006; Wong, Bymaster, & Engleman, 1995). Fluoxetine (Prozac) was one of the first SSRIs developed; it was developed at Lilly Laboratories in 1972. Although it was not the first SSRI created and released on the market, it had fewer side effects than earlier SSRIs; two early SSRIs were withdrawn from the market because of their side effects. Eli Lilly implemented highly effective marketing, therefore fluoxetine is often perceived as the first SSRI. Prozac was approved by the U.S. Food and Drug Administration in 1987 (Wong et al., 1995). Other types of antidepressants include serotonin and norepinephrine reuptake inhibitors (SNRIs), norepinephrine reuptake inhibitors (NRIs), and atypical antidepressants. Sometimes stimulants (e.g., Ritalin) are used to treat depression. One type of antidepressant may be used to augment treatment with an antidepressant of a different type. The antidepressant effect of SSRIs is thought to be achieved by inhibiting the reuptake of the neurotransmitter serotonin, a chemical messenger in the brain. This inhibition allows more serotonin to be available for neurotransmission. While development of new antidepressant medications continues, the mechanism of action of many antidepressant medications is not clearly understood (Patterson, 2006).

Common side effects of SSRIs include anxiety, sedation, insomnia, nausea, gastrointestinal upset, sweating, headache, restlessness, and sexual dysfunction (Preston, O'Neal, & Talaga, 2008). A disadvantage of many antidepressants is that side effects are often experienced before therapeutic effects. For example, someone taking an SSRI may have to endure uncomfortable side effects for six to eight weeks before seeing any therapeutic benefits (i.e., reduction of target symptoms). This can cause some people to discontinue antidepressant treatment before realizing any benefits.

Serotonin syndrome is a potentially lethal condition that results from toxic levels of serotonin in the central nervous system. Serotonin syndrome can be caused by combining antidepressants with each other or with some opioids, antimigraine medications, stimulants (e.g., amphetamines, cocaine), empathogens (e.g., MDMA or Ecstasy), some herbs (e.g., St. John's wort), and various other medications and over-the-counter products. Symptoms of serotonin syndrome may include rapid heart rate, sweating, shivering, dilated pupils, tremor or twitching, muscular rigidity, elevated temperature, confusion, agitation, delirium, hallucinations, coma, or death. Combining antidepressants and alcohol is not advisable; alcohol, a depressant, can worsen clinical depression and increase the toxicity of some SSRIs.

Sudden discontinuation of some SSRIs can result in a withdrawal syndrome. Withdrawal symptoms may include dizziness, nausea, sweating, insomnia, tremor, or confusion. A schedule for tapering off antidepressants should be discussed with a doctor. Taking SSRIs during pregnancy may increase the risk of prenatal complications and could have adverse effects on newborns (Preston et al., 2008); potential risks should be discussed with a doctor. To avoid potentially harmful side effects and drug interactions, health care consumers should be sure that their doctors and pharmacists are aware of *all* medications they are taking, including over-the-counter medications, herbs and natural remedies, and dietary supplements.

See also atypical antidepressants, depression, generalized anxiety disorder, monoamine oxidase inhibiter, obsessive-compulsive disorder, posttraumatic stress disorder, Prozac (fluoxetine), serotonin, social anxiety disorder, St. John's wort, tricyclic antidepressant.

Further Readings:

American Psychiatric Association—Healthy Minds Web site: http://www.healthyminds.org/
Depression and Bipolar Support Alliance Web site: http://www.dbsalliance.org/
How SSRIs work: http://www.humanillnesses.com/Behavioral-Health-Fe-Mu/Medications.html
National Alliance on Mental Illness Web site: http://www.nami.org/

References:

Patterson, J. (2006). *Therapist's guide to psychopharmacology: Working with patients, families, and physicians to optimize care.* New York: Guilford.
Preston, J. D., O'Neal, J. H., & Talaga, M. C. (2008). *Handbook of clinical psychopharmacology for therapists* (5th ed.). Oakland, CA: New Harbinger.
Wong, D. T., Bymaster, F. P., & Engleman, E. A. (1995). Prozac (fluoxetine, Lilly 110140), the first selective serotonin uptake inhibitor and an antidepressant drug: Twenty years since its first publication. *Life Sciences, 57,* 411–441.

Self-Esteem

Self-esteem (also known as *self-regard* or *self-worth*) is one's attitude, opinion, or evaluation toward oneself; it may be positive (high), neutral, or negative (low; Colman, 2001). While the term is often used interchangeably with *self-image*, *self-esteem* means how much one values oneself, while *self-image* refers to one's conception or perception of oneself.

Parenting practices and styles are important to the development of self-esteem in children. In a study looking at construction of family narratives (stories), it was found that a higher level of engagement in emotional narratives by mothers was related to the development of positive self-esteem in pre-adolescent children. This was true when the mothers were telling stories about both positive and negative emotions (Bohanek, Mann, & Fivush, 2008). Peer relationships are very important during adolescence to help form a healthy degree of self-esteem. In particular, negative peer relationships and victimization by peers (being bullied) has been associated with low self-esteem in children and adolescents (Reynolds & Repetti, 2008).

In societies that put pressure on young females to be thin (e.g., North American), girls who are heavier (or think they do not conform to societal concepts of attractiveness) may suffer low self-esteem. Low self-esteem and distorted body image have been found in adolescent girls suffering from eating disorders (e.g., bulimia, anorexia nervosa; O'Dea, 2006).

Self-esteem is a feature of several disorders described in the *Diagnostic and Statistical Manual of Mental Disorders* (American Psychiatric Association, 2000). Individuals with *avoidant personality disorder* have low self-esteem and are shy, quiet, anxious, inhibited, and reluctant to take personal risks. They tend to be inhibited in social or interpersonal situations, have a fear of rejection and failure, and are hypersensitive to criticism. Individuals with *narcissistic personality disorder* exhibit inflated (grandiose) self-image, a need for admiration, and a lack of empathy. These individuals enhance their self-esteem by the value they assign to people with whom they associate. They believe their associates to be powerful, important, or the "best"; they minimize the credentials of anyone who disappoints them. Individuals with narcissistic personality disorder have very fragile self-esteem, as manifested by an excessive need for admiration (e.g., fishing for compliments) and constant attention from others. Fragile self-esteem makes these individuals vulnerable and sensitive to criticism and failure. They tend to form intimate relationships or friendships only if the other person is likely to enhance their self-esteem (American Psychiatric Association, 2000). If self-esteem is threatened, narcissistic individuals are likely to retaliate with anger, hostility, rage, shame, or humiliation (Stucke & Sporer, 2002). Inflated self-esteem—a feature of manic episodes in *bipolar disorder*—may be characterized by grandiosity or uncritical self-confidence that may reach delusional proportions. Grandiose delusions are common (e.g., having a special relationship with a public figure, an exaggerated sense of unlimited personal power). Low self-esteem may be a feature of *depression* (e.g., in major depressive disorder, dysthymic disorder, or bipolar disorder). This may be evidenced by excessive self-criticism; individuals may see themselves as uninteresting or incapable. *Social phobia* may involve low self-esteem, including feelings of inferiority. Individuals with social phobia may fear evaluation or judgment by others, such as taking a test (American Psychiatric Association, 2000).

See also bipolar disorder, depression, dysthymia, major depressive disorder, gender and emotions, personality disorder, Rosenberg Self-Esteem Scale, self-image.

Further Reading:

Nemours Foundation. (n.d.). *Body image and self-esteem.* Retrieved from http://kidshealth.org/teen/food_fitness/problems/body_image.html.

References:

American Psychiatric Association. (2000). *Diagnostic and statistical manual of mental disorders* (4th ed., text rev.). Washington, DC: Author.

Bohanek, J. G., Mann, K. A., & Fivush, R. (2008). Family narratives, self, and gender in early adolescence. *Journal of Early Adolescence, 28,* 153–176.

Colman, A. M. (2001). *Oxford dictionary of psychology.* New York: Oxford University Press.

O'Dea, J. A. (2006). Self-concept, self-esteem and body weight in adolescent females. *Journal of Health Psychology, 11,* 599–611.

Reynolds, B. M., & Repetti, R. L. (2008). Contextual variations in negative mood and state self-esteem: What role do peers play? *Journal of Early Adolescence, 28,* 405–427.

Stucke, T. S., & Sporer, S. L. (2002). When a grandiose self-image is threatened: Narcissism and self-concept clarity as predictors of negative emotions and aggression following ego-threat. *Journal of Personality, 70,* 509–532.

Self-Image

Self-image is the idea or conception one has about oneself (Colman, 2001). While the term is often used interchangeably with self-esteem, *self-image* refers to one's perception of oneself, while *self-esteem* indicates the value one places on oneself (i.e., positive or negative). Adolescents and young adults often experience an identity crisis as they struggle to figure out who they are as individuals, and what social role best fits with their self-image. This has to do with the transition from a dependent child, whose identity is largely shaped by family, to an independent young adult, who is discovering his interests, abilities, and social role in relation to peers.

Society may promote body image ideals, suggesting through media images that males should be big and strong, while females should be thin and beautiful. These pressures can result in distorted body images. People who perceive themselves as heavier than societal ideals (especially adolescent females) may develop eating disorders. Distorted body image may also contribute to substance abuse, with males using steroids to gain muscle mass and both males and females using stimulants (e.g., diet pills, methamphetamine) to get or stay thin (Kumpfer, Smith, & Summerhays, 2008). Severe distortion of body image that results in marked distress and impairment is known as *body dysmorphic disorder*.

Western cultures (such as in the United States) tend to be individualistic, valuing autonomy and promoting independence, achievement of individual goals, attending to the self, and discovering and expressing unique, inner attributes. Asian cultures tend to be more collectivist, emphasizing harmonious interdependence with others, attending to others, and fitting in. Individualistic cultures tend to stress that emotions and personal attributes come from within (internal), while collectivistic cultures consider external factors—the individual's relationships, role, and obligations in relation to family and society. A culture's focus—on individual independence and autonomy (individualistic), or interrelatedness (collectivistic)—helps shape a person's self-image and self-concept (Markus & Kitayama, 1991).

Self-image is a feature of several personality disorders, as described in the *Diagnostic and Statistical Manual of Mental Disorders* (*DSM-IV-TR*; American Psychiatric Association, 2000). The *DSM-IV-TR*, used by mental health professionals in the United States, describes mental health disorders. A feature of *borderline personality disorder* is an unstable self-image as well as impulsivity, self-destructiveness, and unstable interpersonal relationships and mood. Unstable self-image or sense of self is characterized by shifting goals, values, vocational aspirations, sexual identity, and friends. The *DSM-IV-TR* describes individuals with borderline personality disorder as having a self-image based on being bad or evil or feelings of not existing at all. In *narcissistic personality disorder*, self-image is stable but inflated (grandiose). Narcissistic personality disorder is also characterized by a need for admiration and a lack of empathy. Inflated self-image is manifested in a sense of self-importance, exaggeration of achievements and talents, an expectation to be recognized as superior, preoccupation with fantasies of power and success, and a sense of entitlement. *Dissociative identity disorder* (formerly known as *multiple personality disorder*) is characterized by at least two distinct personality or identity states. It reflects a failure to integrate various aspects of identity, memory, and consciousness and is usually associated with a history of trauma. Each personality state may have its own personal history, self-image, identity, gender, and name. Different identities may emerge in specific circumstances (American Psychiatric Association, 2000).

In psychoanalytic terms, the super-ego (or ego ideal) forms an individual's idealized self-image. The super-ego's criticism, prohibitions, and inhibitions form the conscience. Typically developing within the first five years of life, the super-ego reflects internalization of the parent's moral standards and values. Violation of these standards results in shame, guilt, or anxiety. As the child develops through adolescence, values and ideals from peers and society are incorporated into the child's changing self-image.

See also borderline personality disorder, culture, gender and emotions, personality disorder, psychoanalytic perspective, self-esteem.

Further Reading:

Kirberger, K. (2003). *No body's perfect: Stories by teens about body image, self-acceptance, and the search for identity.* New York: Scholastic Paperbacks.

References:

American Psychiatric Association. (2000). *Diagnostic and statistical manual of mental disorders* (4th ed., text rev.). Washington, DC: Author.

Colman, A. M. (2001). *Oxford dictionary of psychology.* New York: Oxford University Press.

Kumpfer, K. L., Smith, P., & Summerhays, J. F. (2008). A wakeup call to the prevention field: Are prevention programs for substance use effective for girls? *Substance Use & Misuse, 43*, 978–1001.

Markus, H. R., & Kitayama, S. (1991). Culture and the self: Implications for cognition, emotion and motivation. *Psychological Review, 98*, 224–253.

Sensation-Seeking and Risk-Taking

In the 1970s, American Psychologist Marvin Zuckerman began publishing articles and book chapters about sensation-seeking, a personality trait he had been studying for a number of years. Zuckerman (1979) defined *sensation- seeking* as "the need for varied, novel, and complex sensations and experiences and the willingness to take physical and social risks for the sake of such experiences" (p. 10). Sensation-seeking has four components: (1) thrill and adventure seeking (an attraction to activities that are physically risky), (2) experience seeking (an interest in novel experiences in the domains of music, art, travel, meeting unusual people, mood-altering drugs, and others), (3) disinhibition (pleasure seeking through parties, gambling, sex with new and various partners, drinking, and so forth), and (4) boredom susceptibility (tendency to become bored by routines and by predictable experiences with people).

Zuckerman has tried to explain the existence of this trait through investigating potential underlying biological factors (Zuckerman & Kuhlman, 2000). He has identified a promising biological mechanism, activity of the enzyme monoamine oxidase (MAO). MAO breaks down neurotransmitters (chemical messengers in the brain), effectively blocking some neurotransmission (firing of neurons); MAO functions to regulate the firing of neurons through decreasing the firing. According to research, individuals who are high in sensation-seeking may have unusually low levels of MAO. Zuckerman reasons that in these individuals, an increase in firing of certain neurons may result, leading to less control over behavior, thoughts, and emotions. Conversely, people who are high in MAO have more control over behavior, inhibiting their risky impulses.

A number of personality trait researchers view sensation-seeking as a component of the broader trait of extraversion (e.g., Eysenck & Zuckerman, 1978; Sutton & Davidson, 1997). Extraversion is one of the most well-known and well-researched traits in personality psychology. It primary components are sociability, positive emotion, activity and assertiveness, and possibly sensation-seeking and impulsivity. Assessing an individual's level of extraversion (typically using self-report questionnaires) can be useful in a variety of contexts, including career counseling, marital or relationship counseling, and team building on the job.

Sensation-seeking has now been studied in many life domains: sport (often extreme sports), social behavior, choice of vocation, sexual behavior, economic behavior such as investing and trading, gambling, drug and alcohol use or abuse, criminal behavior, and others. Zuckerman's (2006) book *Sensation Seeking and Risky Behavior* reviews much of this research. In addition to the attention that sensation-seeking has received in academia, it has also inspired interest among the general public. Numerous Web sites invite browsers to take a sensation-seeking test or discuss sensation-seeking in a particular life context, for example, sports or sexual behavior.

See also affective personality traits, extraversion, PEN model of personality, personality, positive emotions.

Further Reading:

Zuckerman, M. (2006). *Sensation seeking and risky behavior.* Washington, DC: American Psychological Association.

References:

Eysenck, S. B., & Zuckerman, M. (1978). The relationship between sensation-seeking and Eysenck's dimensions of personality. *British Journal of Psychology, 69,* 483–487.

Joseph, J. E., Liu, X., Jiang, Y., Lynam, D., & Kelly, T. H. (2009). Neural correlates of emotional reactivity in sensation seeking. *Psychological Science, 20,* 215–223.

Sutton, S. K., & Davidson, R. J. (1997). Prefrontal brain asymmetry: A biological substrate of the behavioral approach and behavioral inhibition systems. *Psychological Science, 8,* 204–210.

Zuckerman, M. (1979). *Sensation seeking: Beyond the optimal level of arousal.* Hillsdale, NJ: Lawrence Erlbaum Associates.

Zuckerman, M. (2006). *Sensation seeking and risky behavior.* Washington, DC: American Psychological Association.

Zuckerman, M., & Kuhlman, D. M. (2000). Personality and risk-taking: Common biosocial factors. *Journal of Personality, 68,* 999–1029.

Why do some people engage in activities such as bungee jumping, skydiving, riding roller coasters, gambling, or other activities that tend to be exciting (and sometimes risky)? People who seek out adrenaline rushes and risky activities are high sensation-seekers (HSS). HSS seek out thrills and adventures and tend to be less inhibited and more easily bored than people who are low sensation-seekers (LSS). This makes HSS more likely to seek out experiences that involve significant risks; they are more vulnerable to engage in risky sexual behaviors, gambling, or drug abuse than their LSS counterparts. Brain imaging (functional magnetic resonance imaging) studies have shown that HSS show stronger responses to high-arousal stimuli in brain regions associated with arousal and reward (e.g., the right insula and the posterior medial orbitofrontal cortex), while LSS show greater activation in regions related to emotional regulation (anterior medial orbitofrontal cortex and anterior cingulate). This suggests that HSS demonstrate neural responses consistent with a more active approach system, while LSS show more in the area of inhibition (Joseph, Liu, Jiang, Lynam, & Kelly, 2009).

Serotonin

Serotonin is a hormone and neurotransmitter (chemical messenger) found in plants and animals. The chemical name of serotonin is 5-hydroxytryptamine (often abbreviated 5-HT). In the 1930s, Italian pharmacologist Vittorio Erspamer found a substance capable of causing smooth muscles (e.g., in arteries, intestines, bladder, respiratory tract) to contract. He called this substance *enteramine*. In the late 1940s, American scientists Irvine Page, organic chemist Maurice Rapport, and biochemist Arda Green isolated a substance they called *serotonin*. They named the substance serotonin because it was purified from beef serum (*sero-*) and was able to increase the tone of blood vessels (*-tonin*). In 1952, it was determined that enteramine and serotonin were the same substance. In 1952, American biochemist Betty Mack Twarog found serotonin in the brain of mammals, which brought serotonin into the field of neuroscience (Whitaker-Azmitia, 1999).

In humans, serotonin affects the central nervous system and has other functions, including cardiovascular, pulmonary, and energy balance. Behavioral and neurological functions modulated by serotonin include mood, sleep, pain perception, reward, fear, anger, aggression, memory, appetite, sexuality, stress response, addiction, and attention (Berger, Gray, & Roth, 2009). Serotonin plays a role in depression, bipolar disorder, and anxiety.

In the body, serotonin is derived from the amino acid tryptophan, a substance that occurs naturally in foods such as milk and turkey. The body converts tryptophan into serotonin. Advocates of nutritional treatments for depression suggest increasing dietary tryptophan (either through eating tryptophan-rich foods or consuming dietary supplements) as a treatment for depression.

Antidepressants that act on serotonin levels or utilization include monoamine oxidase inhibitors (MAOIs), tricyclic antidepressants (TCAs), selective serotonin reuptake inhibitors (SSRIs), and others. Atypical antipsychotics and buspirone (used to treat anxiety and depression) also act on the serotonin system (Berger et al., 2009). Hallucinogens (e.g., LSD) affect serotonin levels as do empathogens such as MDMA (Ecstasy).

The herb St. John's wort, which is sometimes used as a natural treatment for depression, may affect serotonin levels. Combining medications (e.g., SSRIs and St. John's wort) that affect serotonin levels may result in serotonin syndrome, a potentially life-threatening condition. Symptoms of serotonin syndrome may include fever, sweating, confusion, restlessness, and tremor (Berger et al., 2009).

See also antidepressant, anxiety, bipolar disorder, depression, empathogen, hormones, major depressive disorder, monoamine oxidase inhibitor, neurotransmitter, selective serotonin reuptake inhibitor, tricyclic antidepressants

References:

Berger, M., Gray, J. A., & Roth, B. L. (2009). The expanded biology of serotonin. *Annual Review of Medicine, 60*, 355–366.

Whitaker-Azmitia, P. M. (1999). The discovery of serotonin and its role in neuroscience. *Neuropsychopharmacology, 21*(1 Suppl.), 2S–8S.

Sex and Love Addicts Anonymous

Sex and Love Addicts Anonymous (SLAA) is a 12-step fellowship, modeled after Alcoholics Anonymous (AA), of people who suffer from a compulsive need for sex or who have a desperate attachment to another person. When sexual or emotional obsessive-compulsive patterns exist, relationships or sexual activities can become increasingly destructive to career, family, and a person's sense of self-respect. SLAA members seek to recover from the destructive consequences of addictive behaviors related to sex addiction, love addiction, dependency on romantic attachments, emotional dependency, and sexual, social and emotional anorexia. SLAA defines anorexia as the "compulsive avoidance of giving or receiving social, sexual, or emotional nourishment."

To counter the destructive consequences of addictive behaviors, SLAA members draw on five major resources: sobriety (willingness to stop acting out with addictive behavior on a daily basis), sponsorship and meetings, practicing the 12-step program of SLAA, service (giving back to the SLAA community), and spirituality (developing a relationship with a higher power). The 12 Steps of SLAA are modeled after the 12 Steps of AA. As with other 12-step programs, SLAA emphasizes that its program is spiritual, not religious. SLAA does not have opinions on issues outside of SLAA (e.g., religion, politics), nor is SLAA affiliated with any outside organizations. SLAA espouses the principle of anonymity of members at the public level and emphasizes the need for confidentiality. The SLAA fellowship is self-supporting through voluntary member contributions.

Other 12-step programs designed to help people recover from sexual compulsions or addictions include Sex Addicts Anonymous, Sexaholics Anonymous, Sexual Compulsives Anonymous (SCA), and Sexual Recovery Anonymous (SRA). Programs intended for family or friends of sex addicts (codependents) include Codependents of Sexual Addiction, Co-Sex and Love Addicts Anonymous, Love Addicts Anonymous, S-Anon International Family Groups (S-Anon & S-Ateen), SCA-Anon, and SRA-Anon.

See also 12-step programs.

Further Readings:
Augustine Fellowship. (1986). *Sex and Love Addicts Anonymous.* San Antonio, TX: Author.
Sex and Love Addicts Anonymous Web site: http://www.slaafws.org/
Sex and Love Addicts Anonymous, Fellowship-Wide Services. (1992). *Anorexia: Sexual, social, emotional.* Retrieved from http://www.slaafws.org/pamphlets/anorexia.pdf

Shame

Shame may be defined as "the negative emotion felt when one fails or does something morally wrong and then focuses on one's own global, stable inadequacies in explaining the transgression" (Kalat & Shiota, 2007, p. 239). Shame, one of the emotions that involves an evaluation of the self (often called the *self-conscious emotions*), bears some similarity to guilt, another self-conscious emotion. Shame and guilt overlap in at least two important ways. First, the circumstances that lead to a feeling of either shame or guilt are often the same. In general, people tend to feel either shame or guilt when they have (1) done something that violates their sense of morality or (2) fallen short of living up to their own expectations or the expectations of others (Tangney, Miller, Flicker, & Barlow, 1996). Additionally, the facial and bodily expression of shame and guilt are similar. The individual looks down, either does not smile or has a very slight frown, and has a hunched or slumped posture (although some disagree with this last quality, saying that shame involves a slumped posture, whereas guilt involves a posture that suggests that the individual anticipates moving forward in space; e.g., Lewis, 2008).

The main aspect that seems to distinguish shame and guilt is the individual's own interpretation of the negative event that evoked shame or guilt. Specifically, when experiencing shame, the individual feels that what happens to him reflects on his whole self, thinking, "I am a bad person." Conversely, when feeling guilt, the individual feels badly about an action that he did, thinking, "My behavior was bad," but does not feel badly about the whole self. Lewis (1992) calls this a *global* self-attribution (shame) versus a *specific* self-attribution (guilt). Because the attribution in shame is global, it is difficult to "get rid of" the emotion. The person feels that he wants to hide, disappear, or die. As Lewis (2008) states, the experience is so negative that the individual becomes confused and unable to speak, and the emotion interferes with behavior, especially with potentially proactive, corrective, or other positive behavior.

According to Lewis (2008), Sigmund Freud and neo-Freudian Erik Erikson were only moderately successful in distinguishing between shame and guilt. Freud focused more on guilt than on shame. In his model, guilt becomes a part of the personality (part of the superego) in young childhood, when the child internalizes the morality of his or her parent following his or her Oedipal/Electra complex (experience that involves falling in love with the opposite-sexed parent). As Lewis states, Freud, like modern guilt researchers, saw guilt as a reaction to one's behavior, without an attribution to one's whole self. Therefore, with guilt, an individual can make amends for the behavior through a penance, which may include either an actual attempt to help the injured party or through self-punishment or abstinence.

Erikson discussed shame and guilt in his psychosocial development theory. According to him, shame develops during toddlerhood (about one-and-a-half to four years old) as the child learns toilet training and other developmental achievements, especially those involving control of the muscles. Shame arises largely when the child is unable to have muscular control, particularly anal muscle control (which will happen in varying degrees to all children, and thus nearly all people will develop some degree of shame). Guilt develops during the stage immediately following, when the child locomotes more than in the prior stage, is able to take more initiative, and is able to be more destructive. A prototypical example is the child who, at this age (approximately four to six years), wants to push every button or switch that he comes across—such behavior can lead to disaster. Guilt serves to control this initiative, with the child's realization that he can be destructive and hurt others. Thus, for Erikson, shame and guilt can be distinguished from one another, and shame occurs earlier in development. In other writings, however, Erikson spoke of shame in such a way that it is not clearly differentiated from guilt (e.g., Erikson, 1950).

As Lewis (2008) suggests, shame has the potential to cripple people psychologically. He and others have been particularly interested in studying the shame that may (or may not) result from sexual abuse or other extreme maltreatment. Why do some people (but not others) blame themselves, such that they believe the abuse means that they are bad people? Lewis and others study this topic with the goal of learning how to help liberate people from the psychological suffering that can occur with shame.

See also embarrassment, Sigmund Freud, guilt, human development, pride, psychoanalytic perspective.

Further Reading:
Lewis, M. (1992). *Shame: The exposed self.* New York: Free Press.

References:
Erikson, E. H. (1950). *Childhood and society.* New York: W. W. Norton.
Kalat, J. W., & Shiota, M. N. (2007). *Emotion.* Belmont, CA: Thomson Wadsworth.
Lewis, M. (1992). *Shame: The exposed self.* New York: Free Press.
Lewis, M. (2008). Self-conscious emotions: Embarrassment, pride, shame, and guilt. In M. Lewis, J. M. Haviland-Jones, & L. F. Barrett (Eds.), *Handbook of emotions* (3rd ed., pp. 742–756). New York: Guilford.
Tangney, J. P., Miller, R. S., Flicker, L., & Barlow, D. H. (1996). Are shame, guilt, and embarrassment distinct emotions? *Journal of Personality and Social Psychology, 70,* 1256–1269.

Shyness

Shyness is an emotional state involving feelings of nervousness, awkwardness, and inhibition in social settings. Shyness bears some similarity to the self-conscious emotions shame, embarrassment, and guilt; however, shyness is an anticipatory emotion: individuals experiencing shyness are worrying about potentially embarrassing or awkward situations and the negative judgments that others will make of their behavior. Shyness may be a temporary emotional state that may occur to nearly everyone or it may operate as a personality trait (disposition). People with dispositional shyness feel tense and awkward across a wide variety of social situations. If shyness is extreme and it greatly impacts social interactions and other social behavior, the individual may be diagnosable with a social phobia.

Experiencing shyness involves feeling, physiological, cognitive (thinking), and behavioral aspects. An individual's feelings of nervousness and awkwardness are typically accompanied by bodily symptoms such as blushing, dry mouth, sweating, pounding heart, upset stomach, or dizziness. Fear that others will observe these physical symptoms intensifies the feelings of nervousness and awkwardness. An individual's thoughts are worrisome and self-preoccupied. Some of these thoughts are *meta-cognitions*, meaning thoughts about thoughts or other symptoms (Hendin & Cheek, 1999). For instance, while engaged in a social interaction, the individual may think, "I always say such stupid things" or "I wish I could be relaxed and normal like everybody else." Shy people's thoughts and beliefs tend to vary from those of most other people in that shy people believe others are constantly evaluating social interactions, that they themselves will be evaluated negatively, and that others are paying a great deal of attention to them. Additionally, they selectively remember aspects of interactions that reflect negatively on them, blame themselves for failures in social contexts, and believe successes are due to external factors such as luck. Behaviorally, the shy person tends to be withdrawn, unassertive, and nonconfrontational. She may have awkward body language such as fidgeting, avoiding direct eye contact, or maintaining a large personal space (Hendin & Cheek, 1999).

The shy person may or may not be low in sociability. Being low in sociability means that an individual does not desire much social interaction. However, some people who are shy have moderate to high sociability needs. These individuals experience a conflict between approach and avoidance, and their shyness, which inhibits their sociability, can be experienced as painful.

Shyness is associated with both positive and negative traits. For instance, shyness has been correlated with interpersonal warmth, modesty, and sensitivity (Hendin & Cheek, 1999). Additionally, some evolutionary psychologists view shyness as having survival value in humans and other animals (e.g., Hendin & Cheek, 1999). From this perspective, shyness is seen as related to subordination and submissiveness. The body language of shyness, including blushing, can be perceived by others as appeasement. Additionally, shyness is related to fear of strangers and of new situations. This vigilance and suspiciousness can save an individual's life. Overall, however, shyness tends to be viewed as negative in American culture, which values traits such as extraversion and assertiveness. Shy people tend to have relatively low self-esteem (Cheek & Melchior, 1990) and inferior social skills (e.g., Bruch, 2001). Shyness can has negative life effects, including lower achievement in school or work settings compared to individuals who are more outgoing or assertive. Additionally, shy people have more difficulty with friendship and romantic relationships (Nelson et al., 2008). Shy men are at an even greater disadvantage than women since in many cultures men are supposed to approach women when they are romantically interested; the same expectation is not placed on women.

It is possible for the shy person to change her attitudes about self and others and develop effective ways of interacting socially. Techniques that can decrease shyness include challenging and ultimately changing one's ways of thinking about oneself and about others, forcing oneself to behave in an outgoing or assertive fashion, learning social skills (communication in particular), taking medication, and other means (e.g., Antony & Swinson, 2008).

See also embarrassment, generalized anxiety disorder, guilt, introversion, loneliness, phobia, relationships, self-esteem, shame, social phobia.

Further Reading:
Antony, M. M., & Swinson, R. P. (2008). *The shyness and social anxiety workbook: Proven, step-by-step techniques for overcoming your fear.* Oakland, CA: New Harbinger.

References:
Antony, M. M., & Swinson, R. P. (2008). *The shyness and social anxiety workbook: Proven, step-by-step techniques for overcoming your fear.* Oakland, CA: New Harbinger.
Bruch, M. A. (2001). Shyness and social interaction. In W. R. Crozier & L. E. Alden (Eds.), *International handbook of social anxiety: Concepts, research and interventions relating to the self and shyness* (pp. 195–215). Chichester, England: John Wiley.
Cheek, J. M., & Melchior, L. A. (1990). Shyness, self-esteem, and self-consciousness. In H. Leitenberg (Ed.), *Handbook of social and evaluation anxiety* (pp. 47–82). New York: Plenum.
Hendin, H. M., & Cheek, J. M. (1999). Shyness. In D. Levinson, J. J. Ponzetti, & P. F. Jorgensen (Eds.), *Encyclopedia of human emotions* (2nd ed., pp. 611–618). New York: Macmillan Reference USA.
Nelson, L., Padilla-Walker, L., Badger, S., Barry, C., Carroll, J., & Madsen, S. (2008). Associations between shyness and internalizing behaviors, externalizing behaviors, and relationships during emerging adulthood. *Journal of Youth and Adolescence, 37,* 605–615.

Single Photon Emission Computed Tomography

Single photon emission computed tomography (SPECT) is a body-imaging technique that produces two- or three-dimensional images of a subject. The SPECT technique involves administering radioactive particles to a subject so that activity of certain cells or chemicals in the body may be viewed. The pictures of cell or chemical activity are made available for viewing on a computer screen. During the scanning, a gamma camera, which detects radioactive gamma rays, rotates around the subject, producing multiple pictures. The multiple two-dimensional pictures are then reconstructed by the computer to produce a two- or three-dimensional image.

In studying emotion, SPECT typically involves a picture of activity of the brain. For instance, in the study of schizophrenia, particular brain cells may be observed to determine if they are receiving appropriate amounts of a particular neurotransmitter (chemical messenger, e.g., dopamine). In a review of imaging techniques, Wong, Grunder, and Brasic (2007) concluded that the SPECT and positron emission tomography (PET) techniques hold a great deal of promise for aiding in the diagnosis, treatment, and prevention of a number of psychiatric disorders. Thus far, PET and SPECT techniques have been helpful in understanding schizophrenia, alcoholism and other drug abuse, attention-deficit hyperactivity disorder, depression, and other disorders.

SPECT and PET technology are similar to one another. SPECT produces longer-lasting images and therefore can monitor longer-lasting brain activity; the radioactivity used in PET scanning decays too rapidly for viewing of long-lasting activity. However, PET scans can produce images of a wider variety of brain activity than SPECT scans. SPECT has the benefit of being much less expensive to use. Resolution is better with PET (than SPECT). However, both PET and SPECT provide only limited visualization of brain structures, so sometimes fMRI (functional magnetic resonance imaging) is a better option (Hales, Yudofsky, & Gabbard, 2008). Both types of scans have contributed greatly to neuroscience, with new applications of the techniques being developed on a regular basis.

See also functional magnetic resonance imaging, positron emission tomography.

References:

Hales, R. E., Yudofsky, S. C., & Gabbard, G. O. (2008). *The American Psychiatric Publishing textbook of psychiatry.* Arlington, VA: American Psychiatric Publishing.

Wong, D. F., Grunder, G., & Brasic, J. R. (2007). Brain imaging research: Does the science serve clinical practice? *International Review of Psychiatry, 19*, 541–558.

B. F. Skinner (1904–1990)

Burrhus Frederick Skinner ("Fred") was born in Susquehanna, Pennsylvania. His father, a lawyer, was a gentle, conventional person. His mother, a homemaker, was described by Skinner as dominant, critical, sociable, and pretentious. Although Skinner was closer to his father than to his mother, the father-son relationship became more distant when Skinner's father became depressed during his late teens. Skinner's father had suffered some professional difficulties as a lawyer and was devastated by the death of Skinner's only sibling, a younger brother who passed away suddenly from what was most likely a cerebral hemorrhage.

Skinner attended Hamilton College in New York and graduated with a degree in English. Within a few months, he entered what he called his "Dark Year." For this "year" (actually about 18 months), he had convinced his reluctant parents to support him as he attempted to become a writer. The year became one of social isolation: his relationship with both parents was distant, he no longer had his brother, and he had no close connections other than correspondence relationships with some people from college. He spent much of his time alone, in the library in his parents' house, writing, attempting to write, or working on crafts that he enjoyed. Although he had some encouragement from the poet Robert Frost, Skinner did not become a successful writer during this period of time; he produced only a few articles and short pieces of fiction and was not satisfied with his writing. It became clear to him that he would not become a professional writer. After reading works by John Watson, Ivan Pavlov, Bertrand Russell, and others, he realized he was interested in psychology. He entered graduate school at Harvard, studying psychology and physiology. During these years, Skinner was exposed to more behaviorist ideas and began research on conditioning squirrels and rats. He had found a philosophy that resonated perfectly. Behaviorism is an approach to psychology that emphasizes external causes of behavior (such as reinforcement or punishment) over internal causes (such as feelings or thoughts).

At age 32, Skinner was awarded a PhD, moved to the University of Minnesota to begin his first teaching position, and met Yvonne Blue. They soon married and had two daughters. The behaviorist work that Skinner began in graduate school continued at Minnesota, then at the University of Indiana, and at Harvard, where Skinner worked until his death. During his career, Skinner published prolifically on the conditioning of animals, primarily rats and pigeons. He achieved what John Watson, the founder of behaviorism, had not fully achieved: proof that behaviorism can be made into a science that is applicable. By the 1960s, with Skinner as its primary champion, behaviorism became the leading paradigm in American psychology. Its popularity has waned since then, as other approaches to psychology, such as cognitive science and neuroscience, have risen to the forefront. In a study ranking the 100 most eminent psychologists of the 20th century in the *Review of General Psychology* (Haggbloom et al., 2002), B. F. Skinner was ranked first, followed by Jean Piaget and Sigmund Freud. Among his influential books are *Beyond Freedom and Dignity* (1972), which presents Skinner's philosophy of determinism, and *Walden Two* (1948), a novel in which behaviorist principles are used to produce a utopian society. In 1990, 10 days before he died of leukemia, he was awarded a Lifetime Achievement Award by the American Psychological Association.

See also Animal Behavior Society, behavior therapy, behaviorism, conditioned emotional response, exposure with response prevention, pet therapy, John Watson.

Further Readings:

Bjork, D. W. (1993). *B. F. Skinner: A life.* New York: Basic Books.
Skinner, B. F. (1948). *Walden two.* New York: Macmillan.
Skinner, B. F. (1972). *Beyond freedom and dignity.* New York: Alfred A. Knopf.
Skinner, B. F. (1984). *The shaping of a behaviorist.* New York: New York University Press.

References:

Haggbloom, S. J., Warnick, R., Warnick, J. E., Jones, V. K., Yarbrough, G. L., Russell, T. M., et al. (2002). The 100 most eminent psychologists of the 20th century. *Review of General Psychology, 6,* 139–152.
Lanza, R. P., Starr, J., & Skinner, B. F. (1982). "Lying" in the pigeon. *Journal of the Experimental Analysis of Behavior, 38,* 201–203.
Skinner, B. F. (1948). *Walden two.* New York: Macmillan.
Skinner, B. F. (1972). *Beyond freedom and dignity.* New York: Alfred A. Knopf.

Skinner's early behavior experiments taught pigeons to dance and play tennis. He also taught two pigeons (Jack and Jill) to have a "conversation," in which they used labeled keys to communicate information, including asking what color a key was and asking the other pigeon for help, to obtain food rewards (Lanza, Starr, & Skinner, 1982).

Smiling

A smile is a facial expression formed by contracting muscles around the mouth and eyes. It often involves upturned lips and sometimes an open mouth. In humans, a smile may signify feelings of happiness, pleasure, or amusement, but it can also be a sign of anxiety, embarrassment, or fear. Smiles may serve to communicate greeting, appeasement, or apology. In animals (including humans and other primates), a snarl (which resembles a smile) may communicate fear, submission, or threatening intentions. For example, a dog baring the teeth might signify a warning. A chimpanzee "smile," or a grimace with bared teeth, generally signifies fear (Waller, Vick, Bard, & Smith Pasqualini, 2007).

A smile can be produced deliberately, by contracting the facial muscles, or spontaneously, in response to emotional or social stimuli. In 1862, French neurologist Guillaume-Benjamin-Amand Duchenne (also known as Duchenne de Boulogne, 1806–1875) studied the muscles involved in different types of smiles. Specifically, Duchenne differentiated between involuntary smiles (usually expressing enjoyment) and intentional, deliberate smiles. Duchenne observed that natural, involuntary smiles contracted both the zygomaticus major muscle (raising the corners of the mouth) and the orbicularis oculi muscle (raising the cheeks and forming crow's feet around the eyes). Charles Darwin referred to Duchenne's work in his 1872 book *The Expression of the Emotions in Man and Animals*. Later, American psychologist Paul Ekman suggested that the spontaneous smile described by Duchenne (and Darwin) be referred to as a *Duchenne smile* (Ekman, Davidson, & Friesen 1990). A non-Duchenne (or polite) smile only involves the zygomatic major muscle. Ekman has researched facial expressions extensively using the Facial Action Coding System (FACS; Ekman, Friesen, & Hager, 2002). Ekman notes that Duchenne smiling is more often associated with actual positive feelings such as enjoyment, amusement, happiness, excitement, or interest. Non-Duchenne smiles are more often associated with negative emotions, may function as social markers (e.g., to communicate appeasement), or may be used to mask feelings or to deceive (Papa & Bonanno, 2008). Duchenne smiles tend to correspond with activation of left, anterior (front) brain regions, while non-Duchenne smiles more activate right anterior brain regions. Other research has shown that positive emotions tend to activate left brain regions, while negative feelings more often activate the right side (Ekman et al., 1990). Duchenne smiles have been associated with higher levels of social integration and better health and well-being (Papa & Bonanno, 2008).

Human infants have been observed to smile from birth, with a large increase after 10 days of age and a further increase after about two months of age. Younger infants tend to have unilateral (one-sided) smiles, while bilateral smiling (engaging both sides of the mouth) occurs in older infants (Kawakami et al., 2006). Typically developing infants usually engage in *anticipatory smiling*—smiling at an object then continuing to smile while gazing at a nearby person—between 8 and 12 months. Anticipatory smiling is a precursor to developing joint attention (coordinating visual attention between an object and a social partner), which is a crucial milestone in intentional communication (Venezia, Messinger, Thorp, & Mundy, 2004).

There is a widespread belief that lower social status is associated with more smiling. However, studies questioning this belief have found no relationship between self-perception of social status and smiling (Hall, Horgan, & Carter, 2002). While studies show that girls and women tend to smile more, the degree to which boys and men smile less varies by culture, role, and social expectations (LaFrance, Hecht, & Levy Paluck, 2003).

Gelotology—the study of laughter—has led to several types of therapy that make use of humor, laughter, and smiling. These include humor therapy, clown therapy, laughter therapy, laughter meditation, and laughter yoga. Promising health benefits (physical and psychological) have been demonstrated for some of these therapies (MacDonald, 2004).

See also amusement, anxiety, culture, embarrassment, Facial Action Coding System, facial expressions, fear, gender and emotions, happiness, human development, joy, negative emotions, positive emotions, primates.

Further Readings:

Darwin, C. (1998). *The expression of the emotions in man and animals* (3rd ed.). New York: Oxford University Press. (Original work published 1872). Available from at http://darwin-online.org.uk/pdf/1872_Expression_F1142.pdf

Duchenne, G.-B. (1862). *Le Mécanisme de la Physionomie Humaine* [Mechanism of human physiognomy]. Paris: J.-B. Baillière et Fils.

References:

Ekman, P., Davidson, R.J., & Friesen, W. V. (1990). The Duchenne smile: Emotional expression and brain physiology: II. *Journal of Personality and Social Psychology, 58,* 342–353.

Ekman, P., Friesen, W. V., & Hager, J.C. (2002). *The Facial Action Coding System* (2nd ed.). Salt Lake City, UT: Research Nexus eBook.

Hall, J.A., Horgan, T.G., & Carter, J.D. (2002). Assigned and felt status in relation to observer-coded and participant-reported smiling. *Journal of Nonverbal Behavior, 26,* 63–81.

Kawakami, K., Takai-Kawakami, K., Tomonaga, M., Suzuki, J., Kusaka, T., & Okai, T. (2006). Origins of smile and laughter: A preliminary study. *Early Human Development, 82,* 61–66.

LaFrance, M., Hecht, M.A., & Levy Paluck, E. (2003). The contingent smile: A meta-analysis of sex differences in smiling. *Psychological Bulletin, 129,* 305–334.

MacDonald, C.M. (2004). A chuckle a day keeps the doctor away: Therapeutic humor & laughter. *Journal of Psychosocial Nursing & Mental Health Services, 42,* 18–25.

Papa, A., & Bonanno, G.A. (2008). Smiling in the face of adversity: The interpersonal and intrapersonal functions of smiling. *Emotion, 8,* 1–12.

Venezia, M., Messinger, D.S., Thorp, D., & Mundy, P. (2004). The development of anticipatory smiling. *Infancy, 6,* 397–406.

Waller, B.M., Vick, S.-J., Bard, K.A., & Smith Pasqualini, M.C. (2007). Perceived differences between chimpanzee (*Pan troglodytes*) and human (*Homo sapiens*) facial expressions are related to emotional interpretation. *Journal of Comparative Psychology, 121,* 398–404

Social Learning

People learn new behaviors in many different ways; one of these ways is through *social learning*, which is learning through observing others. American psychologist Albert Bandura published a series of classic studies in the 1960s in which he showed that children can learn aggressive behavior simply through observing an adult behaving aggressively, especially if the adult is rewarded for the behavior (e.g., Bandura, Ross, & Ross, 1963). Bandura's theory of observational learning (social learning) supplemented the behavioral theory of learning, which held that people learn through direct, personal experience with situations; that is, people learn through reinforcement or punishment for their behavior (called operant conditioning) or through classical conditioning, which is when an organism associates two external stimuli, thereby learning to react very similarly to the stimuli. For instance, associating a painful dog bite with the dog itself, and therefore developing a fear of both dog bites and dogs, is an example of classical conditioning.

In addition to aggression, people can learn a variety of emotion-related behaviors through social learning. For example, phobias (fears) of specific objects or situations (such as fear of heights or snakes) can be learned through observing others react with fear to these situations (e.g., Bandura & Rosenthal, 1966). Attempts to reverse phobias can also utilize social learning approaches; a therapist can model counterphobic behavior toward a snake, for instance, moving close to the snake's aquarium and eventually handling the snake. Prosocial behaviors can also be learned through social learning. For instance, Poulos, Rubinstein, and Liebert (1975) found in an experiment that children who watched a prosocial episode of the *Lassie* television program in the lab behaved in a more helpful way toward puppies in a kennel than children who had watched television programs without particular prosocial themes. Social learning even extends to the animal kingdom; Heyes and Galef (1996) discuss a number of mammal and bird species that learn some behaviors through social learning.

See also aggression, animals, behavior therapy, behaviorism, phobia.

References:
Bandura, A., & Rosenthal, T. L. (1966). Vicarious classical conditioning as a function of arousal level. *Journal of Personality and Social Psychology, 3*, 54–62.
Bandura, A., Ross, D., & Ross, S. A. (1963). Imitation of film-mediated aggressive models. *Journal of Abnormal and Social Psychology, 66*, 3–11.
Heyes, C. M., & Galef, B. G. (1996). *Social learning in animals: The roots of culture.* San Diego, CA: Academic Press.
Poulos, R., Rubinstein, E., & Liebert, R. (1975). Positive social learning. *Journal of Communication, 25*(4), 90–97.

Social Support

Relationships are among the most rewarding and fulfilling aspects of human experience. One of the most important benefits provided by relationships is *social support*, the assistance and encouragement that people receive from others as they cope with both everyday living and with tragedy. One way to think about social support is to identify the types of assistance that are provided in supportive relationships. When viewed this way, many scholars (e.g., Cohen, Gottlieb, & Underwood, 2000) identify three categories of social support: *emotional*, *informational*, and *tangible* (also called *instrumental*). *Emotional support* involves expressions of caring, affection, acceptance, reassurance, and the like. *Informational support* is information, guidance, and advice. *Tangible support* means assistance in the form of money, goods, or time. In an example illustrating these types of support, an individual calls her friend and describes a tough day at work; her boss criticized the quality of her work and a coworker accused her of undermining him. An individual providing emotional support may listen closely to her friend, validate her feelings, and tell her that everything will be OK. To provide informational support, the friend may talk about how she responded in similar situations, resulting in successful outcomes. When providing tangible support, the friend may offer to lend her friend a computer program that may improve her work efficiency or bring dinner over to her friend's house on the weekend to reduce the total amount of work that her friend has to do. These categories are not necessarily completely distinct; for instance, someone receiving tangible or informational support may also feel that she is also being cared for and that she is therefore receiving emotional support.

Another way to view social support is to consider an individual's social networks (e.g., Cohen et al., 2007). Many researchers have investigated the types of connections that people have with others in which social support may be provided. For instance, individuals may receive social support from family members, friends, coworkers, neighbors, other community members (such as fellow churchgoers), health providers, therapist, and others. Individuals' connections with others vary widely, both in terms of quantity and quality.

Social support can provide significant benefits. The area in which the benefits of social support have been studied most extensively has been physical health. Seeman and colleagues (2002) found that people who have partners who provide affection have lower blood pressure, cholesterol, and stress hormone levels than people who receive lower levels of affection and encouragement from others. Additionally, evidence is relatively strong that social support boosts immune function, and evidence suggests that social support may decrease mortality from cancer and from HIV/AIDS (for reviews of research on social support and physical health, see Uchino, 2004, 2006).

Social support also potentially improves close relationships for the recipients, and possibly for the providers. For example, when an individual provides social support, the recipient feels closer to that individual (Gleason, Iida, Shrout, & Bolger, 2008). However, support is not always beneficial and may sometimes cause a degree of harm. For instance, people may view a need for support as a sign of weakness or feel burdened because they feel obligated to reciprocate support. Bolger, Zuckerman, and Kessler (2000) have shown that often, the most effective support is "invisible." An individual receives *invisible support* without even being aware that support was provided. Bolger and colleagues studied this type of support in couples who lived together. All participants kept diaries in which they recorded the support that they provided and received during a period of time when one member of the couple was studying for the bar examination. The support that most effectively reduced test anxiety was reported by the support provider but not reported by the recipient. In other words, it appears that the recipient did not notice these provisions of support. Bolger and colleagues concluded that if an individual wants to help his family member, friend, or anyone else to cope effectively, it would be best to offer the support with as much subtlety and unobtrusiveness as possible.

Social support has been researched extensively in psychology and other fields, with an acceleration of interest in the 1970s. Other topics studied in relation to social support include gender, culture, stress, mental illness, and social support in work contexts.

See also family, friendship, intimacy, loneliness, relationships.

References:

Bolger, N., Zuckerman, A., & Kessler, R. C. (2000). Invisible support and adjustment to stress. *Journal of Personality and Social Psychology, 79*, 953–961.

Cohen, S., Gottlieb, B. H., & Underwood, L. G. (2000). Social relationships and health. In S. Cohen, L. G. Underwood, & B. H. Gottlieb (Eds.), *Social support measurement and intervention* (pp. 3–25). New York: Oxford University Press.

Gleason, M., Iida, M., Shrout, P., & Bolger, N. (2008). Receiving support as a mixed blessing: Evidence for dual effects of support on psychological outcomes. *Journal of Personality and Social Psychology, 94*, 824–838.

Seeman, T. E., Singer, B. H., Ryff, C. D., Love, G. D., & Levy-Storms, L. (2002). Social relationships, gender, and allostatic load across two age cohorts. *Psychosomatic Medicine, 64*, 395–406.

Uchino, B. N. (2004). *Social support and physical health: Understanding the health consequences of relationships.* New Haven, CT: Yale University Press.

Uchino, B. (2006). Social support and health: A review of physiological processes potentially underlying links to disease outcomes. *Journal of Behavioral Medicine, 29*, 377–387.

State-Trait Anger Expression Inventory

The State-Trait Anger Expression Inventory (STAXI) was developed by American psychologist Charles Spielberger, who has produced several other psychological measures, including the State-Trait Anxiety Inventory. Spielberger identified several aspects of anger that may be relevant for psychological health and well-being and physical health. The first aspect is *state anger*, a measure of a subjective, short-term experience ranging from annoyance or irritation to rage. With state anger, physiological reactions occur, that is, the stress response, otherwise known as the fight-or-flight response. *Trait anger* is a measure of a general tendency to experience anger, or anger proneness. In addition to evaluating state and trait anger, the STAXI looks at *anger expression* (inward and outward) and *anger control* (inward and outward). *Anger expression inward* is the frequency of holding anger in when experiencing anger. *Anger expression outward* is the frequency of expressing anger outward, physically or verbally. *Anger control outward* is the tendency to experience anger and express it outwardly in a controlled fashion. *Anger control inward* is the general tendency to suppress anger by calming oneself down.

STAXI scores are helpful for understanding many aspects of anger in individuals, as described by Spielberger, Sydeman, Owen, and Marsh (1999). For instance, people who score at or above the 75th percentile in trait anger may have greater difficulty in interpersonal relationships or proneness to psychological or physical illness. A low score on trait anger (below the 25th percentile) combined with high scores on the measures of anger control inward and anger control outward may indicate high use of defense mechanisms to protect oneself from the unpleasantness or perceived "badness" of experiencing anger. The STAXI has been particularly useful in assessing the roles different aspects of anger play in several disorders, including alcoholism, heart disease, and cancer (Spielberger, 1988).

The STAXI was developed for use with individuals aged 16 and over (although a child and adolescent version is also available). It is used in a wide variety of contexts, as both a research and a clinical instrument, to assess both normal and abnormal personality. It has been translated into many different languages.

See also anger, defense mechanisms, State-Trait Anxiety Inventory, stress.

Further Reading:
Spielberger, C. D. (n.d.). *State-Trait Anger Expression Inventory: Measure the experience, expression, and control of anger.* Retrieved from www.mindgarden.com/products/staxs.htm.

References:
Spielberger, C. (1988). *Manual for the State-Trait Anger Expression Inventory (STAXI).* Odessa, FL: Psychological Assessment Resources.
Spielberger, C., Sydeman, S., Owen, A., & Marsh, B. (1999). Measuring anxiety and anger with the State-Trait Anxiety Inventory (STAI) and the State-Trait Anger Expression Inventory (STAXI). In M. Maruish (Ed.), *The use of psychological testing for treatment planning and outcomes assessment* (2nd ed., pp. 993–1021). Mahwah, NJ: Lawrence Erlbaum Associates.

State-Trait Anxiety Inventory

American psychologist Charles Spielberger's interest in anxiety led him to develop the State-Trait Anxiety Inventory (STAI) in 1970. *State anxiety* is a temporary emotional reaction to an event or circumstance, and *trait anxiety* is a personality characteristic. The STAI uses 20 items to measure state anxiety and 20 items to measure trait anxiety. The primary difference between the two types of test items is the directions that are given to assessees (people taking the test). For state anxiety, assessees are asked to respond in terms of how they feel right now, at this moment, and for trait anxiety, they respond in terms of how they generally feel. Examples of items are "I feel upset" and "I am a steady person."

Research with the STAI has shown that state anxiety and trait anxiety are different concepts. For example, in one study (Spielberger, Auerbach, Wadsworth, Dunn, & Taulbee, 1973), patients awaiting surgery took the STAI before surgery and again afterward. When, after surgery, patients were told that their recovery was good, they showed less state anxiety than they had shown prior to the procedure. This result is consistent with the idea that state anxiety is temporary and changes with the situation. Trait anxiety levels were the same before and after surgery; the same individuals who had high levels before surgery had high levels after surgery, whereas some individuals had low levels both before and after surgery. Thus state anxiety operated as a state and trait anxiety operated as a trait in this context.

The STAI was developed for use with high school and college students and adults (a children's version is also available). It is used in a wide variety of contexts, as both a research and a clinical instrument. It has been translated into many languages and is widely used. It is the most frequently utilized measure of anxiety by health psychologists (Piotrowski & Lubin, 1990). Furthermore, it is frequently cited in the research literature (Plake & Impara, 1999).

See also anxiety, Beck Anxiety Inventory, Depression Anxiety and Stress Scales, Revised Children's Manifest Anxiety Scale.

Further Readings:
Hackfort, D., & Spielberger, C. D. (1989). *Anxiety in sports: An international perspective.* New York: Hemisphere.
Spielberger, C. D. (1983). *State-Trait Anxiety Inventory for Adults sampler set: Manual, test, scoring key.* Redwood City, CA: Mind Garden.

References:

Piotrowski, C., & Lubin, B. (1990). Assessment practices of health psychologists: Survey of APA Division 38 clinicians. *Professional Psychology: Research and Practice, 21*, 99–106.

Plake, B.S., & Impara, J.C. (1999). *Supplement to the thirteenth mental measurements yearbook.* Lincoln: University of Nebraska Press.

Spielberger, C.D., Auerbach, S.M., Wadsworth, A.P., Dunn, T.M., & Taulbee, E.S. (1973). Emotional reactions to surgery. *Journal of Consulting and Clinical Psychology, 40*, 33–38.

Spielberger, with D. Hackfort, wrote the book *Anxiety in Sports: An International Perspective* (1989). In 1972, as incoming president of the Southeastern Psychological Association, Spielberger appointed the first Task Force on the Status of Women for that organization.

Stereotype. *See* Prejudice.

Stimulant

Stimulants are substances (drugs or medications) that stimulate the central nervous system. These include major stimulants, such as amphetamines and cocaine (including crack cocaine), and minor stimulants, such as caffeine and nicotine.

Cocaine (also known as snow, blow, flake, and toot) is a naturally occurring alkaloid found in the leaves of the coca shrub, which is indigenous to the Andes Mountains in Peru and Bolivia. Peruvian Indians used to chew coca leaves mixed with lime. In 1886, cocaine was mixed with caffeine from African kola nuts to create Coca-Cola. In 1903, Coca-Cola removed the cocaine from the formula. In 1914, cocaine came under strict control in the United States with the Harrison Narcotics Act. Cocaine is typically taken through nasal inhalation (snorting), intravenous injection, or smoking (freebasing and crack). Side effects may include heart attacks, respiratory failure, strokes, and seizures. Large amounts (or long-term use) can cause psychotic behavior, hallucinations, and bizarre or violent behavior (National Institute on Drug Abuse, 2008). Cocaine is highly addictive. Moderate cocaine use can result in withdrawal (marked by depression and intense cravings for the drug) on discontinuation of the drug.

Amphetamines include methamphetamine (speed, crank, meth, ice), dextroamphetamine (e.g., diet pills such as Dexedrine), some attention-deficit hyperactivity disorder (ADHD) medications, and MDMA (Ecstasy). Adderall, a combination of dextroamphetamine and dextro/levo-amphetamine, is a medication used to treat ADHD and narcolepsy. Amphetamines have characteristics similar to cocaine in terms of physiological and psychological effects, side effects, addictive potential, and withdrawal. Amphetamines can be taken through snorting (nasally), smoking, injection, and anal insertion.

Stimulant diet pills (also referred to as anorectic medications) include benzphetamine (Didrex), diethylproprion (Tenuate, Tepanil), mazindol (Sanorex, Mazanor), phendimetrazine (Bontril, Prelu-27), phentermine (Lonamin, Fastin, Apidex), and fenfluramine and dexfenluramine (Fen-Phen, which was removed from U.S. market in the 1990s). These medications can cause insomnia, irritability, hyperactivity, personality changes, and psychosis. Abrupt cessation can result in extreme fatigue and depression. It is dangerous to take these medications with other stimulants or with alcohol. Methylphenidate (Ritalin, Concerta) is a stimulant medication used to treat ADHD, chronic fatigue syndrome, narcolepsy, and depression. Street names include *kibbles and bits*, *vitamin R*, *kiddie cocaine*, and *study drugs*. Side effects may include insomnia, stomachache, diarrhea, headache, dry mouth, and appetite suppression, and psychosis. Methylphenidate should not be used in patients being treated with MAO inhibitors (a type of antidepressant) because of possible side effects on blood pressure. Methylphenidate has addiction and abuse potential.

Minor stimulants—including caffeine, nicotine, guarana, and ephedra—are less potent central nervous system stimulants than the major stimulants (e.g., cocaine or amphetamines). Other minor stimulants include theophylline (found in tea) and theobromine (found in cocoa beans). Caffeine is most potent in coffee and is also found in tea, cocoa, and kola nuts (used to make cola drinks). Excessive caffeine intake can lead to a rapid heart rate, increased urination, nausea, vomiting, restlessness, anxiety, confusion, depression, tremors, or difficulty sleeping. Caffeine use should be restricted or avoided in people with coronary heart disease or peptic ulcers, children, and women who are pregnant or nursing. Caffeine may interact with other stimulant medications or substances that contain stimulants. While caffeine has little addictive potential, abrupt discontinuation of caffeine can result in headaches, drowsiness, irritability, nausea, vomiting, and fatigue. Guarana, a plant with a high caffeine content, is often found in energy drinks. Ephedra (from the plant *Ephedra sinica*) is found in some teas or herbs used to treat asthma and other breathing problems; it is also found in some herbal weight loss products. Until 2004, many herbal weight loss and quick energy products combined caffeine or caffeine-containing herbs with ephedra. This combination may lead to dangerously increased heart rate and blood pressure and should be avoided by people with heart conditions, high blood pressure, diabetes, or thyroid disease.

Stimulants affect several neurotransmitters (chemical messengers in the brain) including epinephrine, norepinephrine, dopamine, and serotonin. Effects on epinephrine and norepinephrine can cause increased heart rate, blood pressure, respiration, and body temperature. Stimulants may increase alertness (also causing insomnia or sleeping difficulties) and energy and decrease appetite. They can also cause euphoria or a sense of well-being. One reason stimulants can be so addictive is that they flood the brain's "reward" (limbic) system with the neurotransmitter dopamine (National Institute on Drug Abuse, 2007).

Nicotine (found in tobacco) differs from other stimulants in that it acts as both a stimulant and a depressant. It produces a feeling of relaxation or satisfaction rather than the euphoria produced by major stimulants. Tolerance to nicotine develops rapidly, necessitating increased amounts of nicotine to produce similar pleasurable effects. Nicotine is highly addictive; discontinuation causes withdrawal effects, including cravings, irritability, anxiety, depression, sleep disturbance, increased appetite, and restlessness. Tobacco may be ingested through smoking, chewing, or nasal inhalation (snuff).

Treatment for stimulant dependence may include some combination of inpatient or outpatient programs for the initial stages of treatment, cognitive-behavioral therapy, ni tiotan

12-step programs (such as Narcotics Anonymous), other psychotherapeutic approaches (such as motivational interviewing), and/or pharmacotherapy (medication). Medications sometimes used to treat cocaine addiction include topiramate, modafinil, baclofen, and some antidepressant medications (National Institute on Drug Abuse, 2004). Bupropion (the antidepressant medication Wellbutrin) is being explored as a component of treatment for methamphetamine dependence (National Institute on Drug Abuse, 2006).

See also Narcotics Anonymous, neurotransmitter, Substance Abuse and Mental Health Services Administration, substance abuse, sympathetic nervous system, 12-step programs.

Further Reading:

National Institute on Drug Abuse. (2005). *Research report series—Prescription drugs: Abuse and addiction* (NIH Publication No. 01-4881). Washington, DC: U.S. Department of Health and Human Services. Retrieved from http://www.drugabuse.gov/ResearchReports/Prescription/Prescription.html.

References:

National Institute on Drug Abuse. (2004). *NIDA research report: Cocaine: Abuse and addiction* (NIH Publication No. 99-4342). Washington, DC: U.S. Department of Health and Human Services. Retrieved from http://www.nida.nih.gov/ResearchReports/Cocaine/Cocaine.html

National Institute on Drug Abuse. (2006). *NIDA research report: Methamphetamine: Abuse and addiction* (NIH Publication No. 06-4210). Washington, DC: U.S. Department of Health and Human Services. Retrieved from http://www.nida.nih.gov/ResearchReports/methamph/methamph.html

National Institute on Drug Abuse. (2007). *Drugs, brains, and behavior—The science of addiction* (NIH Publication No. 07-5605). Washington, DC: U.S. Department of Health and Human Services. Retrieved from http://www.nida.nih.gov/scienceofaddiction/sciofaddiction.pdf

National Institute on Drug Abuse. (2008). *NIDA InfoFacts: Crack and cocaine.* Washington, DC: U.S. Department of Health and Human Services. Retrieved from http://www.nida.nih.gov/infofacts/cocaine.html

St. John's Wort

St. John's wort (*Hypericum perforatum*) is an herbal product marketed as a dietary supplement. It is frequently used as a treatment for depression; it has also been used to treat nerve pain, anxiety, sleep disorders, malaria, insect bites, wounds, and burns.

St. John's wort is also known as amber touch-and-heal, balm-of-warrior's wound, balsana, bassant, Blutkraut, corancillo dendlu, devil's scourge, Eisenblut, flor de Sao Joa, fuga daemonum, goatweed hartheu, heofarigo on herba de millepertius, herba hyperici, herrgottsblut, hexenkraut, hierba de San Juan, hipericao, hiperico hipericon, isorhamnetin, Jarsin, Johanniskraut, klammath weed, liebeskraut, millepertius pelicao, perforate, pinillo de oro, pseudohypericin, rosin rose, tenturotou, Teufelsflucht, touch and heal Walpurgiskraut, and witcher's herb.

A study with 340 participants found that St. John's wort was not more effective than a placebo (sugar pill) in the treatment of major depression of moderate severity (Hypericum Depression Trial Study Group, 2002). However, an evidence-based monograph from the Natural Standard Research Collaboration (2009) claims that scientific evidence supports the effectiveness of St. John's wort to treat mild to moderate depression. Research does *not* support the effectiveness of St. John's wort as a treatment for severe depression, seasonal affective disorder, anxiety, obsessive-compulsive disorder, premenstrual syndrome, menopause symptoms, social phobia, or HIV.

A photo of St. John's Wort. St John's wort is widely known as a herbal treatment for depression. Its effects are also being studied to treat alcoholism, ADHD, and Parkinson's disease. (iStockPhoto)

Common side effects of St. John's wort include dry mouth, dizziness, gastrointestinal symptoms, increased sensitivity to sunlight, fatigue, sexual dysfunction, swelling, and urinary frequency. There are reports of St. John's wort causing suicidal or homicidal thoughts. Use of St. John's wort may reduce the effectiveness of certain other drugs, including indivir (a protease inhibitor used to treat HIV), cyclosporine, birth control pills, and medications for heart disease and depression.

Combining St. John's wort with other selective serotonin reuptake inhibitor (SSRI) antidepressants can be dangerous, causing serotonin syndrome or precipitating mania. *Serotonin syndrome* is characterized by muscle rigidity, fever, confusion, increased blood pressure and heart rate, and coma (Henney, 2000).

See also complementary and alternative medicine, depression, major depressive disorder, nutritional therapies.

Further Readings:

Brennan, C. (2000, January 2). *St. John's wort—A natural remedy for depression?* Retrieved from http://www.netdoctor.co.uk/special_reports/depression/stjwort.htm

National Center for Complementary and Alternative Medicine. (2002). *Study shows St. John's wort ineffective for major depression of moderate severity.* Retrieved from http://nccam.nih.gov/news/2002/stjohnswort/pressrelease.htm

National Center for Complementary and Alternative Medicine. (2004). *St. John's wort (Hypericum perforatum) and the treatment of depression* (NIH NCCAM Publication No. D005). Retrieved from http://nccam.nih.gov/health/stjohnswort/ataglance.htm

References:

Henney, J. E. (2000). Risk of drug interactions with St John's wort. *Journal of the American Medical Association, 283*, 1679.

Hypericum Depression Trial Study Group. (2002). Effect of *Hypericum perforatum* (St. John's wort) in major depressive disorder: A randomized controlled trial. *Journal of the American Medical Association, 287*, 1807–1814.

Natural Standard Research Collaboration. (2009, August 26). *St. John's wort (Hypericum perforatum L.).* Retrieved from http://www.nlm.nih.gov/medlineplus/druginfo/natural/patient-stjohnswort.html

The Stoics

Stoicism was founded by the Greek philosopher Zeno (ca. 336–265 BC) around 300 BC. Stoicism is so named because of the building in which Zeno used to teach, the *stoa.* Zeno, like the Epicureans who were contemporaneous with him, taught that the key to the good life—a life of compassion and kindliness toward others—comes from managing our emotions. Emotions can often interfere with the good life. Zeno and Epicurus (the founder of Epicureanism) recognized the difficulty in simply suppressing an emotion once it has begun. Therefore we must control what happens before our problematic emotions occur; that is, we must control our desire.

The Epicureans held that it is unnatural, ultimately ungratifying, and potentially destructive to desire dramatic, unattainable things such as power or large quantities of money. They promoted the enjoyment of simple pleasures such as a good meal, an enjoyable time with a friend, and a little bit of lightheadedness that may come with drinking a glass of wine. The Stoics, however, were more extreme in their admonition to eliminate emotions. They argued that practically any desire can potentially be harmful. One of the most influential Stoics, Chrysippus (ca. 280–206 BC) distinguished between the "two movements" of an emotion. The first movement is reflexive, bodily, and uncontrollable. Charles Darwin (1872/1998), who wrote a classic book about emotion, *The Expression of the Emotions in Man and Animals*, describes this emotional aspect in an experiment he conducted on himself. He went to the London Zoo and pressed his face against the glass window cage holding a puff adder snake. Darwin was determined that since he knew he was safe behind the glass, he would not startle when the snake struck at him. The snake did strike, and Darwin "jumped a yard or two back with astonishing rapidity" (p. 40). Like Chrysippus, Darwin realized that he could not control this reaction no matter how hard he tried. According to Chrysippus, the second movement of an emotion is real emotion. This is when we freely choose to translate our desires into behavior. At this point, one can make a decision as to what truly matters. By eliminating wrong desires, we can eliminate the second movements.

We must therefore consider our desires and decide what is important. As we are making these assessments, we will realize that the sources of some desires are worthless—of no real value—and that pursuing these desires would lead to outcomes that are of no real worth. Pursuing some desires may even lead to strong negative emotions such as anger or jealousy. According to Stoics, the worthwhile in life is really only character, rationality (our ability to reason), and kindness. These aspects are permanent and of substance. But many of our desires come from valuing things that are empty and fleeting. For instance, as the Stoic Marcus Aurelius (AD 121–180) described, feeling outraged when someone insults us, or even feeling proud when recognized for a generous act, comes from valuing the transitory in life, which the Stoics called *indifferents*. A Stoic, then, is supposed to distinguish between what may feel immediate and pressing (but that has no real value) and what is truly important. In this way, any inappropriate second movements can be eliminated. The goal of Stoicism was an inner peace that was achieved through self-control of one's emotions. True Stoics practiced their philosophy as a way of life, and this involved introspection that is similar to Eastern meditation.

Stoicism, a way of life for some Greeks during the remainder of the Greek Age, survived through much of the Roman Era as well. Stoicism bears some similarity to modern approaches that advocate the control of emotions through cognition, such as Albert Ellis's ABC model of emotional reaction and other ancient philosophies such as Buddhism.

See also ABC model of emotional reaction, Buddhism, cognitive therapy and cognitive-behavioral therapy, the Epicureans.

Further Reading:
Graver, M. R. (2007). *Stoicism and emotion.* Chicago: University of Chicago Press.

Reference:
Darwin. C. (1998). *The expression of the emotions in man and animals* (3rd ed.). New York: Oxford University Press. (Original work published 1872)

Stress

People have an intuitive understanding of the concept of stress but may not be aware of all of its facets. Stress is most commonly thought of as psychological tension ("I feel stressed"); this description is partly accurate. Stress is also a physical response to a threatening or challenging situation (a stressor) and involves activation of most body systems. This physical response, called the *stress response* or the *fight-or-flight response*, is quite dramatic and includes elevated heart rate, elevated blood pressure, release of stress hormones including adrenaline, mobilization of energy stores in the body (i.e., glucose in the liver), a slowing of digestion, enhanced blood flow to large muscles, pupil dilation, and many other physical changes. In short, stress is experienced both physically and psychologically; it is an arousal of both body and mind.

The study of stress is popular largely because stress is costly to individuals. It can cause damage to the body that is severe enough to contribute to both physical and psychological disease states. Both Sapolsky (2004) and McEwen and Lasley (2002) wrote highly informative and readable books about the relationship between stress and disease. As they (and others) describe, it is clear that stress contributes to heart disease. When under stress, the stress hormones cortisol and epinephrine (adrenaline) mobilize cholesterol and fats for energy. The cholesterol and fats that are not used during the stress response may continue to circulate through the bloodstream, adhering to the inside of blood vessels. This adhesion, called *atherosclerosis*, reduces the circumference of the blood vessels, leading to an increase in blood pressure which can damage the entire circulatory system including the heart. This is only one of many ways that stress can contribute to heart disease.

Stress often suppresses the immune system, increasing susceptibility to many types of infections (possibly multiple infections). As Sapolsky (2004) describes, the evidence is clearest regarding the common cold: immune suppression related to stress increases common cold risk. Additionally, stress is probably related to the worsening of AIDS. More research is needed to determine the precise relationships between stress, immune suppression, and susceptibility to infections of various kinds.

Stress contributes to psychiatric disease. A clear connection has been found between stress and clinical depression, which is more common among people who have experienced significant stress. Research on the relationship between stress and psychiatric diseases including depression is currently active and promising. Additionally, stress has been associated with symptoms that are not considered disorders, for example fatigue states (because the stress response is highly energy consuming) and irritability and interpersonal problems, both of which may be related to fatigue. Even if stress does not cause a disease, it can affect an individual's well-being. In sum, stress is related to many types of diseases, both physical and psychiatric, and general dysfunction.

A variety of stress management techniques are available to mitigate the damaging effects of stress, or even to prevent negative effects. As Monat, Lazarus, and Reevy

(2007) describe, stress management techniques can be divided into three basic categories: (1) a change in one's environment or lifestyle, for example, maintaining proper nutrition, quitting smoking, or avoiding stressors; (2) a change in one's personality or perception, for example, choosing to see the silver lining in the cloud, using one's sense of humor, or taking an anger management course; and (3) a modification of the physiological effects of stress, for example, meditation, deep breathing, or massage. A number of excellent books provide how-to descriptions of many potentially helpful stress management techniques, including Davis, Eshelman, and McKay's (2008) *The Relaxation and Stress Reduction Workbook*, which has sold over 700,000 copies.

As a number of stress experts, including Lazarus (1999), have noted, stress and emotion are interconnected: when one experiences an emotion, especially one of the negative emotions, a stress response ensues. (In general, strong emotions produce strong stress responses and mild emotions produce less intense stress responses.) This is true regardless of the specific negative emotion—fear, anger, and sadness are all associated with increased heart rate, increased blood pressure, release of stress hormones, and so on. Lazarus therefore recommended that stress researchers and emotion researchers collaborate to better understand these psychological phenomena.

See also autogenic training, deep breathing, meditation, mindfulness, progressive muscle relaxation, stress hormones, yoga.

Further Readings:
Davis, M., Eshelman, E. R., & McKay, M. (2008). *The relaxation and stress reduction workbook* (6th ed.). Oakland, CA: New Harbinger.
McEwen, B., & Lasley, E. N. (2002). *The end of stress as we know it.* Washington, DC: Joseph Henry Press.
Monat, A., Lazarus, R. S., & Reevy, G. (Eds.). (2007). *The Praeger handbook on stress and coping.* Westport, CT: Praeger.
Sapolsky, R. M. (2004). *Why zebras don't get ulcers.* New York: Henry Holt.

References:
Anxiety Disorders Association of America. (2008, November). *Stress, anxiety, and exercise.* Retrieved from http://www.adaa.org/StressOutWeek/stress_anxiety_exercise.asp
Davis, M., Eshelman, E. R., & McKay, M. (2008). *The relaxation and stress reduction workbook* (6th ed.). Oakland, CA: New Harbinger.
Lazarus, R. S. (1999). *Stress and emotion: A new synthesis.* New York: Springer.
McEwen, B., & Lasley, E. N. (2002). *The end of stress as we know it.* Washington, DC: Joseph Henry Press.
Monat, A., Lazarus, R. S., & Reevy, G. (Eds.). (2007). *The Praeger handbook on stress and coping.* Westport, CT: Praeger.
Sapolsky, R. M. (2004). *Why zebras don't get ulcers.* New York: Henry Holt.

In the United States, 7 out of 10 adults report experiencing stress or anxiety daily and say that it interferes at least moderately with their lives. A 2008 online poll by the Anxiety Disorders Association of American (ADAA) found that 14 percent of people make use of regular exercise to cope with stress. Others reported talking to friends or family (18%), sleeping (17%), watching movies or TV (14%), eating (14%), and listening to music (13%). Health care professionals recommend exercise to reduce stress. Studies have shown that exercise can effectively reduce fatigue, improve alertness and concentration, and enhance overall cognitive function. Exercise and other physical activity produces endorphins (brain chemicals that act as natural painkillers) and improves the ability to sleep, which reduces stress. Meditation, acupuncture, massage therapy, and deep breathing also prompt the release of endorphins and help to cope with stress (Anxiety Disorders Association of America, 2008).

Stress Hormones

Several hormones play a key role in the complex mind-body reaction that is the stress response. Most stress hormones are secreted from the adrenal glands which are located above each kidney.

The stress response is initiated by a part of the brain called the *hypothalamus*. The hypothalamus, through both nerve connections and hormone-releasing factors that are released into the bloodstream, stimulates the pituitary gland, the *master gland* located immediately below the hypothalamus. In turn, the pituitary gland releases hormones into the bloodstream. These hormones stimulate the adrenal glands to release the hormones that more directly cause the stress response.

Two of the first hormones released by the adrenal glands, adrenaline (epinephrine) and noradrenalin (norepinephrine), primarily affect the cardiovascular system. Adrenaline increases the heart rate and the force of the heartbeat. Noradrenaline initiates contraction of blood vessels which increases blood pressure. With these actions, the heart becomes quite effective at delivering large quantities of blood, rapidly, to needed muscles and other parts of the body that are critically involved in the stress response. In addition, adrenaline increases muscle tension.

A few moments later, the adrenal glands release cortisol and aldosterone. Cortisol primarily mobilizes energy for the stress response. Specifically, it mobilizes fat stores, protein stores (using amino acids from muscle tissue), and increases blood glucose (sugar) through a metabolic process called *gluconeogenesis*. Aldosterone increases sodium retention, which causes water retention. The purpose of the increased water retention is to stimulate the elimination of body waste. Many other hormones are involved in the stress response, including prolactin, endorphins, enkephalins, and vasopressin (an antidiuretic hormone). The stress response is dramatic and extremely complex.

Stress and stress hormones are associated with moods and emotions (Wallenstein, 2003). Cortisol has been linked with several emotions, including fear and depression. Adrenaline is linked with fear and anger. Much is still unknown about the precise relationships between stress hormones and emotion; a good starting point for investigating this topic is Gene Wallenstein's (2003) book *Mind, Stress, and Emotions: The New Science of Mood.*

See also anger, depression, fear, hormones, hypothalamus, physiology of emotion, stress, sympathetic nervous system.

Further Reading:

McEwen, B., & Lasley, E. N. (2002). *The end of stress as we know it.* Washington, DC: Joseph Henry Press.

Reference:

Wallenstein, G. (2003). *Mind, stress, and emotions: The new science of mood.* Boston: Commonwealth Press.

Subjective Experience of Emotion

An emotion is a complex phenomenon involving a physiological component (e.g., autonomic nervous system responses, brain activity), thoughts, often a behavioral or action component, and the subjective experience, which is called an emotional *feeling.*

There are several prominent theories regarding the origin of the subjective experience component of an emotion and how it is related to other emotion components. In the classic James-Lange theory (Lange & James, 1922/1962), first discussed in the late 1800s, a quick cognitive judgment, physiological response, and behavior all occur before emotional feeling; the individual notices a stimulus (e.g., a bear running toward him) and makes a quick judgment of "good" or "bad"; a physiological response occurs (e.g., his heart races, he perspires, and so forth), often accompanied by a behavioral response (e.g., he runs away); then the emotional feeling occurs last. An alternative view is the Cannon-Bard theory (Cannon, 1915/1929): an event occurs (a bear runs toward an individual), and the aspects of emotion—cognitive appraisal or assessment, action (behavior and physiology), and emotional feeling—occur simultaneously and practically independently of one another.

A number of modern emotion theorists agree at least with the appraisal-first-then-feeling aspect of the James-Lange theory (e.g., Lazarus, 2001), although not necessarily with other aspects of the theory. Evidence does exist that people form quick "good" or "bad" judgments prior to experiencing emotional feelings. For instance, in one experiment, people who were presented with a fearful face responded with slight sweating and trembling, even if the photo was presented so briefly that people reported that they did not see the photo at all (Vuilleumier, Armony, Driver, & Dolan, 2001). In another study, researchers recorded brain activity with an electroencephalogram (EEG) while participants looked at photographs of happy, angry, or neutral faces. Seeing an angry face was associated with a strong EEG reaction 200 to 300 milliseconds after the presentation of the photograph, whereas seeing a happy or neutral face did not produce that response (Schupp et al., 2004). However, as Kalat and Shiota (2007) point out, cognition can certainly occur after an emotional feeling. For instance, sometimes people have sudden angry outbursts, perhaps yelling at a person in an impulsive manner. In this case, the person may not know exactly why he yelled and may have to come up with a reason (perhaps a rationalization) later. For example, maybe he yelled at the person because the person is always self-centered (and was reminded of that in the moment). In sum, Kalat and Shiota suggest that the basic identification of good or bad usually occurs very quickly, usually followed by an emotional feeling, but in some situations the emotional feeling may come first.

Emotion scholars also discuss whether physiological response is necessary for emotional feeling. In a review of relevant research, Kalat and Shiota (2007) describe research findings as few and inconclusive. The best evidence would come from individuals who suffer from a condition called locked-in syndrome (sometimes associated with stroke or traumatic brain injury), in which they have lost almost all nerve signals from the brain to both the muscles and the autonomic nervous system. James had hypothesized that emotional feeling comes from the physiological response of the autonomic nervous system. If his theory is correct, patients with locked-in syndrome would have very little emotional feeling. However since these patients also can communicate only minimally, for example, through eye blinks, it is difficult to tell what they are feeling. The issue of the relationship between physiological response and emotional feeling is thus unresolved.

See also appraisal, behavior and emotion, feeling, James-Lange theory of emotion, physiology of emotion.

References:

Cannon, W. B. (1929). *Bodily changes in pain, hunger, fear, and rage* (2nd ed.). New York: D. Appleton. (Original work published 1915)

Kalat, J. W., & Shiota, M. N. (2007). *Emotion*. Belmont, CA: Thomson Wadsworth.

Lange, C. G., & James, W. (1962). *The emotions.* New York: Hafner. (Original work published 1922)

Lazarus, R. S. (2001). Relational meaning and discrete emotions. In K. R. Scherer, A. Schorr, & T. Johnstone (Eds.), *Appraisal processes in emotion* (pp. 37–67). New York: Oxford University Press.

Schupp, H. T., Öhman, A., Junghöfer, M., Weike, A. I., Stockburger, J., & Hamm, A. O. (2004). The facilitated processing of threatening faces: An ERP analysis. *Emotion, 4*, 189–200.

Vuilleumier, P., Armony, J. L., Driver, J., & Dolan, R. J. (2001). Effects of attention and emotion on face processing in the human brain: An event-related fMRI study. *Neuron, 30*, 829–841.

Substance Abuse

One of the most common psychological maladies affecting people in many cultures throughout the world is abuse of drugs that affect psychological functioning (known as psychoactive drugs). Abuse of these drugs may also affect physical functioning over time (e.g., the abuse may eventually cause liver damage). Examples of commonly abused psychoactive drugs are alcohol, amphetamines, cannabis, cocaine, hallucinogens, inhalants, opioids, and sedative-hypnotics.

Use of drugs does not necessarily imply abuse. The *Diagnostic and Statistical Manual of Mental Disorders* (*DSM-IV-TR*; American Psychiatric Association, 2000) lists specific criteria for substance abuse, as follows: a maladaptive pattern of substance use that results in considerable impairment or distress, as characterized by one or more of (1) repeated substance use leading to deficiency in performing important role obligations at work, school, or home (e.g., failure to show up at work or school or neglecting one's children); (2) recurrent substance use in contexts in which the use causes physical hazards (e.g., substance use while driving); (3) repeated legal problems due to the substance use (e.g., arrests for disturbing the peace); and (4) persistent substance use despite awareness of social or interpersonal problems associated with the substance use (e.g., arguments with domestic partner about the substance use).

Substance abuse does not imply substance dependence, although dependence does imply abuse. The *DSM-IV-TR* describes substance dependence as a maladaptive pattern of substance use leading to considerable impairment or distress, with at least three of the following symptoms: (1) tolerance for the substance, as indicated by a need for greater amounts of the substance to produce the desired psychological state, or notably decreased effect as one continues to use the same amount of the substance; (2) withdrawal symptoms; (3) use of larger amounts of the substance, or over a longer period, than planned; (4) unsuccessful attempts to decrease or control substance use; (5) large amounts of time spent attempting to obtain, use, or recuperate from the effects of the substance; (6) significant social, occupational, or recreational activities are decreased or abandoned because of use of the substance; and (7) substance use is continued despite awareness of physical or psychological problems associated with the use.

Large numbers of people in the United States display substance abuse or dependence. According to the National Survey on Drug Use and Health, 19 percent of Native Americans; between 9 and 10 percent of Caucasian Americans, Hispanic Americans, and African Americans; and 4.3 percent of Asian Americans abuse or are dependent on a substance or substances. In total, 9.2 percent of teens and adults in the United States abuse or are dependent on substances in any given year (National Survey on Drug Use and Health, 2008).

There is likely more than one cause of substance abuse or dependence. According to the sociocultural viewpoint, substance abuse is related to socioeconomic stress and to cultural values and customs. Some evidence supports these assertions. For instance, people from lower socioeconomic groups abuse substances at a higher rate than people with higher socioeconomic status (e.g., Franklin & Markarian, 2005). Rates of alcoholism are relatively high in Ireland and Eastern Europe, where alcohol use is more culturally entrenched and accepted, and where people may communicate less clearly about limiting substance use than people from other cultural backgrounds (e.g., Ksir, Hart, & Oakley, 2008; Ledoux, Miller, Choquet, & Plant, 2002). Behavioral and cognitive factors may also contribute to substance abuse and dependence. Behaviorists suggest that drug use is reinforced by being rewarding both through producing pleasurable feelings and by reducing tense feelings (e.g., Ksir et al., 2008). Cognitive theorists further reason that the *anticipation* of pleasurable effects from using substances further encourages substance use (Chassin, Collins, Ritter, & Shirley, 2001). Some evidence has supported these behavioral and cognitive perspectives. For instance, it appears that people are more likely to seek out substances such as alcohol or heroin when they feel stress (e.g., Cooper, 1994).

Both genetic and biological factors probably contribute to substance abuse and dependence. Studies of children who are adopted shortly after birth support a genetic contribution. In these studies, children whose biological parents suffered from alcohol dependence were compared to children whose biological parents had no alcohol dependence. By the time the children reached adulthood, those with alcohol-dependent biological parents had higher rates of alcohol abuse (e.g., Walters, 2002). Drugs also operate on neurotransmitters (chemical messengers in the brain), which have varying functions, including lifting mood, reducing pain, and increasing alertness. The effects that drugs have on these neurotransmitters partially explains why using drugs is often experienced as pleasurable, and why people would seek drugs to achieve these effects.

Substance abuse and dependence are treated through a variety of modalities. Some treatments work at the biological level, such as detoxification, which is withdrawal from a drug while under medical supervision, and drug maintenance therapy, in which a person who is dependent on a high-risk drug such as heroin is given a similar, but less dangerous drug (typically, methadone in place of heroin) as a substitute for the dangerous drug. Treatment may also operate at the behavioral level. For instance, aversion therapy involves associating the drug with something highly unpleasant. When treating alcohol addiction, a medication may be administered that produces nausea and vomiting if alcohol is used. The natural aversion for nausea and vomiting may lead to an aversion for the substance that is being abused. Support groups (such as Alcoholics Anonymous, Narcotics Anonymous, and other 12-step programs) and residential treatment programs are also used to treat abuse and dependence. A variety of authors in Francis, Miller, and Mack's (2008) edited volume describe these treatments and others. As discussed in these chapters, treatments require hard work on the part of the addicted individual and are most often moderately successful rather than highly successful. It is important to fully understand abuse and addiction to further alleviate the suffering and cost associated with this relatively common form of mental illness.

See also Alcoholics Anonymous, aversion therapy, cognitive therapy and cognitive-behavioral therapy, depressant drugs, detoxification, empathogen, stimulant, 12-step programs.

Further Readings:

Francis, R. J., Miller, S. I., & Mack, A. (Eds.). (2008). *Clinical textbook of addictive disorders.* New York: Guilford.

Ksir, C., Hart, C. L., & Oakley, R. (2008). *Drugs, society, and human behavior* (12th ed.). Boston: McGraw-Hill.

References:

American Psychiatric Association. (2000). *Diagnostic and statistical manual of mental disorders* (4th ed., text rev.). Washington, DC: Author.

Chassin, L., Collins, R. L., Ritter, J., & Shirley, M. C. (2001). Vulnerability to substance use disorders across the life span. In R. E. Ingram & J. M. Price (Eds.), *Vulnerability to psychopathology: Risk across the lifespan* (pp. 165–172). New York: Guilford.

Comer, R. J. (2010). *Abnormal psychology.* New York: Worth.

Cooper, M. L. (1994). Motivations for alcohol use among adolescents: Development and validation of a four-factor model. *Psychological Assessment, 6,* 117–128.

Francis, R. J., Miller, S. I., & Mack, A. (Eds.) (2008). *Clinical textbook of addictive disorders.* New York: Guilford.

Franklin, J., & Markarian, M. (2005). Substance abuse in minority populations. In R. J. Frances, A. H. Mack, & S. I. Miller (Eds.), *Clinical textbook of addictive disorders* (3rd ed., pp. 321–339). New York: Guilford.

Ksir, C., Hart, C. L., & Oakley, R. (2008). *Drugs, society, and human behavior* (12th ed.). Boston: McGraw-Hill.

Ledoux, S., Miller, P., Choquet, M., & Plant, M. (2002). Family structure, parent-child relationships, and alcohol and other drug use among teenagers in France and the United Kingdom. *Alcohol and Alcoholism, 37,* 52–60.

National Survey on Drug Use and Health. (2008). *National survey on drug use.* Washington, DC: Department of Health and Human Services, Substance Abuse and Mental Health Services Administration, Office of Applied Sciences.

United Nations Office on Drugs and Crime. (2009). *World drug report.* Retrieved from http://www.unodc.org/documents/wdr/WDR_2009/Executive_summary_LO-RES.pdf

Walters, G. D. (2002). The heritability of alcohol abuse and dependence: A meta-analysis of behavior genetic research. *American Journal of Drug and Alcohol Abuse, 28,* 557–584.

- The United Nations Office on Drugs and Crime estimates that in 2007, between 172 and 250 million persons used illicit drugs at least once in that year and that there were between 18 and 38 million problem drug users from 15 to 64 years of age in 2007. In Africa and Oceania, more people sought treatment for problems with cannabis than any other drug (63% in Africa; 47% in Australia and New Zealand), while opiates were the primary drug treated in Asia (65%) and Europe (60%). Cocaine was more prominent in North America (34%) and South America (52%) than in other regions. Amphetamines were more prominent in Asia (18%), North America (18%), and Oceania (20%). Cannabis has been playing an increasingly large role in drug treatment in Europe, South America, and Oceania since the late 1990s, while amphetamines account for a greater share of drug treatment in North and South America than in the past (United Nations Office on Drugs and Crime, 2009).
- Many celebrities have died as a result of substance abuse, including Elvis Presley, John Belushi, and Chris Farley (Comer, 2010, p. 397).
- The theme of substance abuse has been depicted in countless movies, including *Basketball Diaries* (1995), *Fear and Loathing in Las Vegas* (1998), *Pulp Fiction* (1994), *Requiem for a Dream* (2000), *Synanon* (1965), *Traffic* (2000), and *Trainspotting* (1996).

Source: http://www.imagiscape.ca/research/art/Movies%20and%20Mental%20Illness%20 Filmography.htm

Substance Abuse and Mental Health Services Administration

The Substance Abuse and Mental Health Services Administration (SAMHSA), a division of the U.S. Department of Health and Human Services, was established in 1992. The purpose of SAMHSA is to devote energy, programs, and funding to improve the lives of people at risk for or suffering from a mental illness or addictive disorder. Specifically, SAMHSA was created with the vision that all people, including those with or at risk for mental or addictive disorder, deserve satisfying lives that include a home, a job, and fulfilling relationships with family and friends.

To work toward these ends, SAMHSA offers a wide variety of services, most of which are described and presented on the organization's Web site. SAMHSA collects and compiles epidemiological data on mental illness and addiction at federal and state levels. The SAMHSA Web site lists federal grant opportunities available to researchers studying mental illness or addiction. SAMHSA offers a variety of programs and campaigns, for instance, Building Blocks for a Healthy Future, designed to teach caregivers of three- to six-year-olds about prevention; the "Mental Health Services Locator," a searchable directory of mental health treatment centers; and the Suicide Prevention Resource Center. SAMHSA publishes information about mental disorders and addiction in many forms, including newsletters, brochures, and reports.

SAMHSA is a resource for mental health workers, researchers, people suffering from mental illness or addiction and their families, and the general public.

See also substance abuse.

Further Reading:
Substance Abuse and Mental Health Services Administration Web site: http://www.samhsa.gov/

Surprise

Surprise is a reaction that occurs when one's expectations have been violated. Surprise may or may not qualify as an emotion. According to Hadwin (1999), it meets many of the criteria for a basic emotion: it is characterized by a unique facial expression, behavior, physiological change, and subjective experience. American psychologist Paul Ekman, who conducted classic cross-cultural studies on emotion and facial expression, classified it as one of only six basic emotions, which also include happiness, sadness, fear, anger, and disgust (Ekman, 1984). However, an alternative way of viewing surprise is that it is not an emotion but rather a cognitive state. Ortony, Clore, and Collins (1988) defined emotion as a "valenced" reaction, which means that the reaction is either positive or negative. They state that surprise is neutral and is therefore not an emotion at all; surprise is unexpectedness only. They further state that events can occur that include reactions of both surprise and happiness, which they call *pleasant surprise*. For example, a child could be (unexpectedly) presented with a new rocking pony. Her first, very quick reaction is related to the unexpected nature of the gift—she is surprised. Very soon after this reaction, she feels pleasure or happiness.

Regardless of whether surprise is an emotion or a cognitive state, many have argued that surprise is functional. In his classic book on emotional expression, *The Expression of the Emotions in Man and Animals*, Charles Darwin (1872) stated that the facial expression of surprise, with highly elevated eyebrows and eyes wide open, allows people to see and react to events. Similarly and more recently, Tomkins (1962) asserted that the surprised expression allows for an interruption of the individual's present activity, which means that she can attend to new events and analyze them. According to Steinsmeier-Pelster, Martini, and Reisenzein (1995), surprise functions to motivate people to examine and explore the event or situation that was surprising.

See also basic emotions, facial expression.

Further Reading:
Hadwin, J. A. (1999). Surprise. In D. Levinson, J. J. Ponzetti, & P. F. Jorgensen (Eds.), *Encyclopedia of human emotions* (2nd ed., pp. 645–651). New York: Macmillan Reference USA.

References:
Darwin, C. (1998). *The expression of the emotions in man and animals* (3rd ed.). New York: Oxford University Press. Retrieved from http://darwin-online.org.uk/pdf/1872_Expression_F1142.pdf
Ekman, P. (1984). Expression and the nature of emotion. In K. Scherer & P. Ekman (Eds.), *Approaches to emotion* (pp. 319–344). Hillsdale, NJ: Lawrence Erlbaum Associates.
Hadwin, J. A. (1999). Surprise. In D. Levinson, J. J. Ponzetti, & P. F. Jorgensen (Eds.), *Encyclopedia of human emotions* (2nd ed., pp. 645–651). New York: Macmillan Reference USA.
Ortony, A., Clore, G. L., & Collins, A. (1988). *The cognitive structure of emotions.* Cambridge, England: Cambridge University Press.

Steinsmeier-Pelster, J., Martini, A., & Reisenzein, R. (1995). The role of surprise in the attribution process. *Cognition & Emotion, 9*, 5–31.

Tomkins, S. S. (1962). *Affect, imagery, consciousness: Vol. 1. The positive affects.* New York: Springer.

Sympathetic Nervous System

The sympathetic nervous system (SNS) is a division of the autonomic nervous system (ANS). Neurons in the ANS monitor the organs and internal activities such as heart rate, digestion, breathing, energy mobilization, and glandular activity. The ANS regulates these internal body functions to maintain the body's homeostasis (balance). The SNS and the other primary division of the ANS, the parasympathetic nervous system (PNS), immediately respond to environmental circumstances and work together to achieve the body's homeostasis. The SNS and PNS have different yet complementary functions: the SNS is involved in the functioning of the active body, whereas the PNS is involved in the functioning of the body at rest. Both systems operate automatically without the involvement of human consciousness.

The SNS originates in the thoracic and lumbar (middle and lower) regions of the spinal cord. Most sympathetic neurons are part of the peripheral nervous system. The peripheral nervous system mainly controls the functioning of internal organs and muscles in the periphery of the body. Through chains of sympathetic ganglia (nerve complexes), sympathetic neurons of the spinal cord connect to peripheral sympathetic neurons. This connection leads to the physiological reactions throughout one's body.

The primary function of the SNS is to prepare the body for action and stress. Known as the fight-or-flight system, the SNS is active in a state of arousal or emergency.

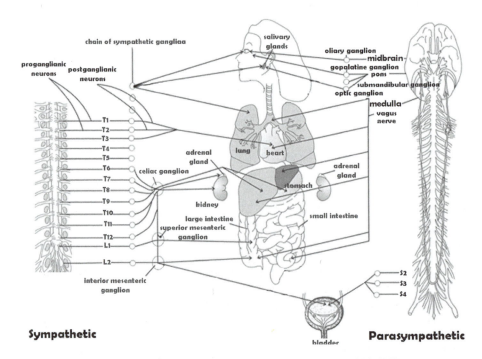

A diagram of the human sympathetic and parasympathetic nervous system. (ABC-CLIO)

Epinephrine and norepinephrine, hormones secreted by the adrenal glands (which are controlled by the SNS), help produce general arousal and emotional reactions. Other actions that occur when the SNS is aroused are increased heart rate, increased blood pressure, release of glucose by the liver (so that glucose may be used as an energy source), slowing down of digestion, dilation of the pupils, and other effects. Most of the physiological changes found in the state of arousal arise from SNS activity.

Experiencing a negative emotion (e.g., anger, sadness, fear) typically involves activation of the SNS; the stronger the emotion, the more intense the fight-or-flight response can be. In contrast, a negative emotion that appears to be associated with a different physiological response—that is, activation of the PNS—is disgust (Levenson, Ekman, & Friesen, 1990). The physiology of positive emotions may also differ from the general physiology of negative emotions. For instance, happiness is associated with both sympathetic and parasympathetic nervous system response (Levenson et al., 1990).

See also autonomic nervous system, hormones, negative emotions, parasympathetic nervous system, stress, stress hormones.

Reference:

Levenson, R. W., Ekman, P., & Friesen, W. V. (1990). Voluntary facial action generates emotion-specific autonomic nervous system activity. *Psychophysiology, 27*, 363–384.

Sympathy

Emotion scholars do not all agree about the meaning of sympathy. Some describe sympathy as a feeling of caring and empathic sadness for another person who is in distress (e.g., Eisenberg et al., 1989). Another way to describe it is to say that it may include any of a number of negative feelings (e.g., sadness, fear, worry, concern, or indignation) and/or behaviors (e.g., concerned facial expression, hugs) that one individual directs toward another who is suffering or experiencing bad fortune or trouble (Clark, 1999). According to both of these descriptions, sympathy occurs if another person is suffering or in distress. Other elements of the descriptions differ somewhat. One point of difference is whether sympathy must involve a feeling of caring; according to Eisenberg et al. (1989) caring is present, whereas in Clark's (1999) view, sympathy may be present without a feeling of caring toward the suffering individual. Additionally, according to Eisenberg et al. (1989), sympathy involves empathic sadness, whereas Clark (1999) says that sympathy may involve either negative feelings directed toward another (such as sadness), or sympathetic behavior; according to Clark, a person could behave in a sympathetic fashion without actually feeling anything, and this is still called sympathy.

According to Clark (1999), "getting to" sympathy is a process. First, an individual must take the perspective of another person. The next step toward sympathy is feeling the inner experience of the other person, especially her emotions, or acting on the cognitive understanding of the person's situation, without necessarily feeling anything—or both feeling and acting. According to the definition of Eisenberg et al. (1989), an additional step would be to care about the suffering.

If feelings of sympathy are present, they may be experienced in many ways. Sympathy may be felt as intense sadness for a friend whose child died. Another example is righteous anger on hearing about a case of racial discrimination. Or sympathy may be a brief pang of uneasiness that the individual pushes away and forgets quickly. As mentioned, sympathy may or may not be translated into behavior. The sympathetic person may have sympathetic feelings, and do nothing. Or, she may engage in behavior ranging from empathic, supportive listening, to providing tangible expressions of sympathy such as sending cards or flowers, to behavior that may be costly in terms of energy and time invested, such as intervening on behalf of the person to help him to pursue a racial discrimination claim.

Clark (1999) discusses how societies vary in terms of average amounts of sympathy of their citizens. Additionally, rules for expressing sympathy are very particular to cultures. She briefly describes anthropologist Nancy Scheper-Hughes's depiction of a society in which little sympathy is present. In *Death without Weeping*, Scheper-Hughes (1992) recounts her experience with the Alto do Cruzeiro people of Brazil, who were so impoverished that they were not able to feed all their children. Fewer than half of the Alto children survived to adulthood. If an infant became sick, family members would not attempt to nurse the infant to good health, nor would they report feeling sympathy. Instead, they would give a greater share of food, clothing, and other necessities to healthier children. If an infant died, people would not cry when the infant was buried. Clark (1997) discusses the relationship between culture and sympathy in her book *Misery and Company: Sympathy in Everyday Life*.

See also culture, empathy, sadness, theory of mind.

Further Readings:
Clark, C. (1997). *Misery and company: Sympathy in everyday life*. Chicago: University of Chicago Press.
Clark, C. (1999). Sympathy. In D. Levinson, J. J. Ponzetti, & P. F. Jorgensen (Eds.), *Encyclopedia of human emotions* (2nd ed., pp. 651–656). New York: Macmillan Reference USA.
Scheper-Hughes, N. (1992). *Death without weeping*. Berkeley: University of California Press.

References:
Clark, C. (1997). *Misery and company: Sympathy in everyday life*. Chicago: University of Chicago Press.
Clark, C. (1999). Sympathy. In D. Levinson, J. J. Ponzetti, & P. F. Jorgensen (Eds.), *Encyclopedia of human emotions* (2nd ed., pp. 651–656). New York: Macmillan Reference USA.
Eisenberg, N., Fabes, R. A., Miller, P. A., Fultz, J., Shell, R., Mathy, R. M., et al. (1989). Relation of sympathy and personal distress to prosocial behavior: A multimethod study. *Journal of Personality and Social Psychology, 57*, 55–66.
Scheper-Hughes, N. (1992). *Death without weeping*. Berkeley: University of California Press.

Systematic Desensitization

Systematic desensitization, developed by Joseph Wolpe (e.g., Wolpe & Lazarus, 1966), is a behavioral therapy that is used primarily to treat phobias (fears). The technique involves learning how to relax while gradually being exposed to a feared object or situation. Common phobias include fear of various animals, heights, blood, enclosed spaces, flying, and water, and systematic desensitization can be applied with any of these fears.

Treatment of the phobic client involves (1) training in a relaxation technique such as progressive muscle relaxation, relaxing imagery, or meditation; (2) the client's creation of an anxiety hierarchy, which is a list of feared situations, ordered from least fear inducing to most fear inducing; and (3) pairing the relaxation with the feared situations, beginning with the least fear inducing and gradually ending with the most fear inducing. The idea is that after treatment, the client will have a relaxation response when encountering the formerly feared object or situation rather than a fear response.

Suppose a client is afraid of snakes. First, the client will be trained to relax. Next, he will produce an anxiety hierarchy, which might look something like the following:

10. I'm in a room that has an aquarium against the far wall. A snake is inside the aquarium. (least feared)
9. I'm in the room with the snake in the aquarium, and the snake is hissing.
8. I'm watching a documentary about snakes.
7. I'm watching the scary scene in *True Grit* (a John Wayne movie in which a character gets bitten by a rattlesnake).
6. I'm inside my house and saw a huge snake outside.
5. I'm outside, and a snake slithered within a few feet of me.
4. My cat brought what appears to be a dead snake into the house.
3. A snake is loose in the room in which I am sitting.
2. A snake slithered over my foot.
1. A snake is crawling on my neck. (most feared)

After constructing this hierarchy, the following procedure is implemented. The client is instructed to relax. Then, the client is exposed to situation 10 (least feared) on the anxiety hierarchy. This exposure can be real or in vivo (imagined). If the client is exposed to situation 10 and remains relaxed, the therapist will instruct him to move to situation 9. If the client becomes anxious at any point, he self-induces relaxation, or the therapist may induce relaxation. With each success, the client moves up the hierarchy toward situation 1 (most feared). Systematic desensitization may be of short duration, involving only 6 or so sessions, or longer lasting, up to 100 or more sessions, depending on the severity of the phobia, the number of phobias from which the client suffers, and other factors. This therapy is an effective treatment for phobias and is associated with improvement in most sufferers (Wiederhold & Wiederhold, 2005).

See also behavior therapy, exposure with response prevention, fear, phobia.

References:
Wiederhold, B. K., & Wiederhold, M. D. (2005). Specific phobias and social phobia. In M. D. Wiederhold & B. K. Wiederhold, *Virtual reality therapy for anxiety disorders: Advances in evaluation and treatment* (pp. 125–138). Washington, DC: American Psychological Association.
Wolpe, J., & Lazarus, A. A. (1966). *Behavior therapy techniques: A guide to the treatment of neuroses.* London: Pergamon Press.

T

Tarantism

Tarantism was a disease that afflicted people in some parts of Europe from about the 1300s through the 1700s. Symptoms included melancholy, delusions, hallucinations, stupor, and an uncontrollable need to dance. The illness was thought to be caused by the bite of the "tarantula" spider (actually a wolf spider, *Lycosa tarantula*, originally named "tarantula" but different from the tarantulas, *L. theraphosidae*, of which we speak today), and the only cure (it was believed) was to engage in the energetic dancing that the sufferer felt so strongly compelled to do. The common belief currently is that tarantism was psychologically caused. Another possibility is that it may have been caused by ingestion of a toxin.

The disease was centered in a city in southern Italy, Taranto. Both the disease and the spider were named for this city. Tarantism is an example of mass hysteria, which was relatively common during the Middle Ages and early part of the Renaissance. Another example of mass madness is the behavior and symptoms (e.g., "fits," hallucinations) exhibited by girls in Salem, Massachusetts, around 1691, which led to the infamous Salem witchcraft trials. Theories about causes of this behavior include convulsive ergot poisoning (caused by a mold that grows on rye) or encephalitis (Norton, 2003).

When mass hysteria occurs, large numbers of people share the same symptoms. There are usually a variety of somatic (physical) symptoms, including dramatic ones (e.g., excessive motor activity, hyperventilation, convulsions, fainting). Common characteristics of groups susceptible to mass hysteria include closely knit social groups, often united by strong religious beliefs, with atmospheres of tension and restraint, and those that have are paranoid or suspicious of outsiders or have a grudge against specific groups of people. Theories about causes of the behavior or outbreak included possession, poisoning (by a food or gas), or an epidemic infection (Trimble, 2004).

Further Readings:
Sidky, H. (1997). *Witchcraft, lycanthropy, drugs and disease: An anthropological study of the European witch hunts.* New York: Peter Lang.
Sigerist, H. E. (1965). *Civilization and disease.* Ithaca, NY: Cornell University Press.

Mexican Redknee Tarantula. One of the most sought after tarantulas due to its color and mild temperament. It will throw hairs from its abdomen when threatened. (iStockPhoto)

Franca Riela and Elvira Ferrara from Cantania, Sicily perform the Tarantella while on a pilgrimage to the Vatican City in Rome, October 3, 1950. The Tarantella, a frenzied, whirling dance, is believed to be derived from the frenzied dancing that was supposed to be a cure for the effects of a tarantula bite. (AP/Wide World Photos)

References:
Norton, M. B. (2003). *In the devil*. Westminster, MD: Knopf.
Trimble, M. (2004). *Somatoform disorders: A medicolegal guide*. West Nyack, NY: Cambridge University Press.

Temperament

The word *temperament* is used in everyday language, referring to the characteristic behavior of a baby or child, or emotional qualities of a person of any age. This popular conception is similar to the way social scientists construe temperament. According to American psychologist Gordon Allport (1961), the father of trait psychology,

> Temperament refers to the characteristic phenomena of an individual's nature, including his susceptibility to emotional stimulation, his customary strength and speed of response, the quality of his prevailing mood, and all the peculiarities of fluctuation and intensity of mood, these being phenomena regarded as dependent on constitutional make-up, and therefore largely hereditary in origin. (p. 34)

Primary characteristics of this description are that temperament refers to attributes that (1) distinguish a person from other people, (2) are largely hereditary, and (3) are largely of an emotional nature. Although not explicit in Allport's definition, temperament is also presumed to be at least relatively stable over time, perhaps over most or all of a person's lifetime, just like other personality traits.

Developmental and personality psychologists have produced a number of different models for understanding the nature of temperament traits. Among the most well known is Thomas, Chess, and Birch's (1970) model. The researchers interviewed mothers of babies and identified three patterns of temperament. *Easy* babies typically express positive emotions, have emotional reactions that are low to moderate in intensity, and experience regular sleeping and eating patterns. *Difficult* babies are frequently in a negative mood, experience intense emotional reactions, and have sleeping and eating patterns that are irregular. *Slow-to-warm-up* babies possess combinations of the easy and difficult patterns. Their moods are relatively negative, their emotional reactions are low in intensity, and they will approach new objects or events only after an initial period of hesitation and timidity.

Other researchers (e.g., Buss, 1991) have argued that three particular traits—sociability, emotionality, and activity level—qualify as temperament traits because they appear to be present at birth and are stable across time. Long-term longitudinal studies, in which the same participants are researched over a period of time, have provided evidence for stability of sociability and emotionality. For instance, Caspi, Elder, and Bem (1988) studied very unsociable children and followed them for 30 years. They found general tendencies toward unsociable or shy behavior through adulthood. Men in the study took longer than other men to marry, become parents, and become stable in their careers. Women research participants were more likely than other women to choose a traditionally feminine life path, getting married, having children, and becoming homemakers. Chess and Thomas (e.g., Chess & Thomas, 1990) researched emotionality in a general sample of people for a period of 30 years, beginning in infancy. They found that most participants had established a general emotional pattern in the first few months of life and that the pattern continued through adulthood.

Many psychologists who study personality or emotion are convinced, based on the evidence, that people possess temperaments. Beginning in the 1990s, temperament research evolved in complexity; researchers now study the ways in which temperament and environmental factors interact to produce behavior. Researchers may now begin to address important clinical questions such as, "Under what circumstances will an impulsive child develop into an adult who channels impulses into productive (rather than destructive) behavior?" Circumstances that are studied could include general parenting styles, discipline styles, socioeconomic status, and so forth. Bates, Goodnight, and Fite (2008) review some of the research on temperament-environment interactions.

See also affective personality traits, attachment, extraversion, genetics, human development, neuroticism, personality, shyness.

References:
Allport, G. W. (1961). *Pattern and growth in personality*. New York: Holt, Rinehart, and Winston.
Bates, J. E., Goodnight, J. A., & Fite, J. E. (2008). Temperament and emotion. In M. Lewis, J. M. Haviland-Jones, & L. F. Barrett (Eds.), *Handbook of emotions* (3rd ed., pp. 485–496). New York: Guilford.
Buss, A. H. (1991). The EAS theory of temperament. In J. Strelau & A. Angleitner (Eds.), *Explorations in temperament: International perspectives on theory and measurement* (pp. 43–60). New York: Plenum Press.
Caspi, A., Elder, G. H., & Bem, D. J. (1988). Moving away from the world: Life-course patterns of shy children. *Developmental Psychology, 24*, 824–831.
Chess, S., & Thomas, A. (1990). The New York Longitudinal Study (NYLS): The young adult periods. *Canadian Journal of Psychiatry, 35*, 557–561.
Stelmack, R. M., & Stalikas, A. (1991). Galen and the humor theory of temperament. *Personality and Individual Differences, 12*, 255–264.
Thomas, A., Chess, S., & Birch, H. G. (1970). The origin of personality. *Scientific American, 223*, 102–109.

Greek physician Galen of Pergamum (AD 130–200) used the idea of the humors (bodily fluids) to explain individual differences in temperament or character. The four humors, and their associated characteristics, were sanguine (buoyant; blood), phlegmatic (sluggish; phlegm), choleric (quick tempered; bile), and melancholic (dejected; black bile). Physical and psychological characteristics were determined by the balance of the four humors, which were understood in terms of a general cosmological theory in which fire, earth, air, and water were the four basic elements of all things. From Galen's ideas, theories of personality types emerged in the 18th and 19th centuries (Stelmack & Stalikas, 1991).

Thematic Apperception Test

The Thematic Apperception Test (TAT) was introduced by American artist Christiana Morgan and American psychologist Henry Murray in 1935. The TAT is a projective test that involves presenting people with ambiguous stimuli or situations (e.g., inkblots, pictures of people interacting, incomplete sentences, etc.) and asking for responses (e.g., telling a story, completing a sentence, drawing a picture, etc.). Projective tests may be used to assess any of a wide variety of psychological attributes, including general personality traits, needs, unconscious conflicts and defenses, general psychological adjustment, and psychiatric disorders.

The TAT was the brainchild of Murray, who wished to measure people's fantasies and other deeply hidden characteristics. Prior to deciding on the TAT as his method, he had experimented with other approaches, for instance, an odor imagination test, in which assessees (people taking a test) sniffed a variety of substances and were asked to create anecdotes based on the odors, and a musical reverie test, wherein assesses sat in a comfortable chair, listened to classical music, and were asked to "allow their minds to drift."

The TAT consists of 31 cards depicting scenes involving individual people, people interacting, or objects. To select the pictures, Murray, Morgan, and other staff members of the Harvard Psychological Clinic (where Murray worked as a professor) looked through magazines. About 2,000 photographs and illustrations were chosen and were shown to students, colleagues, and family members to evaluate the illustrations' capacity to evoke fantasies. After 29 were selected, Morgan redrew them and pasted them to cardboard. The remaining two were original art work by Morgan and a blank card. Some examples of TAT pictures are a boy sitting down at a table, looking at a violin placed on the table; a close-up of two faces, one older and one younger, with ambiguous expressions; and a muscular man climbing up a rope.

Clinical psychologists administering the TAT typically choose 5 to 12 cards for a particular assessee. During administration the assessor presents the cards one at a time, with instructions to tell a story that describes what is happening now, what happened before, and what will happen next. The assessor writes down what the assessee says verbatim or tape-records the session. The resultant 5 to 12 stories are interpreted. TAT interpretation is generally loose, but typical aspects that might be evaluated are needs, motives, and themes of relationships with people.

The TAT has been criticized for lack of reliability (consistency) of administration and scoring (e.g., Lilienfeld, Wood, & Garb, 2000, 2001). Although some standardized administration and scoring systems exist, research suggests that most psychologists do not utilize these systems, but rather, interpret in an impressionistic fashion, based on their own intuitions. For instance, in a study of 100 North American psychologists who practice in the court systems, only 3 percent said that they used standardized scoring (Camara, Nathan, & Puente, 1998). Lilienfeld and his colleagues also conclude that the TAT has not yet demonstrated validity for identifying any particular psychological attributes, although two areas are promising. Specifically, the TAT may do a good job of assessing achievement motivation and an individual's typical ways of perceiving others (called *object relations*).

The TAT is a popular test among clinical psychologists, ranking in the top 10 in frequency of use (Camara, Nathan, & Puente, 2000). The only projective test that is more frequently used is the Rorschach Inkblot Test. Although the TAT has been criticized along with other projective tests, the ongoing research may provide solid evidence for its utility and validity for some purposes. Additionally the TAT has expanded in use; marketing researchers have found that it can be helpful in identifying effective forms of advertisement (see Soley & Smith, 2008).

See also Children's Apperception Test, defense mechanisms, projective test, psychoanalytic perspective, Rorschach psychodiagnostic technique, the unconscious mind.

Further Readings:

Gieser, L., & Stein, M. I. (Eds.). (1999). *Evocative images: The Thematic Apperception Test and the art of projection.* Washington, DC: American Psychological Association.

Lilienfeld, S. O., Wood, J. M., & Garb, H. N. (2001). What's wrong with this picture? *Scientific American, 284*(5), 80–87.

Paul, A. M. (2004). *The cult of personality: How personality tests are leading us to miseducate our children, mismanage our companies, and misunderstand ourselves.* New York: Free Press.

Soley, L., & Smith, A. L. (2008). *Projective techniques for social science and business research.* Milwaukee, WI: Southshore Press.

References:

Camara, W. J., Nathan, J. S., & Puente, A. E. (1998). *Psychological test usage in professional psychology.* Report to the American Psychological Association Practice and Science Directorates.

Camara, W. J., Nathan, J. S., & Puente, A. E. (2000). Psychological test usage: Implications in professional psychology. *Professional Psychology: Research and Practice, 31*, 141–154.

Lilienfeld, S. O., Wood, J. M., & Garb, H. N. (2000). The scientific status of projective techniques. *Psychological Science in the Public Interest, 1*, 27–66.

Lilienfeld, S. O., Wood, J. M., & Garb, H. N. (2001). What's wrong with this picture? *Scientific American, 284*(5), 80–87.

Morgan, C. D., & Murray, H. H. (1935). A method for investigating fantasies: The thematic apperception test. *Archives of Neurology and Psychiatry, 34*, 289–306.

Soley, L., & Smith, A. L. (2008). *Projective techniques for social science and business research.* Milwaukee, WI: Southshore Press.

Theory of Mind

Theory of mind (ToM) refers to the ability to infer the emotional state, beliefs, desires, or intentions of others from nonverbal signals (e.g., facial expressions or body language) or linguistic cues (prosody). This awareness of another's perspective is related to social cognition which is found in normally developing humans, other primates (e.g., chimpanzees and orangutans; Call & Tomasello, 1998), and some other animals (e.g., dogs; Horowitz, 2009). Sometimes referred to as *mind-blindness*, ToM deficits describe an inability to take another person's perspective. Individuals with a ToM deficit may have difficulty determining others' intentions, understanding how their own behavior affects other people, or have a difficult time with social reciprocity. *Social reciprocity* is involved in activities such as taking turns when playing games or engaging in conversation.

ToM research burgeoned after the 1978 publication of an article by American psychologists David Premack and Guy Woodruff ("Does the Chimpanzee Have a Theory of Mind?"). Both an understanding of attention in others and awareness of others' intentions are precursors to development of ToM. Normally developing human infants usually understand attention in others by seven to nine months of age. An understanding of others' intentions or goals may also be a precursor to ToM; this understanding has been observed in children ages two and three years (Call & Tomasello, 1998). Empathy is a concept related to ToM. It may be necessary to understand that other people have their own thoughts, emotions, and intentions before being able to put oneself in another person's shoes. ToM deficits are a key characteristic of individuals with autistic spectrum disorders (ASD), including Asperger's syndrome. However, this does not mean that people with ASD do not experience emotions, including empathy. ToM deficits have also been observed in individuals with schizophrenia (Phillips, Drevets, Rauch, & Lane, 2003) and have been posited in some cases of bipolar disorder and dementia (Brüne & Brüne-Cohrs, 2006).

There are several types of tasks or tests to determine whether an individual has ToM. In the *false-belief task*, test subjects are told a story involving two characters. In an example of the false-belief story, there are two children in a room (Bob and Anne), two containers (a box and a basket), and a marble. Bob places the marble in the basket, then leaves the room. While Bob is gone, Anne moves the marble from the basket to the box. Bob returns. The examiner asks the test subject where Bob will look for the marble. The test subject passes the task if he or she says that Bob will look in the basket for the marble. Someone without this ability might answer incorrectly that Bob will look for the marble in the box (where the marble has actually been moved). To pass the false-belief task, an individual needs to understand that Bob does not know about the marble being moved from the basket to the box. The *appearance-reality* task test subjects are shown a box that has a label (for example) with a picture of candies. The test subject is asked what he or she thinks is in the box. The test subject answers correctly, "candies." Then the examiner opens the box and shows that it actually contains pencils. The experimenter closes the box and asks the test subject what another person, who has not been shown the true contents, will think is in the box (the correct answer is "candies").

A drawback with many ToM tests is that it is difficult to distinguish between language abilities, desire for social interaction, and ToM. There is a strong relationship between the development of language abilities and ToM abilities. It has been found that Deaf children—even those with language delays (sign language or oral language)—develop ToM abilities similar to those of hearing children. This is not true for children with autism, who exhibit significant deficits in ToM abilities (Astington & Baird, 2005). It may also be difficult to discern ToM abilities in individuals who have little or no interest in social interactions, which is the case with many individuals with autism. Behaviors such as pretend play and imitation have been associated with the development of ToM. While it was previously thought that an individual either had or did not have ToM, ToM deficits may exist on a continuum: an individual may have deficits to some degree in some areas, while being capable in other areas.

Special types of brain cells called *mirror neurons* may be involved in ToM abilities. It has been found that the mirror neuron systems of children with autism differ from those of typically developing children, and are associated with deficits in imitation, ToM, and social communication (Dapretto et al., 2006).

See also autistic spectrum disorders, body language, empathy, facial expressions, human development, primates, schizophrenia, sympathy.

Further Readings:

Lantz, J. (2002). Theory of mind in autism: Development, implications, and interventions. *The Reporter,* 7(3), 18–25.

Soraya, L. (2008, May 19). Empathy, mindblindness, and theory of mind: Do people with autism truly lack empathy? *Psychology Today: Asperger's Diary.* Retrieved from http://www.psychologytoday.com/blog/aspergers-diary/200805/empathy-mindblindness-and-theory-mind

References:

Astington, J. W., & Baird, J. A. (2005). *Why language matters for theory of mind.* Cary, NC: Oxford University Press.

Brüne, M., & Brüne-Cohrs, U. (2006). Theory of mind—Evolution, ontogeny, brain mechanisms and psychopathology. *Neuroscience and Biobehavioral Reviews, 30,* 437–455.

Call, J., & Tomasello, M. (1998). Distinguishing intentional from accidental actions in orangutans (*Pongo pygmaeus*), chimpanzees (*Pan troglodytes*), and human children (*Homo sapiens*). *Journal of Comparative Psychology, 112,* 192–206.

Dapretto, M., Davies, M. S., Pfeifer, J. H., Scott, A. A., Sigman, M., Bookheimer, S. Y., et al. (2006). Understanding emotions in others: Mirror neuron dysfunction in children with autism spectrum disorders. *Nature Neuroscience, 9,* 28–30.

Horowitz, A. (2009). Attention to attention in domestic dog (*Canis familiaris*) dyadic play. *Animal Cognition, 12,* 107–118.

Phillips, M. L., Drevets, W. C., Rauch, S. L., & Lane, R. (2003). Neurobiology of emotion perception II: Implications for major psychiatric disorders. *Biological Psychiatry, 54,* 515–528.

Premack, D. G., & Woodruff, G. (1978). Does the chimpanzee have a theory of mind? *Behavioral and Brain Sciences, 1,* 515–526.

Thought Control Questionnaire

All people experience some thoughts that they regard as unpleasant and unwanted, and for most people such thoughts can become highly distracting at certain points during their lifetimes. Thoughts can be disturbing enough to reach a clinically significant level, forming a major component of a number of psychiatric disorders, including major depression, eating disorders, substance-related disorders, and anxiety disorders such as obsessive-compulsive disorder and posttraumatic stress disorder.

In 1994, British psychiatrists Adrian Wells and Mark Davies published the Thought Control Questionnaire (TCQ) to assess ways people cope with unwanted, intrusive thoughts. To identify common thought control strategies that people use for unwanted thoughts—information that would be used to create the items for the TCQ—the researchers conducted interviews with two groups of people: patients diagnosed with an anxiety disorder or hypochondriasis and nonpatients who had no history of treatment for psychiatric disorders.

Wells and Davies initially identified 59 techniques that people use to control unwanted thoughts. They conducted further research and utilized a statistical procedure called *factor analysis*, designed to summarize information, on the 59 items and determined that 30 items should be retained for the final questionnaire. The 30 items were grouped into five categories of thought control: *distraction* (e.g., I think about something else), *social control* (e.g., I don't talk about the thought to anyone), *worry* (e.g., I think about past worries instead), *punishment* (e.g., I punish myself for thinking the thought), and *reappraisal* (e.g., I try to reinterpret the thought).

In their original study on these thought control techniques, Wells and Davies found that two of the categories, worry and punishment, were broadly associated with mental disorders or emotional vulnerability. Later research conducted by Fehm and Hoyer (2004) led to the same general conclusions. The TCQ is used in clinical assessments but is not yet used widely in research; Fehm and Hoyer (2004) suggest that the utility of this measure is likely to increase if some modifications are made to instructions and to the items themselves. Research on the various thought control strategies may eventually lead to a better understanding of the broad functionality or dysfunctionality of different techniques. Additionally, certain techniques may be helpful in certain situations or for certain people, but not for other situations or people. At this point, much remains unknown about the particular benefits and shortcomings of specific thought control strategies.

See also anxiety, obsessive-compulsive disorder, generalized anxiety disorder, posttraumatic stress disorder, regulation of emotion, thought stopping.

Further Reading:

TCQ from Mental Health Nurse: www.mentalhealthnurse.co.uk/images/Assessment%20Tools/Thought%20Control%20Questionnaire.pdf

References:

Fehm, L., & Hoyer, J. (2004). Measuring thought control strategies: The Thought Control Questionnaire and a look beyond. *Cognitive Therapy and Research, 28,* 105–117.

Wells, A., & Davies, M.I. (1994). The Thought Control Questionnaire: A measure of individual differences in the control of unwanted thoughts. *Behaviour Research and Therapy, 32,* 871–878.

Thought Stopping

Thought stopping is a simple coping technique whereby one consciously stops negative thoughts that occur. When a person has a run or chain of negative thoughts, he says to himself, "Stop!" then shifts his thoughts to something different. The bothersome thought may occur again (perhaps immediately), and the individual repeats the technique. Thought stopping can be helpful for a variety of negative ruminations. It can be used with the self-disparaging ideation from which some people frequently suffer (such as saying to oneself, "I'm ugly," "I'm worthless," and "I'm such a loser"). The approach is also helpful with obsessive anxiety, for example, continuously worrying about the children while on a dinner date with your spouse (and effectively ruining the dinner) or obsessive thoughts of anger or revenge wherein a person cannot stop thinking about the wrongs that her boss inflicted on her. Other examples of situations that can be alleviated with thought stopping include depression, smoking, and phobias.

Thought stopping was popularized by Wolpe and Lazarus in their 1966 book *Behavior Therapy Techniques.* The authors state that the technique was introduced by J. G. Taylor in 1955. On the basis of research results indicating enhanced effectiveness, when implemented, thought stopping may also include utilizing a relaxation technique (such as deep breathing or muscle relaxation) prior to saying "Stop!" McKay, Davis, and Fanning (2007) have written a well-received workbook, *Thoughts & Feelings: Taking Control of your Moods & your Life*, that describes numerous general stress management, cognitive, and behavioral techniques, including thought stopping, as methods for coping with negative thoughts and feelings.

See also anxiety, behavior therapy, cognitive therapy and cognitive-behavioral therapy, deep breathing, depression, Arnold A. Lazarus, progressive muscle relaxation, regulation of emotion.

Further Reading:

McKay, M., Davis, M., & Fanning, P. (2007). *Thoughts & feelings: Taking control of your moods & your life* (3rd ed.). Oakland, CA: New Harbinger.

References:

McKay, M., Davis, M., & Fanning, P. (2007). *Thoughts & feelings: Taking control of your moods & your life.* Oakland, CA: New Harbinger.

Wolpe, J., & Lazarus, A. A. (1966). *Behavior therapy techniques: A guide to the treatment of neuroses.* London: Pergamon Press.

Transference

Transference is a phenomenon in which a patient in therapy projects feelings onto the therapist. For example, a patient may feel dependence, rebellion, hatred, resentment, or sexual feelings toward the therapist or may feel rejected or judged by the therapist. In psychoanalysis (Freudian psychotherapy), this is thought to reflect feelings the patient has experienced in earlier significant relationships. Transference feelings may be a reflection of conflicts experienced with a parent, sibling, employer, or significant other. Transference feelings may be disturbing, and the patient may blame distressing feelings on the therapist. Identifying and working through transference allows the patient the opportunity to develop insights about patterns of interaction and to change these patterns in subsequent relationships. Transference feelings may occur in many relationships, not just in therapy, when attitudes and feelings about people or situations from the past are unconsciously transferred to another person or situation in the present (Jones, 2005).

Sigmund Freud first described transference in 1905 and noted it as an essential part of the psychoanalytic process (Clarkson & Nuttall, 2000). While many different types of therapy are attuned to the interactions and relationship between therapist and client, not all believe that transference is essential to the therapeutic process (Clarkson & Nuttall, 2000). From a psychoanalytic perspective, it is believed that unconscious feelings affect behavior. *Resistance* is a defense mechanism that protects the ego (conscious part of the psyche) by keeping upsetting material out of the conscious mind (repressed). By working through feelings of transference and resistance, the patient may discover and acknowledge unconscious feelings and be freed from the effects of unconscious feelings on future behavior. By maintaining a neutral stance, the therapist becomes a blank screen onto which the patient can project feelings. The psychoanalyst analyzes and interprets the psychological meaning behind repressed material and transference feelings.

Countertransference describes feelings the therapist may project onto the patient. For example, if the therapist begins to have strong feelings of annoyance or irritation toward a patient, it may be because the patient reminds the therapist of a previous troublesome relationship (e.g., with a family member). The manner in which the patient interacts with the therapist may set off unconscious response patterns in the therapist. It is important for the therapist to acknowledge feelings of countertransference and to work through these feelings. Dealing with countertransference allows the therapist to regulate his emotions within the therapeutic relationship and may provide insight into the client's issues. If therapeutically appropriate, countertransference issues may be dealt with directly with the patient. For example, the therapist may say to the patient, "When you say things in that manner, I feel ——." However, it is better to handle some types of countertransference, such as feelings of sexual attraction for a patient, outside the therapeutic relationship. Some therapists consult with their own therapists, with whom they can discuss these feelings. Unresolved transference or countertransference can cause misunderstandings and damage the therapeutic relationship.

See also defense mechanisms, Sigmund Freud, psychoanalytic perspective, psychodynamic psychotherapy and psychoanalysis, the unconscious mind.

Further Reading:
Encyclopædia Britannica. (2009). Mental disorder. *Encyclopædia Britannica Online.* Available from http://www.britannica.com/

References:
Clarkson, P., & Nuttall, J. (2000). Working with countertransference. *Psychodynamic Counselling, 6,* 359–379.
Jones, A. C. (2005). Transference, counter-transference and repetition: Some implications for nursing practice. *Journal of Clinical Nursing, 14,* 1177–1184.

Traumatic Brain Injury

Traumatic brain injury (TBI) is a type of brain injury that occurs when an external trauma damages the brain, resulting in neurological dysfunction. TBI may be caused if the head suddenly and violently strikes an object (e.g., from a fall or car accident) or if an object pierces the skull and enters the brain (e.g., a gunshot). Other types of brain injury (e.g., acquired brain injury) may be caused by disease (e.g., meningitis), surgery, toxins, anoxia (e.g., lack of oxygen resulting in cerebral palsy), or stroke. Shaken-baby syndrome is a severe form of physical child abuse caused by vigorously shaking an infant or small child (up to five years of age), causing bleeding in the eyes or brain. Shaken-baby syndrome can result in developmental delays, cognitive impairment, paralysis, severe motor difficulties, spasticity, blindness, seizures, or death. Boxers and football players may sustain a type of TBI known as *dementia pugilistica* (which used to be called *punch drunk*). Now referred to as *chronic traumatic encephalopathy*, it is caused by repeated blows to the head (Masel, 2009). Repeated mild TBIs occurring over months or years can result in cumulative neurological damage and cognitive impairment; occurring over a period of days or weeks, TBI can be fatal (National Center for Injury Prevention and Control [NCIPC], 2009).

TBI severity can be mild, moderate, or severe. With mild TBI, a person may remain conscious or lose consciousness briefly (for a few seconds or minutes). Mild TBI symptoms may include headache, confusion, dizziness, lightheadedness, vision changes (e.g., blurred vision or tired eyes), ringing in the ears, bad taste in the mouth, fatigue, lethargy, change in sleep patterns, mood swings, cognitive difficulties (e.g., trouble with memory, concentration, attention, or thinking), and changes in behavior (National Institute of Neurological Disorders and Stroke [NINDS], 2009). In addition to these symptoms, moderate or severe TBI may result in headache that gets worse or does not go away, repeated vomiting or nausea, seizures, inability to awaken from sleep, dilation of the pupils, slurred speech, weakness or numbness in the extremities, loss of coordination, increased confusion, restlessness, or agitation. Symptoms may not manifest for days or weeks following the injury (NINDS, 2009).

In the United States, 1.4 million people sustain a TBI each year. Of these, 4 percent die, 17 percent are hospitalized, and 79 percent are treated in an emergency room and released. The leading causes of TBI are falls (28%), motor vehicle crashes (20%), struck by/against accidents (colliding with a moving or stationary object; 19%), and assaults (11%). Males are 1.5 times more likely than females to sustain a TBI. Those at highest risk of sustaining a TBI are those aged 0 to 4 years and 15 to 19 years. Firearm use is the leading cause of death from TBI. African Americans have the highest death rate from TBI (NCIPC, 2009).

TBI can result in many disabilities, including problems with cognition (e.g., thinking, memory, reasoning), sensory processing, communication, mental health (e.g., depression, anxiety, personality changes) and behavior (e.g., aggression, acting out, social inappropriateness). Serious head injury can result in *stupor* (an unresponsive state from which an individual can be aroused with a strong stimulus), *coma* (an unresponsive and unaware state), or *vegetative state* (unresponsive and unaware but continuing to have sleep-wake cycles and periods of alertness). A *persistent vegetative state* (PVS) is when an individual stays in a vegetative state for over a month. PVS is not the same thing as brain death, which occurs when the brain stem dies and all brain activity (including periods of alertness and wake-sleep cycles) ceases.

Prompt treatment of moderate or severe TBI may lessen severity of consequences or prevent further injury. Treatment focus is on stabilization to ensure proper oxygen supply (to the brain and the rest of the body), maintain blood flow, and control blood pressure. Imaging studies, such as X-rays, computed tomography (CT) scan, or functional magnetic resonance imaging (fMRI), can detect skull fractures and locate specific areas of injury in the brain. About half of individuals with severe TBI need surgery to repair hematomas (ruptured blood vessels) or contusions (bruised brain tissue; NINDS, 2009). Rehabilitation may include physical therapy, occupational therapy, speech and language therapy, physiatry (physical medicine), pharmacotherapy (medication), psychotherapy, and social support. The U.S. Centers for Disease Control (2006) estimates that at least 5.3 million Americans with TBI will have a long-term or lifelong need for assistance with activities of daily living (e.g., dressing, basic hygiene) because of their disability. TBI can cause seizure disorder and increase the risk for Parkinson's disease and Alzheimer's disease (NCIPC, 2009).

See also functional magnetic resonance imaging, mood swings, National Institute of Neurological Disorders and Stroke, Parkinson's disease, right hemisphere syndrome.

Further Readings:

Brain Injury Association of America Web site: http://www.biausa.org/
Brain Injury Resource Foundation Web site: http://www.birf.info/
Gladwell, M. (2009, October 19). Offensive play: How different are football and dogfighting? *The New Yorker*. Retrieved from http://www.newyorker.com/reporting/2009/10/19/091019fa_fact_gladwell?currentPage=all
Interactive brain map: http://www.birf.info/home/bi-tools/brainmap/qlinks_bramap.html

References:

Centers for Disease Control and Prevention. (2006, July). *Facts about traumatic brain injury*. Retrieved from http://www.cdc.gov/ncipc/tbi/FactSheets/Facts_About_TBI.pdf

Masel, B. (2009). *Conceptualizing brain injury as a chronic disease.* Vienna, VA: Brain Injury Association of America.

National Center for Injury Prevention and Control. (2009). *What is traumatic brain injury?* Retrieved from http://www.cdc.gov/ncipc/tbi/TBI.htm

National Institute of Neurological Disorders and Stroke. (2009). *What is traumatic brain injury?* Retrieved from http://www.ninds.nih.gov/disorders/tbi/tbi.htm

Winslade, W. J., & Brady, J. S. (1998). *Confronting traumatic brain injury: Devastation, hope, and healing.* Binghamton, NY: Vail-Baillou Press.

- When John Hinkley attempted to assassinate President Reagan in 1981, James Brady (U.S. White House press secretary) sustained a gunshot wound to the head, resulting in traumatic brain injury. Since the shooting, Mr. Brady has made great efforts lobbying for handgun control. The Brady Bill—a U.S. handgun control bill requiring a waiting period and background check before purchasing a handgun—was signed into law in 1993. Mr. Brady's head injury caused significant impairment, including difficulties with speech, paralysis affecting much of his body, and chronic pain (Winslade & Brady, 1998).
- *Locked-in syndrome* is a rare neurological disorder that may result from traumatic brain injury or stroke; it may also be caused by poison (e.g., tetrodotoxin from a puffer fish), circulatory system disease, medication overdose, or diseases that destroy the myelin sheath surrounding nerve cells. It causes complete paralysis of all voluntary muscles in the body, except those that control eye movement. People with locked-in syndrome are conscious but cannot speak or move; communication may be possible through eye blinks.

Tricyclic Antidepressant

When imipramine (Tofranil) was developed as an antipsychotic in the 1950s, it was also found to have antidepressant properties. This was followed by the development of amitriptyline (Elavil) and other cyclic antidepressants in the 1960s (Preston, O'Neal, & Talaga, 2008). The cyclic antidepressants include the tricyclics (TCAs; e.g., desipramine, Sinequan) and tetracyclics (e.g., amoxapine, Serzone, Trazodone). Heterocyclic antidepressants, which have molecular structures of three or more rings, include the tricyclics, which have three rings, and the tetracyclics, which have four.

TCAs are used to treat clinical depression and chronic pain. TCAs have also been used to treat obsessive-compulsive disorder, bipolar disorder, headache, bulimia, irritable bowel syndrome, narcolepsy, insomnia, persistent hiccups, pathological crying or laughing, smoking cessation, attention-deficit hyperactivity disorder, and panic disorders and as an adjunctive treatment for schizophrenia. The TCA opipramol (Neuraxpharm, Insidon) is used to treat anxiety. In addition to the TCAs, other types of antidepressants include monoamine oxidase inhibitors (MAOIs), selective serotonin reuptake inhibitors (SSRIs), serotonin and norepinephrine reuptake inhibitors (SNRIs), norepinephrine reuptake inhibitors (NRIs), and atypical antidepressants.

The monoamine hypothesis—the main theory spurring development of TCAs—holds that the antidepressant effects are achieved by inhibiting the reuptake of specific neurotransmitters (such as serotonin and norepinephrine). These neurotransmitters are chemical messengers involved in communication between neurons in the brain. With reuptake, a neurotransmitter is absorbed (or recycled) back into a neuron and is no longer available for use. Inhibiting reuptake allows more of these neurotransmitters to be available for neurotransmission (Patterson, 2006). TCAs are being prescribed less often since the advent of effective SSRIs and atypical antidepressants, which can be more effective and have fewer side effects. However, TCAs are still useful for treatment-resistant clinical depression that has not responded to treatment with SSRIs.

Side effects of TCAs can be grouped into four categories: anticholinergic (e.g., dry mouth, dry skin, blurred vision, constipation), adrenergic (e.g., sweating, sexual dysfunction, sudden drop in blood pressure), antihistaminic (e.g., sedation, weight gain), and miscellaneous (e.g., lowered seizure threshold, cardiac arrhythmia, elevated heart rate, hepatitis, rashes, sweating, anxiety; Preston et al., 2008). The TCA iprindole can be fatal when combined with Ecstasy (MDMA). TCAs are very toxic—even small overdoses can be lethal. For this reason, it is not advisable to prescribe TCAs to individuals who are suicidal. *Serotonin syndrome*—a potentially lethal condition resulting from toxic levels of serotonin in the central nervous system—can be caused by combining antidepressants with each other or with some opioids (e.g., tramadol, fentanyl), antimigraine medications, stimulants (e.g., amphetamines, cocaine), psychedelics (e.g., MDMA), herbs (e.g., St. John's wort), and various other medications and over-the-counter products. Symptoms of serotonin syndrome may include rapid heart rate, sweating, shivering, dilated pupils, tremor or twitching, muscular rigidity, elevated temperature, confusion, agitation, delirium, hallucinations, coma, or death. Risk of taking TCAs while pregnant varies by medication. Some TCAs show evidence of maternal harm or harm to the fetus, and risk cannot be ruled out for other TCAs (Preston et al., 2008). To avoid potentially harmful side effects and drug interactions, health care consumers should be sure that their doctors and pharmacists are aware of *all* medications they are taking, including over-the-counter medications, herbs and natural remedies, and dietary supplements.

See also antidepressant, atypical antidepressants, depression, major depressive disorder, monoamine oxidase inhibiter, neurotransmitter, Prozac (fluoxetine), selective serotonin reuptake inhibitor, serotonin, St. John's wort.

Further Readings:

American Psychiatric Association—Healthy Minds Web site: http://www.healthyminds.org/
Depression and Bipolar Support Alliance Web site: http://www.dbsalliance.org/
National Alliance on Mental Illness Web site: http://www.nami.org/

References:

Patterson, J. (2006). *Therapist's guide to psychopharmacology: Working with patients, families, and physicians to optimize care.* New York: Guilford.
Preston, J. D., O'Neal, J. H., & Talaga, M. C. (2008). *Handbook of clinical psychopharmacology for therapists* (5th ed.). Oakland, CA: New Harbinger.

Triune Brain

In 1970, following about two decades of research, American physician and neuroscientist Paul MacLean introduced the triune brain theory (MacLean, 1970). This theory attempts to explain anatomy and functioning of the human brain (and brains of other animals) from an evolutionary perspective. MacLean proposed that the brain is actually three brains in one, each with its own particular type of intelligence, perception of time and space, memory, and other functions. The three layers of the brain each developed at different points in evolutionary history. The first layer, called the *reptilian brain* or *physical brain*, controls basic, immediate survival functions such as breathing and heart rate and survival-motivated behaviors such as food procurement and mating. All vertebrate animals have this layer of the brain, which developed first in evolutionary history. The second layer, called the *paleomammalian brain* or the *emotional brain*, and identified by MacLean as the limbic system, is present in mammals but not other vertebrates (fish, amphibians, reptiles, and birds), although the other vertebrates have some analogous structures. The final layer, called the *mammalian brain* or *thinking brain*, developed last and is involved in higher-level thinking and behavior, including problem solving, planning, language, and other functions. Only the more recently evolved mammals have this brain: humans, other primates, and advanced mammals.

The paleomammalian or emotional brain integrates sensory information coming from the external environment and sensations from inside the body and produces

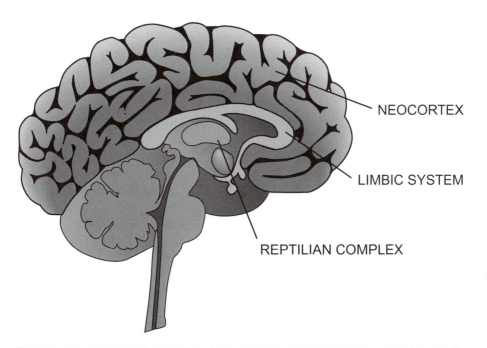

The triune brain theory, introduced by Paul MacLean in 1970, proposed that the human brain is actually three layers that developed at different points in evolutionary history. (ABC-CLIO)

emotional feelings. In work that MacLean did prior to unveiling his triune brain theory (e.g., MacLean, 1949), he proposed that a particular brain structure, the hippocampus, was the central structure involved in this integration. MacLean had recognized that emotions can be experienced as "irrational" and that people are not always easily able to verbalize their emotions. (In fact, we often express our emotions by screaming, crying, and so forth.) He stated that the anatomy of the hippocampus does not allow for sophisticated (i.e., verbal) expression of emotion. Hippocampal nerve cells are large, crude cells, unlike the nerve cells of the thinking brain (cortex), which are more complex. Hippocampal cells can allow for representing information symbolically but not verbally. MacLean gives the example of representing the color red. The hippocampus could not conceive of it as a particular wavelength of light or a three-letter word but could perhaps associate red with blood, flowers, the sun right before nighttime, danger, and so on. Humans have a thinking brain but still also have an emotional brain. Therefore some, perhaps many, emotions are experienced in this crude, symbolic, nonverbal way.

Many brain experts and emotion scholars have agreed that many aspects of MacLean's theory are valid. LeDoux (1996) expressed his admiration of MacLean's work, stating that MacLean's theory was an outstanding synthesis of the most current research and knowledge in brain science, psychology, and psychiatry at the time. LeDoux agrees that an emotional brain exists similar to the way that MacLean described it, except that based on research evidence, MacLean's concept of the emotional brain is probably too simple. That is, when researchers have attempted to find the emotional brain using MacLean's thesis—that scientists should be able to locate the emotional brain based on knowledge of how the brain evolved—this has worked out well sometimes and not so well at other times. Supporting MacLean's thesis, the amygdala, which is located in the appropriate area of the brain to qualify as an emotional brain structure, has clear emotional functions. For instance, the amygdala is active when people see fearful facial expressions on other people (Breiter et al., 1996), and depressed people have elevated activity in their amygdalas (e.g., Nofzinger et al., 1999). However, some of the areas that MacLean originally identified as the emotional brain or limbic system appear to have little to do with emotion. For instance, the hippocampus is associated primarily with memory functions rather than with emotion (e.g., Eichenbaum, Otto, & Cohen, 1992). LeDoux (1996) discusses other criticisms and support for MacLean's theory, particularly in regard to the emotional brain concept. MacLean's theory has inspired large amounts of research and further thinking on the functions of various parts of the brain, on the emotional brain in particular, and on the way that evolution is related to brain function. As LeDoux (1996) says, however, a more complex model is needed to more fully understand the emotional brain.

See also amygdala, hippocampus, hypothalamus, limbic system, physiology of emotion.

Further Readings:

LeDoux, J. (1996). *The emotional brain: The mysterious underpinnings of emotional life.* New York: Touchstone.

MacLean, P. D. (1970). The triune brain, emotion, and scientific bias. In F. O. Schmitt (Ed.), *The neurosciences: Second study program* (pp. 336–349). New York: Rockefeller University Press.

References:

Breiter, H. C., Etcoff, N. L., Whalen, P. J., Kennedy, W. A., Rauch, S. L., Buckner, R. L., et al. (1996). Response and habituation of the human amygdala during visual processing of facial expression. *Neuron, 17*, 875–887.

Eichenbaum, H., Otto, T., & Cohen, N. J. (1992). The hippocampus: What does it do? *Behavioral and Neural Biology, 57*, 2–36.

LeDoux, J. (1996). *The emotional brain: The mysterious underpinnings of emotional life.* New York: Touchstone.

MacLean, P. D. (1949). Psychosomatic disease and the "visceral brain": Recent developments bearing on the Papez theory of emotion. *Psychosomatic Medicine, 11*, 338–353.

MacLean, P. D. (1970). The triune brain, emotion, and scientific bias. In F. O. Schmitt (Ed.), *The neurosciences: Second study program* (pp. 336–349). New York: Rockefeller University Press.

Nofzinger, E. A., Nichols, T. E., Meltzer, C. C., Price, J., Steppe, D. A., Miewald, J. M., et al. (1999). Changes in forebrain function from waking to REM sleep in depression: Preliminary analyses of [18F] FDG PET studies. *Psychiatry Research, 91*(2), 59–78.

Trust

Trust is an individual's collection of expectations that another individual or group of individuals will behave in favorable and accepting ways toward him. When trust is present, an individual can have faith that the trusted one will take care not to harm him. Trust can be selective, with an individual trusting one individual or group in some contexts and other individuals or groups in other contexts.

Mutual trust is essential for the effective functioning of both individual relationships and of social groups, including whole societies. At the societal and social group level, trust allows the group to develop and increase in complexity; conversely, societal or group development is hindered without trust. At the most fundamental level, trust is necessary for the initial formation of a group, and later, trust impacts the group's ability to solve problems collectively. In our evolutionary history, we faced many threats and hardships such as need for shelter, need for food and other resources, and need for protection against the elements, predatory animals, and perhaps other humans. Gathering together in groups and forming societies created superior protection for people. Many trust scholars therefore make the argument that the human capacity for trust enhances survival, and we can reasonably assume that this capacity developed through natural selection (e.g., Couch, 1999).

Not only is trust valuable for forming social groups, it is also valuable for the formation of bonds in intimate relationships. According to research by Wilson and Carroll (1991), trust is necessary for self-disclosure, which in turn is necessary for the development of intimacy. A number of scholars have theorized about the way that trust originates and develops in an individual. For instance, German-born American psychologist Eric Erikson (1950) and British psychiatrist John Bowlby (1973) emphasized that trust begins to develop in infancy through interactions with one's caregivers (usually the mother and father). According to Erikson, trust arises when the caregiver reliably and appropriately responds to the needs of the infant. For instance, if the infant is crying because she is hungry, feeding the infant will help her to feel trust. Trust will develop over time with many need-satisfying interactions with the caregivers. Conversely, if the caregiver does not respond appropriately to the baby's needs, for example, through responding as if the need were different (e.g., changing the diaper when the baby is crying because of hunger), or if the caregiver is neglectful toward the infant, mistrust develops. Erikson pointed out that no parent is perfect, and therefore some mistrust will develop in all infants. Furthermore, some degree of mistrust is healthy for individuals. If people fail to develop an awareness that others could hurt or disappoint them, this creates vulnerability. The ideal development is one is which both trust and mistrust develop, with a higher proportion of trust than mistrust.

According to Bowlby, development of trust is closely interconnected with the attachment relationship. Bowlby argued that a drive toward attachment is inborn and a survival mechanism. The attachment drive induces the infant to remain physically close to caregivers, who in turn will protect the infant from physical and psychological harm. In the infant's early interactions with caregivers, she receives information from caregivers about their responsiveness to her needs. The infant processes this information, developing an expectation about the future behavior (e.g., reliability, responsiveness) of caregivers. This expectation she has developed is a sense of trust. Furthermore, Bowlby states that the sense of trust with caregivers is generalized to other relationships; the child now has a general sense of trust of others. Future behaviors can and generally do impact the sense of trust; however, early information is most important because once a sense of trust has become a part of the child's worldview, future interactions are interpreted through this lens.

American psychologist Julian Rotter (1967) had a view similar to Bowlby's but with at least two major differences. Like Bowlby, Rotter believed that trust emerges and evolves through interactions with others. For Rotter, however, the "others" can be any social agents, including parents, other family members, peers, teachers, and so on. Similar to Bowlby's perspective, Rotter argued that a *generalized expectancy* regarding trustworthiness of others develops through experiencing positive and negative outcomes in interaction with others. Unlike Bowlby, however, Rotter stated that the generalized expectancy can come from another source: observing the behavior of others and hearing about the expectations of others. Therefore direct experience with others is only part of what creates trust; children and adults may also learn some of their attitudes about trust simply from hearing what others think or from observing the trustworthy or untrustworthy behavior of one person toward another.

Research has supported Erikson's, Bowlby's, and Rotter's claims that trust develops early in life and that this early trust concept possesses some stability and impacts later relationships. For instance, Ainsworth, Blehar, Waters, and Wall (1978) showed that infants can be identified as exhibiting different attachment styles that are differentially related to trust (i.e., the secure type experiences high trust and the anxious-ambivalent and avoidant types exhibit must less trust), and later research has shown that these attachment styles are stable over time and associated with relatively trusting or relatively untrusting romantic relationships in adulthood (see Grossman, Grossman, & Waters, 2005).

See also Mary D. Salter Ainsworth, attachment, John Bowlby, developmental crisis, emotional abuse, evolutionary psychology (human sociobiology), friendship, human development, intimacy, loneliness, relationships, social learning.

References:
Ainsworth, M. S., Blehar, M. C., Waters, E., & Wall, S. (1978). *Patterns of attachment: A psychological study of the strange situation.* Hillsdale, NJ: Lawrence Erlbaum Associates.
Bowlby, J. (1973). *Attachment and loss: Vol 2. Separation.* New York: Basic Books.

Couch, L. L. (1999). Trust. In D. Levinson, J. J. Ponzetti, & P. F. Jorgensen (Eds.), *Encyclopedia of human emotions* (2nd ed., pp. 662–667). New York: Macmillan Reference USA.

Erikson, E. H. (1950). *Childhood and society.* New York: W. W. Norton.

Grossmann, K. E., Grossmann, K., & Waters, E. (Eds.). (2005). *Attachment from infancy to adulthood: The major longitudinal studies.* New York: Guilford.

Rotter, J. B. (1967). A new scale for the measurement of interpersonal trust. *Journal of Personality, 35,* 651–665.

Valhouli, C. (n.d.). *Cutting down the dissonance: The psychology of gullibility.* Retrieved from http://www.columbia.edu/cu/21stC/issue-3.4/valhouli.html

Wilson, J. M., & Carroll, J. L. (1991). Children's trustworthiness: Judgments by teachers, parents, and peers. In K. J. Rotenberg (Ed.), *Children's interpersonal trust: Sensitivity to lying, deception, and promise violations* (pp. 100–117). New York: Springer.

- A lack of trust can cause someone to be suspicious of others and hinder development of meaningful social relationships. Extreme suspiciousness may rise to the level of paranoia, which is associated with some mental disorders (e.g., paranoid schizophrenia, paranoid personality disorder, and delusional disorder, persecutory type) and the use of some stimulant drugs (e.g., methamphetamine).
- Can someone be too trusting? Being gullible can make an individual vulnerable to being taken advantage of. Gullibility can make one prey to cults, scam artists, and more likely to believe urban legends, Internet rumors, and pseudoscientific claims. In 1997, 14-year-old Nathan Zohner won a junior high school science fair for a project called "How Gullible Are We?" Zohner had circulated a report to other students warning of the dangers of the chemical dihydrogen monoxide. He said that this chemical caused excessive sweating, was lethal if inhaled, and caused erosion. He was asking what should be done about it. Most students favored banning the substance; only one correctly identified it as water (H_2O). For more about gullibility, see Valhouli (n.d.).

12-Step Programs

Alcoholics Anonymous (AA), founded in 1935, was the first 12-step program. In the 12 Steps of AA, the first step is admitting that there is a problem: that one is powerless over alcohol (or another addiction). The second and third steps are spiritual in nature; believing that a higher power (of one's own understanding) can help relieve one's problems (i.e., alcoholism or other addiction) and deciding to turn one's life over to the care of that higher power. In the fourth and fifth steps, one creates and shares a list of one's behaviors with another person. Then, in the sixth and seventh steps, one identifies what personal characteristics (referred to as shortcomings) have contributed to the behaviors recounted in the fifth step inventory and asks one's higher power to remove those shortcomings. The eighth and ninth steps involve making amends (e.g., apologies and reparations) to people one has harmed. The 10th step is a maintenance step, involving examining one's behaviors and making any necessary amends on a daily basis. The 11th step involves maintaining contact with one's higher power through daily meditation and prayer. The 12th step involves giving back to others recovering from alcoholism through service (e.g., sponsoring others, sharing the AA message, or doing service in AA groups).

All subsequent 12-step programs are based on modified versions of AA's 12 Steps. Many 12-step programs also incorporate AA's 12 Traditions, especially the principle of anonymity at the public level.

Twelve-step programs established to help people with addictions, behaviors, or issues other than alcoholism include Narcotics Anonymous (established in 1953), Gamblers Anonymous (1957), Overeaters Anonymous (1960), Debtors Anonymous (1968), Emotions Anonymous (1971), Sexaholics Anonymous (1979), Cocaine Anonymous (1982), Recoveries Anonymous (1983), Workaholics Anonymous (1983), and Obsessive Compulsive Anonymous (1988). Twelve-step programs established to help support the family and friends of people with addictive or disordered behaviors include Al-Anon and Alateen (1951), Nar-Anon (for families of addicts, 1968), Adult Children of Alcoholics (established in 1978), Co-Dependents Anonymous (1986), and Families Anonymous. As long as enough people share a particular addiction, behavior, or mood problem and want to form support groups to help each other recover from their mutual problem, there is a 12-step program for them.

The 12-step programs emphasize that they are spiritual rather than religious. However, some people seeking recovery from alcoholism or other addictions are put off by the concept of a higher power (referred to as God in several of AA's 12 Steps). Other people do not believe that it is necessary or desirable to admit powerlessness (part of AA's first step) to recover. People seeking a nonspiritual mutual-help approach to recovery from alcoholism and drug addiction established Secular Organization for Sobriety (SOS) and LifeRing as alternatives to 12-step programs. Other alternatives include self-recovery methods that do not involve group meetings such as the method espoused by Rational Recovery.

See also Al-Anon and Alateen, alcohol abuse and alcoholism, Alcoholics Anonymous, Emotions Anonymous, Narcotics Anonymous, Overeaters Anonymous, Sex and Love Addicts Anonymous, substance abuse.

Further Readings:

Alcoholics Anonymous World Services Inc. (2001). *Alcoholics Anonymous.* New York: Author. (Original work published 1935)

Christopher, J. (1988). *How to stay sober: Recovery without religion.* Amherst, NY: Prometheus Books.

Humphreys, K. (2003). *Circles of recovery: Self-help organizations for addictions.* Cambridge, England: Cambridge University Press.

Type A Behavior Pattern

A Type A behavior pattern is a cluster of personality traits identified by American cardiologists Ray Rosenman and Meyer Friedman in the early 1960s. In their medical practice, they observed that their patients manifested behaviors and attitudes that distinguished them from other people; specifically, they appeared anxious, focused on their work lives and achievement, and overly concerned with time. In 1974, Rosenman and Friedman clearly identified this personality pattern as one they began to suspect was a risk factor for coronary heart disease. Characteristics of the Type A personality are (1) achievement orientation; (2) aggressiveness and competitiveness, sometimes turning into hostility; and (3) time urgency. Time urgency is a cluster of three subtraits: (1) multitasking (doing more than one task at a time), (2) time urgency (overconcern with time such that one has to be in the fastest line at the grocery store, the fastest driver on the highway, etc.), and (3) chronic activation (a continual state of being keyed up or physiologically aroused, creating an appearance of anxiety or intensity in the individual).

Friedman and Rosenman (1974) discussed a series of studies investigating 3,411 men over a number of years. Results of the research indicated that the Type A behavior pattern preceded the diagnosis of coronary heart disease in 72 to 85 percent of research participants. Leading cardiologists found these results strongly suggestive, if not convincing, which led to the question of mechanism: how might Type A personality cause or contribute to heart disease? By the 1990s, researchers (see Cooper, 1995; Williams & Williams, 1993) found that individuals with the Type A behavior pattern have sympathetic nervous systems (SNS) that are more reactive to stimuli than people who possess none of the Type A traits. Greater SNS activity, which occurs with the stress response, is associated with a variety of symptoms that predispose individuals to heart disease such as increased blood pressure, elevated cholesterol levels in the blood, and decreased flexibility of the blood vessels.

Further study of the Type A behavior pattern has led many to conclude that only one Type A component is reliably associated with heart disease. The primary pathogenic component is anger/hostility (e.g., Miller, Smith, Turner, Guijarro, & Hallet, 1996). The hostility component of Type A can be reduced through counseling or therapy, and reducing hostility can decrease the severity of future damage to the cardiovascular system (e.g., Friedman et al., 1996). At present, researchers disagree over whether the time urgency component also increases heart disease risk (Girdano, Dusek, & Everly, 2009).

See also anger, stress, stress hormones, sympathetic nervous system.

Further Readings:

Friedman, M., & Rosenman, R. H. (1974). *Type A behavior and your heart.* New York: Knopf.
Williams, R. B., & Williams, V. (1993). *Anger kills: Seventeen strategies for controlling the hostility that can harm your health.* New York: HarperPerennial Library.

References:

Cooper, C. L. (Ed.). (1995). *Handbook of stress medicine and health.* Boca Raton, FL: CRC Press.
Friedman, M., Breall, W. S., Goodwin, L., Sparagon, B. J., Ghandour, G., & Fleischmann, N. (1996). Effect of Type A behavioral counseling on frequency of episodes of silent myocardial ischemia in coronary patients. *American Heart Journal, 132,* 933–937.
Friedman, M., & Rosenman, R. H. (1974). *Type A behavior and your heart.* New York: Knopf.
Girdano, D. A., Dusek, D. E., & Everly, G. S., Jr. (2009). *Controlling stress and tension* (8th ed.). San Francisco: Benjamin Cummings.
Griffin, R. W., & Moorhead, G. (2009). *Organizational behavior: Managing people and organizations.* Mason, OH: Cengage Learning.
Miller, T. Q., Smith, T. W., Turner, C. W., Guijarro, M. L., & Hallet, A. J. (1996). A meta-analytic review of research on hostility and physical health. *Psychological Bulletin, 119,* 322–348.
Williams, R. B., & Williams, V. (1993). *Anger kills: Seventeen strategies for controlling the hostility that can harm your health.* New York: HarperPerennial Library.

American cardiologists Ray Rosenman and Meyer Friedman first got the idea about Type A personality when a worker repairing the upholstery on their waiting room chairs commented that the upholstery only seemed to be worn on the front of the seats. After further observation, Rosenman and Friedman realized that many of their patients were anxious and had a hard time sitting still; they were literally sitting on the edges of their seats! These informal observations led to more detailed study and discovery of the Type A personality (Griffin & Moorhead, 2009).

U

The Unconscious Mind

Emotional aspects of the unconscious mind have been of concern to researchers and theorists in diverse fields, including clinical/personality psychology, evolutionary biology, and social psychology. Although the idea of an unconscious mind can be traced to the ancient Greeks, in more modern times, the concept was popularized by Sigmund Freud from the clinical/personality psychology perspective and by Charles Darwin and others from the evolutionary perspective (Bargh & Morsella, 2008).

The unconscious mind is a central idea in Freudian theory and permeates his writings. In one of Freud's early publications, *Studies on Hysteria*, coauthored with Josef Breuer in 1895, the authors discussed several case histories illustrating the power of the unconscious mind. Their central theme was that the intense suffering of the mentally ill patient is caused by her inability to face personal characteristics or realities that may generate disturbing emotions such as shame, guilt, fear, or self-loathing. One patient described in the book, Katharina, suffers a variety of anxiety symptoms, including panic attacks, vomiting, and a feeling of suffocating. In therapy with Freud, she accepts what she has been repressing for a number of years: her father had attempted to molest her when she was a child. Because this memory caused her pain, she had repressed it into the unconscious mind for several years. Furthermore, Freud suggests, when Katharina became an adolescent, she was better able to understand what her father had been trying to do to her. At that point, she felt some attraction to her father but was horrified by that feeling and had to repress her own attraction as well. Thus the unconscious, which included the disturbing memory and her own feelings of attraction, expressed itself through her symptoms. In therapy with Freud, she was able to accept the memory and her own feelings, and her symptoms were relieved.

In another early case, the patient, Fräulein Elizabeth, was (unconsciously) in love with her brother-in-law and at some level wished that her ill sister would die. These thoughts and feelings distressed her intensely, so she repressed them. The unconscious mind produced symptoms, including intense leg pain, as a way of expressing the forbidden emotions. In Freud's theory, the unconscious mind is composed of disturbing mental products such as thoughts, emotions, memories, and impulses.

The unconscious mind must find a manner of expression, and the expression must be indirect or disguised so as not to reveal the unconscious contents. The expressions may take many forms, including symptoms, dreams, slips of the tongue, jokes, projection of one's characteristics onto other persons, and artistic productions. According to Freud, the key to a cure for a mentally ill person is knowing oneself, or bringing the unconscious mind into consciousness. When one is aware of her emotions, thoughts, impulses, and so on, she can consciously decide how to express them rather than passively allowing the unconscious mind to have control.

Another perspective on the unconscious mind was introduced by evolutionary biologists, including Darwin (1859) in *On the Origin of Species by Means of Natural Selection*, and was further elaborated by Dawkins (1976) in *The Selfish Gene*. According to this perspective, characteristics that enhance the survival of the organism will likely survive themselves. For example, if an individual tends to emotionally bond with other humans and this emotional bonding enhances his survival, then the characteristic "tendency to bond emotionally" will likely survive. Many of our inherited characteristics are preferences or feelings for or against something (emotions). As another example, people who naturally feared snakes may have been more likely to survive than people who did not. The individual person may not know why he dislikes snakes. More precisely, he may not even always know that he *does* dislike snakes but may simply try to avoid them. These preferences and dislikes (which we could call *approach tendencies* and *avoidance tendencies*) can certainly operate at a level that is below consciousness, or unconscious. In the evolutionary biology point of view, most animal (including human) behavior is caused by motives that are not conscious (unconscious). As our characteristics have evolved, there is no requirement that we are aware of their utility or even of their existence.

A third perspective on the unconscious mind comes from social psychologists. The relevant social psychology field is called *social cognition*, which focuses on our attitudes, judgments, and decision-making processes about social affairs. Topics included in this field are prejudice, persuasion (including how advertisements persuade people to buy products), group decision making, conformity, and attraction and relationships. Research has focused on the degree to which people are aware of aspects that influence their decisions and of the reasons for their behavior. A review of this research concluded that the unconscious mind significantly and powerfully affects people's experiences, decisions, and judgments in the social realm (Bargh, 2007). Chen, Fitzsimons, and Andersen (2007) reviewed research and theory on how the unconscious influences our close relationships. Unconscious factors may affect each major phase of a relationship, from the initial attraction to experiences and behaviors that occur in a well-established relationship to the way that we feel and behave when ending a relationship.

Historically, psychology has tended to focus on consciousness and conscious processes and has relatively neglected unconscious processes. Conversely, the perspective of evolutionary biology has always been that in the animal kingdom, unconscious causes of behavior are predominant. The unconscious mind has gained a new respect in psychology as well.

See also ambivalence, appraisal, attitude, conditioned emotional response, Charles Darwin, defense mechanisms, evolutionary psychology (human sociobiology), Sigmund

Freud, prejudice, psychoanalytic perspective, psychodynamic psychotherapy and psychoanalysis, Edward O. Wilson.

Further Readings:

Bargh, J. A. (Ed.). (2007). *Social psychology and the unconscious: The automaticity of higher mental processes.* New York: Psychology Press.

Freud, S., & Gay, P. (Ed.). (1989). *The Freud reader.* New York: W. W. Norton.

References:

Bargh, J. A. (Ed.). (2007). *Social psychology and the unconscious: The automaticity of higher mental processes.* New York: Psychology Press.

Bargh, J. A., & Morsella, E. (2008). The unconscious mind. *Perspective on Psychological Science, 3*, 73–79.

Breuer, J., & Freud, S. (1955). Studies on hysteria. In J. Strachey (Ed. & Trans), *The standard edition of the complete psychological works of Sigmund Freud* (Vol. 2). London: Hogarth Press. (Original work published 1895)

Chen, S., Fitzsimons, G. M., & Andersen, S. M. (2007). Automaticity in close relationships. In J. A. Bargh (Ed.), *Social psychology and the unconscious: The automaticity of higher mental processes* (pp. 133–172). New York: Psychology Press.

Darwin, C. (1859). *On the origin of species by means of natural selection.* London: John Murray.

Dawkins, R. (1976). *The selfish gene.* New York: Oxford University Press.

Universal Signals

Famed emotion researcher Paul Ekman (1984) originated the concept of universal signal to describe his supposition that each distinct emotion has a distinct universal signal, or sign, that reveals its presence. The signal is communicated in various modes through facial expression, voice, and possibly others ways such as posture or body movement.

Interrelated with and fundamental to Ekman's discussion of universal signals were Ekman and colleagues' arguments that emotions are universal or common across cultures. Ekman and Friesen (1975) presented evidence that at least six emotions are present across cultures, with highly similar or identical facial expressions: happiness, sadness, fear, anger, disgust, and surprise.

Ekman (1999) states that these hypothesized universal signals have a function, which is to aid in the development and regulation of interpersonal relationships. Universal signals convey a great deal of information to the perceiver in a highly efficient way. Ekman (1999) used the specific example of disgust to illustrate his point. He said that when we see a person with a disgust expression, we already know that the person is reacting to a stimulus that is distasteful in taste or smell (or could be morally distasteful); the person may produce vocalizations such as "yuck," and the person will likely turn away or move away from the offensive source. Ekman gives some examples of the association between nonverbal emotional expressions and interpersonal relationships. For instance, facial expressions are likely crucial in the formation of attachments between infants and caregivers and between romantic partners. As another example, people who suffer from facial paralysis since birth report that forming and maintaining interpersonal relationships, even casual ones, is difficult, and they have attributed this difficulty to their inability to produce facial expressions.

Ekman (1984, 1999) discussed detailed aspects of his theory of universal signals, addressing many questions that might be asked by a skeptic. For instance, he explained that sometimes the emotional signal may not be present, even when the individual is experiencing the emotion, because an individual can often intentionally suppress this signal. Conversely, he explains that emotional expressions can be simulated in ways that are convincing.

See also basic emotions, body language, culture, display rules, Paul Ekman, facial expression, nonverbal expression, primary emotions, relationships, vocal expression

References:
Ekman, P. (1984). Expression and the nature of emotion. In K. Scherer & P. Ekman (Eds.), *Approaches to emotion* (pp. 319–344). Hillsdale, NJ: Lawrence Erlbaum Associates/
Ekman, P. (1999). Basic emotions. In T. Dalgleish & M. J. Power (Eds.), *Handbook of cognition and emotion* (pp. 45–60). New York: John Wiley/
Ekman, P., & Friesen, W. V. (1975). *Unmasking the face.* Englewood Cliffs, NJ: Prentice Hall.

V

Valium

Before the 1950s, the medications most commonly used to treat anxiety conditions were the barbiturates (sedative-hypnotics). Their use involves relatively high risk because of their side effects, which include extreme drowsiness, high potential for physical dependence, and risk of overdose that can lead to death. In the late 1940s, pharmaceutical treatment of anxiety was improved with the development of a new sedative-hypnotic, meprobomate (brand name Miltown), which tends to have fewer side effects than the older drugs of its type.

In the 1950s, benzodiazepines—a superior type of antianxiety medication (anxiolytic)—were discovered. Dr. Leo Sternbach, a chemist from Croatia who was working at the Hoffmann–La Roche laboratories in Nutley, New Jersey, developed the first benzodiazepine in 1954. Sternbach had originally been working with this group of chemicals in the 1930s in Poland and then had abandoned his work. He resumed his work at Hoffman–LaRoche in the early 1950s when he hypothesized that these drugs could have psychoactive effects. He created a promising compound called Ro-5-0690, then shelved the project. One and a half years later, an associate chemist found Ro-5-0690 while cleaning the lab; he suggested that it be tested for psychoactive properties. Two months later, Dr. Lowell O. Randall, director of pharmacologic research at Hoffman–LaRoche, reported that the new medication had relaxing and sedative effects on mice and cats and was safe. The new medication was named chlordiazepoxide (brand name Librium).

Librium was more effective than Miltown, producing therapeutic effects at a smaller dosage, and had fewer side effects, including less sedation and lower risk of overdose. With its discovery, a large investigation began into benzodiazepines. Within a few years, diazepam (Valium) was created from the Librium molecule; it was approved for sale by the U.S. Food and Drug Administration in 1963 (Bakalar, 2005). Valium was more powerful than Librium and was prescribed widely throughout the 1960s and 1970s, reaching peak sales in the United States in 1978 (Bakalar, 2005). From 1969 to 1982, it was the top-selling medication in the United States (Kennedy, n.d.). Valium had a mixed reputation: at times it was promoted as a harmless panacea. It gained cultural notoriety in the Rolling Stones song "Mother's

Little Helper." Some of the dangers of Valium (e.g., addiction and withdrawal) were described in the 1979 book *I'm Dancing as Fast as I Can* (Gordon, 1979).

Currently Valium is used for treating a wide variety of psychological and physical conditions, including anxiety, alcohol withdrawal, seizures, muscle spasms, and insomnia. It is used worldwide and remains a frequently prescribed medication. Benzodiazepines should not be used during pregnancy or while nursing (Preston, O'Neal, & Talaga, 2008). Baenninger and Baenninger (2003) wrote a compelling biography of Leo Sternberg that includes a history of the development of Valium and other benzodiazepines, titled *Good Chemistry: The Life and Legacy of Valium Inventor Leo Sternbach.*

See also anxiety, anxiolytic, benzodiazepine.

Further Readings:

Baenninger, A., & Baenninger, A. (2003). *Good chemistry: The life and legacy of Valium inventor Leo Sternbach.* New York: McGraw-Hill.

Gordon, B. (1979). *I'm dancing as fast as I can.* New York: Harper and Row.

References:

Baenninger, A., & Baenninger, A. (2003). *Good chemistry: The life and legacy of Valium inventor Leo Sternbach.* New York: McGraw-Hill.

Bakalar, N. (2005, February 22). A host of anxiety drugs, begat by valium. *New York Times.* Retrieved from http://query.nytimes.com/gst/fullpage.html?res=9F03E0DF1F3AF931A15751C0A9639C8B63&sec=health

Gordon, B. (1979). *I'm dancing as fast as I can.* New York: Harper and Row.

Kennedy, B. (n.d.). The tranquilizing of America: How mood-altering prescription drugs changed the cultural landscape. *CNN Interactive.* Retrieved from http://www.cnn.com/SPECIALS/1999/century/episodes/06/currents/

Preston, J.D., O'Neal, J.H., & Talaga, M.C. (2008). *Handbook of clinical psychopharmacology for therapists* (5th ed.). Oakland, CA: New Harbinger.

Vocal Expression

Humans have many different ways of expressing their emotions nonverbally. These include facial expression, body posture, body movements, vocal expression, and other methods. Vocal expressions of emotion encompass acoustics of speech (e.g., a person changes the loudness of her voice while she is saying something) and specific vocalizations such as laughing and screeching. Some examples of potential means of vocal expression are general tone of voice, pitch of voice, loudness, speed of speech, varying inflections, and other means. Although vocal expression has not been studied as extensively as other forms of nonverbal expression of emotion (facial expression in particular), a respectable body of research has now accumulated, mostly since the 1980s and 1990s.

Two general perspectives exist regarding the nature of the relationship between the use of one's voice and emotion. The first perspective is that one's voice is used to express emotion; it is a means to communicate the way one feels to other people. Scherer and his colleagues have been the main proponents of this view. The second perspective is that the voice is used to induce emotion in the listener and therefore to influence his behavior. This approach is termed the *affect induction* view (e.g., see Owren, Rendall, & Bachorowski, 2003). This latter approach was initially developed based on research on nonhuman primates and the functionality of the calls that they make to one another (e.g., Owren & Rendall, 1997, 2001). As Bachorowski and Owren (2008) discuss, the first view would be strongly supported if research showed that specific acoustic features of the voice were associated with specific emotions (e.g., a sudden increase in pitch reliably means happiness or a sudden decrease in pitch means anger, or particular changes in loudness are associated with particular emotions), or possibly in other ways. However, they state that the evidence is not strong to support this position. Bachorowski and Owren claim instead that compelling evidence exists that vocal features have a strong effect on the emotions of the target (person listening to the speech or vocalization), supporting the affect induction view. An implication of their view is that vocal expressions most clearly function as tactics of social influence rather than as external communications or representations of the way one is feeling internally.

The research on the relationship between emotion and use of the voice is complex. Neither the emotional expression nor the affect induction perspective, as competing perspectives, has been endorsed by a majority of emotion researchers.

See also aprosodia, basic emotions, body language, facial expression, nonverbal expression, primates, prosody.

Further Reading:
Bachorowski, J., & Owren, M. J. (2008). Vocal expressions of emotion. In M. Lewis, J. M. Haviland-Jones, & J. F. Barrett (Eds.), *Handbook of emotions* (3rd ed., pp. 196–210). New York: Guilford.

References:
Bachorowski, J., & Owren, M. J. (2008). Vocal expressions of emotion. In M. Lewis, J. M. Haviland-Jones, & J. F. Barrett (Eds.), *Handbook of emotions* (3rd ed., pp. 196–210). New York: Guilford.

Johnstone, T., & Scherer, K. R. (2000). Vocal communication of emotion. In M. Lewis & J. M. Haviland-Jones (Eds.), *Handbook of emotions* (2nd ed., pp. 220–235). New York: Guilford.

Owren, M. J., & Rendall, D. (1997). An affect-conditioning model of nonhuman primate vocal signaling. In D. H. Owings, M. D. Beecher, & N. S. Thompson (Eds.), *Perspectives in ethology: Vol. 12. Communication* (pp. 299–346). New York: Plenum Press.

Owren, M. J., & Rendall, D. (2001). Sound on the rebound: Bringing form and function back to the forefront in understanding nonhuman primate vocal signaling. *Evolutionary Anthropology: Issues, News, and Reviews, 10,* 58–71.

Owren, M. J., Rendall, D., & Bachorowski, J. (2003). Nonlinguistic vocal communication. In D. Maestripieri (Ed.), *Primate psychology* (pp. 359–394). Cambridge, MA: Harvard University Press.

W

John Watson (1878–1958)

John Watson is one of the most significant figures in the history of psychology. He has three major contributions to his credit: he wrote the revolutionary paper that started the behaviorist movement, he conducted the famous (or infamous) Little Albert study, and he demonstrated the broad range of applications of classical conditioning.

Watson was born in rural South Carolina, one of six children in the Watson family. His father was an alcoholic who had alienated himself from his community with his unpredictable and aggressive behavior. By the time Watson was born, the family lived in poverty; his father jumped from one job to the next and periodically abandoned the family. When Watson was 12, his deeply religious and practical mother sold the farm they owned and moved the family to Greenville, South Carolina, where she believed they would have better economic and educational opportunities. Watson went to college and, despite poor grades, graduated from Furman University. He wrote a letter to the president of the University of Chicago, asking to be accepted as a doctoral student. This letter, along with a letter of recommendation from the president of Furman University, gained him admission, and he earned a doctorate in psychology at the age of 25, becoming the university's youngest PhD. He received several professional offers and accepted a full professorship at the Johns Hopkins University in Baltimore, Maryland.

During his graduate school years at the University of Chicago, Watson married Mary Ickes, a young woman from a prominent family. Watson was unfaithful to Mary within the first year of marriage, the beginning of a series of infidelities. The couple had two children. In 1919, Watson began an affair with his graduate student research assistant, Rosalie Rayner. The affair became scandalous and ruined his academic career. He and Mary divorced, he married Rosalie Rayner, and he left Johns Hopkins University to pursue a career in advertising. His advertising career was extremely successful, and the couple lived a luxurious life for a time. They too had two children. Watson loved Rosalie deeply, perhaps more than anyone is his life, and fell into a depression when she died of dysentery in her mid-thirties (Watson was 58). When Watson was 79, the year before his death, he was awarded the American Psychological

Association gold medal for contributions to psychology. At the ceremony, fearing that he might burst into tears when accepting the award, one of Watson's sons accepted the award for him. He died at age 80, having become somewhat unkempt and solitary in his later years.

In 1913, Watson wrote a paper, "Psychology as the Behaviorist Views It," that established behaviorism as a paradigm in psychology. In the paper, Watson argued that behavior—observable actions—should be the only subject matter of psychology. He argued for exclusion of all "mental processes," which include emotions, thoughts, motives, and dreams, as objects of study. His rationale was that behavior can be observed objectively (i.e., two or more individuals can observe an individual's behavior and come to some agreement regarding the nature of the behavior), whereas all mental processes cannot be observed objectively (because the person experiencing the mental process is the only person who can actually report on it). Therefore, to create a serious science, like physics, chemistry, or biology, the methods must be tightened up. Furthermore, Watson argued that the goal of psychology should be to predict and control behavior. His paper was powerful but not entirely convincing because Watson did not present real-life examples of how behaviorism could actually be practiced. So he set out to conduct some studies that could establish behaviorism as a science.

Watson's most famous study, published in 1920 with his future wife as coauthor, was the Little Albert study. Watson and Rayner set out to demonstrate that an emotion could be conditioned in an infant, thus showing that emotions are not entirely inborn and can be manipulated. In the study, Watson and Rayner took nine-month-old Albert and conditioned him to fear a white rat. They started by demonstrating that Albert was not initially afraid of the rat. In fact, before the conditioning procedures, Albert happily allowed the rat to walk near him as he sat and to touch him. Next, the researchers presented Albert with a stimulus that he naturally feared (a loud noise, produced behind Albert's head) and presented the white rat simultaneously. The loud noise and the rat were presented to Albert together (paired) several times. Albert cried during these conditioning trials. After seven pairings of the noise and rat, Albert began to cry and show other fear behaviors when the rat was presented by itself. Watson and Rayner had demonstrated that they could condition an infant to fear a previously unfeared object. This study showed that behaviorism could be a real science; research utilizing behaviorist principles and methodologies could produce results and could include real-life, practical, and significant topics. Shortly after the study was published, however, Watson left academia. Behaviorism had lost its primary champion. For this reason, behaviorism was in a lull until another enthusiastic, perhaps dogmatic figure entered the scene in the 1930s: B. F. Skinner.

Watson was also well known for warning against the dangers of spoiling children with too much love and pampering. Watson believed that human emotions could be, and should be, controlled. We can condition our children to behave in ways that minimize their individual suffering and that benefit society. The conditioning he promoted would be called *tough love* today. The book he published in 1928, *The Psychological Care of Infant and Child*, was well received in both academic and popular circles.

See also attachment, behavior therapy, behaviorism, conditioned emotional response, fear, phobia, B. F. Skinner.

Further Readings:

Beck, H. P., Levinson, S., & Irons, G. (2009). Finding little Albert: A journey to John B. Watson's infant laboratory. *American Psychologist, 64,* 605–614.

Buckley, K. W. (1989). *Mechanical man: John Broadus Watson and the beginnings of behaviorism.* New York: Guilford.

Watson, J. B. (1997). *Behaviorism.* Edison, NJ: Transaction. (Original work published 1925)

References:

Watson, J. B. (1913). Psychology as the behaviourist views it. *Psychological Review, 20,* 158–177.

Watson, J. B. (1928). *The psychological care of infant and child.* London: Allen.

Watson, J. B., & Rayner, R. (1920). Conditioned emotional reactions. *Journal of Experimental Psychology, 3,* 1–14.

Watson's Little Albert study sparked discussion among researchers about the ethics involved in using human participants in research. These discussions eventually led to professional practice and research guidelines. Most research institutions (e.g., at universities and medical centers) now have institutional review boards that go over proposed research methods to ensure participants' well-being and researchers' compliance with professional ethical guidelines.

Edward O. Wilson (1929–)

Edward O. Wilson is a representative of evolutionary psychology, which focuses on understanding human psychology (behaviors, thoughts, and emotions) from an evolutionary standpoint. The assumption behind evolutionary psychology (also called human sociobiology) is that psychological traits have evolved through natural selection in the same way that physical traits have evolved. For example, the fact that aggressive behavior exists in current human behavior is most likely indicative of aggressive behavior serving a purpose in the evolutionary history of our species; aggressiveness enhanced our survival.

Edward O. Wilson was born in Birmingham, Alabama, and spent his childhood in several southern cities and towns. He was an only child to Inez and Edward Wilson, a government accountant. At age seven, while his parents were going through a divorce, he was sent to live with friends in Paradise Beach, Florida. During that summer, he explored the nature surrounding his temporary home, the beginning of his intense interest in nature. One of his investigations resulted in an accident with a fish; as Wilson pulled the fish out of the water, it flew into his face, and one of the spines cut his eye, leaving him blind in that eye.

In his autobiography *Naturalist*, Wilson (1994) explained that his decision to focus his study on ants resulted partly from his physical challenge. He said, "I would thereafter celebrate the little things of the world, the animals that can be picked up between thumb and forefinger and brought close for inspection" (Wilson, 1994, p. 15). After his parents' divorce, he lived with his father and stepmother, who moved a number of times. He remained an only child. Wilson earned BS and MS degrees in biology from the University of Alabama. He earned his PhD in entomology, specializing in myrmecology (the study of ants), at Harvard University in 1955. In the same year,

Wilson married Irene Kelley, and they had a daughter. In 1956, he was appointed to a faculty position at Harvard University, where he remained for four decades, until his retirement.

Wilson is credited with making sociobiology into both a popular and a controversial subject of study. Although Wilson's predecessors or contemporaries had applied the natural selection concept to social behavior—for example, Richard Dawkins (1976) in his book *The Selfish Gene* and Darwin, who discussed the evolutionary origin of emotional expression—Wilson was the first to summarize sociobiology principles in a wide variety of species, ranging from bacteria and insects to the great apes and humans. His book *Sociobiology: The New Synthesis* (Wilson, 1975) provided this survey and touched the surface of what he would later say about evolution, social behavior, and humans. In *On Human Nature*, Wilson (1978) examined a wide variety of human behaviors from the evolutionary point of view, including aggression, altruism, bonding, gender differences, heroism, love, the soul, and warfare. Some people, including a few colleagues, reacted with anger to Wilson's book. During the 1970s, socialization theories prevailed in psychology, and Wilson's suppositions were taken by some to mean that people cannot change their behavior; that our genes create immutable characteristics. Some even accused him of racism and sexism, and at the 1978 annual meeting of the American Association for the Advancement of Science, a young woman poured a pitcher of ice water over his head.

In today's world, most agree that Wilson has become a less controversial figure. He has received over 100 awards, some for his scholarly contributions and others for his service to humanity. His awards include membership in the National Academy of Science (1969), two Pulitzer prizes (1979, 1991), the Crafoord Prize (the highest award given in ecology, 1990), recognition among *Time Magazine*'s 25 most influential people in America (1995), the Audubon Medal of the National Audubon Society (1995), and the gold medal of the Worldwide Fund for Nature (1990). He has written 20 books and over 400 articles. Edward Wilson currently resides in Lexington, Massachusetts, with his wife, Irene.

See also Charles Darwin, Paul Ekman, evolutionary psychology (human sociobiology).

Further Readings:

Dawkins, R. (1976). *The selfish gene.* New York: Oxford University Press.

Wilson, E. O. (1975). *Sociobiology: The new synthesis.* Cambridge, MA: Harvard University Press.

Wilson, E. O. (1978). *On human nature.* Cambridge, MA: Harvard University Press.

Wilson, E. O. (1994). *Naturalist.* Washington, DC: Island Press.

References:

Dawkins, R. (1976). *The selfish gene.* New York: Oxford University Press.

Wilson, E. O. (1975). *Sociobiology: The new synthesis.* Cambridge, MA: Harvard University Press.

Wilson, E. O. (1978). *On human nature.* Cambridge, MA: Harvard University Press.

Wilson, E. O. (1994). *Naturalist.* Washington, DC: Island Press.

Y

Yale-Brown Obsessive Compulsive Scale

The Yale-Brown Obsessive Compulsive Scale (Y-BOCS) was developed in 1989 by Drs. Wayne Goodman, Lawrence H. Price, Steven A. Rasmussen, and colleagues (Goodman et al., 1989a, 1989b). It is designed to rate the severity of symptoms in obsessive-compulsive disorder (OCD). The original Y-BOCS is a 10-item scale, with 5 of the items addressing obsessions and the other 5 asking about compulsions. Questions ask about time spent on, interference from, distress from, resistance to, and control over obsessions or compulsions. Each item is rated on a scale from 0 (none) to 4 (extreme), yielding a total score ranging from 0 to 40. Separate subtotals can be generated for obsessions and compulsions, allowing treatment to be tailored to the individual's specific manifestation of OCD. The scale, originally intended to be administered by professional clinicians (e.g., therapists), can also be self-administered. The Y-BOCS is considered the most widely used OCD scale (Deacon & Abramowitz, 2005). It is used in research and in treatment to measure changes in OCD symptom severity. It was not originally designed as a diagnostic instrument. While the Y-BOCS is popular and considered the gold standard in measurement of OCD symptoms, some researchers have questions about its validity and have suggested scoring changes (Deacon & Abramowitz, 2005).

Prior to development of the Y-BOCS, other rating scales for OCD existed, but they all had limitations: they were cumbersome to administer, did not have established validity, or were otherwise unsuitable for use in drug trial research. Some scales included non-OCD symptoms (e.g., depression). Other scales focused only on certain types of obsessions or compulsions (e.g., fear of contamination or hand washing). The Y-BOCS does not focus on the content of the patient's symptoms, only on the severity. It is based on symptoms of OCD as defined in the *Diagnostic and Statistical Manual of Mental Disorders* (*DSM-III-R*; American Psychiatric Association, 1987).

A companion tool is the Yale-Brown Obsessive Compulsive Scale Symptom Checklist (Goodman et al., 1989a, 1989b). It is a clinician- or self-administered checklist of common types of OCD symptoms. Unlike the Y-BOCS, it does focus on the content of symptoms. For example, it asks about obsessions related to aggression, contamination, sex, religion, hoarding/saving, and need for exactness or symmetry. The checklist has been criticized as discriminatory because one of the items asks about obsession with homosexual content. A Swedish patient filed a complaint with the Ombudsman against Discrimination on Grounds of Sexual Orientation (a Swedish public agency), which determined that the Y-BOCS checklist is discriminatory and should be discontinued (Rûck & Bergström, 2006). However, Swedish doctors Rûck and Bergström stress that interpreted within the appropriate context, the Y-BOCS checklist is useful and not discriminatory.

See also Diagnostic and Statistical Manual of Mental Disorders, obsessive-compulsive disorder.

Further Reading:
Y-BOCS (online version): http://www.brainphysics.com/ybocs.php

References:
American Psychiatric Association. (1987). *Diagnostic and statistical manual* of *mental disorders* (3rd ed., rev.). Washington, DC: Author.
Deacon, B. J., & Abramowitz, J. S. (2005). The Yale-Brown Obsessive Compulsive Scale: Factor analysis, construct validity, and suggestions for refinement. *Journal of Anxiety Disorders, 19*, 573–585.
Goodman, W. K., Price, L. H., Rasmussen, S. A., Mazure, C., Fleischmann, R. L., Hill, C. L., et al. (1989a). The Yale-Brown Obsessive Compulsive Scale I: Development, use, and reliability. *Archives of General Psychiatry, 46*, 1006–1011.
Goodman, W. K., Price, L. H., Rasmussen, S. A., Mazure, C., Delgado, P., Heninger, G. R., et al. (1989b). The Yale-Brown Obsessive Compulsive Scale II: Validity. *Archives of General Psychiatry, 46*, 1012–1016.
Rûck, C., & Bergström, J. (2006). Letter to the editor: Is the Y-BOCS discriminatory against gays and lesbians? *American Journal of Psychiatry, 163*, 1449.

Yerkes-Dodson Law

The Yerkes-Dodson law is a theory that emphasizes the relation between arousal and task performance. Specifically, the theory states that the optimal task performance is accomplished at a moderate level of arousal and that low or high levels of arousal result in relatively poorer task performance, leading to an inverted (upside down) U-shaped relation between arousal and task performance. The Yerkes-Dodson law originally derived from propositions by American psychologists Robert Mearns Yerkes and John Dillingham Dodson in an article published in the *Journal of Comparative Neurology and Psychology* in 1908.

The arousal that Yerkes and Dodson described can also be thought of as emotion or motivation. The change of arousal from a drowsy state (low arousal) to an alert state (moderate arousal) produces enhanced efficiency of performance. However, in other cases, the change of arousal from an alert state to an extremely emotional state (high arousal) leads to impaired responding or performance. This theory indicates that one needs to be moderately aroused when studying for an upcoming exam because with extreme arousal, one becomes too anxious about the exam, and the anxiety might interfere with performance. The Yerkes-Dodson law further proposes that increasing task difficulty decreases the optimal levels of arousal for its performance; that is, an easy or simple task requires moderate to high arousal for an optimal performance, whereas a complex or difficult task needs lower levels of arousal for an optimal performance.

The inverted U-shaped function relating arousal to task performance proposed in the Yerkes-Dodson law has been criticized by some researchers. For instance,

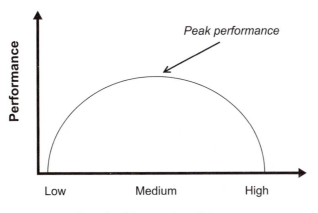

Level of Arousal or Stress

The Yerkes-Dodson law is an empirical relationship between arousal and performance, originally developed by psychologists Robert M. Yerkes and John Dillingham Dodson in 1908. The law dictates that performance increases with physiological or mental arousal, but only up to a point. When levels of arousal become too high, performance decreases. (Courtesy of Yvette Malamud Ozer)

Bäumler (1994) argues that with regard to arousal levels in the extensive middle ground (neither extreme of very low nor very high arousal), research evidence does not clearly implicate a constant or predictable best level for optimal performance. Furthermore, as Mendl (1999) argues, the law is not particularly helpful because it is too broad and general.

See also motivation.

Further Reading:
Bambrick, L. (2006). *The Yerkes-whatzy law of who now?* Retrieved from http://www.secretgeek.net/ydlaw.asp

References:
Bäumler, G. (1994). On the validity of the Yerkes-Dodson law. *Studia Psychologica, 36,* 205–209.
Mendl, M. (1999). Performing under pressure: Stress and cognitive function. *Applied Animal Behaviour Science, 65,* 221–244.
Yerkes, R. M., & Dodson, J. D. (1908). The relation of strength of stimulus to rapidity of habit formation. *Journal of Comparative Neurology and Psychology, 18,* 459–482.

Yoga

Yoga is an ancient Sanskrit word meaning "union" or "reunion," referring to the union of body, mind, and soul or spirit. Historically, the practice of yoga has been rooted in spiritual enlightenment. However, as yoga was exported to the West, particularly the United States, yoga has also come to be known as flexibility exercises and stretch relaxation, and spirituality is often not a necessary aspect of the practice.

The roots of yoga have been traced as far back as the sixth century BC. Patanjali was probably the first person to describe the yoga postures in writing in a text called the *Yoga Sutras*, written in India in the second century BC. Yoga was brought to the United States in the late 1800s when Swami Vivekananda spoke to the World Parliament of Religions in Chicago. In the 1970s, Swami Rama, a yogi master from the Himalayan Institute, visited the United States, further popularizing yoga. Enthusiasm for the practice has continued to increase in the decades that followed. Over time, a number of yoga paths have developed, each focusing on a unique route toward enlightenment. Yogi master Swami Rama has identified five paths: karma yoga (the path of action), bhakti yoga (the path of devotion), jnana yoga (the path of knowledge), kundalini yoga (the path of spiritual awakening), and hatha yoga (the path of physical balance).

According to a study conducted by the *Yoga Journal* in 2008 (Ruiz, 2008), about 15.8 million Americans practice yoga. The primary reason cited for practicing yoga was maintenance and improvement of health. Since about 2000, the health benefits of yoga, particularly hatha (physical balance) yoga, have been studied extensively. For instance, results of research have indicated that regular practice of hatha yoga helps with decreasing menopausal symptoms (Khalsa, 2004), coping with breast cancer (Carson et al., 2007), coping with diabetes (Mercuri, Olivera, Souto, Guidi, & Gagliardino, 2000), and carpal tunnel syndrome (Garfinkel et al., 1998). Additionally, yoga clearly increases flexibility (Ruiz, 2000). Smith, Hancock, Blake-Mortimer, and Eckert (2007) showed that hatha yoga is helpful for stress management.

Practicing each hatha yoga asana (posture) involves three steps: moving into the posture, maintaining it, and moving out of it. Moving into and out of the poses should be slow and gradual. Conscious breathing is typically an aspect of hatha yoga practice. Some examples of yoga poses are the mountain, fish, cobra, human triangle, spinal twist, and corpse. A number of books clearly describe how to do hatha yoga postures, for instance, Girdano, Dusek, and Everly's (2009) *Controlling Stress and Tension* and Seaward's (2009) *Managing Stress.*

See also stress.

Further Readings:
Feuestein, G. (2001). *The yoga tradition: Its history, literature, philosophy, and practice.* Prescott, AZ: Holm Press.
Girdano, D. A., Dusek, D. E., & Everly, G. S., Jr. (2009). *Controlling stress and tension* (8th ed.). San Francisco: Benjamin Cummings.
International Journal of Yoga Web site: http://www.ijoy.org.in/
Seaward, B. L. (2009). *Managing stress* (6th ed.). Sudbury, MA: Jones and Bartlett.

References:
Carson, J. W., Carson, K. M., Porter, L. S., Keefe, F. J., Shaw, H., & Miller, J. M. (2007). Yoga for women with metastatic breast cancer: Results from a pilot study. *Journal of Pain and Symptom Management, 33*, 331–341.
Garfinkel, M. S., Singhal, A., Katz, W. A., Allan, D. A., Reshetar, R., & Schumacher, H. R., Jr. (1998). Yoga-based intervention for carpal tunnel syndrome: A randomized trial. *Journal of the American Medical Association, 208*, 1601–1603.
Girdano, D. A., Dusek, D. E., & Everly, G. S., Jr. (2009). *Controlling stress and tension* (8th ed.). San Francisco: Benjamin Cummings.

Khalsa, H. K. (2004). How yoga, meditation, and a yogic lifestyle can help women meet the challenges of perimenopause and menopause. *Sexuality, Reproduction, and Menopause, 2*, 169–175.

Mercuri, N., Olivera, E. M., Souto, A., Guidi, M. L., & Gagliardino, J. J. (2000). Yoga practice in people with diabetes. *Diabetes Research and Clinical Practice, 50*(Suppl. 1), 234–235.

Ruiz, F. P. (2008, March/April). What science can teach us about flexibility. *Yoga Journal, 209*, 92–101.

Seaward, B. L. (2009). *Managing stress* (6th ed.). Sudbury, MA: Jones and Bartlett.

Smith, C., Hancock, H., Blake-Mortimer, J., & Eckert, K. (2007). A randomised comparative trial of yoga and relaxation to reduce stress and anxiety. *Complementary Therapies in Medicine, 15*, 77–83.

APPENDIX A: PSYCHOPHARMACOLOGY

The authors have worked to ensure that all information concerning medications in this book is accurate at the time of publication. This information is intended to generally describe different classes and types of medication used to treat mental health disorders. It is not a comprehensive list of medications or side effects. It is not intended to recommend the use of certain medications, suggest treatment, or substitute for the care of a qualified health care professional. Specific situations may require specific therapeutic approaches not included in this book. For these reasons, we recommend that readers follow the advice of qualified health care professionals directly involved in their care.

Yvette Malamud Ozer

Psychopharmacology: Medications (By Class)

Category/*Class*	Drug	Brand names	Indications/uses	Comments
Antidepressants				
Tricyclic antidepressants (TCAs)			Clinical depression, pain, attention-deficit hyperactivity disorder (ADHD)	Also used successfully for headache, bulimia, irritable bowel syndrome, narcolepsy, insomnia, persistent hiccups, pathological laughing or crying, smoking cessation, and as an adjunct in schizophrenia; high risk of overdose; TCAs may be involved in up to 33% of all fatal poisonings, second only to analgesics

(*continued*)

Category/*Class*	Drug	Brand names	Indications/uses	Comments
Antidepressants				
Tricyclic antide- pressants (TCAs) *(continued)*				
	amitriptyline	*Elavil, Endep, Tryptanol, Trepiline*		
	butriptyline	*Evadene, Evadyne*		Sedative properties
	clomipramine	*Anafranil*	Obsessive- compulsive disorder (OCD)	
	desipramine	*Norpramin, Pertofrane*	Mood disorders, especially bipolar disorder	
	dothiepin	*Prothiaden, Thaden*		
	doxepin	*Adapin, Sinequan*		
	imipramine	*Tofranil*	Migraine	
	iprindole			Can be fatal when combined with Ecstasy (MDMA)
	lofepramine	*Gamanil, Lomont*		
	melitracen			
	nortriptyline	*Pamelor, Aventyl, Nortrilen*		
	opipramol	*Neuraxpharm, Insidon*	Anxiety	
	protriptyline	*Vivactil*		
	trimipramine	*Surmontil*		
Tetracyclic antidepressants			Depression, panic disorders, bipolar disorders	
	amoxapine	*Asendin, Asendis, Defanyl, Demolox, Moxadil*		Not publicly available
	maprotiline	*Ludiomil*		
	mianserin	*Tolvon*		Phased out in favor of mirtazapine

Category/*Class*	Drug	Brand names	Indications/uses	Comments
Antidepressants				
Tetracyclic antidepressants (continued)				
	setiptiline	*Tecipul*		Not publicly available
	trazodone	*Desyrel*		
Monoamine oxidase inhibitors (MAOIs)			Especially potent in refractory (treatment-resistant) depressions	*Disadvantages:* drug-drug and drug-food interactions can be dangerous
	iproniazid	*Marsilid, Iprozid, Ipronid, Rivivol, Propilniazida*		Originally developed to treat tuberculosis
	isocarboxazid	*Marplan*	Depression (not responsive to SSRIs), bulimia	
	nialamide	*Psicodisten, Niaquitil, Nialamid, Niamidal, Niamide, Novazid, Nuredal, Niamid, Niazin, Nyazin, Surgex, Mygal, Delmoneurina, Isalizina, Espril, Nyezin*	Depression; off-label uses: trigeminal neuralgia	
	pargyline	*Eutonyl*	Moderate to severe hypertension (high blood pressure)	
	phenelzine	*Nardil*	Anxiety disorder, social phobia, generalized anxiety disorder (GAD), social anxiety disorder, atypical depression, refractory depression, bulimia	Side effects may include sedation, hypotension (low blood pressure), insomnia, weight gain; low-tyramine diet required to prevent hypertensive reaction

(continued)

Category/*Class*	Drug	Brand names	Indications/uses	Comments
Antidepressants				
Monoamine oxidase inhibitors (MAOIs) (continued)				
	selegiline	*Deprenyl, Emsam (transdermal patch)*	Major depression (transdermal patch), early-stage Parkinson's disease, senile dementia	Under investigation for ADHD treatment and smoking cessation aid; *off-label uses:* narcolepsy, as a nootropic (to improve thinking, memory, and learning), for its purported life-extending effects, and to positively affect libido in older men; *veterinary uses:* symptoms of Cushing's disease and cognitive dysfunction in dogs
	tranylcypromine	Parnate	Major depressive episodes without melancholia, refractory depression and anergic (low-energy) atypical depression; off-label uses: post-traumatic stress disorder (PTSD)	
Reversible inhibitors of monoamine oxidase A (RIMAs)				*Benefit:* no special diet necessary (as with MAOIs)
	brofaromine	*Consonar*	Depression, anxiety	
	harmaline			Harmaline is a naturally occurring alkaloid found in the hallucinogenic plant yage (*Banisteriopsis caapi*), also known as ayahuasca; can cause tremors
	moclobemide	*Aurorix, Manerix*	Depression, social anxiety	Reversible MAO-A inhibitor; available in Europe and Canada; not available in United States

Category/*Class*	Drug	Brand names	Indications/uses	Comments
Antidepressants				
Reversible inhibitors of mono-amine oxidase A (RIMAs) (continued)				
	toloxatone	*Humoryl*		
Selective serotonin reuptake inhibitors (SSRIs)			Depression, OCD, GAD, social anxiety disorder, PTSD	Side effects may include sexual dysfunction, nausea, sedation, insomnia, sweating, withdrawal syndrome
	alaproclate		Depression; also used to suppress cocaine cravings	
	citalopram	*Celexa, Cirpam, Cirpamil, Elopram*		Minimal documented interaction with other drugs; minimal seda-tion/weight gain; may cause anxiety initially
	escitalopram	*Lexapro*	Depression, GAD, social anxiety	Minimal documented interaction with other drugs; minimal seda-tion/weight gain; may cause anxiety initially
	etoperidone	*Etonin*		Used in the 1970s to impede the effects of LSD
	fluoxetine	*Prozac, Sarafem*		First SSRI on the market (1986); *advantages:* activating (energizing), long half-life; *disadvantages:* may cause initial anxiety, may interact with other medications
	fluvoxamine	*Luvox*	OCD (patients with obsessive symptoms), GAD, social anxiety disorder	

(*continued*)

Category/*Class*	Drug	Brand names	Indications/uses	Comments
Antidepressants				
Selective serotonin reuptake inhibitors (SSRIs) (continued)				
	paroxetine	*Paxil, Pexeva*	GAD, social anxiety disorder	Good antianxiety benefit; more prone to withdrawal symptoms, weight gain, may interact with other medications; contraindicated in pregnancy
	sertraline	*Zoloft*	Depression, extreme shyness, GAD, social anxiety disorder, PTSD	*Advantages:* not too sedating, does not typically cause anxiety; *disadvantages:* more prone to gastrointestinal side effects
	zimelidine	*Normud, Zel*		Synthesized from the antihistamine brompheniramine
Atypical antidepressants				
Serotonin-norepinephrine reuptake inhibitors (SNRIs, NSRIs, SSNRIs)				
	desvenlafaxine	*Pristiq*	Major depressive disorder (MDD), vasomotor symptoms of menopause	Currently in regulatory review process; also being tested for use in treatment of fibromyalgia and neuropathic pain
	duloxetine	*Cymbalta*	Depression, diabetic nerve pain	Good for severe depression; may cause nausea, sedation
	milnacipran	*Ixel*	Depression, chronic pain	

Category/*Class*	Drug	Brand names	Indications/uses	Comments
Antidepressants				
Serotonin-norepinephrine reuptake inhibitors (SNRIs, NSRIs, SSNRIs) (continued)				
	nefazodone	*Serzone*	Good at reducing anxiety	Fewer sexual side effects; *disadvantages:* sedating, prone to medication interactions, rare reports of liver damage; no longer available in United States (withdrawn in 2004 because of safety concerns)
	venlafaxine	*Effexor*	Severe depression, GAD, social anxiety disorder, chronic pain	Side effects may include sexual dysfunction, nausea, sedation, insomnia, sweating, withdrawal syndrome, hypertension
Selective serotonin reuptake enhancers (SSREs)				
	tianeptine	*Stablon, Coaxil, Tatinol*	Antidepressant, anxiolytic; off-label use: asthma, erectile dysfunction	Particularly suitable for use in elderly patients and following alcohol withdrawal
Noradrenergic and specific serotonergic antidepressants (NaSSAs)				
	mirtazapine	*Remeron, Avanza, Axit, Mirtabene, Mirtaz, Norset, Organon, Remergon, Remergil, Rexer, Promyrtil, Zispin*	Mild to severe depression; off-label use: insomnia, panic disorder, OCD, GAD, social anxiety disorder, PTSD	Free of serotonin-related side effects; less sexual dysfunction; side effects include sedation, dry mouth, and weight gain; indicated in treating depressed geriatric patients who often show marked weight loss

(continued)

Category/*Class*	Drug	Brand names	Indications/uses	Comments
Antidepressants				
Muscarinic antagonists				
	dibenzepin	*Noveril*	Depression	
Dopamine reuptake inhibitors (DARIs)				
	amineptine	*Maneon, Survector*		May have abuse potential for stimulant properties
	phenmetrazine	*Preludin, Defenmetrazin, Fenmetrazin, Oxazimedrine, Phenmetraline*	Anorectic (promotes weight loss)	A CNS stimulant; removed from market due to abuse potential
	vanoxerine			Under investigation as treatment for cocaine addiction
Norepinephrine-dopamine reuptake inhibitors (NDRIs)				
	bupropion	*Wellbutrin, Budeprion, Zyban*	Depression, smoking cessation	*Advantages:* energizing, few sexual side effects, less weight gain; *disadvantages:* may increase anxiety and insomnia; can cause seizures (especially if dose >400 mg/day)
	nomifensine maleate	*Merital*		Abuse potential; can cause anemia, liver, and kidney toxicity; used mainly for research

Category/*Class*	Drug	Brand names	Indications/uses	Comments
Antidepressants				
Norepinephrine reuptake inhibitors (NRIs, NERIs, NARIs)				
	atomoxetine	*Strattera, Attentin*	ADHD; good for cognitive symptoms	Nonstimulant treatment for ADHD; originally intended to be a new antidepressant drug, however, no clinical benefits could be shown; minimal sexual side effects; *disadvantages:* may cause sedation or anxiety
	maprotiline	*Deprilept, Ludiomil, Psymion*	Depression, anxiety, insomnia	Second-generation antidepressant; may worsen psychotic conditions (e.g., schizophrenia); should not be used during manic phase of bipolar disorder
	reboxetine	*Edronax, Norebox, Prolift, Solvex, Vestra*	Clinical depression, panic disorder, ADD/ADHD	
	viloxazine	*Emovit, Vivalan, Vivarint, Vicilan*	Depression; off-label uses: narcolepsy, alcoholism	
Stimulants			Has been used as antidepressant (alone or to augment other antidepressant medications)	High abuse potential; side effects include insomnia, appetite suppression, anxiety, and agitation
	dextroamphetamine	*Dexedrine*		
	methamphetamine	*Desoxyn*		
	methylphenidate	*Ritalin, Rubifen, Concerta*		

(continued)

Category/*Class*	Drug	Brand names	Indications/uses	Comments
Antidepressants				
Alternative antidepressants				
	5-HTP			5-hydroxytryptophan (a serotonin precursor)
	L-Tryptophan		Natural antidepressant found in turkey, potatoes, and milk	
	melatonin		Depression, seasonal affective disorder (SAD)	Serotonin is a parent to melatonin (N-acetyl-5-methoxytryptamine); inadequate serotonin production affects melatonin production, affecting sleep patterns
	Omega-3 fatty acids		Unipolar depression; also claimed to be effective in treatment of bipolar disorder, premenstrual syndrome (PMS), fibromyalgia, chronic fatigue syndrome (CFS), Huntington's disease, schizophrenia, ADD/ADHD	Eicosapentaenoic acid; an omega-3 fatty acid found in fish oil, seafood, flaxseed, and eggs
	St. John's wort		Minor to moderate depression	*Hypericum perforatum*
	tyrosine			
	vitamins and minerals			Lack of well-designed, controlled studies showing efficacy
Anxiolytics				
Benzodiazepines			Severe anxiety, psychosis, anticonvulsant, sedative, skeletal muscle relaxant	Side effects may include sedation, cognitive impairment, ataxia, withdrawal symptoms

Category/*Class*	Drug	Brand names	Indications/uses	Comments
Anxiolytics				
Benzodiazepines (continued)				
	adinazolam	*Deracyn*		
	alprazolam	*Xanax (also known by many other brand names in countries other than the United States)*	Panic disorder, panic attacks, severe anxiety disorder, nongeneralized (performance-type) social anxiety disorder, adjunctive treatment for depression (with SSRIs), sometimes used to treat borderline personality disorder	
	bentazepam	*Thiadipone*		
	bromazepam	*Calmepam, Compendium, Creosedin, Durazanil, Lectopam, Lexaurin, Lexomil, Lexotan, Lexotanil, Normoc, Somalium*		
	brotizolam	*Lendormin*		
	camazepam	*Albego, Limpidon, and Paxor*		
	chlordiazep-oxide	*Librium, Librax, Librocol, Librelease, Libritabs, Limbitrol, Menrium, Novo-Poxide, Poxidium, Risolid, Defobin*		*Street name:* lib; first benzodiazepine developed (1957)
	cinolazepam	*Gerodorm*		
	clobazam	*Frisium, Urbanyl, Mystan*	Anxiety, seizure disorder, adjunctive treatment for schizophrenia	

(continued)

Category/*Class*	Drug	Brand names	Indications/uses	Comments
Anxiolytics				
Benzodiazepines (*continued*)				
	clonazepam	*Klonopin, Rivotril*	Anxiety disorders, panic attacks, GAD, social anxiety disorder, seizure disorder, restless leg syndrome, initial treatment of mania (together with lithium, haloperidol, or risperidone), chronic fatigue syndrome, night terrors, Tourette's syndrome, side effects of schizophrenia agents; off-label use: hallucinogen-persisting perception disorder	
	clorazepate	*Tranxene, Tranxilium*	Alcohol withdrawal, seizure disorder, anxiety	
	clotiazepam	*Trecalmo*		Not approved for sale in United States or Canada
	cloxazolam	*Sepazon, Olcadil*		Not approved for sale in United States or Canada
	cyprazepam	*Somelin*		Not approved for sale in United States or Canada
	diazepam	*Valium, Stesolid, Diazemuls, Seduxen, Bosaurin, Diapam, Antenex, Ducene, Apozepam, Pax*	Alcohol withdrawal, seizure disorder, anxiety, muscle spasms, insomnia, veterinary uses	*Street names:* V, blue
	doxefazepam	*Doxans*		Not approved for sale in United States or Canada
	ethyl loflazepate	*Meilax*		
	etizolam	*Sedekopan*		Not approved for sale in United States or Canada

Category/*Class*	Drug	Brand names	Indications/uses	Comments
Anxiolytics				
Benzodiazepines (continued)				
	fludiazepam	*Erispan*		
	flunitrazepam	*Rohypnol*		Abused as a date rape drug; *street names:* rophy, rufflels, roofies, ruffies, ruff up, rib, roach 2, R2, R2-Do-U, roche, rope, ropies, circles, circes, forget it, forget-me-pill, Baptist Communion, Mexican Valium
	flurazepam	*Dalmane, Dalmadorm*	Insomnia	Primarily used as a hypnotic (for insomnia); longest half-life of all the benzodiazepines; may stay in the bloodstream up to four days
	flutazolam	*Coreminal*		
	flutoprazepam	*Restas*		
	gidazepam	*Gidazepamum*	Anxiety, seizure disorders, sedative, muscle relaxant	
	halazepam	*Alapryl, Pacinone, Paxipam, Paxipam*		
	haloxazolam	*Somelin*		Not approved for sale in United States or Canada
	ketazolam	*Anseren, Anxon, Contamex, Loftran, Marcen, Sedotime, Solatran, Unakalm*		Not approved for sale in United States or Canada
	loprazolam	*Dormonoct, Havlane, Sonin, Somnovit*	Severe insomnia	

(continued)

Category/*Class*	Drug	Brand names	Indications/uses	Comments
Anxiolytics				
Benzodiazepines (*continued*)				
	lorazepam	*Ativan and Temesta are most common*	Anxiety, nongeneralized (performance-type) social anxiety disorder, insomnia, seizure disorder, alcohol withdrawal, adjunct antinausea drug	Banned in United Kingdom since 1991
	lormetazepam	*Noctamid, Ergocalm, Loramet, Dilamet, Sedaben, Stilaze, Nocton, Pronoctan, Noctamide, Loretam, Minias, Aldosomnil*		Sometimes known as methyllorazepam; not approved for sale in United States or Canada
	medazepam	*Nobrium, Rudotel, Raporan*		
	mexazolam	*Melex*		Not approved for sale in United States or Canada
	midazolam	*Versed, Hypnovel, Dormicum, Dormonid*	Sedation prior to surgery, rapid treatment of prolonged-seizures-status epilepticus	*Street name:* dazzle
	nimetazepam	*Erimin*		Subject to abuse, especially by people addicted to amphetamines or opiates; no longer sold in most Western nations
	nitrazepam	*Mogadon, Alodorm*	Insomnia, myoclonic seizures	
	nordazepam	*Stilny, Madar, Vegesan, Calmday*	Anxiety	
	oxazepam	*Alepam, Murelax, Oxascand, Serax, Serepax, Seresta, Sobril*	Anxiety disorders with associated tension, irritability, and agitation; drug and alcohol withdrawal; anxiety associated with depression	

Category/*Class*	Drug	Brand names	Indications/uses	Comments
Anxiolytics				
Benzodiazepines (continued)				
	oxazolam	*Hializan, Serenal, Tranquit*		
	phenazepam		Seizure disorder, alcohol withdrawal, insomnia, pre-op anesthesia	Developed in Soviet Union; used in Russia
	pinazepam	*Domar*		
	prazepam	*Centrax*		
	temazepam	*Restoril, Normison, Tenox, Temaze*	Insomnia and other sleep disorders	One of the most addictive benzodiazepines; high abuse potential; *street names:* rugby balls, terms, jellies, mazzies, beans, eggs, yellow jackets; primarily used as a hypnotic (for insomnia)
	tetrazepam	*Clinoxan, Myolastan, Musaril, Relaxam, Spasmorelax*	Muscle spasm, anxiety disorders such as panic attacks; more rarely: depression, PMS, agoraphobia	
	tofisopam	*Emandaxin, Grandaxin*	Anxiety, alcohol withdrawal	
	triazolam	*Halcion, Novodorm, Songar*	Acute insomnia, jet lag	Banned in the United Kingdom since 1991; primarily used as a hypnotic (for insomnia)
	zolazepam	*Flupyrazapon*	Veterinary anesthetic	
Atypical and nonbenzodiazepines				
	estazolam	*ProSom, Eurodin*	Insomnia	A triazolobenzodiazepine with rapid onset and limited daytime sedation

(continued)

Category/*Class*	Drug	Brand names	Indications/uses	Comments
Anxiolytics				
Atypical and nonbenzo-diazepines (continued)				
	eszopiclone	*Lunesta*		Short-acting nonbenzodiazepine
	quazepam	*Doral, Dormalin*	Insomnia	A benzodiazepine derivative that selectively targets GABA-A type 1 receptors; has hypnotic and anticonvulsant properties; less over-dose and dependence potential and fewer side effects than typical benzodiazepines
	zaleplon	*Sonata*		Short-acting nonbenzo-diazepine hypnotic
	zolpidem	*Ambien*		Short-acting nonbenzo-diazepine
Partial serotonin 1A agonists			Anxiety; also used as augmentative treat-ment for depression	A class of drugs with anxiolytic effects; fewer side effects than benzodiazepines; not addictive; tolerance does not develop
	buspirone	*BuSpar, Ansial, Ansiced, Anxiron, Axoren, Bespar, Buspimen, Buspinol, Buspisal, Narol, Spitomin*		Delayed onset of action (1–2 weeks); side effects may include nausea, dizziness, and anxiety
	gepirone	*Ariza, Variza*		A pyridinyl piperazine partial 5-HT 1A agonist; not approved by the U.S. Food and Drug Administration (FDA)
	ipsapirone			

Category/*Class*	Drug	Brand names	Indications/uses	Comments
Anxiolytics				
Partial serotonin 1A agonists (*continued*)				
	tiospirone		Antipsychotic	
Barbiturates			Anxiety, seizure disorders, sedative	Anxiolytic effects linked to sedation; high risk of abuse; nontherapeutic uses include physicianassisted suicide and capital punishment
	allobarbital			
	alphenal			
	amobarbital	*Amytal*		*Street names:* downers, blue heavens, blue velvet, blue devils
	aprobarbital			
	barbexaclone			
	barbital			
	butabarbital			
	butalbital			
	butallylonal			
	butobarbital			
	Combination of secobarbital sodium and amobarbital sodium in equal proportions	*Tuinal*		*Street names:* rainbows, reds and blues, tooies, double trouble, gorilla pills, F-66s
	cyclobarbital			
	cyclopal			
	ethallobarbital			
	heptabarbital			
	hexethal			

(*continued*)

Category/*Class*	Drug	Brand names	Indications/uses	Comments
Anxiolytics				
Barbiturates (*continued*)				
	hexobarbital			
	mephobarbital			
	metharbital			
	methohexital			
	methylpheno-barbital			
	pentobarbital	*Nembutal*		*Street names:* nembies, yellow jackets, abbots, Mexican yellows
	phenobarbital	*Luminal*		Used by Nazi doctors to kill children born with disease or deformity (code-named "Operation T-4"); *street names:* purple hearts, goof balls
	probarbital			
	propallylonal			
	proxibarbital			
	reposal			
	secobarbital	*Seconal*		*Street names:* reds, red birds, red devils, lilly, F 40s, pinks, pink ladies, seggy
	talbutal			
	thialbarbital			
	thiamylal			
	thiobarbital			
	thiobutabarbi-tal thiopental			

Category/*Class*	Drug	Brand names	Indications/uses	Comments
Anxiolytics				
Barbiturates (continued)				
	vinbarbital			
	vinylbital			
Minor tranquilizers				
	ethchlorvynol	*Placidyl*	Insomnia	A sedative-hypnotic tertiary carbinol; addictive properties; causes withdrawal; side effects may include rash, faintness, restlessness, euphoria, nausea and vomiting, numbness, blurred vision, stomach pains, temporary dizziness, convulsions, hallucinations, memory loss; *street name:* jellybellies; not available in United States since 1999
	glutethimide	*Doriden*	Insomnia	Introduced in 1954 as a sedative-hypnotic to treat insomnia; abuse and addiction potential; causes severe withdrawal symptoms; rarely prescribed today
	meprobamate	*Miltown, Equanil, Meprospan*	Anxiety	Anxiolytic effects linked to sedation; high risk of abuse; largely replaced by benzodiazepines; *street name:* happy pills

(continued)

Category/*Class*	Drug	Brand names	Indications/uses	Comments
Anxiolytics				
Minor tranquilizers (continued)				
	methyprylon	*Noludar*	Insomnia	Sedative in the piperidinedione family; side effects include rash, fever, depression, ulcers/sores in mouth or throat, bleeding or bruising, confusion, fast heartbeat, respiratory depression, edema, dizziness, drowsiness, headache, double vision, clumsiness, constipation, diarrhea, nausea, vomiting, weakness; withdrawn from U.S. market in 1965; withdrawn from Canadian market in 1990; rarely prescribed today
	tybamate	*Solacen, Tybatram*		
Beta blockers			Hypertension, congestive heart failure, abnormal heart rhythms, chest pain	Off-label use to combat physical symptoms of anxiety; side effects include hypotension, bradycardia (slow heart rate), and depression
	alprenolol	*Alfeprol, Alpheprol, Alprenolol, Alprenololum, Apllobal, Aptine, Aptol, Duriles, Gubernal, Regletin, Yobir*		
	atenolol	*Tenormin*		
	carteolol	*Carteololum, Cartrol, Ocupress*	Eyedrops used to treat glaucoma	
	levobunolol	*Betagan*	Eyedrops used to treat glaucoma	

Category/*Class*	Drug	Brand names	Indications/uses	Comments
Anxiolytics				
Beta blockers (*continued*)				
	mepindolol			
	metipranolol	*OptiPranolol*	Eyedrops used to treat glaucoma	
	nadolol	*Corgard*	Hypertension, chest pain	
	oxprenolol		Angina, arrhythmia, hypertension	Should not be used by people with asthma
	penbutolol	*Levatol*	Hypertension	
	pindolol	*Visken, Betapindol, Calvisken, De-creten, Durapindol*	Angina, arrhythmia, hypertension, acute stress reactions	Investigational use as augmentative treatment for depression
	propranolol	*Inderal*	Hypertension, angina, tachycardia, myocardial infarction, essential tremor, migraines	*Experimental use:* PTSD; *off-label use:* performance-type social anxiety disorder
	sotalol	*Betapace*	Arrhythmia, hypertension	
	timolol	*Blocadren*	Hypertension, to prevent heart attacks, to prevent migraines; ophthalmic use: (Timoptic) to treat glaucoma	
Other anxiolytics				
	clonidine	*Catapres*	Insomnia, hypertension, nerve pain, night sweats	A direct-acting alpha-2 adrenergic agonist; also used for anesthesia, opioid detoxification, Tourette's syndrome, and to counteract the effects of stimulant medications (e.g., methylphenidate, amphetamine); used in conjunction with stimulants to treat ADHD

(*continued*)

618   APPENDIX A: PSYCHOPHARMACOLOGY

Category/Class	Drug	Brand names	Indications/uses	Comments
Anxiolytics				
Other anxiolytics (continued)				
	diphenhy-dramine	*Benadryl, Dimedrol*	Anxiety, insomnia, allergic reactions, anaphylaxis, nausea, motion sickness	Antihistamine of the ethanolamine class; has sedative-hypnotic properties; used to treat extrapyramidal side effects (EPS) of antipsychotic medications and cholinergic effects of some medications; can be abused to induce delirium or hallucinations
	hydroxyzine	*Atarax, Alamon, Aterax, Durrax, Equipose, Masmoran, Orgatrax, Paxistil, Quiess, Tran-Q, Tranquizine, Vistaril*	Anxiety, itches and irritations, nausea	First-generation antihistamine of the piperazine class; synthesized in 1950s; also used as a weak analgesic and an opioid potentiator; has sedative, hypnotic, and tranquilizing properties; very little abuse potential
Alternative anxiolytics				
	Ashwagandha		Sedative, sexual vitality	*Withania somnifera;* also known as Indian ginseng, winter cherry, ajagandha, kanaje Hindi, and Samm Al-Ferakh; a plant in *Solanaceae* or nightshade family
	Coastal water hyssop			*Bacopa monnieri;* another common name is brahmi; clinical evidence of efficacy (comparable to lorazepam) with no amnesic or other side effects
	Kava kava		Anxiety, insomnia, menopausal symptoms	*Piper methysticum;* a euphoric, tension-relieving herb; limited reliable evidence of efficacy; may cause liver disease/failure

Category/*Class*	Drug	Brand names	Indications/uses	Comments
Anxiolytics				
Alternative anxiolytics (continued)				
	Lavender		Anxiety, restlessness, insomnia, depression, headache, upset stomach	*Lavandula angustifolia;* used in aromatherapy or dried flowers made into tea; small studies on lavender for anxiety show mixed results
	Marijuana			*Cannabis sativa*
	Passionflower		Insomnia, hysteria, seizure disorder, painkiller	*Passiflora incarnata and P. edulis;* contains beta-carboline harmala alkaloids, which are MAOIs with antidepressant properties; limited reliable evidence of efficacy for anxiety disorders
	St. John's wort			*Hypericum perforatum;* limited reliable evidence of efficacy for anxiety
	Valerian root		Anxiety, seizure disorder, sedative	*Valeriana officinalis*
Mood stabilizers				
Anticonvulsants			Mood stabilizers/ antimanics (e.g., for bipolar disorder), GAD, social anxiety disorder, seizure disorders	
	carbemazepine	*Tegretol, Equetro*		
	felbamate	*Felbatol*	Seizure disorders	Use associated with aplastic anemia and acute liver failure; FDA warnings to only use as anticonvulsant for severe refractory seizure disorders

(continued)

Category/*Class*	Drug	Brand names	Indications/uses	Comments
Mood Stabilizers				
Anticonvulsants (contined)				
	gabapentin	*Neurontin*	Seizure disorders; off-label uses: bipolar disorder, GAD, social anxiety disorder	Not FDA approved for bipolar disorder; research suggests it is not an effective first- or second-line treatment for bipolar disorder, however, many psychiatrists continue to prescribe it; may be useful as an adjunctive treatment for refractory bipolar disorder with comorbid panic disorder or alcohol abuse; side effects may include sedation, ataxia, dizziness, dry mouth, nausea, asthenia (weakness), flatulence, decreased libido
	lamotrigine	*Lamictal, Lamictin, Lamogine*	Seizure disorders, bipolar disorder; off-label uses: PTSD, borderline personality disorder	Successful in controlling rapid cycling and mixed bipolar states in people who have not received adequate relief from lithium, carbamazepine, and/or valproate
	levetiracetam	*Keppra*		Research does not support use for bipolar disorder
	lithium carbonate	*Carbolith, Cibalith-S, Duralith, Eskalith, Lithane, Lithizine, Lithobid, Lithonate, Lithotabs*	Bipolar disorder	

Category/*Class*	Drug	Brand names	Indications/uses	Comments
Mood Stabilizers				
Anticonvulsants (continued)				
	oxcarbazepine	*Trileptal*		Not FDA approved for bipolar disorder
	pregablin	*Lyrica*	GAD, social anxiety disorder, nerve pain	No research to support its use for bipolar disorder; may be used for comorbid anxiety and bipolar disorder; side effects may include sedation, ataxia, dizziness, dry mouth, nausea, asthenia, flatulence, decreased libido
	tiagabine	*Gabitril*	Anxiety disorders	Selective GABA reuptake inhibitor
	topiramate	*Topamax*		Not FDA approved for bipolar disorder; side effects may include weight loss
	valproate (divalproex, valproic acid)	*Depakene, Depakote, Depacon*		
Alternative mood stabilizers				
	Omega-3 fatty acids		Unipolar depression, bipolar disorder, schizophrenia	Eicosapentaenoic acid; an omega-3 fatty acid found in fish oil, seafood, flaxseed, and eggs; some studies suggest effectiveness in treating depressive symptoms in bipolar disorder (no effect on manic symptoms), but results are not conclusive

(continued)

Category/*Class*	Drug	Brand names	Indications/uses	Comments
Mood Stabilizers				
Alternative mood stabilizers (continued)				
	St. John's wort		Minor to moderate depression, bipolar disorder	*Hypericum perforatum;* some concerns about risk of triggering a manic or hypomanic episode in individuals with bipolar disorder
Antipsychotics			Bipolar disorder, schizophrenia, other psychoses	
Typical antipsychotics				Also referred to as first-generation or conventional antipsychotics, classical neuroleptics, or major tranquilizers
	chlorpromazine	*Thorazine, Largactil*		The first antipsychotic medication; first used in 1952 as a post-operative sedative
	fluphenazine	*Prolixin*		Available in time-release intramuscular (IM) formulation
	haloperidol	*Haldol, Serenace*		Available in time-release IM formulation
	loxapine	*Loxapac, Loxitane*		
	mesoridazine	*Serentil*		
	molindone	*Moban*		
	perphenazine	*Trilafon*		
	pimozide	*Orap*		
	prochlorpera-zine	*Compazine, Buccastem, Stemetil*		
	thioridazine	*Mellaril*		
	thiothixene	*Navane*		
	trifluoperazine	*Stelazine*		
	zuclopenthixol	*Clopixol*		

Category/*Class*	Drug	Brand names	Indications/uses	Comments
Mood Stabilizers				
Atypical antipsychotics				Also referred to as second-generation or novel antipsychotics
	amisulpride	*Solian*		Selective dopamine antagonist; not approved for use in United States
	aripiprazole	*Abilify*		Dopamine partial agonist (third-generation antipsychotic)
	asenapine			
	bifeprunox			Not approved for use in United States
	clozapine	*Clozaril*		First atypical antipsychotic developed
	iloperidone	*Fanapta, Zomaril*		
	melperone	*Buronil, Burnil, Eunerpan*		Approved for use in Europe
	olanzapine	*Zyprexa*		
	paliperidone	*Invega*		
	quetiapine	*Seroquel*		
	risperidone	*Risperdal*		
	sertindole	*Serlect*		
	ziprasidone	*Geodon*		
	zotepine	*Nipolept, Losizopilon, Lodopin, Setous*		Not approved for use in United States
Alternative antipsychotics				
	Betel nuts			*Areca catechu;* a muscarinic agonist; some studies show effective on positive symptoms of schizophrenia
	glycine			

(continued)

Category/*Class*	Drug	Brand names	Indications/uses	Comments
Mood Stabilizers				
Alternative antipsychotics (continued)				
	Omega-3 fatty acids		Depression, bipolar disorder, schizophrenia	Found in fish oil, seafood, flaxseed, and eggs; some studies suggest effectiveness in treating schizophrenia, but results are inconsistent and inconclusive
	Rauwolfia			*Rauwolfia serpentina* extract was used before the first antipsychotics were synthesized in the 1950s; can cause depression
	Vitamin B$_3$ (niacin)			
Antiparkinsonian/anticholinergic drugs			Used to counteract side effects of antipsychotics	
	amantadine	*Symmetrel*		Dopamine agonist
	benztropine mesylate	*Cogentin*		Antimuscarinic for parkinsonian symptoms
	biperiden	*Akineton*		Antimuscarinic for parkinsonian symptoms
	diphenhydramine	*Benadryl, Dimedrol*	Anxiety, insomnia, allergic reactions, anaphylaxis, nausea, motion sickness	Antihistimine/anticholinergic; used to treat EPS of antipsychotics
	ethopropazine	*Parsidol*		Antimuscarinic for parkinsonian symptoms
	orphenadrine			Antimuscarinic for parkinsonian symptoms
	procyclidine	*Kemadrin*		Antimuscarinic for parkinsonian symptoms
	trihexyphenidyl	*Artane*		Antimuscarinic for parkinsonian symptoms

APPENDIX B: ORGANIZATIONS

The authors have made every attempt to ensure the accuracy of the information about the following organizations, including contact information. Descriptions are based on information provided by each organization. The information presented here is not intended to endorse or promote these organizations, nor is it intended to recommend specific treatments for conditions or for individuals.

Yuri Ito and Yvette Malamud Ozer

Organization Types: P = Professional, R = Research/Scientific, S = Self-Help/Support, C = Consumer Resources/Referrals, E = education/advocacy/policy

Organization	Type	Contact information	Description
Adult Children of Alcoholics (ACA)	S	(562) 575-7831 http://www.adultchildren.org/	12-step support group for adult children of alcoholics
Adult Survivors of Child Abuse (ASCA)	S, C	info@ascasupport.org http://www.ascasupport.org/	International self-help support group program for adult survivors of neglect, physical, sexual, or emotional abuse
Agoraphobics Building Independent Lives (ABIL)	S, C	(804) 257-5591 mhav@mhav.org http://www.mhav.org/ programs.html#ABIL	Provides hope, support, and advocacy to people affected by panic attacks, phobias, or agoraphobia; has nationwide self-help groups; provides public education
AirCraft Casualty Emotional Support Services (ACCESS)	S	(877) 227-6435 info@accesshelp.org http://www.accesshelp.org/	Air disaster bereavement support network that connects people who have survived or lost loved ones in plane crashes and other aviation tragedies with individuals who have lived through similar losses

(continued)

Organization	Type	Contact information	Description
Al-Anon Family Groups	S	U.S.: (757) 563-1600 Canada: (613) 723-8484 http://www.al-anon.alateen.org/	Mutual support group for friends and relatives of alcoholics; members share their experience, strength, and hope to solve their common problems
Alateen	S	U.S.: (757) 563-1600 Canada: (613) 723-8484 http://www.al-anon.alateen.org/alateen.html	Part of Al-Anon Family Groups, Alateen is a mutual support group for teenagers who have an alcoholic friend or family member
Alcoholics Anonymous (AA)	S	(212) 870-3400 http://www.aa.org/	12-step program for recovery from alcoholism
Alternatives to Violence Project (AVP Britain)	C	44 020 7324 4755 http://www.avpbritain.org.uk/	Organizes low-cost anger management workshops for people in the community, schools, prisons, and the workplace in Britain
American Academy of Child and Adolescent Psychiatry (AACAP)	P, R	(202) 966-7300 http://www.aacap.org/	Professional medical association; active in research, prevention, and ensuring treatment and access to services for children, adolescents, and families affected by mental, behavioral, or developmental disorders
American Association for Marriage and Family Therapy (AAMFT)	P	(703) 838-9808 http://www.aamft.org/	A professional organization for marriage and family therapists, AAMFT develops standards for graduate education and training, clinical supervision, professional ethics, and the clinical practice of marriage and family therapy
American Association of Anger Management Providers (AAMP)	C	(310) 207-3591 georgeanderson@aol.com http://www.aaamp.org/	Directory listing anger management providers in the United States
American Association of Retired Persons (AARP)	E, C	(888) 687-2277 http://www.aarp.org/	Nonprofit, nonpartisan organization helping people 50 and over improve the quality of their lives; leads positive social change through advocacy; provides information and discounts on services
American Institute of Stress (AIS)	E	(914) 963-1200 Stress125@optonline.net http://www.stress.org/	Clearinghouse for information on all stress-related subjects
American Psychiatric Association (APA)	P	(888) 357-7924 (703) 907-7300 apa@psych.org http://www.psych.org/	Professional organization of psychiatrists that promotes high-quality care for individuals with mental disorders, promotes psychiatric education and research, and advances the profession of psychiatry in the United States

Organization Types: P = Professional, R = Research/Scientific, S = Self-Help/Support, C = Consumer Resources/Referrals, E = education/advocacy/policy

Organization	Type	Contact information	Description
American Psychological Association (APA)	P, R	(800) 374-2721 http://www.apa.org/	Scientific and professional organization representing psychology in the United States
American Psychosocial Oncology Society (APOS)	P	(434) 293-5350 info@apos-society.org http://www.apos-society.org/	Professional organization advancing the science and practice of psychosocial care for people with cancer; provides a forum for professionals and individuals interested in the psychological, social, behavioral, and spiritual aspects of cancer
American Red Cross	C	(800) RED-CROSS (202) 303-5000 http://www.redcross.org/	Provides domestic disaster relief, community services for the needy, support and comfort for military members and their families, educational health and safety programs, and international relief and development programs; collects, processes, and distributes blood and blood products
American Society of Group Psychotherapy and Psychodrama (ASGPP)	P	(609) 737-8500 asgpp@asgpp.org http://www.asgpp.org/	Fosters national and international cooperation among all who are concerned with the theory and practice of psychodrama, sociometry, and group psychotherapy
Animal Behavior Society (ABS)	R	(812) 856-5541 aboffice@indiana.edu http://animalbehaviorsociety.org/	A nonprofit scientific group that encourages and promotes the study of animal behavior
Anxiety Disorders Association of America (ADAA)	C	(240) 485-1001 information@adaa.org http://www.adaa.org/	Nonprofit organization that informs the public, health care professionals, and media that anxiety disorders are real, serious, and treatable; provides information and referrals
Association for Death Education and Counseling (ADEC)	E, C	(847) 509-0403 http://www.adec.org/	Interdisciplinary organization in the field of dying, death, and bereavement; provides education, a certification program, and referrals
Association for Play Therapy (APT)	P	(559) 294-2128 info@a4pt.org http://www.a4pt.org/	A national professional society advancing the usefulness of play, play therapy, and credentialed play therapists
Association for Psychological Science (APS)	R	(202) 293-9300 http://www.psychologicalscience.org/	A nonprofit organization that promotes, protects, and advances the interests of scientifically oriented psychology in research, application, teaching, and the improvement of human welfare

Organization Types: P = Professional, R = Research/Scientific, S = Self-Help/Support, C = Consumer Resources/Referrals, E = education/advocacy/policy

(continued)

Organization	Type	Contact information	Description
Aurora Dawn Foundation	C	adf_support@earthlink.net http://www.auroradawnfoundation.org/	Offers housing, support, and community and social advocacy for persons with HIV/AIDS who have nowhere else to go; has a residence for men, a women's outreach program, and a rural retreat for healing; located in San Francisco, California
Autism Network International (ANI)	S, E	http://www.autreat.com/	Autistic-run self-help and advocacy organization for autistic people
Autism Society of America (ASA)	C, E	(800) 3-AUTISM http://www.autism-society.org/	Grassroots autism organization that improves the lives of people affected by autism by increasing public awareness, advocating for appropriate services, and providing information regarding treatment, education, and research
Awareness Foundation for OCD & Related Disorders (AFOCD)	C	http://www.ocdawareness.com/	Educates the public and individuals about OCD and related disorders through lectures, e-mails, private coaching, consulting, films, and books
Batterers Anonymous	S	(951) 312-1041 jerrygoffman@hotmail.com http://batterersanonymous.com/	Self-help program for men who want to control their anger and eliminate their abusive behavior toward women
Borderline Personality Disorder Resource Center (BPDRC)	C	(888) 694-2273 bpdresourcecenter@nyp.org http://bpdresourcecenter.org/	Provides information and resources about borderline personality disorder
Cancer Hope Network	C	(877) 467-3638 info@cancerhopenetwork.org http://www.cancerhopenetwork.org/	Not-for-profit organization providing free, confidential, one-to-one support to cancer patients and their families
CancerCare	C	(800) 813-HOPE info@cancercare.org http://www.cancercare.org/	Nonprofit organization providing free, professional support services to people with cancer, caregivers, children, loved ones, and the bereaved; services include counseling, education, financial assistance, and practical help and are provided by trained oncology social workers
Center on Addiction and the Family (CoAF)	C, E	(718) 222-6641 coaf@phoenixhouse.org http://www.coaf.org/	Formerly Children of Alcoholics Foundation; helps children from alcoholic and substance-abusing families break the cycle of addition and reach their full potential; develops curriculum and educational materials, provides information about substance abuse to the general public, trains professionals, and promotes research

Organization Types: P = Professional, R = Research/Scientific, S = Self-Help/Support, C = Consumer Resources/Referrals, E = education/advocacy/policy

Organization	Type	Contact information	Description
Chemically Dependent Anonymous (CDA)	S	(888) CDA-HOPE http://www.cdaweb.org/	12-step program to help people stay clean and sober
Child & Adolescent Bipolar Foundation (CABF)	S, C	(847) 492-8519 cabf@bpkids.org http://www.bpkids.org/	Parent-led organization of families raising children and teens living with bipolar disorder and related conditions; provides education, support, advocacy, and referrals to Internet and local support groups
Cocaine Anonymous (CA)	S	(310) 559-5833 cawso@ca.org http://www.ca.org/	12-step recovery program for cocaine
Co-Dependents Anonymous (CoDA)	S	(602) 277-7991 outreach@coda.org http://www.codependents. org/	12-step program for men and women whose common purpose is to develop healthy relationships
COLAGE	S, E	(415) 861-5437 colage@colage.org http://www.colage.org/	National movement of children, youth, and adults with one or more lesbian, gay, bisexual, transgender, and/or queer parents; builds community and works toward social justice through youth empowerment, leadership development, education, and advocacy
Compass, Inc.	C, E	(561) 533-9699 http://www.compassglcc. com/	Diminishes stereotypes by challenging long-standing misconceptions about the character of the lesbian, gay, bisexual, and transgender community through education and advocacy, providing health services, and community organizing; located in Palm Beach County, Florida
Council on Anxiety Disorders	C, S	(706) 947-3854 slvau@stc.net	Two groups in Georgia that hold meetings to provide education, support, and encouragement for people with anxiety disorders
Crystal Meth Anonymous (CMA)	S	(213) 488-4455 http://www.crystalmeth. org/	12-step recovery program for crystal meth users (methamphetamine)
Daily Strength Anger Management Support Group	S	http://www.dailystrength. org/c/Anger-Management/ support-group/	Online anger management support group

Organization Types: P = Professional, R = Research/Scientific, S = Self-Help/Support, C = Consumer Resources/Referrals, E = education/advocacy/policy

(continued)

Organization	Type	Contact information	Description
Delta Society	E, C	info@DeltaSociety.org http://www.deltasociety.org/	Delta Society educates health care and other professionals about how to incorporate animals into goal-directed treatment or visiting animal activities, provide high-standard therapy animal training and curricula, and inspire people to volunteer with their pets in their local communities to improve people's health and well-being through positive interactions with animals
Depressed Anonymous (DA)	S	(502) 569-1989 info@depressedanon.com http://www.depressedanon.com/	12-step program for depression
Depression and Bipolar Support Alliance (DBSA)	S, R, C	(800) 826-3632 http://www.dbsalliance.org/	Patient-directed national organization focusing on mood disorders; provides up-to-date, scientifically based tools and information for the general public; supports research to promote more timely diagnosis, develop more effective and tolerable treatments, and discover a cure
Drug Free America Foundation (DFAF)	E	(727) 828-0211 http://www.dfaf.org/	Drug prevention and policy organization committed to developing, promoting, and sustaining global strategies, policies, and laws to reduce illegal drug use, drug addiction, and drug-related injury and death; opposes legalization of drugs and permissive drug policies
Emotional Health Anonymous (EHA)	S	(626) 287-6260 sgveha@hotmail.com http://home.flash.net/~sgveha/	12-step program for people who suffer from emotional and mental problems not related to substance abuse
Emotions Anonymous (EA)	S	(651) 647-9712 infodf3498fjsd@emotionsanonymous.org http://www.emotionsanonymous.org/	12-step program for people working toward recovery from emotional difficulties
Families for Depression Awareness	C, E	(781) 890-0220 info@familyaware.org http://www.familyaware.org/	Helps families recognize and cope with depressive disorders to get people well and prevent suicides; activities include education, advocacy, and referrals

Organization Types: P = Professional, R = Research/Scientific, S = Self-Help/Support, C = Consumer Resources/Referrals, E = education/advocacy/policy

Organization	Type	Contact information	Description
Families Helping Families (FHF)	C	(619) 294-8000 fhf@jennadruck.org http://jdf-fhf.org/	Part of the Jenna Druck Foundation; provides comprehensive support services to bereaved families, individuals, and communities who have experienced the loss of a loved one; provides support groups, community education, and support and education for the workplace and classroom
Freedom From Fear (FFF)	E, C	(718) 351-1717 (ext. 19) help@freedomfromfear.org http://www.freedomfrom fear.org/	National not-for-profit mental health advocacy association that positively impacts the lives of people affected by anxiety, depressive, and related disorders through advocacy, education, research, referrals, and community support
Friends for Survival	S	(800) 646-7322 (916) 392-0664 ffs@truevine.net http://www.friendsforsur-vival.org/	Provides peer support services to those who have lost friends or family to suicide
Friendship Network	S	info@friendshipnetwork.org http://www.friendshipnet work.org/	Introduces people with mental illness to each other to help them develop friendships, social skills, and self-confidence
Gamblers Anonymous (GA)	S	(213) 386-8789 isomain@gamblersanony mous.org http://www.gamblersanony mous.org/	A 12-step fellowship whose members come together at meetings to help themselves and each another to stop compulsive gambling
Gift From Within (GFW)	C, S	(207) 236-8858 JoyceB3955@aol.com http://www.giftfromwithin. org/	International nonprofit organization for people who have, are at risk for, or care for individuals with posttraumatic stress disorder; develops and disseminates educational material; peer support network of survivors
Gilda's Club	C	(888) GILDA-4-U info@gildasclub.org http://www.gildasclub.org/	Creates welcoming communities of free support for people living with cancer; provides networking and support groups, workshops, education, and social activities
Global and Regional Asperger Syndrome Partnership (GRASP)	E, S	(888) 474-7277 info@grasp.org http://www.grasp.org/	Educational and advocacy group serving individuals on the autism spectrum; provides a support group network, educational outreach, and information

Organization Types: P = Professional, R = Research/Scientific, S = Self-Help/Support, C = Consumer Resources/Referrals, E = education/advocacy/policy

(continued)

Organization	Type	Contact information	Description
Gray Panthers	E	(800) 280-5362 info@graypanthers.org http://www.graypanthers.org/	Advocacy organization seeking intergenerational approaches to achieving social and economic justice and peace; strives to create a humane society that puts the needs of people over profits, responsibility over power, and democracy over institutions
GriefNet	C, S	cendra@griefnet.org http://www.griefnet.org/	Internet community of persons dealing with grief, death, and major loss; has resources, referrals, and support groups
GriefShare	C	(800) 395-5755 info@griefshare.org http://www.griefshare.org/	Holds seminars and support groups led by trained group leaders for people grieving the death of a loved one; part of the Church Initiative based in North Carolina
GROW in America	S	(888) 741-GROW http://www.growinamerica.org/	International mental health movement with a network of member-run support groups in four different countries (United States, Australia, New Zealand, and Ireland)
HealthyWomen (HW)	E	(877) 986-9472 http://www.healthywomen.org/	Independent health information source for women, providing unbiased and accurate health information
Hospice Foundation of America	C, E	(800) 854-3402 (202) 457-5811 info@hospicefoundation.org http://www.hospicefoundation.org/	Provides leadership in the development and application of hospice and its philosophy of care with the goal of enhancing the U.S. health care system and the role of hospice; provides professional development, public education and information, research, and publications
International Critical Incident Stress Foundation Inc. (ICISF)	C, E	(410) 750-9600 info@icisf.org http://www.icisf.org/	Provides leadership, education, training, consultation, and support services in comprehensive crisis intervention and disaster behavioral health services to the emergency response professions, other organizations, and communities worldwide
International OCD Foundation	S, C, R	(617) 973-5801 info@ocfoundation.org http://www.ocfoundation.org/	Formerly the Obsessive-Compulsive Foundation; not-for-profit organization of people with obsessive-compulsive disorder (OCD) and related disorders, their families, friends, professionals, and other concerned individuals; educates the public and professional communities, provides assistance to individuals with OCD, and supports research into the causes and effective treatments of OCD
International Stress Management Association (ISMA)	E	44 01179 697284 stress@isma.org.uk http://www.isma.org.uk/	Registered charity with a multidisciplinary professional membership that includes the United Kingdom and the Republic of Ireland; promotes best practice in the prevention and reduction of human stress; sets professional standards and disseminates information

Organization Types: P = Professional, R = Research/Scientific, S = Self-Help/Support, C = Consumer Resources/Referrals, E = education/advocacy/policy

Organization	Type	Contact information	Description
Kara	S, C	(650) 321-5272 http://www.kara-grief.org/	Helps people deal with loss and grief through support and education; individual peer counseling and support groups provided by trained volunteers are free of charge; located in Palo Alto, California
Kempe Postpartum Depression Intervention Program	C	(303) 864-5300 questions@kempe.org http://www.kempe.org/	Provides evidenced-based group psychotherapy and mental health evaluations for mothers with postpartum depression; located in Aurora, Colorado
LifeRing Secular Recovery	S	(510) 763-0779 service@lifering.org http://www.unhooked.com/	Nonreligious self-help recovery organization for individuals who seek group support to achieve abstinence from alcohol and other addictive drugs
Marijuana Anonymous (MA)	S	(800) 766-6779 office@marijuana-anonymous.org http://www.marijuana-anonymous.org/	A 12-step recovery program for marijuana
Mental Health America (MHA)	C	(800) 969-6642 infoctr@mentalhealthamerica.net http://www.nmha.org/	Provides advocacy, public education, and support for Americans with mental health conditions; formerly known as the National Mental Health Association
Mental Health Gap Action Programme (mhGAP)	E	41 22 791 21 11 mnh@who.int http://www.who.int/mental_health/mhgap/	World Health Organization program to increase services for mental, neurological, and substance use disorders in countries with low and middle incomes
Moderation Management (MM)	S	mm@moderation.org http://www.moderation.org/	Behavioral change program and national support group network for people who have made the decision to reduce their drinking
Mothers Against Drunk Driving (MADD)	C, E	(800) 438-6233 http://www.madd.org/	Advocacy and education activities to stop drunk driving, support the victims of drunk driving, and prevent underage drinking; provides services to help victims cope with grief
NAADAC: The Association for Addiction Professionals	P	(800) 548-0497 naadac@naadac.org http://www.naadac.org/	Professional organization serving addiction counselors, educators, and other addiction-focused health care professionals
Nar-Anon Family Groups	S	(800) 477-6291 (310) 534-8188 naranonWSO@gmail.com http://www.nar-anon.org/	A 12-step fellowship whose members are relatives and friends who are concerned about the addiction or drug problem of another
Narconon Exposed	S	dst@cs.cmu.edu http://www.cs.cmu.edu/~dst/Narconon/	Provides information about Narconon and keeps a watchful eye on Narconon activities around the world

Organization Types: P = Professional, R = Research/Scientific, S = Self-Help/Support, C = Consumer Resources/Referrals, E = education/advocacy/policy

(continued)

Organization	Type	Contact information	Description
Narconon International	S	(800) 391-4893 info@narconon.org http://www.narconon.org/	Nonprofit public benefit organization dedicated to eliminating drug abuse through prevention, education, and rehabilitation; based on the work of Church of Scientology founder L. Ron Hubbard
Narcotics Anonymous (NA)	S	U.S. (California): (818) 773-9999 Europe (Brussels): 32 2 646 6012 fsmail@na.org http://www.na.org/	International 12-step recovery program for addiction with more than 43,900 weekly meetings in over 127 countries worldwide
National Alliance for Research on Schizophrenia and Depression (NARSAD)	R	(516) 829-0091 info@narsad.org http://www.narsad.org/	Supports research into prevention and treatment of mental illnesses such as schizophrenia, depression, and bipolar disorder
National Alliance on Mental Illness (NAMI)	S, C	Phone: (703) 524-7600 Help line: (800) 950-6264 info@nami.org http://www.nami.org/	Provides support, education, and advocacy to people with mental illness and their families
National Anger Management Association (NAMA)	P, C	(646) 485-5116 namass@namass.org http://www.namass.org/	Nonprofit professional organization for the advancement of anger management services, research, and professional anger management services; has a code of ethical standards, a certification program, and a directory of anger management specialists
National Association of School Psychologists (NASP)	P, E	(866) 331-NASP center@naspweb.org http://www.nasponline.org/	A professional organization that supports school psychologists and provides resources and services to enhance the mental health and educational needs of all children and youth; promotes prevention and early intervention, problem-solving approaches and collaboration, and research-based strategies and programs
National Center for Trauma-Informed Care (NCTIC)	E	(866) 254-4819 NCTIC@NASMHPD.org http://mentalhealth.samhsa.gov/nctic/	Technical assistance center that builds awareness of trauma-informed care and promotes the implementation of trauma-informed practices in programs and services; part of Center for Mental Health Services

Organization Types: P = Professional, R = Research/Scientific, S = Self-Help/Support, C = Consumer Resources/Referrals,
E = education/advocacy/policy

Organization	Type	Contact information	Description
National Child Traumatic Stress Network (NCTSN)	E, C	California: (310) 235-2633 North Carolina: (919) 682-1552 http://www.nctsnet.org/nccts/	Collaboration of academic and community-based service centers that raise the standard of care and increase access to services for traumatized children and their families across the United States; develops and disseminates evidence-based interventions, trauma-informed services, and public and professional education
National Coalition for the Homeless (NCH)	E, C	(202) 462-4822 info@nationalhomeless.org http://www.nationalhomeless.org/	A national organization committed to ending homelessness; NCH helps those who are currently experiencing homelessness or who are at risk for being homeless; main activities include public education, policy advocacy, and grassroots organizing
National Council on Alcoholism and Drug Dependence (NCADD)	C	(212) 269-7797 national@ncadd.org http://www.ncadd.org/	Fights the stigma and disease of alcoholism and drug addiction; provides education, information, and help to the public; and advocates prevention, intervention, and treatment through a nationwide network of affiliates
National Eating Disorders Association (NEDA)	C, E	(206) 382-3587 http://www.nationaleatingdisorders.org/	A nonprofit organization that provides support and resources to those affected by eating disorders and to educate concerned individuals and the general public about eating disorders
National Education Alliance for Borderline Personality Disorder (NEA-BPD)	C	info@neabpd.org http://www.borderlinepersonalitydisorder.com/	Raises public awareness, provides education, promotes research, and enhances the quality of life of those affected by borderline personality disorder
National Empowerment Center (NEC)	S, C	(800) 769-3728 info4@power2u.org http://www.power2u.org/	A consumer/survivor/ex-patient-run organization that carries a message of recovery, empowerment, hope, and healing by providing referrals and information to people who have been labeled with mental illness
National Family Caregivers Association (NCFA)	C, E	(800) 896-3650 info@thefamilycaregiver.org http://www.thefamilycaregiver.org/	Educates, supports, empowers, and speaks up for Americans who care for loved ones with a chronic illness, disability, or old age; offers caregiving resources and advocacy
National Institute of Mental Health (NIMH)	R	(866) 615-6464 (301) 443-4513 nimhinfo@nih.gov http://www.nimh.nih.gov/	Generates research on the causes of mental disorders and develops new and better interventions to prevent and treat mental illnesses

Organization Types: P = Professional, R = Research/Scientific, S = Self-Help/Support, C = Consumer Resources/Referrals, E = education/advocacy/policy

(continued)

Organization	Type	Contact information	Description
National Institute of Neurological Disorders and Stroke (NINDS)	R	(800) 352-9424 http://www.ninds.nih.gov/	Conducts and supports research on brain and nervous system disorders
National Institute on Alcohol Abuse and Alcoholism (NIAAA)	R	(301) 443-3860 http://www.niaaa.nih.gov/	Provides leadership in the national effort to reduce alcohol-related problems by conducting and supporting research in genetics, neuroscience, epidemiology, health risks and benefits of alcohol consumption, prevention, and treatment; disseminates research findings to health care providers, researchers, policy makers, and the public
National Institute on Drug Abuse (NIDA)	R	English: (301) 443-1124 Spanish: (240) 221-4007 information@nida.nih.gov http://www.nida.nih.gov/	Supports and conducts research on drug abuse and addiction; disseminates research results to improve drug abuse and addiction prevention, treatment, and policies
National Mental Health Consumers' Self-Help Clearinghouse	S, C	(800) 553-4539 info@mhselfhelp.org http://mhselfhelp.org/	Extensive library of information on self-help and advocacy topics, including peer counseling, deinstitutionalization, fund-raising, involuntary treatment, patient rights, and using the media
National Organization for Victim Assistance (NOVA)	C, E	(800) 879-6682 nova@try-nova.org http://www.trynova.org/	Private, nonprofit organization of victim and witness assistance programs and practitioners, criminal justice agencies and professionals, mental health professionals, researchers, former victims and survivors, and others committed to the recognition and implementation of victim rights and services
National Transportation Safety Board (NTSB)	E	(202) 314-6000 http://www.ntsb.gov/	Investigates every civil aviation accident in the United States and significant accidents in the other modes of transportation (railroad, highway, marine, and pipeline) and issues safety recommendations aimed at preventing future accidents
Neurotics Anonymous	S	(310) 516-1051 http://www.neuroticosanonimosusa.com/neurotics.html	12-step program for people dealing with emotional problems
Nicotine Anonymous (NicA)	S	(877) 879-6422 info@nicotine-anonymous. org http://www.nicotine-anony mous.org/	12-step recovery program for nicotine

Organization Types: P = Professional, R = Research/Scientific, S = Self-Help/Support, C = Consumer Resources/Referrals, E = education/advocacy/policy

Organization	Type	Contact information	Description
North American Riding for the Handicapped Association (NARHA)	C, E	(800) 369-7433 http://www.narha.org/	Provides equine-assisted activity and therapy programs in the United States and Canada; fosters safe, professional, ethical, and therapeutic equine activities through education, communication, research, and standards
Obsessive Compulsive Anonymous (OCA)	S	(516) 739-0662 west24th@aol.com http://obsessivecompulsiveanonymous.org/	12-step program for people with obsessive-compulsive disorder
ONE Freedom	C	(888) 334-VETS http://www.onefreedom.org/	Offers military personnel and families resources, referrals, and training to build strength, resilience, and an understanding of how to maintain balance in the face of military deployments and other lifestyle challenges
Overeaters Anonymous (OA)	S	(505) 891-2664 http://www.oa.org/	12-step program for compulsive eaters
Pacific Post Partum Support Society (PPPSS)	C	(604) 255-7999 http://www.postpartum.org/	Nonprofit society providing support to women and families experiencing depression or anxiety related to the birth or adoption of a baby; provides training and information for professionals and community education on postpartum depression
Parents Anonymous Inc.	R, C, S	(909) 621-6184 Parentsanonymous@parentsanonymous.org http://www.parentsanonymous.org/	Child abuse prevention organization providing training, technical assistance, research, and publications
Pathways to Peace	E	(415) 461-0500 nfo@pathwaystopeace.org http://www.pathwaystopeace.org/	International peace-building, educational, and consulting organization; collaborates with other organizations and participates in United Nations conferences
Postpartum Health Alliance (PHA)	C	(619) 254-0023 info@postpartumhealthalliance.org http://www.postpartumhealthalliance.org/	Nonprofit organization of health professionals who educate other health professionals and the public about the mood disorders that can follow childbirth; provides educational materials and referrals
Postpartum Support International (PSI)	C, E	(800) 944-4773 http://postpartum.net/	Educates and builds awareness of the emotional and psychological changes women go through during and after pregnancy; provides information, resources, and education and advocates for research and legislation to support perinatal mental health; a help line provides referrals

Organization Types: P = Professional, R = Research/Scientific, S = Self-Help/Support, C = Consumer Resources/Referrals, E = education/advocacy/policy

(continued)

Organization	Type	Contact information	Description
Rainbows International	C	(847) 952-1770 info@rainbows.org http://www.rainbows.org/	International, not-for-profit organization fostering emotional healing among children grieving a loss from a life-altering crisis; offers comprehensive grief support curricula and training
Rational Recovery (RR)	S	(530) 621-2667 http://www.rational.org/	Source of counseling, guidance, and direct instruction on self-recovery from addiction to alcohol and other drugs through planned, permanent abstinence
Recovery International	S	(866) 221-0302 info@lowselfhelpsystems.org http://www.lowselfhelpsystems.org/	Formerly Recovery Inc.; through community, telephone, and online meetings, helps individuals manage feelings or impulses that impair the ability to live a normal life using a cognitive-behavioral, peer-to-peer, self-help training system
San Francisco Bay Area Center for Cognitive Therapy	C	(510) 652-4455 http://www.sfbacct.com/	Group of clinical psychologists working together in a partnership; provides cognitive-behavioral therapy (CBT), conducts training and research, and disseminates information about CBT; located in Oakland, California
Schizophrenia: Open the Doors	E	http://www.openthedoors.com/english/	International program to fight stigma and discrimination of schizophrenia; provides information and list of resources; advocates for change
Self-Help for Women with Breast or Ovarian Cancer (SHARE)	C	(866) 891-2392 info@sharecancersupport.org http://www.sharecancersupport.org/	Brings women affected by breast or ovarian cancer, their families, and friends together with others who have experienced breast or ovarian cancer; provides participants with the opportunity to receive and exchange information, support, strength, and hope
Sex and Love Addicts Anonymous (SLAA)	S	http://www.slaafws.org/	12-step program of people helping each other deal with sex addiction or love addiction
SMART Recovery	S	(440) 951-5357 http://www.smartrecovery.org/	Offers free face-to-face and online mutual help groups for people recovering from all types of addictive behaviors
Substance Abuse and Mental Health Services Administration (SAMHSA)	R, C	(877) 726-4727 SHIN@samhsa.hhs.gov http://www.samhsa.gov/	Supports state and community efforts to expand and enhance prevention and early intervention programs and to improve the quality, availability, and range of substance abuse treatment, mental health, and recovery support services in local communities

Organization Types: P = Professional, R = Research/Scientific, S = Self-Help/Support, C = Consumer Resources/Referrals, E = education/advocacy/policy

Organization	Type	Contact information	Description
Substance Abuse Treatment Facility Locator	C	English: (800) 662-HELP Spanish: (800) 662-9832 TDD: (800) 228-0427 http://dasis3.samhsa.gov/	Referral help lines (phone) and Internet referrals for substance abuse treatment programs in the United States
Survivors Art Foundation (SAF)	C	safe@survivorsartfoundation.org http://www.survivorsartfoundation.org/	Nonprofit organization empowering trauma survivors with effective expressive outlets via an Internet art gallery, outreach programs, national exhibitions, publications, and development of employment skills
Survivors of Bereavement by Suicide (SOBS)	S	National Office: 44 0115 944 1117 National Helpline (UK): 44 0844 561 6855 sobs.admin@care4free.net http://www.uk-sobs.org.uk/	Self-help organization breaking the isolation of those bereaved by the suicide of a close relative or friend; provides group meetings, a telephone help line, and information; located in England
The Bright and Beautiful Therapy Dogs, Inc.	C	(888) PET-5770 Info@Golden-Dogs.org http://www.golden-dogs.org/	Evaluates and trains therapy dogs; located in New Jersey
The Center for Victims of Violence and Crime (CVVC)	C, E	(412) 392-8582 information@cvvc.org http://www.cvvc.org/	Provides victim advocacy and support services, crisis intervention, counseling, and community education programs that address the causes and impacts of all types of violence and crime
The Compassionate Friends (TCF)	S	(877) 969-0010 http://www.compassionatefriends.org/	Assists families toward the positive resolution of grief following the death of a child
The Dougy Center for Grieving Children and Families	C	(866) 775-5683 help@dougy.org http://www.dougy.org/	Through peer support groups, education, and training, provides a safe place for children, teens, young adults, and their families who are grieving a death to share their experiences
The Jenna Druck Foundation	E, C	(619) 294-8000 info@jennadruck.org http://jennadruck.org/	Includes two programs: Young Women's Leadership (YWL) provides leadership training to upcoming young women, and Families Helping Families (FHF) serves people in their journey through grief
The Latham Foundation for the Promotion of Humane Education	E	(510) 521-0920 info@latham.org http://www.latham.org/	Clearinghouse for information about humane issues and activities, the human–companion animal bond, animal-assisted therapy, and connections between child and animal abuse and other forms of violence

Organization Types: P = Professional, R = Research/Scientific, S = Self-Help/Support, C = Consumer Resources/Referrals, E = education/advocacy/policy

(continued)

Organization	Type	Contact information	Description
The Mood Disorders Support Group of New York City (MDSG)	S	(212) 533-MDSG info@mdsg.org http://www.mdsg.org/	Nonprofit self-help organization for individuals with depression and bipolar disorder, their families, and friends; helps people accept and manage their illness and improve the quality of their lives; an independent affiliate of DBSA
The Shaken Baby Alliance	E	(877) 6-END-SBS info@shakenbaby.com http://shakenbaby.org/	Provides support to victim family members of shaken baby syndrome; has information and training programs for professionals and advocates for legislation to enact laws and policies to protect children, prevent abuse, and hold perpetrators criminally responsible for the abuse of children
The Wellness Community	C	(202) 659-9709 help@thewellnesscommunity.org http://www.thewellnesscommunity.org/	International nonprofit organization providing free support, education, and hope to people with cancer and their loved ones; holds professionally led support groups, educational workshops, nutrition and exercise programs, and stress-reduction classes
Therapet Animal Assisted Therapy Foundation	E	therapet@embarqmail.com http://www.therapet.com/	Establishes and communicates standards of practice for use of specially trained animals in health care settings; educates health care professionals, facility leaders, and communities on opportunities and benefits of animal-assisted therapy; trains, certifies, and assures competency of human-animal volunteer teams
Therapy Dogs International Inc. (TDI)	E	(973) 252-9800 tdi@gti.net http://www.tdi-dog.org/	Regulates, tests, and registers therapy dogs and their volunteer handlers for the purpose of visiting nursing homes, hospitals, and other institutions
Therapy Dogs Inc. (TDInc)	E	(877) 843-7364 therapydogsinc@qwestoffice.net http://www.therapydogs.com/	Provides registration, support, and insurance for members involved in volunteer animal–assisted activities, including visits to hospitals, special needs centers, schools, and nursing homes
Tragedy Assistance Program for Survivors (TAPS)	C, S	(202) 588-8277 info@taps.org http://www.taps.org/	Provides comfort and care to families of military men and women through peer-based emotional support, case work assistance, crisis intervention, and grief and trauma resources

Organization Types: P = Professional, R = Research/Scientific, S = Self-Help/Support, C = Consumer Resources/Referrals, E = education/advocacy/policy

Organization	Type	Contact information	Description
U.S. VETS	C	(213) 542-2600 http://www.usvetsinc.org/	Provides housing, counseling, and job assistance to homeless veterans; programs foster the skills necessary for veterans to return to the community and remain self-sufficient
Voice of the Retarded (VOR)	E	(877) 399-4VOR info@vor.net http://www.vor.net/	Advocates, educates, and assists families, organizations, public officials, and individuals concerned with the quality of life of and choice for persons with mental retardation within residential options, including home, community-based, and facility-based care
Wings of Light	S, C	http://www.wingsoflight.org/	Nonprofit organization serving as a united voice for those whose lives have been touched by aircraft accidents; provides support networks and referrals
Women For Sobriety, Inc. (WFS)	S	(215) 536-8026 http://www.womenforsobriety.org/	Self-help program for women with alcoholism; based on a 13-statement program that encourages emotional and spiritual growth
World Fellowship for Schizophrenia and Allied Disorders (WFSAD)	C, S, E	(416) 961-2855 info@world-schizophrenia.org http://www.world-schizophrenia.org/	Increases knowledge, understanding, and compassion and reduces the fear, stigma, discrimination, and abuse that accompany schizophrenia and other serious mental illnesses; provides self-help groups, workshops, and education and advocates for better treatment and appropriate services
Young Women's Leadership (YWL)	E	(619) 294-8000 ywl@jennadruck.org http://jdfleadership.org/	Part of the Jenna Druck Foundation; provides leadership training and opportunities to upcoming young women
Youth Enrichment Services (YES)	S, C	(212) 620-7310 YES@gaycenter.org http://www.gaycenter.org/youth/	Provides lesbian, gay, bisexual, and transgender young people with community support to foster healthy development in a safe, affirming, sex-positive, alcohol- and drug-free environment; located in New York City

Organization Types: P = Professional, R = Research/Scientific, S = Self-Help/Support, C = Consumer Resources/Referrals, E = education/advocacy/policy

APPENDIX C: SUGGESTED READINGS

This appendix contains a list of suggested books for those who are interested in pursuing emotion topics in more depth. The books are organized into several categories: self-help, first-person accounts, general emotion books for general audiences, general emotion books for academic audiences, biographies, and textbooks. This list is not intended to be comprehensive; the books listed are those that are believed to be most relevant and accessible to a general audience or classics in the field (or both). The two categories of general emotion books (for general and for academic audiences) were created as a guide; however, some books fit in both categories. The interested reader should check both lists.

Gretchen M. Reevy

Self-Help

Antony, M. M., & Swinson, R. P. (2008). *The shyness and social anxiety workbook: Proven, step-by-step techniques for overcoming your fear.* Oakland, CA: New Harbinger.

Beattie, M. (1992). *Codependents' guide to the twelve steps.* New York: Fireside.

Begley, S. (2007). *Train your mind, change your brain.* New York: Ballantine.

Behary, W. T. (2008). *Disarming the narcissist: Surviving and thriving with the self-absorbed.* Oakland, CA: New Harbinger.

Bourne, E. J. (2005). *The anxiety and phobia workbook.* Oakland, CA: New Harbinger.

Bower, S. A., & Bower, G. H. (2004). *Asserting yourself—A practical guide for positive change* (Updated ed.). Cambridge, MA: De Capo Press.

Christopher, J. (1988). *How to stay sober: Recovery without religion.* Amherst, NY: Prometheus Books.

Dalai Lama, H. H., & Cutler, H. C. (1998). *The art of happiness: A handbook for living.* New York: Riverhead Books.

Davis, M., Eshelman, E. R., & McKay, M. (2008). *The relaxation and stress reduction workbook* (6th ed.). Oakland, CA: New Harbinger.

Elliott, C. H., & Smith, L. L. (2002). *Overcoming anxiety for dummies.* New York: John Wiley.

Ellis, A., & Harper, R. A. (1975). *A guide to rational living.* Chatsworth, CA: Wilshire.

Frankl, V. E. (1988). *The will to meaning: Foundations and applications of logotherapy.* New York: Penguin Books.

Gordon, J. S. (2008). *Unstuck: Your guide to the seven-stage journey out of depression.* New York: Penguin Press.

Hyman, B. M., & Pedrick, C. (2005). *The OCD workbook: Your guide to breaking free from obsessive-compulsive disorder* (2nd ed.). Oakland, CA: New Harbinger.

Kabat-Zinn, J. (2005). *Wherever you go, there you are: Mindfulness meditation in everyday life.* Concord, NH: Hyperion.

McDermott, D., & Snyder, C. R. (2000). *The great big book of hope.* Oakland, CA: New Harbinger.

McKay, M., Davis, M., & Fanning, P. (2007). *Thoughts & feelings: Taking control of your moods & your life* (3rd ed.). Oakland, CA: New Harbinger.

Miller, T. (1996). *How to want what you have.* New York: Harper Perennial.

Pines, A. M. (1998). *Romantic jealousy: Causes, symptoms, cures.* New York: Routledge.

Rahula, W. (1974). *What the Buddha taught.* New York: Grove Press.

Rolfe, S. (2005). *Rethinking attachment for early childhood practice: Promoting security, autonomy, and resilience in young children.* Crows Nest, Australia: Allen and Unwin.

Rubin, K. H., with Thompson, A. (2003). *The friendship factor: Helping our children navigate their social worlds and why it matters for their success.* New York: Penguin.

Seligman, M. (2007). *What you can change and what you can't: The complete guide to successful self-improvement.* New York: Vintage.

Snyder, C. R. (2003). *The psychology of hope: You can get there from here.* New York: Free Press.

Torrey, E. F. (2006). *Surviving schizophrenia: A manual for families, patients, and providers* (5th ed.). New York: HarperCollins.

Williams, R. B., & Williams, V. (1993). *Anger kills: Seventeen strategies for controlling the hostility that can harm your health.* New York: HarperPerennial Library.

First-Person Accounts

Bell, J. (2007). *Rewind, replay, repeat: A memoir of obsessive-compulsive disorder.* Center City, MN: Hazelden.

Bridge, A. (2008). *Hope's boy.* New York: Hyperion. (emotional abuse)

Casey, N. (2002). *Unholy ghost: Writers on depression.* New York: Harper Perennial.

Colas, E. (1999). *Just checking: Scenes from the life of an obsessive-compulsive.* New York: Washington Square Press.

Dodds, M. (2007). *Schizoaffective: A happier and healthier life.* Frederick, MD: PublishAmerica.

Dully, H., & Fleming, C. (2007). *My lobotomy.* New York: Crown.

Fox, M. J. (2002). *Lucky man: A memoir.* New York: Hyperion. (Parkinson's disease)

Gordon, B. (1979). *I'm dancing as fast as I can.* New York: Harper and Row. (addiction to Valium)

Grandin, T. (2006). *Thinking in pictures: My life with autism* (Exp. ed.). New York: Vintage.

Jamison, K. R. (1997). *An unquiet mind: A memoir of moods and madness.* New York: Random House. (bipolar disorder)

Kaysen, S. (1994). *Girl, interrupted.* New York: Vintage. (borderline personality disorder)

Kirberger, K. (2003). *No body's perfect: Stories by teens about body image, self-acceptance, and the search for identity.* New York: Scholastic Paperbacks.

McFall, E. E. (2007). *I can still hear their cries, even in my sleep: A journey into PTSD.* Parker, CO: Outskirts Press.

Rand, R. (2004). *Dancing away an anxious mind: A memoir about overcoming panic disorder.* Madison: University of Wisconsin Press.

Reiland, R. (2004). *Get me out of here: My recovery from borderline personality disorder.* Center City, MN: Hazelden.

Shepard, J. (2009). *The meaning of Matthew: My son's murder in Laramie, and a world transformed.* New York: Hudson Street Press.

Snyder, K. (2007). *Me, myself, and them: A firsthand account of one young person's experience with schizophrenia.* New York: Oxford University Press.

Tammet, D. (2007). *Born on a blue day: Inside the extraordinary mind of an autistic savant.* New York: Free Press.

Wandzilak, K., & Curry, C. (2006). *The lost years: Surviving a mother and daughter's worst nightmare.* Santa Monica, CA: Jeffers Press. (alcoholism)

General Books for General Audiences

Alcoholics Anonymous World Services Inc. (2001). *Alcoholics Anonymous.* New York: Author. (Original work published 1935)

Barber, C. (2009). *Comfortably numb: How psychiatry medicated a nation.* New York: Vintage.

Barnes, D. S. (2006). *The great stink of Paris and the marriage of filth and germs.* Baltimore: Johns Hopkins University Press.

Barton, W. E. (1987). *The history and influence of the American Psychiatric Association.* Arlington, VA: American Psychiatric Publishing.

Beam, A. (2003). *Gracefully insane: Life and death inside America's premier mental hospital.* Cambridge, MA: Perseus Books Group.

Beck, A. T. (2000). *Prisoners of hate: The cognitive basis of anger, hostility, and violence.* New York: HarperCollins.

Becker, M. (2002). *The healing power of pets: Harnessing the amazing ability of pets to make and keep people happy and healthy.* New York: Hyperion.

Bernstein, P. L. (1998). *Against the gods: The remarkable story of risk.* New York: John Wiley.

Breggin, P. R. (2001). *The antidepressant fact book: What your doctor won't tell you about Prozac, Zoloft, Paxil, Celexa, and Luvox.* Cambridge, MA: De Capo Press.

Briggs, J. L. (1970). *Never in anger: Portrait of an Eskimo family.* Cambridge, MA: Harvard University Press.

Brockman, J. (Ed.). (2004). *Curious minds: How a child becomes a scientist.* New York: Vintage Books.

Buss, D. M. (1994). *The evolution of desire: Strategies of human mating.* New York: Basic Books.

Buss, D. M. (2000). *The dangerous passion: Why jealousy is as necessary as love and sex.* New York: Free Press.

Carr, A. (2004). *Positive psychology: The science of happiness and human strengths.* New York: Brunner-Routledge.

Cooper, R. (2005). *Classifying madness: A philosophical examination of the diagnostic and statistical manual of mental disorders.* Dordrecht, Netherlands: Springer.

Csikszentmihalyi, M. (1991). *Flow: The psychology of optimal experience.* New York: Harper Perennial.

Csikszentmihalyi, M. (1996). *Creativity: Flow and the psychology of discovery and invention.* New York: HarperCollins.

Damasio, A. (1994). *Descartes' error: Emotion, reason and the human brain.* New York: Putnam.

Dawkins, R. (1976). *The selfish gene.* New York: Oxford University Press. (evolutionary psychology)

Dukakis, K., & Tye, L. (2006). *Shock: The healing power of electroconvulsive therapy.* New York: Penguin.

Ehrenreich, B. (2009). *Bright-sided: How the relentless promotion of positive thinking has undermined America.* New York: Metropolitan Books.

Ekman, P. (2007). *Emotions revealed: Recognizing faces and feelings to improve communication and emotional life* (2nd ed.). New York: Holt Paperbacks.

Ekman, P. (2009). *Telling lies: Clues to deceit in the marketplace, politics, and marriage* (Rev. ed.). New York: W. W. Norton.

Ekman, P., & Friesen, W. V. (1975). *Unmasking the face.* Englewood Cliffs, NJ: Prentice Hall. (evolutionary basis of facial expression)

Emotions Anonymous Ltd. (1994). *Emotions Anonymous.* St. Paul, MN: Author.

Festinger, L., Riecken, H. W., & Schachter, S. (1956). *When prophecy fails.* Minneapolis: University of Minnesota Press. (cognitive dissonance)

Feuestein, G. (2001). *The yoga tradition: Its history, literature, philosophy, and practice.* Prescott, AZ: Holm Press.

Frankl, V. E. (1962). *Man's search for meaning.* New York: Washington Square. (logotherapy)

Frey, W. H. (1985). *Crying: The mystery of tears.* Minneapolis, MN: Winston Press.

Goleman, D. (1995). *Emotional intelligence: Why it can matter more than IQ.* New York: Bantam.

Haidt, J. (2006). *The happiness hypothesis: Finding modern truth in ancient wisdom.* New York: Basic Books.

Harary, K., & Robinson, E. D. (2005). *Who do you think you are?* London: Penguin Group. (Five Factor model of personality)

Harris, J. R. (2009). *The nurture assumption: Why children turn out the way they do.* New York: Free Press.

Healy, J. (2008). *Mania: A short history of bipolar disorder.* Baltimore: Johns Hopkins University Press.

Heyes, C. M., & Galef, B. G. (1996). *Social learning in animals: The roots of culture.* San Diego, CA: Academic Press.

Humphreys, K. (2003). *Circles of recovery: Self-help organizations for addictions.* Cambridge, England: Cambridge University Press.

Hunt, M. (2007). *The story of psychology.* New York: Doubleday Anchor.

Kagan, J. (2008). *What is emotion? History, measures, meanings.* New Haven, CT: Yale University Press.

Kesey, K. (1962). *One flew over the cuckoo's nest.* New York: Viking.

Kirschenbaum, H., & Henderson, V. L. (1989). *The Carl Rogers reader.* Boston: Houghton Mifflin.

Kramer, P. D. (1997). *Listening to Prozac: The landmark book about antidepressants and the remaking of the self.* New York: Penguin.

Kübler-Ross, E. (1969). *On death and dying.* New York: Macmillan.

LeDoux, J. (1996). *The emotional brain: The mysterious underpinnings of emotional life.* New York: Touchstone.

Levin, J., & McDevitt, J. (2002). *Hate crimes revisited: America's war on those who are different.* Boulder, CO: Westview Press.

Lewis, M. (1992). *Shame: The exposed self.* New York: Free Press.

Lutz, T. (2001). *Crying: A natural and cultural history of tears.* New York: W. W. Norton.

Macmillan, M. (2000). *An odd kind of fame: Stories of Phineas Gage.* Cambridge, MA: MIT Press.

Maslow, A. H. (1962). *Toward a psychology of being.* Princeton, NJ: Van Nostrand. (humanistic psychology)

McEwen, B., & Lasley, E. N. (2002). *The end of stress as we know it.* Washington, DC: Joseph Henry Press.

McMahon, D. M. (2006). *Happiness: A history.* New York: Atlantic Monthly Press.

Mitchell, S. A., & Black, M. J. (1996). *Freud and beyond: A history of modern psychoanalytic thought.* New York: Basic Books.

Morris, T. (1999). *Philosophy for dummies.* Foster City, CA: IDG Books.

Oatley, K. (2004). *Emotions: A brief history.* Malden, MA: Blackwell.

Overall, K. L. (1997). *Clinical behavioral medicine for small animals.* Portland, OR: Mosby.

Paul, A. M. (2004). *The cult of personality: How personality tests are leading us to miseducate our children, mismanage our companies, and misunderstand ourselves.* New York: Free Press.

Payne, C. (2009). *Asylum: Inside the closed world of state mental hospitals.* Boston: MIT Press.

Pease, B., & Pease, A. (2006). *The definitive book of body language.* New York: Bantam Dell.

Peck, M. D. (1978). *The road less travelled.* New York: Touchstone.

Pert, C. B. (1997). *Molecules of emotion.* New York: Scribner.

Peterson, G. W., & Fabes, R. (2003). *Emotions and the family.* Binghamton, NY: Haworth Press.

Regan, P. C., & Berscheid, E. (1999). *Lust: What we know about human sexual desire.* Newbury Park, CA: Sage.

Rogers, C. R. (1961). *On becoming a person: A therapist's view of psychotherapy.* Boston: Houghton Mifflin.

Sacks, O. (2007). *Musicophilia: Tales of music and the brain.* New York: Vintage Books.

Sapolsky, R. M. (2004). *Why zebras don't get ulcers.* New York: Henry Holt. (stress)

Scheper-Hughes, N. (1992). *Death without weeping.* Berkeley: University of California Press. (cultural perspective on sympathy; case study of a culture)

Seligman, M.E.P. (1991). *Learned optimism.* New York: Knopf.

Sharples, R. W. (2007). *Stoics, Epicureans, and Skeptics: An introduction to Hellenistic philosophy.* Boca Raton, FL: Taylor and Francis.

Shorter, E., & Healy, D. (2007). *Shock therapy: A history of electroconvulsive treatment in mental illness.* New Brunswick, NJ: Rutgers University Press.

Sidky, H. (1997). *Witchcraft, lycanthropy, drugs and disease: An anthropological study of the European witch hunts.* New York: Peter Lang.

Skinner, B. F. (1948). *Walden Two.* New York: Macmillan.

Snyder, C. R. (2003). *The psychology of hope: You can get there from here.* New York: Free Press.

Solomon, A. (2001). *The noonday demon.* New York: Touchstone. (depression)

Stevenson, J. (2005). *The complete idiot's guide to philosophy.* New York: Alpha.

Tart, C. T. (2001). *States of consciousness.* Available from http://backinprint.com (Original work published 1979)

Temple-Raston, D. (2001). *A death in Texas: A story of race, murder, and a small town's struggle for redemption.* New York: Henry Holt.

Tick, E. (2005). *War and the soul: Healing our nation's veterans from post-traumatic stress disorder.* Wheaton, IL: Quest Books.

Tone, A. (2009). *The age of anxiety: A history of America's turbulent affair with tranquilizers.* New York: Basic Books.

Tsu, L. (1989). *Tao te ching.* New York: Vintage.

Wallenstein, G. (2003). *Mind, stress, and emotions: The new science of mood.* Boston: Commonwealth Press.

Yalom, I. (1980). *Existential psychotherapy.* New York: Basic Books.

Yalom, I. D., & Leszcz, M. (2005). *Theory and practice of group psychotherapy* (5th ed.). New York: Basic Books.

General Books for Academic Audiences

Allport, G. W. (1954). *The nature of prejudice.* Reading, MA: Addison-Wesley.

Andersen, P., Morris, R., Amaral, D., Bliss, T., & O'Keefe, J. (Eds.). (2007). *The hippocampus book.* New York: Oxford University Press.

Arnold, M. B. (1960). *Emotion and personality.* New York: Columbia University Press.

Bargh, J. A. (Ed.). (2007). *Social psychology and the unconscious: The automaticity of higher mental processes.* New York: Psychology Press.

Binswanger, L. (1942). *Foundations and knowledge of human existence.* Zurich, Switzerland: M. Niehaus.

Bowlby, J. (1969). *Attachment and loss: Vol. I. Attachment.* New York: Basic.

Cannon, W. B. (1929). *Bodily changes in pain, hunger, fear, and rage* (2nd ed.). New York: D. Appleton. (Original work published 1915).

Cramer, P. (2006). *Protecting the self: Defense mechanisms in action.* New York: Guilford.

Darwin, C. (1859). *On the origin of species by means of natural selection.* London: John Murray.

Darwin, C. (1998). *The expression of the emotions in man and animals* (3rd ed.). New York: Oxford University Press. (Original work published 1872)

Dovidio, J. F., Glick, P., & Rudman, L. (2005). *On the nature of prejudice: Fifty years after Allport.* Malden, MA: Blackwell.

Durkheim, E., Simpson, G., & Spaulding, J. A. (1997). *Suicide: A study in sociology.* New York: Free Press. (Original work published 1897)

Ekman, P., & Davidson, R. J. (Eds.). (1994). *The nature of emotion: Fundamental questions.* New York: Oxford University Press.

Ekman, P., & Rosenberg, E. L. (Eds.). (2005). *What the face reveals: Basic and applied studies of facial expression using the Facial Action Coding System (FACS)* (2nd ed.). New York: Oxford University Press.

Erhlich, H. (2009). *Hate crimes and ethnoviolence: The history, current affairs, and future of discrimination in America.* Boulder, CO: Westview Press.

Evans, R. B., Sexton, V. S., & Cadwallader, T. C. (Eds.). (1992). *The American Psychological Association: A historical perspective.* Washington, DC: American Psychological Association.

Freud, A. (1936). *The writings of Anna Freud: Vol. 2. The ego and the mechanisms of defense.* New York: International Universities Press.

Freud, S. (1997). *Sexuality and the psychology of love.* New York: Touchstone. (Original work published 1963)

Freud, S., & Gay, P. (Ed.). (1989). *The Freud reader.* New York: W. W. Norton.

Frijda, N. H. (1986). *The emotions.* Cambridge, England: Cambridge University Press.

Friedman, M., & Rosenman, R. H. (1974). *Type A behavior and your heart.* New York: Knopf.

Galovsky, T. E., Malta, L. S., & Blanchard, E. B. (Eds.). (2006). *Road rage: Assessment and treatment of the angry, aggressive driver.* Washington, DC: American Psychological Association.

Geen, R. G. (2001). *Human aggression (mapping social psychology).* Berkshire, England: Open University Press.

Gross, J. J. (2006). *Handbook of emotion regulation.* New York: Guilford.

Hoffman, M. L. (2000). *Empathy and moral development: Implications for caring and justice.* New York: Cambridge University Press.

Izard, C. E. (1971). *The face of emotion.* East Norwalk, CT: Appleton-Century-Crofts.

James, W. (1890). *The principles of psychology* (2 Vols.). New York: Henry Holt.

Jung, C. G., & Hull, R.F.C. (1992). *Two essays on analytical psychology* (Vol. 7). New York: Routledge.

Lange, C. G., & James, W. (1962). *The emotions.* New York: Hafner. (Original work published 1922)

Lazarus, R. S. (1966). *Psychological stress and the coping process.* New York: McGraw-Hill.

Lazarus, R. S. (1991). *Emotion and adaptation.* New York: Oxford University Press.

Lazarus, R. S. (1999). *Stress and emotion: A new synthesis.* New York: Springer.

Lewis, M., Haviland-Jones, J. M., & Barrett, L. F. (Eds.). (2008). *Handbook of emotions* (3rd ed.). New York: Guilford.

Maslow, A. H. (1977). *The healthy personality.* New York: Van Nostrand.

Mayne, T. J., & Bonnano, G. A. (Eds.). (2001). *Emotions: Current issues and future directions.* New York: Guilford.

Miller, W. I. (1997). *The anatomy of disgust.* Cambridge, MA: Harvard University Press.

Monat, A., Lazarus, R. S., & Reevy, G. (Eds.). (2007). *The Praeger handbook on stress and coping.* Westport, CT: Praeger.

Murray, H. A. (1938). *Explorations in personality.* New York: Oxford University Press.

Nelson, R. J. (Ed.). (2005). *Biology of aggression.* New York: Oxford University Press.

Novaco, R. (1975). *Anger control: The development and evaluation of an experimental treatment.* Lexington, MA: D.C. Health.

O'Connell, A. N., & Russo, N. F. (Eds.). (1983). *Models of achievement: Reflections of eminent women in psychology.* New York: Columbia University Press.

Patterson, J. (2006). *Therapist's guide to psychopharmacology: Working with patients, families, and physicians to optimize care.* New York: Guilford.

Peterson, C., Maier, S. F., & Seligman, M.E.P. (1993). *Learned helplessness: A theory for the age of personal control.* New York: Oxford University Press.

Peterson, C., & Seligman, M.E.P. (2004). *Character strengths and virtues: A handbook and classification.* New York: Oxford University Press.

Preston, J. D., O'Neal, J. H., & Talaga, M. C. (2008). *Handbook of clinical psychopharmacology for therapists* (5th ed.). Oakland, CA: New Harbinger.

Reisberg, D., & Hertel, P. (2003). *Memory and emotion.* New York: Oxford University Press.

Roazen, P. (1974). *Freud and his followers.* New York: New York University Press.

Rogers, C. R. (1942). *Counseling and psychotherapy.* Boston: Houghton Mifflin.

Rogers, C. R. (1951). *Client-centered therapy, its current practice, implications, and theory.* Boston: Houghton Mifflin.

Shields, S. A. (2002). *Speaking from the heart: Gender and the social meaning of emotion.* Cambridge, England: Cambridge University Press.

Skinner, B. F. (1938). *The behavior of organisms: An experimental analysis.* New York: Macmillan.

Skinner, B. F. (1976). *About behaviorism.* New York: Vintage.

Sternberg, R. J., & Sternberg, K. (2008). *The nature of hate.* New York: Cambridge University Press.

Stets, J. E., & Turner, J. H. (Eds.). (2007). *Handbook of the sociology of emotions.* New York: Springer.

Uchino, B. N. (2004). *Social support and physical health: Understanding the health consequences of relationships.* New Haven, CT: Yale University Press.

Walker, J. (2001). *Control and the psychology of health: Theory, measurement, and applications.* Buckingham, England: Open University Press.

Washton, A. M., & Zweben, J. E. (2008). *Treating alcohol and drug problems in psychotherapy practice: Doing what works.* New York: Guilford.

Watson, J. B. (1997). *Behaviorism.* Edison, NJ: Transaction. (Original work published 1925)

Wierzbicka, A. (1999). *Emotions across languages and cultures: Diversity and universals.* Cambridge, England: Cambridge University Press.

Wilson, E. O. (1975). *Sociobiology: The new synthesis.* Cambridge, MA: Harvard University Press.

Wolpe, J., & Lazarus, A. A. (1966). *Behavior therapy techniques: A guide to the treatment of neuroses.* New York: Pergamon Press.

Zuckerman, M. (2006). *Sensation seeking and risky behavior.* Washington, DC: American Psychological Association.

Biographies

Baenninger, A., & Baenninger, A. (2003). *Good chemistry: The life and legacy of Valium inventor Leo Sternbach.* New York: McGraw-Hill.

Bjork, D. W. (1993). *B. F. Skinner: A life.* New York: Basic Books.

Blum, D. (2002). *Love at Goon Park: Harry Harlow and the science of affection.* New York: Berkley Books.

Bowlby, J. (1990). *Charles Darwin: A new life.* New York: W. W. Norton.

Buckley, K. W. (1989). *Mechanical man: John Broadus Watson and the beginnings of behaviorism.* New York: Guilford.

Cannon, W. B. (1945). *The way of an investigator.* New York: W. W. Norton.

Clark, R. W. (1980). *Freud: The man and the cause—a biography.* New York: Random House.

Clarke, D. M. (2006). *Descartes: A biography.* New York: Cambridge University Press.

Darwin, F. (Ed.). (1958). *An autobiography of Charles Darwin and selected letters.* New York: Dover.

El-Hai, J. (2007). *The lobotomist: A maverick medical genius and his tragic quest to rid the world of mental illness.* Hoboken, NJ: John Wiley.

Ellis, A. (2010). *All Out!* Amherst, NY: Prometheus.

Freud, S., & Freud, E. D. (2007). *Living in the shadow of the Freud family.* Westport, CT: Praeger.

Freud, S., & Gay, P. (1988). *Freud: A life for our time.* New York: W. W. Norton.

Gillham, N. W. (2001). *A life of Sir Francis Galton: From African exploration to the birth of eugenics.* New York: Oxford University Press.

Gollaher, D. L. (1995). *Voice for the mad: The life of Dorothea Dix.* New York: Free Press.

Holmes, J. (1993). *John Bowlby and attachment theory.* London: Routledge.

Jones, E. (1953–1958). *The life and work of Sigmund Freud* (3 Vols.). New York: Basic Books.

Maslow, B. G. (1972). *Abraham H. Maslow: A memorial volume.* Monterey, CA: Brooks/Cole.

Maslow, A. H. (1979). *The journals of Abraham Maslow* (R. J. Lowry, Ed.). Lexington, MA: Lewis.

Quinn, S. (1987). *A mind of her own: The life of Karen Horney.* New York: Summit Books/ Simon and Schuster.

Rubins, J. L. (1978). *Karen Horney: Gentle rebel of psychoanalysis.* New York: Dial.

Simon, L. (1998). *Genuine reality: A life of William James.* New York: Harcourt Brace.

Skinner, B. F. (1984). *The Shaping of a Behaviorist.* New York: New York University Press.

Weishaar, M. (1993). *Aaron T. Beck.* Thousand Oaks, CA: Sage.

Wilson, E. O. (1994). *Naturalist.* Washington, DC: Island.

Young-Bruehl, E. (1988). *Anna Freud.* New York: Summit Books.

Textbooks

Benjamin, L. T., Jr. (2007). *A brief history of modern psychology.* Malden, MA: Blackwell.

Bornstein, M. H., & Davidson, L. (2003). *Well-being: Positive development across the life course.* Mahwah, NJ: Lawrence Erlbaum Associates.

Buss, D. (2007). *Evolutionary psychology: The new science of the mind.* Needham Heights, MA: Allyn and Bacon.

Crosson-Tower, C. (2009). *Understanding child abuse and neglect.* Englewood Cliffs, NJ: Prentice Hall.

Funder, D. C. (2010). *The personality puzzle* (5th ed.). New York: W. W. Norton.

Girdano, D. A., Dusek, D. E., & Everly, G. S., Jr., (2009). *Controlling stress and tension* (8th ed.). San Francisco: Benjamin Cummings.

Hothersall, D. (2004). *History of psychology.* San Francisco: McGraw-Hill.

Kalat, J. W., & Shiota, M. N. (2007). *Emotion.* Belmont, CA: Thomson Wadsworth.

Ksir, C., Hart, C. L., & Oakley, R. (2008). *Drugs, society, and human behavior* (12th ed.). Boston: McGraw-Hill.

McAdams, D. P. (2008). *The person: An introduction to the science of personality psychology.* Hoboken, NJ: John Wiley.

Miller, R. S., Perlman, D., & Brehm, S. S. (2007). *Intimate relationships* (4th ed.). New York: McGraw-Hill.

Nichols, M. P. (2008). *Family therapy: Concepts and methods* (8th ed.). Boston: Allyn and Bacon.

Oatley, K., Keltner, D., & Jenkins, J. M. (2006). *Understanding emotions.* Malden, MA: Blackwell.

Richard, D.C.S., & Huprich, S. K. (Eds.). (2009). *Clinical psychology: Assessment, treatment, and research.* San Francisco: Elsevier.

Sollod, R. N., Wilson, J. P., & Monte, C. F. (2009). *Beneath the mask: An introduction to theories of personality.* Hoboken, NJ: John Wiley.

Spiegler, M. D., & Guevremont, D. C. (2009). *Contemporary behavior therapy* (5th ed.). Belmont, CA: Wadsworth.

Yalom, I. D., & Leszcz, M. (2005). *Theory and practice of group psychotherapy* (5th ed.). New York: Basic Books.

INDEX

ABC model of emotional reaction, 31–33, 420, 542

Abdominal breathing, 184

Abraham H. Maslow: A Memorial Volume (Maslow), 368

Abramson, Lyn, 344

Academy of Dance Therapists (ADTR), 181

Acathexis, 154

Acceptance, 33–34, 368; acceptance and commitment therapy, 164; encounter group and, 238; friendship and, 276; mindfulness and, 376; self-acceptance, 238, 289, 368, 505; social support and, 535; unconditional, 263

Ackerman, Nathan, 263

Active agency, 162–63

Active emotions, 3

Actual level, social contact and, 356

Acupuncture, 18, 34–35, 164–65, 545

Acute phase of schizophrenia, 514

Acute stress disorder, 35–37, 189, 210, 458

Adjustment disorder, 37–38, 204, 290

Adler, Alfred, 16, 118

Adult Children of Alcoholics (ACoA), 45, 50

Aesthetic emotion, 179

Affect, 38–39; induction, 584–85

Affective Communication Test (ACT), 91

Affective personality traits, 39–41. *See also* Neuroticism

Affective prosody, 90

Against the Gods: The Remarkable Story of Risk (Bernstein), 111

Agency thinking, 310

Aggression, 41–42, 62–63, 81, 98, 121; autistic spectrum disorders and, 106; bipolar disorder and, 133; borderline personality

disorder and, 139, 309; gender and, 283–84; hate crimes and, 303–4; obsessive-compulsive disorder and, 417; pet therapy and, 435; play therapy and, 444; psychosurgery as treatment for, 463, 486; in road rage, 498–500; serotonin and, 410, 525; social learning and, 534; in traumatic brain injury, 568; Type A personality and, 57

Aggressive driving, 498–99

Agoraphobia, 436, 437

Ainsworth, Leonard, 43

Ainsworth, Mary, 43–44, 101–2, 143, 318, 574

Akinetic mutism, 74

Al-Anon Family Groups, 44–45, 49–50, 576

Alateen, 44–45, 49–50, 576

Alcohol: abuse, 37, 45–47, 48, 87, 98, 106, 191, 404, 424, 548; dependence, 45, 404, 548

Alcoholics Anonymous (AA), 33, 47, 48–50, 191, 232, 283, 398, 421, 525, 549, 575; Al-Anon/Alateen and, 44–45

Alcoholism, 34, 44, 45–47, 48–50; aversive conditioning as treatment for, 113; hormones and, 313

Alexithymia, 50–51, 52; aprosodia and, 90; dysphoria and, 212; emotional intelligence and, 229; feelings chart and, 267

Ali, Muhammad, 428

Alienation, 52–53, 73

Allen, Woody, 484

Allport, Gordon, 464, 559

Alpha test, Army, 22

Altered states of consciousness, 53; primal therapy and, 467

Altered States of Consciousness (Tart), 53

About the Authors

GRETCHEN M. REEVY received her PhD in Psychology from the University of California, Berkeley, in 1994. Since 1994 she has taught in the Department of Psychology at California State University, East Bay, specializing in personality and stress and coping courses. With Alan Monat and Richard S. Lazarus, she coedited the *Praeger Handbook on Stress and Coping.* Her research interests are in personality, stress and coping, social support, and gender differences. She enjoys reading, running, and swimming, and has a love for animals.

YVETTE MALAMUD OZER received her master's degree in clinical child/school psychology from California State University, East Bay, and a certificate in substance abuse counseling from University of California, Berkeley, Extension. Her research and practice interests include neuropsychology, psychopharmacology, psychometrics, and resilience. She plays viola in a community orchestra and enjoys reading and spending time with her family.

YURI ITO received her BA in Psychology from California State University, East Bay, in 2007. She received a master's of business administration degree at California State University, Sacramento in 2010. She enjoys reading, hiking, and painting.